D0893913

DATA TRANSMISSION

INTER-UNIVERSITY ELECTRONICS SERIES

Bennett and Davey. DATA TRANSMISSION

Jamieson et al. INFRARED PHYSICS AND ENGINEERING

DATA TRANSMISSION

WILLIAM R. BENNETT

Head, Data Theory Department
Bell Telephone Laboratories, Incorporated

JAMES R. DAVEY

Head, Data Terminals and Transmission Department
Bell Telephone Laboratories, Incorporated

McGRAW-HILL BOOK COMPANY

New York   San Francisco   Toronto   London   Sydney

PREFACE

The increasing use of mechanized data processing methods has led to an accelerated need for more and better communication channels between machines and between machines and people. These channels must be able to accept and deliver messages in machine language, which is predominantly digital.

The transmission of digital signals has been extensively studied in the past under the subject of telegraphy. Modern data transmission might be considered as an outgrowth of telegraph transmission. The differences are mainly in the trend toward higher information rates and more extensive interconnections by switched networks. Existence of analog facilities which already serve similar needs for other types of communication has given an impetus toward adaptation for data of the many transmission media originally designed for other signals. The telephone network in particular furnishes an attractive source of data channels because of the many points of access and the extensive switching capabilities. Effective utilization of the available facilities requires an understanding of both digital and analog transmission.

The purpose of this book is to present in one volume the important principles of modern data communication. Early digital signaling systems are reviewed, the basic concepts of digital messages and their electrical analogs are presented, and the various transmission methods are described in detail. Emphasis is placed on the optimum spectral shaping of data signals to achieve maximum tolerance to noise. Theoretical error rates are derived for specific kinds of modulation and detection. Commonly encountered transmission impairments and their effects are described. Particular attention is given to the characteristics of the telephone voice channel. Modulation systems are compared as to their bandwidth efficiency and their tolerance to noise and transmission impairments. The important problem areas of coherent detection, synchronization, equalization, and error control are discussed from a realistic point of view. A section is included on methods of measuring the performance of data transmission systems. The book concludes with chapters on optimization theory and the statistics of digital signals.

The material of the present book was first presented by the authors in a series of lectures offered to members of the Data Communications Development Laboratory of the Bell Telephone Laboratories. The primary object was to consolidate the very considerable background of knowledge which had come into being relative to data transmission problems during many man-years of experience. The audience was encouraged to discuss and to criticize the material. The lecture notes were revised to take advantage of the comments received.

It has been the intent of the authors to make the material comprehensible to those who have the equivalent of a bachelor's degree in electrical engineering with emphasis leaning toward applications to communication. Some mathematical maturity is assumed, but explanations are included whenever relatively unfamiliar analytical techniques are introduced.

It is not practical to include individual acknowledgments of all the help received from others in the preparation of this book. Specific instances have been cited in the text where appropriate. An important contribution throughout has been the conscientious editorial assistance of Viola M. Bennett, Technical Editor, Columbia Radiation Laboratory, Columbia University.

William R. Bennett
James R. Davey

CONTENTS

Preface v

Chapter 1. Historical Introduction **1**

1-1. Semaphore-type Systems 1
1-2. Electrostatic Telegraphy 3
1-3. Electrochemical and Other Nonelectromagnetic Systems . . 4
1-4. The Electromagnetic Telegraph 5
1-5. Printing Telegraph Systems 11
1-6. Multiplexing Methods 12
1-7. Submarine Cables 14
1-8. Wireless Telegraphy 16

Chapter 2. Digital Representation of Information . . . **19**

2-1. Symbol Patterns 19
2-2. Timing of Digital Information 20
2-3. Examples of Digital Codes 21

Chapter 3. Electrical Representation of Digital Information **26**

3-1. Basic Information Waveforms 26
3-2. Modulated Carrier Signals 29
3-3. Modulated Pulses 30

Chapter 4. Frequency Analysis of Digital Data Signals . **32**

4-1. Baseband Signals 32
4-2. Sinusoidal Amplitude Modulation 34
4-3. Square-wave Amplitude Modulation 35
4-4. Sinusoidal Phase and Frequency Modulation 36
4-5. Frequency Modulation by Complex Waveforms 38
4-6. Phase Modulation by Complex Waveforms 40
4-7. Pulse Modulation 40
4-8. Calculation of Spectral Components in FM Case 42
   Continuous Phase 43
   Discontinuous Phase 46

Chapter 5. Effects of Restricted Bandwidth **49**

5-1. Illustrative Examples of Pulses Represented by Fourier Integrals 50

vii

5-2. Baseband Signals 53
5-3. Nyquist's First Criterion; Equally Spaced Axis Crossings in the
     Impulse Response 61
5-4. Nyquist's Second Criterion; Equal Times between Transition
     Values 63
5-5. Nyquist's Third Criterion; Preservation of Pulse Areas . . 65
5-6. Generalized Signal Pulse Shapes 65
5-7. Application to AM 66
5-8. Application to FM 70
5-9. Analysis of a Frequency-shift Signal as an AM Signal . . . 77

Chapter 6.   Transmission Impairments 83

6-1. Amplitude-frequency Distortion 83
6-2. Phase-frequency Distortion 84
6-3. Nonlinear Distortion 90
6-4. Frequency Offset 91
6-5. Sudden Amplitude and Phase Jumps 92
6-6. Echoes 92
6-7. Noise and Other Interference 94
6-8. Variable Channels 94

Chapter 7.   Baseband Systems 96

7-1. Basic Functions of a Baseband System 96
7-2. Allowable Distortions 97
7-3. Channel Transmission Characteristic 98
7-4. Optimum Transmitting and Receiving Filters 99
7-5. Probability of Error for Binary Signals 110
7-6. Multilevel Signals 114
7-7. Effect of Phase-frequency Distortion 118
7-8. Binary Signaling above the Nyquist Rate 121
7-9. Regeneration 128

Chapter 8.   Amplitude-modulation Systems 133

8-1. Transmitting Modulator 134
8-2. Synchronous Detection 136
8-3. Envelope Detection 137
8-4. Optimum Filters for Noise Suppression 141
8-5. Optimum Filters for Suppression of Mutual Interference . . 145
8-6. Signal-to-noise Ratio and Error Probability 151
8-7. Effect of Phase-frequency Distortion 161

Chapter 9.   Frequency-modulation Systems 164

9-1. Frequency Modulators 165
9-2. The Limiter 169
9-3. Ideal Frequency Detectors 170

9-4. Actual Frequency Detectors 171
9-5. Additive Gaussian Noise 174
9-6. A General Evaluation of Error Probabilities in Binary Angle
Modulation 177
9-7. Probability of Error in Binary FM 182
9-8. Impulse Noise 190
9-9. Time Jitter 195
9-10. Multilevel FM 196

Chapter 10. Phase-modulation Systems 201

10-1. Generation of Phase-modulation Signals 202
10-2. Fixed-Reference Phase Detection 203
10-3. Differential Phase Detection 204
10-4. Filtering Considerations 208
10-5. Noise Margins 210
10-6. Calculation of Error Probabilities in PM Systems with Additive
Gaussian Noise 212
10-7. Average Signal Power in PM Systems 220

Chapter 11. Comparisons of Modulation Methods . . . 225

11-1. Performance in Presence of Gaussian Noise 225
11-2. Performance in Presence of Delay Distortion . . . 230
11-3. Performance with Level Variations 230
11-4. Performance with Frequency Offset 231
11-5. Effects of Sudden Phase Jumps 231
11-6. Signal Space Diagrams 232
    Amplitude Modulation 232
    Phase Modulation 233
    Vestigial Sideband 233
    Frequency Modulation 234
    Duobinary Frequency Modulation 235
11-7. Factors Affecting Choice of Data System 237

**Chapter 12. Past and Present Data Communication
Systems 240**

12-1. Early Telegraph Systems 240
12-2. Duplex Telegraph Systems 242
12-3. Line Facilities for D-C Telegraphy 244
12-4. Carrier Telegraph Systems 246
12-5. Higher-speed Voice-band Data Transmission 246
12-6. Data Terminals Using Amplitude Modulation . . . 247
    AN/TSQ Data System 247
    A1 Data System 247
    Rixon Sebit 247
    ACF Data Terminal 248

12-7. Data Terminals Using Frequency Modulation   248
       Bell System 202-type Data Sets   248
       Lenkurt Quaternary FM Data Set 248
12-8. Data Terminals Using Phase Modulation   248
       Collins Data Terminals   248
       Bell System 201-type Data Sets   249
       Lincoln Laboratories Phase-modulation Terminal   .   .   . 249
       Hughes Quaternary Phase-modulation Terminal   .   .   . 250
       Robertshaw-Fulton Multi-Lok Terminal 250
12-9. Data Terminals for Wider Than Voice-band Facilities   .   . 250

**Chapter 13.   Methods of Establishing a Reference Carrier
for Synchronous Detection** **252**

13-1. Reference Carrier for Binary Double-sideband AM   .   .   . 252
13-2. Reference Carrier for Binary Vestigial-sideband AM with Suppressed
       Carrier   254
13-3. Reference Carrier for Quadrature AM   258

Chapter 14.   Methods of Synchronization .   .   . **260**

14-1. Symbol Timing for a Synchronous Binary System   .   .   . 260
14-2. Symbol Timing for a Synchronous Multilevel System   .   .   . 262
14-3. Symbol and Character Timing in Start-Stop Systems   .   .   . 263
14-4. Character Timing for a Synchronous Binary System   .   .   . 264
14-5. Methods of Improving Reliability of Synchronization   .   . 264
14-6. Character Timing in Parallel Systems   267

Chapter 15.   Equalization of Data Channels .   .   . **268**

15-1. Equalization Networks   268
15-2. Use of Transversal-type Filters   269
15-3. Equalization by Predistortion 273
15-4. Equalization by Quantized Feedback   274

**Chapter 16.   Measuring the Performance of Data Transmission
Systems** **277**

16-1. Data Signal Distortion   277
16-2. Measurement of Bias Distortion   279
16-3. Measurement of Peak Distortion and Bias of Random Synchronous
       Data Signals 280
16-4. Measurement of Peak Distortion and Bias of Start-Stop Data Signals 282
16-5. Shortest-pulse Distortion Measurements   284
16-6. Measurement of Characteristic Distortion 284
16-7. Methods of Measuring Error Rate   285
16-8. Error Rate in Presence of Random Noise   286
16-9. Use of Eye-pattern Observations   287
16-10. Margin Tests on Digital Receivers   287

Chapter 17.   Error Control 291

17-1. Error Detection 291
17-2. Error Correction 293
17-3. Coding and Decoding by Shift Registers 295
17-4. Recurrent Coding for Burst Error Correction 300
17-5. Sequential Coding and Decoding 301

Chapter 18.   Idealized Optimization Theory 305

18-1. The Idealized Channel of Information Theory 305
18-2. Results from Statistical Decision Theory 307

Chapter 19.   Statistics of Digital Signals 315

19-1. Spectral Density 315
   Relation of Spectral Density and the Fourier Transform . . 316
   Use of a Random Signal Process as a Noise Source . . . 321
   Carrier-type Signals 321
   Binary Phase Modulation 322
   Multilevel Phase Modulation 324
   Frequency-shift Keying with Discontinuous Phase . . . 326
   Continuous-phase FSK 327
   Cross-spectral Density 332
19-2. Correlation 333
   Wiener-Khintchine Relations 334
   Examples of Autocorrelation Functions 336

Name Index 343

Subject Index 346

CHAPTER 1

HISTORICAL INTRODUCTION

The earliest data transmission systems depended on direct sensory perception of visual and acoustic signals. Human repeaters were inserted to extend the distance over which observations could be made. Visual signals were commonly derived from fire by night and smoke by day. ' Drums and gongs were used for acoustic sources. We do not have much information about the primitive codes, bit rates, transmission delays, and error rates.

1-1 SEMAPHORE-TYPE SYSTEMS

One of the oldest written descriptions of a data transmission system is that of Polybius, a Greek general of 300 B.C. At each station there were two walls about 7 feet long and 6 feet high with a space of 3 feet between them. One to five torches were placed on top of each wall. The code was defined by a rectangular array such as shown in Table 1-1. The letter A (alpha) was represented by one torch on each wall, B (beta) by one torch on the right and two on the left, etc.

Table 1-1. Code Used by Polybius, 300 B.C.

		LEFT				
		1	2	3	4	5
	1	A	B	Γ	Δ	E
	2	Z	H	Θ	I	K
RIGHT	3	Λ	M	N	Ξ	O
	4	Π	P	Σ	T	Υ
	5	Φ	X	Ψ	Ω	

This signaling method is the ancestor of the semaphore which was intensely developed in Europe near the end of the eighteenth and beginning of the nineteenth century. The Chappe semaphore system was used particularly in France, Germany, and Russia. The inventor, Claude Chappe, constructed the first model while still in school. The purpose was to communicate with his brothers, who were in another school about a mile from his own. An improved version comprising

1

a number of intermediate stations was installed by the French government in 1794 to cover the 150-mile distance between Paris and Lille. As shown in Fig. 1-1, a crossarm, 14 feet in length, was placed on top of a post and at each end was a shorter arm making an adjustable angle with the main arm.

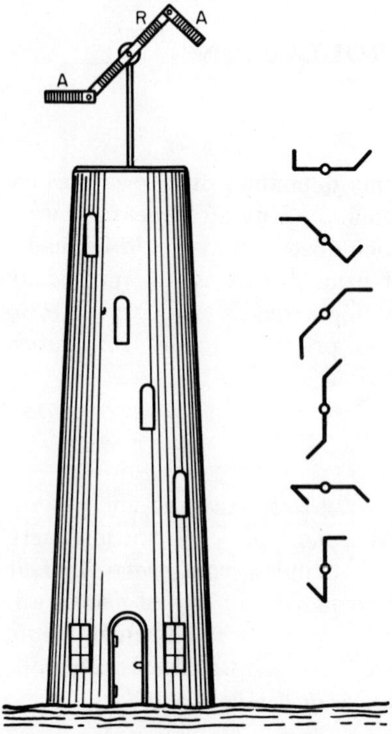

An operator manipulated the shorter arms with ropes and pulleys to obtain different positions representing the letters of the alphabet, numbers, and phrases. With 45-degree steps, it was possible to make 196 distinct signals. The semaphores were placed on stone towers at distances from 6 to 10 miles. A string of 220 towers extended from the Prussian frontier 1,200 miles via Warsaw to Leningrad and employed 1,300 operators. In Germany a line of semaphore stations was established in 1832 from Berlin to Treves via Potsdam, Magdeburg, Cologne, and Coblenz, at a cost of 170,000 thalers.* In France a line from Paris to Toulon was 475 miles long and had 120 stations. Transmission took place at the rate of one signal per minute including time for verification before another signal was transmitted. The transmission time from Paris to Toulon was ten to twelve minutes. The station attendants did not have to be highly skilled and were paid about 25 sous† per day.

FIG. 1-1. Chappe semaphore telegraph on top of a signal tower. (*From* "*Communication through the Ages*" *by Alfred Still. Reproduced by permission of the copyright holders, Holt, Rinehart and Winston, Inc., New York.*)

In 1795 the British Admiralty adopted a six-shutter optical telegraph system invented by Lord George Murray. As shown in Fig. 1-2, there were six panels which could be turned individually to present either a face or an edge to the observer. A 64-valued code was thus obtained. Various versions of optical signaling survive to this day as, for example, the arm and flag signals of military and naval activities.

* A thaler was equal to 3 marks or 71.4 cents.
† A sou was equal to 5 centimes or $1/20$ franc.

1-2 ELECTROSTATIC TELEGRAPHY

The early development of the electric telegraph overlapped that of the visual and acoustic systems. While electric manifestations have been known from antiquity, the only methods of generation were based on friction, and the methods of detection depended on forces exerted on light bodies. In 1747 Dr. William Watson, of England, demonstrated that electricity could be propagated over a wire for a distance of 2 miles. This led a contributor, who signed himself C. M.,* to suggest in the *Scots' Magazine* of February 17, 1753, that a pith-ball telegraph system could be devised with one wire for each letter of the alphabet. At the receiver, a pith ball was to be suspended by a silk thread near the extremity of each wire. When charge from a frictional generator was applied to the proper wire at the transmitter, repulsion of the corresponding pith ball at the receiver identified the letter.

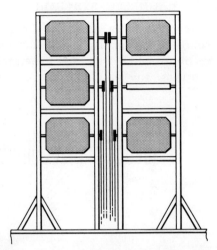

FIG. 1-2. Lord George Murray's six-shutter telegraph. (*From "Communication through the Ages" by Alfred Still. Reproduced by permission of the copyright holders, Holt, Rinehart and Winston, Inc., New York.*)

LeSage is said to have constructed such an apparatus at Geneva in 1774. In 1787 Lomond made and operated a pith-ball telegraph with only one insulated wire between sender and receiver. Chappe experimented around 1790 with what we would now call a pulse position modulation system in which clocks at the two ends of the line registered the times at which sparks occurred, and the code was based on the time readings. Other experiments on telegraphy by static electricity were carried out by Betancourt in 1787 using a battery of Leyden jars, and by Reizen (or Reusser) in 1794, who used electric sparks to mark tinfoil. Cavallo in 1795 used the number of sparks to designate signals.

The practical difficulty with electrostatic telegraphy was that the high voltages and low currents of the sources required high-impedance circuits. No satisfactory solution of the resulting insulation problem

---

* It is conjectured that "C. M." was either Charles Marshall of Renfrew, Scotland, or Charles Morrison of Greenock. The letter was sent from Renfrew.

was found.   In fact, no significant progress was made until a low-impedance source in the form of a primary electric cell or an electromagnetic generator became available.

1-3 ELECTROCHEMICAL AND OTHER NONELECTRO-MAGNETIC SYSTEMS

In 1800 Volta produced his galvanic pile, which was a chemical source of continuous electric current.   This was a considerable improvement over the frictional generators and Leyden jars formerly constituting the only supply.   At first, Volta's discovery stimulated

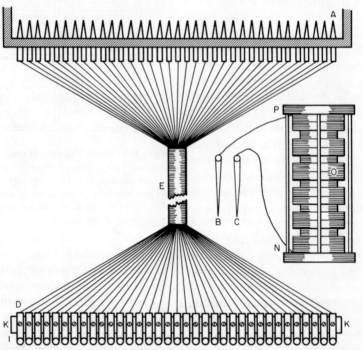

FIG. 1-3. Diagram of Sömmering's proposed electrochemical telegraph. (*From "Communication through the Ages" by Alfred Still. Reproduced by permission of the copyright holders, Holt, Rinehart and Winston, Inc., New York.*)

electrochemical signaling.   For example, in Sömmering's system of 1809 (Fig. 1-3), the electric current was used to decompose water.   The signals were recognized by the presence of gas bubbles at the electrodes. Thirty-five pins, marked with the 25 letters of the German alphabet and the 10 numerals, passed up through the bottom of the glass trough *A* filled with acidulated water.   Signaling was done by touching a pair of wires with the contact points B and C, which supplied current from the voltaic pile O. Bubbles of hydrogen were emitted from one of the wires touched and bubbles of oxygen from the other. More hydrogen was emitted than oxygen, and the operator was directed to read the letter from the pin with greater emission of gas.

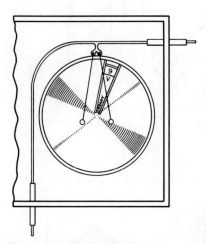

An electrophysiological telegraph in which the signals were received by shocks in the fingers of the observer was proposed by de Heer in 1839. Dyar in 1828 marked litmus paper with electric current. The differences in time between marks on the hand-moved paper constituted a code. An ingenious system of a type similar to that tried earlier by Chappe was successfully operated by Ronalds in 1816 over a distance of 8 miles. At the two ends he installed clocks (Fig. 1-4) carrying light paper disks on which were marked the letters of the alphabet. Perforated covers exposed only one letter at a time. When the clocks were synchronized, the same letter was visible at the two ends simultaneously. An electric spark coincident in time with the exposed letter indicated the intended signal. This was perhaps the first truly synchronous telegraph.

FIG. 1-4. Clockwork indicator at sending and receiving ends of Ronalds's electrical telegraph. (*From "Communication through the Ages" by Alfred Still. Reproduced by permission of the copyright holders, Holt, Rinehart and Winston, Inc., New York.*)

1-4 THE ELECTROMAGNETIC TELEGRAPH

The next substantial forward step came with the discovery of the relation between electricity and magnetism initiated by the experiments of Oersted in 1819 and continued by Ampère in 1820. The latter proposed a telegraph system with a wire and magnetized needle for each letter. By about 1825 Schilling had constructed a single-needle system based on the galvanometer invented by Schweigger in 1820. Schilling attached a paper disk to the needle in such a way that either a white or black face showed depending on the direction of current (Fig. 1-5). Schilling's code, shown in Table 1-2, indicates a considerable advance in efficiency over the earlier schemes. Note that

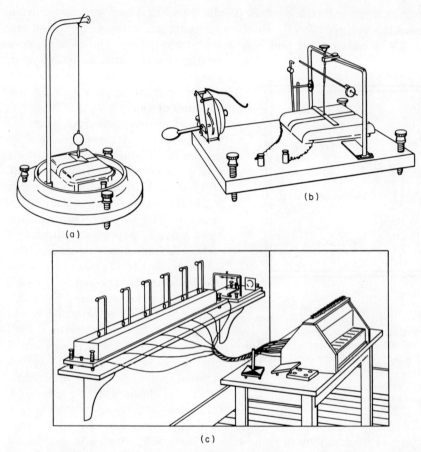

FIG. 1-5. Schilling's telegraph: (a) indicator; (b) alarm mechanism; (c) complete installation. (*Reproduced by permission of the editors of "A History of Technology," published by the Clarendon Press, Oxford.*)

already the information-theoretic principle of shorter codes for more frequently used letters appears to have been recognized.

The basic technology for essentially modern telegraph art was quickly made available during the next two decades from the discovery by Arago and Faraday in 1820 of the magnetization of soft iron by electric currents, the work of Henry in 1830 on electromagnetism, the laws governing current intensity of Ohm and Pouillet, and the invention of improved batteries by Becquerel, Daniell (1836), Bunsen, and Grove (1837).

In 1834 Gauss and Weber constructed a crude electromagnetic telegraph by stringing wire over the housetops of Göttingen to connect

Table 1-2. Schilling's Telegraph Code

b = black   w = white

A	b	w				N	w	b		
B	b	b	b			O	b	w	b	
C	b	w	w			P	w	w	b	b
D	b	b	w			Q	w	w	w	b
E	b					R	w	b	b	
F	b	b	b	b		S	w	w		
G	w	w	w	w		T	w			
H	b	w	w	w		U	w	w	b	
I	b	b				V	w	w	w	
J	b	b	w	w		W	b	w	b	w
K	b	b	b	w		X	w	b	w	b
L	w	b	b	b		Y	w	b	b	w
M	w	b	w			Z	w	b	w	w

the Astronomical Observatory, Physical Cabinet, and Magnetic Observatory. The slow oscillations of magnetic bars to the left or right caused by the passage of current from galvanic batteries furnished the signals, which were viewed through a telescope (Fig. 1-6). The operation was complicated, slow, and inefficient, but sufficed for the intended purpose. The code, shown in Table 1-3, was similar to that of Schilling. A considerably improved system embodying many of the features of the later methods of Morse, Vail, Cooke, and Wheatstone was set up by Steinheil between Munich and Bogenhausen early in 1837. Steinheil demonstrated that the earth could replace one wire of the transmission path. For a source of current he used Faraday's

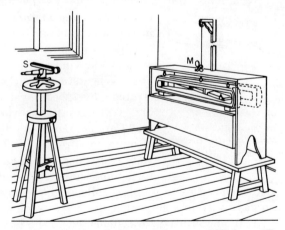

FIG. 1-6. The electromagnetic telegraph of Gauss and Weber. (*From "Communication through the Ages" by Alfred Still. Reproduced by permission of the copyright holders, Holt, Rinehart and Winston, Inc., New York.*)

Table 1-3. The Telegraph Code of Gauss and Weber

l = left r = right

A	r	M	*l r l*	0	*r l r l*
B	*l l*	N	*r l l*	1	*r l l r*
C, K	*r r r*	O	*r l*	2	*l r r l*
D	*r r l*	P	*r r r r*	3	*l r l r*
E	*l*	R	*r r r l*	4	*l l r r*
F, V	*r l r*	S	*r r l r*	5	*l l l r*
G	*l r r*	T	*r l r r*	6	*l l r l*
H	*l l l*	U	*l r*	7	*l r l l*
I, J	*r r*	W	*l r r r*	8	*r l l l*
L	*l l r*	Z	*r r l l*	9	*l l l l*

magnetoelectric generator and for his receiver Schweigger's galvanometer. The needle either struck a bell giving audible sound or made a black spot on paper by means of an ink-filled vessel mounted on the

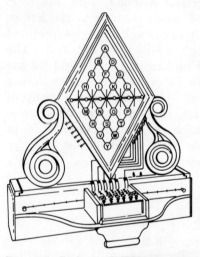

end. The spots appeared in parallel traces, one line showing spots when the deflection was to the left and the other when the deflection was to the right. Steinheil's code in terms of these spot patterns is shown in Table 1-4.

Out of the sixty or more different early methods proposed for telegraphy, there finally emerged the two most widely known land telegraph systems: the needle telegraph of Cooke and Wheatstone, introduced in England; and the electromagnetic telegraph of Morse and Vail, originating in the United States. In July, 1837, Wheatstone and Cooke demonstrated a five-needle system (Figs. 1-7 and 1-8) operating between Euston and Camden Town on the London-Birmingham railway. The needles were controlled by the currents from five line wires. This cumbersome

FIG. 1-7. Cooke and Wheatstone's five-needle telegraph. (*Reproduced by permission of the editors of "A History of Technology," published by the Clarendon Press, Oxford. British Crown Copyright, Science Museum.*)

method was soon replaced by a double-needle system using two wires, and this in turn gave way to a single-needle system with one wire and ground. The galvanometer needle was deflected to the left by current of one polarity and to the right by the reverse current. A code based on left and right deflections required at first that an operator read the

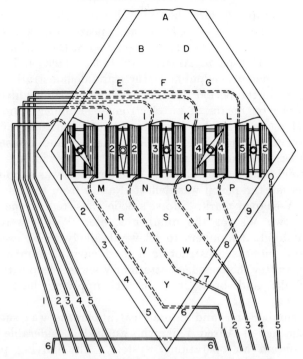

FIG. 1-8. Wiring diagram of Cooke and Wheatstone's telegraph. (*From "Communication through the Ages" by Alfred Still. Reproduced by permission of the copyright holders, Holt, Rinehart and Winston, Inc., New York.*)

motions visually. It was later found that insertion of an ivory stop pin on the left and a metal stop pin on the right enabled distinguishable sounds to be produced by the two deflections. These audible signals could be read with greater speed and less fatigue than the visual ones. Still later, a double-plate sounder in which a hammer struck either a bell or a metal plate was devised.

Table 1-4. Steinheil's Recording Telegraph Code

A	·˙·	L	˙··	0	···
B	·˙··	M	···	1	·˙··
C, K	··˙	N	··	2	·˙··
D	·˙	O	···	3	····
E	·	P	·˙··	4	····
F	·˙·	R	··	5	˙···
G	··˙·	S	··˙·	6	····
H	····	T	·˙	7	··˙·
CH	····	U, V	·˙·	8	···˙
ScH	·˙·˙	W	·˙··	9	··˙
I, J	·	Z	··˙··		

Morse's telegraph system, however, became the most universally accepted one. The genesis of his ideas appears to have been a series of conversations with Charles T. Jackson aboard the packet-ship *Sully* returning from Europe to America in 1832. Jackson in turn was stimulated by the various public lectures and demonstrations given by Joseph Henry in the period from 1828 to 1831. Henry lifted weights and rang bells by means of an electromagnet under remote electric control. Morse's original telegraph receiver consisted of a pencil mounted on the armature of an electromagnet and pressed against moving paper. When there was no current in the winding, the pencil made a straight line on the paper. When current was supplied during a brief interval, the pencil was deflected away from the line and back to make a V-shaped mark. Morse's code consisted of one V for the number 1, two V's for the number 2, etc. Words were sent by assigning individual numbers to all words likely to be used. Morse spent several months constructing a dictionary of numbered words. At the transmitter the message pattern of V's was set up with sawtooth type to make and break the circuit supplying battery to the electromagnet.

Morse's cumbersome and unpractical apparatus was successful in enlisting the aid of Alfred Vail, who applied considerable inventive talent to obtain an operational system. The moving pencil was replaced by a steel pen which, when the current was on, made indentations in the paper. Direct coding of the letters by dots and dashes replaced Morse's V's. It was the intention that the message would be read from the paper record, but the operators themselves discovered that they could read the code much faster by listening to the clicks of the armature. Piquancy is added to the story by describing Vail's visit to the office of the local newspaper in Morristown, New Jersey, to determine letter probabilities by counting the type in the letter boxes. However, we have seen that the advantage of assigning the shortest codes to the letters used oftenest had already been exemplified in the earlier codes of Schilling, Weber and Gauss, and Steinheil.

Morse's first successful demonstration (Fig. 1-9) occurred in 1844 over a 40-mile line between Baltimore and Washington. A competitive electrochemical telegraph invented by Bain in 1846 was put into operation between many cities in the United States and Canada in 1849. Bain's system used sensitive paper prepared by a solution of cyanide of potassium. The electric current from an iron stylus to the paper decomposed the salts and left a light blue mark. Patent litigation during the next three years led to consolidation with the Morse interests and eventual abandonment of the Bain system. An electrothermal system proposed by Horne in which current through a fine platinum wire burned holes in the paper could not get started because the local relay which controlled a sufficient amount of current infringed the Morse patent. Actually, the use of the incoming weak signal to control a larger amount of power in a local circuit was patented by Cooke and Wheatstone in England for their telegraph system on June 12, 1837. The application of the same principle to relay a signal from a long circuit by keying a fresh transmitting source was patented by Edward Davy in England, July 4, 1838. Morse patented the relay for long circuits in the United States, June 20, 1840, and for local circuit operation, April 11, 1846.

Fig. 1-9. Morse's recording electric telegraph as used on the experimental line between Baltimore and Washington. (*From "Communication through the Ages" by Alfred Still. Reproduced by permission of the copyright holders, Holt, Rinehart and Winston, Inc., New York.*)

1-5 PRINTING TELEGRAPH SYSTEMS

The first telegraph which printed words in Roman letters instead of a code at the receiver was invented by Royal E. House of Vermont in 1846. He · was refused a patent at first on account of a claimed infringement of Morse's patent and was forced to replace an electromagnet by a pneumatic system. House used a step-by-step method in which sending and receiving wheels moved together. An impulse was sent over the line for each step in the motion of the sending wheel, and reception of this impulse caused a corresponding motion of the receiving wheel. A pause at the end of each group of impulses allowed the receiving wheel to stop long enough to enable printing of the character corresponding to the position reached. The first line using the House printer was completed in 1849 between New York and Philadelphia. Rapid expansion to other cities followed, and a large proportion of the private telegrams and press reports were soon carried by the House system. The printed slips were particularly satisfying to the business public. The appreciable amount of mechanical power required for this system was supplied in the main by a man called the "grinder," who had the special task of turning a crank.

The Hughes printer, developed by David E. Hughes of Kentucky in 1855, was based on an idea similar to that of the Ronalds synchronous clockwork telegraph of 1816. Hughes used matched vibrating springs to control the machine speeds through escapement mechanisms at 120 rpm. With all the machines running in synchronism, a signal in the line indicated by its time of occurrence which letter should be printed. Printing was accomplished without stopping the machines, and speeds of about thirty words per minute were obtained.

1-6 MULTIPLEXING METHODS

In the early telegraph circuits the transmitter and receiver were in series, and transmission could take place in either direction, but not in both directions simultaneously. Such circuits are called "simplex" in England. "Simplex" in America means a circuit obtained by tapping the midpoints of two-wire terminals and thereby obtaining one line out of the two wires in parallel. This is distinguished from the "metallic" circuit in which the two wires are in series. Duplex systems which permit independent transmission in both directions over the same line were devised at an early date. These employ a Wheatstone bridge principle with the transmitter and receiver of each end in conjugate arms. The line and a balancing network complete the bridge. The bridge duplex is usually distinguished from the differential duplex, in which the receiving relay is protected from outgoing currents by opposing windings, but both depend on balance.* Such circuits are often called "full duplex." The term "half duplex" is used in England when the two directions are obtained by two one-way circuits as, for example, between each wire of a pair and ground. In America "half duplex" means a full duplex system which is operated in only one direction at a time, but with a capability of a break by the receiver to reverse the direction.

Multiplexing the telegraph circuit came in for early consideration. The "diplex" or two-channel circuit was obtained by the use of polarized and nonpolarized relays. The former is sensitive to the

---

* See Figs. 12-5 and 12-6 in Chap. 12 for diagrams of the circuits employed in these systems.

direction of the current in its windings, registering a mark for one direction and a space for the other. The latter operates in the same way on either direction of current. In the diplex application the key of one channel impresses signals by reversing the direction of current, while the key of the other makes independent changes between small and large magnitudes. At the receiver a polarized relay sensitive to the polarity of either small or large current is connected in series with an unpolarized relay operating on large current of either polarity. The ultimate of this kind of polarity-magnitude multiplex was the quadruplex system,* invented by Edison in 1874. It is a duplexed diplex and permits simultaneous two-channel operation in both directions.

Further multiplexing was accomplished by time division of the line. In this method a plurality of sources and their receivers are connected to corresponding contacts of synchronous rotating distributors at the channel terminals. A practical multiplex system produced by Baudot in 1874 enabled up to six operators to work over a single line simultaneously. A five-unit code was employed. Each operator had a keyboard with five keys. To send a character, the operator depressed the keys corresponding to the elements in the code which required marking signals. This connected the marking battery to the corresponding segments of the group of five assigned to that operator on the distributor. The keys remained locked in place until the next trip of the distributor brush over the group of segments. At this time the signals were sent to the line and the keys were unlocked for the next character. Indication of the unlocking was given to the operator by an audible "cadence signal." The manipulation of a Baudot transmitting keyboard called for a high degree of skill. No corresponding attempt was made to read the received message directly. The Baudot receiver was automatic and made a printed record on paper tape.

The Baudot system dominated the field, particularly in Europe, until the advent of carrier-frequency methods in the 1920s. Limitations of bandwidth in the telegraph lines were not a serious problem as long as hand sending was used. The practical speed of a Baudot operator was 30 words per minute. On the basis of the five-unit code used for the letters and an average word length of five letters and one space, six operators could send a total of 90 bits per second over the line. Higher speeds were obtained by automatizing the transmitter. This was done by feeding the input from perforated tape on which the coded message had been previously punched by a machine with a typewriter keyboard.

* See Fig. 12-7 in Chap. 12.

Subsequent developments in land telegraphy will be discussed in Chap. 12.

1-7 SUBMARINE CABLES

A direct limitation on sending speed was found when telegraphy over submarine cables was attempted. Here the early investigators found that the central conductor and return sheath acted like the plates of a Leyden jar in that they had to be charged before the signal could be received at the far end. In cther words, shunt capacitance was an inhibiting factor which cut down the operating speed even when sending by hand. One had to wait until the response to one signal had sufficiently died away before one could send another recognizable pulse. This was the advent of bandwidth limitation with which we are now so familiar.

Successful submarine cables began with the discovery of gutta-percha in 1847. Gutta-percha-covered wires encased in lead tubes were used in the Bain line to cross the Connecticut River at Middletown in 1849. On August 28, 1850, Jacob Brett strung gutta-percha-covered wire from Dover to Calais, a sea distance of 25 nautical miles, and passed signals across the English Channel. The unprotected wire was cut by rocks or by fishermen the first day. In September, 1851, a permanent cable was completed between these points. The Atlantic Telegraph Company organized by Cyrus Field finally succeeded in establishing a cable connection between England and the United States for a brief interval in 1858. The cable had been badly damaged by high-voltage testing. A 90-word message from Queen Victoria to President Buchanan was successfully transmitted in 67 minutes, but after a few more messages the cable failed altogether. Permanent cables were finally established in 1866.

It was found that when land telegraph methods were used on the Atlantic cable the speed could not exceed one or two words per minute. Lord Kelvin's mirror galvanometer used as a receiving instrument raised the speed to seven or eight words a minute. His siphon recorder, perfected in 1870, gave a still further improvement. The received signal current flowed through a light coil of fine wire suspended between the poles of a magnet. The motion of the coil was transmitted by silken fibers to a small glass siphon about the size of a needle. One end of the siphon dipped into a pot of ink, and the other hung close over a moving strip of paper. As the siphon vibrated, the ink splattered on the paper to make a line of fine dots. With this recorder and improved cables, speeds of 20 words per minute were obtained.

The submarine cable as a transmission line was closely approximated by taking into account only the series resistance and shunt capacitance. The transient response of such a system can be calculated by the same methods introduced by Fourier in his study of heat flow. The formulas were worked out by Kelvin in 1855 and led to the famous "KR law." The symbol K was used at that time for capacitance. The law states that the maximum operating speed is inversely proportional to the product CRl^2 where C and R are the capacitance and resistance per unit of length and l is the length. In modern terminology the propagation constant of an RC line of length l is equal to $l\sqrt{j\omega RC}$ at angular frequency ω and the attenuation constant $A(\omega)$ at frequency ω is therefore $l\sqrt{\omega RC/2}$ nepers. It appears then that

$$\frac{1}{CRl^2} = \frac{\omega}{2A^2(\omega)} \tag{1-1}$$

If we define ω_0 as the value of ω at which the attenuation is some specified value A_0, and call ω_0 the bandwidth of the cable, then

$$\frac{1}{CRl^2} = \frac{\omega_0}{2A_0{}^2} \tag{1-2}$$

From this relation, we see that the KR law says that the operating speed is directly proportional to bandwidth. Thus it is a special case of Hartley's[1] law enunciated in 1928. Modification to show the effect of signal-to-noise ratio was made by Shannon[2] in 1948. We shall observe, as we go along, the vital role which bandwidth plays in data transmission.

A substantial improvement in cable transmission was suggested by Oliver Heaviside[3] in 1887 from a study of the complete expression for the propagation constant of a line having series inductance L and shunt conductance G per unit of length in addition to the R and C parameters. The expression is

$$P = l\sqrt{(R + j\omega L)(G + j\omega C)} \tag{1-3}$$

from which if we make

$$\frac{L}{R} = \frac{C}{G} = r \tag{1-4}$$

$$P = l\sqrt{RG}(1 + j\omega r) \tag{1-5}$$

This is equivalent to an attenuation $l\sqrt{RG}$ nepers independent of frequency, and a phase shift $\omega r l\sqrt{RG} = \omega l\sqrt{LC}$ radians proportional to frequency. The waveform is therefore undistorted, and intersymbol interference does not occur. A Heaviside distortionless line permits signaling at an unlimited rate with constant delay $l\sqrt{LC}$

seconds. Practical circumstances limit the range of frequencies over which the realization is possible. In the case of a submarine cable, it was pointed out by Krarup in 1902 that inductance could be added by winding magnetic wire or tape around the central conductor. With the development of high-permeability materials such as permalloy, it was found possible to increase the operating speed by a factor of eight to ten times. For example, the New York–Azores permalloy-loaded submarine cable was operated at 400 words per minute in 1924. Loading was also applied to land cables but the lumped-coil method introduced for telephony was found more suitable than the continuous type. In applications of loading, it is not found best, in general, to go all the way to the Heaviside distortionless line. A smaller amount of added inductance actually gives less loss at the expense of moderate phase distortion. A practical difficulty is that cable parameters vary with frequency. A loaded cable is more difficult to balance for duplex operation than a nonloaded one, but this is a not unreasonable penalty to pay for the wider band.

1-8 WIRELESS TELEGRAPHY

High-frequency oscillations capable of being observed at a distance without the use of wires were produced by Joseph Henry in the United States in 1840. Maxwell's famous mathematical prediction of electromagnetic radiation such as Henry had already generated was made in 1873. Hertz's classical experiments verifying Maxwell's theory were performed in 1887. The coherer, which was the first detector of sufficient sensitivity to observe radio waves at great distances, was devised in 1892 by Edouard Branly in France, following up the phenomena originally discovered by Munk in 1835. The coherer consisted of metallic powder in a tube with attached electrodes. Passage of high-frequency current reduced the resistance of the path through the particles causing an observable increase in direct current from a battery. The powder tended to become fused by the increased current, and a mechanical tapper or decoherer was provided to restore the sensitivity after a signal had been received. In 1894 Sir Oliver Lodge demonstrated a wireless transmitter and receiver before the Royal Society as a part of a lecture commemorating the death of Hertz. The lecture was widely reported and stimulated many investigators in other countries. Among these were Marconi in Italy and Popov in Russia. The controversy over which of these two should receive the greater credit has been analyzed by Susskind,[4] who concludes "if any single individual may be designated as the 'inventor of radio' (i.e., radiotelegraphy), it is Marconi."

Marconi began his experiments in Italy in 1895. After demonstrating that he could transmit and receive over a distance, he went to England in 1896 and formed the Wireless Telegraph and Signal Company in 1897. In 1899 he sent messages across the English Channel and in 1901 across the Atlantic Ocean between Poldhu, England, and St. Johns, Newfoundland. In 1898 Braun in Germany introduced improved coupling circuits to obtain more accurate tuning and avoidance of interference between stations. The importance of Braun's work may be judged from the fact that he shared equally in a Nobel Physics Prize with Marconi. Improved efficiency of the spark-gap transmitter was accomplished in 1906 by Wien, who quenched the oscillations of one circuit, leading to the so-called "quenched-spark" system. In the years 1906 and 1907, Poulsen initiated the generation of continuous-wave oscillations by an electric arc. Alexanderson constructed the first of his high-frequency alternators in 1907. Goldschmidt and von Arco in Germany also constructed high-frequency generators at about this time. These generators used magnetic cores for frequency multiplication with signal amplification and were early examples of what are now called "parametric amplifiers."

For detection the coherer was replaced first by an electrolytic detector and then by a crystal. Fleming's two-electrode vacuum-tube rectifier brought out in 1904 was not at first regarded as superior to a crystal detector, since it was actually less sensitive and required a battery, which the crystal did not. DeForest's "audion," or three-electrode tube, came on the scene in 1907 and soon took over the detection field. Its use as a generator of electric waves was announced by Meissner in Germany in 1913.

In practically all the wireless telegraph applications on-off keying was used. The code was similar to that used on land telegraphy, but some changes were made. The radio telegraphers did not like Morse's use of dots, dashes, and spaces to represent the letters and revised the code to include only dots and dashes. Some early experiments were made with frequency-shift keying because this was in principle an easy thing to do with a wireless transmitter. The frequency could be changed by shorting out part of a tuning coil. A receiver tuned to one of the two frequencies would then give a high and low response for the two conditions. Actually, there were practical difficulties because the high voltages used made this sort of keying somewhat hazardous. The method was successfully applied, however, to the Poulsen arc transmitter. More extensive development of frequency-shift keying awaited the advent of power amplifiers.

With the perfection of the vacuum tube the modern era of communication may be considered to have arrived. We accordingly turn from the historical approach to the exposition of present-day art in data communication. References 5 to 10 give further details concerning the early history of various kinds of signaling.

REFERENCES

1. Hartley, R. V. L.: Transmission of Information, *Bell System Tech. J.*, vol. 7, pp. 535–563, July, 1928.
2. Shannon, C. E.: A Mathematical Theory of Communication, *Bell System Tech. J.*, vol. 27, pp. 379–423, July, 1948; vol. 27, pp. 623–656, October, 1948.
3. Heaviside, O.: "Electrical Papers," Macmillan & Co., Ltd., London, 1892.
4. Susskind, C.: Popov and the Beginnings of Radiotelegraphy, *Proc. IRE*, vol. 50, no. 10, pp. 2036–2047, October, 1962.
5. Prescott, G. B.: "History, Theory, and Practice of the Electric Telegraph," Ticknor and Fields, Boston, 1866.
6. Sabine, R.: "The Electric Telegraph," Virtue Bros. & Co., London, 1867.
7. Fahie, J. J.: "A History of Electric Telegraphy to the Year 1837," E. & F. N. Spon, London, 1884.
8. Still, A.: "Communication through the Ages," Murray Hill Books, Inc., New York, 1946.
9. Freebody, J. W.: "Telegraphy," Sir Isaac Pitman & Sons, Ltd., London, 1958.
10. Leggett, B.: "Wireless Telegraphy," E. P. Dutton & Co., Inc. New York, 1921.

CHAPTER 2

DIGITAL REPRESENTATION OF INFORMATION

Communication of information between human beings is accomplished mainly by a language of speech sounds or written characters and numbers. Language is discrete information as opposed to the continuous type of information obtained from physical measurements of such quantities as distances or angles. Continuous forms of information can be represented by translation to other continuously variable quantities or analogs such as electric current or deflection of a spring. Information flow within a machine system may often remain in this continuous analog form. For human interpretation, however, it is usual to quantize such information to discrete form by digital scales. Here we shall be concerned with the transmission of information already in discrete form and expressed by symbols such as alphabetical characters and numbers. In the transmission of such information or data, we shall use recognizable electrical states as symbols. The term "digital" will be used in connection with such discrete information whether or not there is any number system involved. First we shall consider the general nature of information representation by symbol patterns.

2-1 SYMBOL PATTERNS

To express information a pattern of symbols must have variation. This requires at least two different symbols. However, the differentiation may be either in the nature of the symbol or in its spacing or timing with respect to other symbols. Blank spaces or time intervals can also be regarded as symbols. Today's business language usually makes use of 50 to 100 printed characters. In the electrical transmission of digital data, it is usually desirable to limit the number of signaling symbols to a small number in the interest either of simplicity or of accuracy. Consequently it is usual to group a small number of signaling symbols in patterns or codes which in turn represent the larger number of business characters. These groups of elementary signaling symbols are sometimes called "words" although they may actually represent characters in the original message form.

As an example consider a two-symbol system. By arranging the symbols in groups of six, we obtain $2^6 = 64$ distinct combinations which will suffice for the usual business language. If these two symbols are "1" and "0," the 64 combinations are the binary numbers having the decimal equivalent 0 to 63. The term "bit," a contraction of "binary digit," is commonly applied to binary symbols. In general, if we use n different symbols in groups of m symbols, we obtain n^m distinct combinations.

The term "baud" is often used erroneously as a synonym for "bit." The baud is a unit of signaling speed; the speed in bauds is equal to the number of signaling elements or symbols per second. For binary symbols the signaling rate in bits per second is equal to the speed in bauds.

The transmission of data symbols one at a time is known as serial transmission. The transmission of several symbols simultaneously is known as parallel transmission. Usually the group of simultaneous symbols represents a character.

2-2 TIMING OF DIGITAL INFORMATION

The elements of time and space play important roles in the digital representation of data. It is necessary to be able to separate one symbol from another in order to identify it. This is accomplished in printed symbols by physical separation. In the electrical representation of symbols this same idea of separation has to be planned for, and the data receiver must know the plan. One method of separation of serial symbols involves a fixed time pattern of symbol spacing of which the receiver has prior knowledge. This is called synchronous transmission since the receiver must be in synchronism with the time pattern of the incoming symbol. Methods used in establishing the time base at the receiver will be taken up later.

A second method, known as asynchronous operation, involves no fixed time pattern. Instead, either a particular symbol is used to indicate the separation between message symbols, or else coding arrangements are used which insure that no two successive symbols are alike. In the latter case the receiver knows a new symbol is intended each time a different symbol is recognized. Asynchronous transmission thus requires at least three symbols and requires more symbols to represent a given message than does synchronous transmission. This reduced efficiency, however, can be kept to a minimum by proper coding. For instance, one of the symbols may be used to indicate a repeat of the previous symbol as a means of assuring that each symbol is different from the previous one. This method also applies to parallel transmission where one character combination may be used to indicate a repeat. In such a case where the number of character combinations is large, the loss of efficiency is quite small.

A combination of these two forms of operation known as start-stop is widely used in printing telegraph systems. Here a fixed time pattern is used for the group of symbols representing a character, but each group is preceded by a signal transition which serves as a symbol to denote when the fixed pattern is to start. Thus the spacing of the transmitted characters can be varied without prior knowledge of the receiver. It is of interest to note that the Morse code is in this category. The time pattern is not absolutely fixed, but the receiver must assume that the relative pattern of dot and dash lengths is to be fixed within a character.

Where groups or codes of symbols are used serially, the beginning and end of each group must be found. This is called word or character timing. The start-stop mode of operation is one way of providing this timing. However, the use of additional symbols for each character is sometimes too wasteful of time. Where the operation is synchronous over long sequences of symbols, a distinctive symbol or combination of symbols not used as a message character can mark the beginning of the initial character in a group. If all following characters of the group have a known equal number of symbols, the spacing of the characters can be determined from the symbol timing. Repeating the character synchronizing combination at the start of each group of characters prevents a slip in the timing from persisting.

Word or character synchronization can also be achieved by use of a code having an inherent self-synchronizing property. Minimum-redundancy variable-length binary codes which are self-synchronizing have been described by Huffman[1] and others.[2] There are also classes of equal length codes which have the property that any sequence formed by portions of two adjacent code words differs in at least one symbol from any valid code word. Such codes have been described as comma-free[3,4] since no symbols are required to indicate or initially establish the separation between code words.

In parallel transmission the simultaneous symbols are separated by being carried over some form of multiple channel, and the symbol and character timing become the same.

2-3 EXAMPLES OF DIGITAL CODES

In Table 2-1 some of the more common codes presently in use by business machines are given. All of these codes are binary. Some are restricted in that not all possible combinations are used.

Table 2-1. Business Machine Codes

	5-LEVEL TAPE	8-LEVEL TAPE**	IBM 4-OUT-OF-8	IBM CARD	SPERRY-RAND CARD
A	12	167	1578	12-1	246
B	145	267	2578	12-2	24
C	234	12567	1278	12-3	15
D	14	367	3578	12-4	134
E	1	13567	1378	12-5	13
F	134	23567	2378	12-6	256
G	245	12367	4578	12-7	45
H	35	467	1478	12-8	35
I	23	14567	2478	12-9	34
J	124	157	1568	11-1	234
K	1234	257	2568	11-2	346
L	25	127	1268	11-3	16
M	345	357	3568	11-4	14
N	34	137	1368	11-5	146
O	45	237	2368	11-6	23
P	235	12357	4568	11-7	235
Q	1235	457	1468	11-8	345
R	24	147	2468	11-9	25
S	13	256	2567	0-2	245
T	5	126	1267	0-3	356
U	123	356	3567	0-4	145
V	2345	136	1367	0-5	136
W	125	236	2367	0-6	135
X	1345	12356	4567	0-7	156
Y	135	456	1467	0-8	236
Z	15	146	2467	0-9	456
0	P*	6	3467	0	1
1	Q*	1	1678	1	2
2	W*	2	2678	2	26
3	E*	125	1256	3	3
4	R*	3	3678	4	36
5	T*	135	1356	5	4
6	Y*	235	2356	6	46
7	U*	123	4678	7	5
8	I*	4	1456	8	56
9	O*	145	2456	9	6

*FIGURES SHIFT (UPPER CASE)
**LEVEL 5 IS A PARITY CHECK

The first two columns are codes commonly used in punched paper tape. The terms "5-level" and "8-level" refer to the number of possible hole positions in the tape or, equivalently, the number of binary symbols or bits used in each character code. The numbers listed in the chart indicate the hole positions used for each character. The tape is used to generate binary electrical signals with the presence

Table 2-1. Business Machine Codes (Continued)

	5-LEVEL TAPE	8-LEVEL TAPE	IBM 4-OUT-OF-8	IBM CARD
SPACE	3	5	3456	
CAR. RET.	4	8		
LINE FEED	2			
,	N*	12456	1247	0-3-8
.	M*	12467	1246	12-3-8
/	X*	156	1567	0-1
&	G*	567	3478	12
$	D*	12457	1248	11-3-8
)	L*	0*		
'	J*	1*		
@		2*	1345	4-8
#	H*	3*	1245	3-8
=		4*		
%		5*	1347	0-4-8
¢		6*		
?	B*	7*		
*		8*	1348	11-4-8
(	K*	9*		
:	C*	/*		
;	V*	&*		
_		$*		
"	Z*	-*		
-	A*	7	3468	11
Lower Case (LTRS)	12345	24567		
Upper Case (FIGS)	1245	34567		
TAB		23456		
TAPE FEED		1234567		

*UPPER CASE

Numbers in table indicate hole positions in tape or card except for IBM 4-out-of-8 Code which is used only in transmission for error detection.

and absence of holes controlling the two signaling states. The "7-level" binary-coded decimal code used by IBM on magnetic tape is the same for most characters as that shown for "8-level" paper tape except for the order of the bits. The 1, 2, 4, 8, A, B, C magnetic tape channel designations correspond to the 1, 2, 3, 4, 6, 7, 5 hole positions given in the table.

The 5-level code is the one commonly used with teletypewriters. The 8-level code provides more combinations, permitting the use of uppercase and lowercase alphabet characters and a large number of miscellaneous characters. It also permits the use of codes which enable certain types of transmission errors to be detected. It is for this reason that the fifth level of the 8-level code is used to make each

Table 2-2. American Standard Code for Information Interchange

b7				0	0	0	0	I	I	I	I
	b6			0	0	I	I	0	0	I	I
		b5		0	I	0	I	0	I	0	I
b4	b3	b2	b1								
0	0	0	0	NULL	DC$_0$	ƀ	0	@	P		
0	0	0	I	SOM	DC$_1$	!	I	A	Q		
0	0	I	0	EOA	DC$_2$	"	2	B	R		
0	0	I	I	EOM	DC$_3$	#	3	C	S		U N A S S I G N E D
0	I	0	0	EOT	DC$_4$ (STOP)	$	4	D	T	U N A S S I G N E D	
0	I	0	I	WRU	ERR	%	5	E	U		
0	I	I	0	RU	SYNC	&	6	F	V		
0	I	I	I	BELL	LEM	' (APOS)	7	G	W		
I	0	0	0	FE$_0$	S$_0$	(	8	H	X		
I	0	0	I	HT / SK	S$_1$	)	9	I	Y		
I	0	I	0	LF	S$_2$	*	:	J	Z		
I	0	I	I	V$_{TAB}$	S$_3$	+	;	K	[		
I	I	0	0	FF	S$_4$	, (COMMA)	<	L	\		ACK
I	I	0	I	CR	S$_5$	–	=	M	]		①
I	I	I	0	SO	S$_6$	.	>	N	↑		ESC
I	I	I	I	SI	S$_7$	/	?	O	←		DEL

Standard 7-bit set code positional order and notation are shown with b$_7$ the high-order, and b$_1$ the low-order, bit position.

Example:

	b$_7$	b$_6$	b$_5$	b$_4$	b$_3$	b$_2$	b$_1$
The code for "R" is:	I	0	I	0	0	I	0

NULL	Null/Idle	DC$_1$–DC$_3$	Device control
SOM	Start of message	DC$_4$(Stop)	Device control (stop)
EOA	End of address	ERR	Error
EOM	End of message	SYNC	Synchronous idle
EOT	End of transmission	LEM	Logical end of media
WRU	"Who are you?"	S$_0$–S$_7$	Separator (information)
RU	"Are you...?"	ƀ	Word separator (space, normally non-printing)
BELL	Audible signal		
FE$_0$	Format effector	<	Less than
HT	Horizontal tabulation	>	Greater than
SK	Skip (punched card)	↑	Up arrow (Exponentiation)
LF	Line feed	←	Left arrow (Implies/ Replaced by)
V$_{TAB}$	Vertical tabulation	\	Reverse slant
FF	Form feed	ACK	Acknowledge
CR	Carriage return	①	Unassigned control
SO	Shift out	ESC	Escape
SI	Shift in	DEL	Delete/Idle
DC$_0$	Device control reserved for data link escape		

character have an odd number of holes. The 4-out-of-8 code is a fixed-count type of code with all characters containing four marking and four spacing bits. It is used for error detection in certain IBM data transmission systems.

The fourth column gives the Hollerith code used on IBM punched cards. Each character on the card is represented by holes in a vertical column. There are 12 possible hole positions and 80 column positions. One, two, and sometimes three holes are used as shown in the chart. For serial transmission of this type of code, it is usually translated to one having fewer bits. For example, the 8-bit code shown in the third column has been used for this purpose. The restriction of each code to exactly four marking bits is of value in detecting the more frequent transmission errors.

The fifth column gives the code used on the 90-column Sperry-Rand punched card. This type of card provides for two characters in each of 45 possible column positions. Each character is represented by holes in six possible positions.

An American Standard Code for Information Interchange[5] was approved on June 17, 1963. This code is shown in the chart of Table 2-2. It is a 7-bit code, thus providing for as many as 128 different characters. The blank positions in the table are unassigned and are available for special purposes and for future growth of the standard code. An eighth bit can be added as a parity check for error detection purposes. As this code is generally adopted, it will be possible to exchange digital information among various types and makes of business machines without the code translations which are often necessary at present.

REFERENCES

1. Huffman, D. A.: A Method for the Construction of Minimum-redundancy Codes, *Proc. IRE*, vol. 40, pp. 1098–1101, September, 1952.
2. Gilbert, E. N., and E. F. Moore: Variable-length Binary Encodings, *Bell System Tech. J.*, vol. 38, pp. 933–967, July, 1959.
3. Crick, F. H. C., J. S. Griffith, and L. E. Orgel: Codes without Commas, *Proc. Natl. Acad. Sci. U.S.*, vol. 43, pp. 416–421, May, 1957.
4. Golomb, S. W., B. Gordon, and L. R. Welch: Comma-free Codes, *Can. J. Math.*, vol. 10, no. 2, pp. 202–209, 1958.
5. American Standards Association, Inc.: American Standard Code for Information Interchange, X3.4–1963, New York.

CHAPTER 3

ELECTRICAL REPRESENTATION OF DIGITAL INFORMATION

3-1 BASIC INFORMATION WAVEFORMS

There are a number of ways by which digital symbols can be represented by electrical signals. All these involve assigning a range of values of a continuously variable electrical function to mean some digital symbol. The simplest analog is a multivalued current or voltage wave. In Fig. 3-1 is shown a synchronous two-valued data wave. In each symbol interval a condition of current or no current is

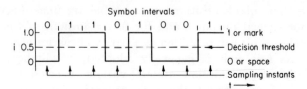

FIG. 3-1. Synchronous two-valued data wave.

transmitted. The two symbols are labeled "1" and "0." In telegraph terminology these are called "mark" and "space," terms which originated from the appearance of the recorded signal of the early Morse telegraph systems. The receiver under control of its clock, properly phased with respect to the incoming data wave, samples the wave at the middle of each symbol interval. If the wave is between half and full amplitude, the symbol is recorded as a 1; if between zero and half amplitude, as a 0. The threshold of decision between 1 and 0 in this case is the half-amplitude level. This type of signal is sometimes referred to as "on-off" and in telegraphy as "neutral" since a neutral relay or sounder can be used which responds to either direction of current.

Instead of current and no current, opposite directions or polarities of current can be used. In Fig. 3-2 is shown a wave having equal positive and negative amplitudes. In this case the decision threshold is zero. This type of signal is referred to as "polar."

26

In the foregoing examples no change in signal occurs when one of the symbols is repeated. It is sometimes desirable to have definite separation between the symbol signals as shown in Fig. 3-3. A rectangular pulse of current is used for a 1 and no pulse for a 0. The

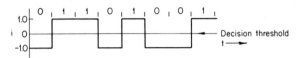

FIG. 3-2. Wave of equal positive and negative amplitudes.

spacing of the symbols is greater than the pulse length so that intervals of no current occur between successive 1 symbols. This type of signal is called "return-to-zero" as opposed to the "nonreturn-to-zero" signals of the previous examples which used full symbol-length pulses.

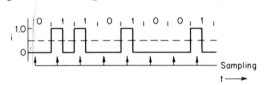

FIG. 3-3. Return-to-zero signal.

An example of a polar return-to-zero type signal is shown in Fig. 3-4. In this case the zero intervals can be considered as a third symbol used to separate the information bearing symbols. The symbol spacing can be varied with this type of signal and operated asynchronously. Such signals are sometimes called "self-clocking" since the receiver needs no symbol time base.

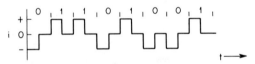

FIG. 3-4. Polar return-to-zero signal.

Still another type of signal is shown in Fig. 3-5 in which alternating polarity pulses are used for 1 symbols and no pulse for 0 symbols. The 1 pulse can be either full or fractional length of the symbol interval.

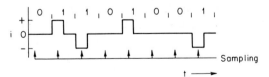

FIG. 3-5. Bipolar signal.

This type of signal is called "bipolar." One reason for using the bipolar type just described is to eliminate the necessity of transmitting d-c and low-frequency components.

It is sometimes desirable to encode the information in terms of signal transitions. For example, a transition in a binary wave may be used to designate a 0; and no transition, a 1, as indicated in Fig. 3-6. Such a signal wave can be inverted in polarity without affecting its

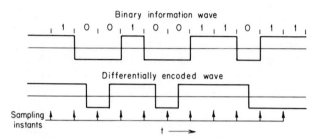

FIG. 3-6. Differential encoding of binary information.

interpretation and is useful in systems which have no sense of absolute polarity. The information can be recovered by sampling the received wave and comparing the polarity of adjacent samples to determine if a transition has occurred. This is termed differential detection and for a serial channel requires synchronous operation.

A type of encoding somewhat inverse to that just described employs polar pulses to indicate transitions of an information wave. This is indicated in Fig. 3-7. The pulse length corresponds to the maximum

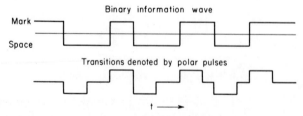

FIG. 3-7. Dicode wave.

rate of transitions which is to be transmitted. This type of signal, like that of Fig. 3-5, has no d-c component. It can be used to transmit asynchronous data. Another feature which is sometimes desirable is that its average power varies proportionally with the density of the transitions of the information wave. This type of signal is sometimes known as "dicode."

As an example of a signal with a larger number of levels, Fig. 3-8 shows a four-level synchronous wave. Since the input and output of such a data channel would most likely be binary data, the four symbols have been given two-digit binary designations. Three thresholds are necessary at the receiver to make the decision among the four states.

The examples discussed refer to serial operation where one symbol at a time is transmitted. Parallel data can be handled by provision of multiple channels.

All the foregoing examples of data waveforms are called baseband signals. They are the basic data waves to be transmitted. They can

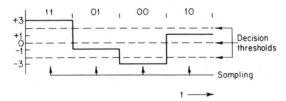

FIG. 3-8. Four-level synchronous data wave.

be transmitted directly in this form, in which case a channel passing frequencies from zero or near zero to a frequency about equal to the symbol rate is required. Alternatively these basic waves can be used to modulate a carrier wave, thus permitting the transmission to take place in a higher-frequency band.

3-2 MODULATED CARRIER SIGNALS

A sinusoidal wave, $A \sin (\omega t + \theta)$, can be used to carry a baseband data signal by varying either the amplitude A, the frequency ω, or the phase θ. An example of simple on-off amplitude modulation is shown in Fig. 3-9. The amplitude can be varied to represent any of

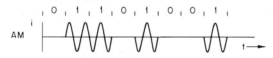

FIG. 3-9. On-off amplitude modulation.

the baseband signals described previously. For polar signals the negative amplitudes result in 180° phase changes of the carrier wave.

An example of a binary frequency-modulated carrier wave is shown in Fig. 3-10. This type of modulation is sometimes called "frequency-shift keying" (FSK) and "carrier-shift keying." Frequency modulation

can be used to carry any of the baseband waveforms previously
described.

Fig. 3-10. Binary frequency-modulated carrier wave.

An example of a binary phase-modulated carrier wave is shown in
Fig. 3-11. A phase change of 180° is depicted. Since phase is an
angular quantity, 180° is the largest possible step change. Thus the
baseband wave must not vary the phase more than $\pm 180°$ to avoid
ambiguity, and furthermore $+180°$ and $-180°$ become the same.
Binary 180° phase modulation is equivalent to polar amplitude
modulation.

Since modulated carrier waves of different frequencies can be readily
separated by filters, several separate channels can be provided over a

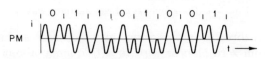

Fig. 3-11. Binary phase-modulated carrier wave.

common facility. This permits several symbols to be transmitted
simultaneously and can be used for parallel-type data.

3-3 MODULATED PULSES

Pulse-modulation systems usually employ short pulses of high peak
power and low duty factor as an effective way of combating noise.
Although such systems are mainly used for analog data, they can also
be used to carry any baseband digital signal. The modulated pulses
may themselves be baseband current pulses, or they may be on-off
keyed carrier signals. Amplitude modulation of pulses (PAM) has

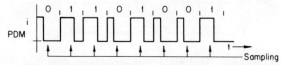

Fig. 3-12. Binary pulse duration modulation.

already been mentioned, but pulses can also be modulated in duration
(PDM) and in time position (PPM). In Fig. 3-12 a pulse signal is
shown duration modulated by binary data. In Fig. 3-13 a pulse

signal is shown position modulated by binary data. It is evident that reception of such data signals involves measurement of variation in the time duration or location of pulses. Pulse duration modulation can readily be operated asynchronously as far as symbol spacing is concerned, but of course the duration coding of the symbols must be fixed. Pulse position modulation is usually operated synchronously

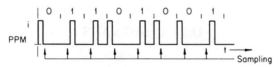

FIG. 3-13. Binary pulse position modulation.

although variable symbol spacing can be used if a time reference pulse precedes each symbol pulse. In this case it becomes essentially the same as pulse duration modulation.

The widely used International Morse Code is an example of binary pulse duration modulation. The shorter pulse is called a "dot" and the longer pulse, which has a duration of three dots, is called a "dash." The pulses are separated by uniform spaces, and hence the pulse rate varies with the signal sequence.

CHAPTER **4**

FREQUENCY ANALYSIS OF DIGITAL
DATA SIGNALS

4-1 BASEBAND SIGNALS

In order to design suitable transmission channels for digital signals, one must know something of the frequency spectrum of the signals. First, we will consider the spectrum of the idealized rectangular pulses previously discussed. The frequency analysis of a regularly repeated pulse such as shown in Fig. 4-1 can be accomplished by means of a

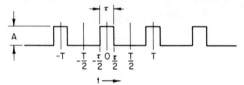

FIG. 4-1. Periodic pulse train.

Fourier series. Such a series expresses any physically important repetitive time function as the sum of a constant and harmonically related sinusoidal terms. This can be written as

$$E(t) = \frac{a_0}{2} + \sum_{n=1}^{\infty} (a_n \cos n\omega t + b_n \sin n\omega t) \qquad (4\text{-}1)$$

where

$$a_0 = \frac{\omega}{\pi} \int_{-\pi/\omega}^{\pi/\omega} E(t)\, dt \qquad (4\text{-}2)$$

$$a_n = \frac{\omega}{\pi} \int_{-\pi/\omega}^{\pi/\omega} E(t) \cos n\omega t\, dt \qquad (4\text{-}3)$$

$$b_n = \frac{\omega}{\pi} \int_{-\pi/\omega}^{\pi/\omega} E(t) \sin n\omega t\, dt \qquad (4\text{-}4)$$

If the time scale can be so chosen that the function is symmetrically oriented about $t = 0$, as in Fig. 4-1, the "b" terms become zero. With

32

a pulse repetition period of T, $\omega = 2\pi/T$. For a rectangular pulse of width τ and amplitude A the coefficients of the terms become

$$a_0 = \frac{2}{T} \int_{-T/2}^{T/2} E(t)\, dt = \frac{2}{T} [At]_{-\tau/2}^{\tau/2} = \frac{2A\tau}{T} \tag{4-5}$$

$$a_n = \frac{2}{T} \int_{-T/2}^{T/2} E(t) \cos \frac{2\pi n t}{T}\, dt = \frac{2}{T}\left[\frac{A \sin (2\pi n t/T)}{(2\pi n/T)}\right]_{-\tau/2}^{\tau/2}$$

$$= \frac{2A}{T} \frac{\sin (\pi n \tau/T)}{(\pi n/T)} \tag{4-6}$$

Multiplying and dividing by τ,

$$a_n = \frac{2A\tau}{T} \frac{\sin (\pi n \tau/T)}{(\pi n \tau/T)} \tag{4-7}$$

The series thus becomes

$$\frac{a_0}{2} + \sum_{n=1}^{\infty} a_n \cos n\omega t = \frac{A\tau}{T} + \sum_{n=1}^{\infty} \frac{2A\tau}{T} \frac{\sin (\pi n \tau/T)}{(\pi n \tau/T)} \cos n\omega t \tag{4-8}$$

The coefficients of the cosine terms follow a $(\sin x)/x$ envelope form where $x = (\pi n \tau)/T$.

For the special case of $\tau = T/2$, representing a train of alternate on-off square-wave pulses, all the even terms fall at zero points of the $(\sin x)/x$ function giving

$$E(t) = A\left(\frac{1}{2} + \frac{2}{\pi} \cos \omega t - \frac{2}{3\pi} \cos 3\omega t + \frac{2}{5\pi} \cos 5\omega t \cdots\right) \tag{4-9}$$

Thus such a wave consists of a d-c term plus a fundamental and odd harmonics thereof. The amplitudes of the harmonics are inversely proportional to their frequencies. This type of signal is often called a "dot signal" or "reversals." If the pulses are shorter or longer than $T/2$, there will be both even and odd harmonics present.

Leaving the pulse width τ constant and increasing the pulse spacing T to a large value results in a large number of spectral components having amplitudes following the $(\sin x)/x$ envelope shape as illustrated in Fig. 4-2. In the limit as T becomes infinite we obtain the continuous frequency spectrum of a single rectangular pulse.

The first zero of the $(\sin x)/x$ function occurs when $x = \pi$ or, in the Fourier series [Eq. (4-8)], when $n = T/\tau$. This corresponds to a frequency of n/T or $1/\tau$. Thus as the pulse is made shorter, the frequency of the first zero increases. In the limit for an infinitesimally short pulse or impulse the spectrum becomes flat.

Equation (4-9) with the d-c term omitted gives the spectrum of a polar dot or reversal signal with a peak-to-peak amplitude of A. The

spectrum of a single polar pulse is the same as for the on-off case
except for an $A/2$ d-c component as the base.

Return-to-zero type signals have a broader frequency spectrum for
a given signaling rate because of the shorter pulses. For this reason
they are usually used only for local transmission paths where the
required bandwidth is readily available. As a result of the wider
spectrum of return-to-zero signals less of the energy is at zero and very
low frequencies. This makes it feasible to transmit such signals
through transformers and other a-c coupled circuits without appreciable
pulse shape distortion. This is often useful in avoiding d-c coupling
problems such as those caused by ground potential differences.

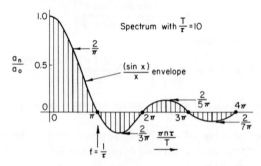

Fig. 4-2. Amplitude of harmonics in Fourier series representation of rectangular
pulse train with pulse spacing equal to ten times pulse width.

4-2 SINUSOIDAL AMPLITUDE MODULATION

Before a carrier modulated by a data signal is considered, the simple
case of sinusoidal modulation will be reviewed. In the general
expression of a carrier signal,

$$E(t) = A \sin (\omega_c t + \theta) \tag{4-10}$$

consider the case of sinusoidal amplitude modulation. If the relative
phase constant θ is assumed to be zero and the amplitude varies from
its unmodulated value A by the factor $1 + m \sin \omega t$, we obtain

$$E(t) = A(1 + m \sin \omega t) \sin \omega_c t = A \sin \omega_c t + (mA \sin \omega t) \sin \omega_c t$$

$$= A \sin \omega_c t + m \frac{A}{2} \cos (\omega_c t - \omega t) - m \frac{A}{2} \cos (\omega_c t + \omega t) \tag{4-11}$$

The modulated signal is thus shown to consist of the unmodulated
carrier plus equal lower and upper side-frequency components which
differ in frequency from the carrier by the modulating frequency
$\omega/2\pi$. The side-frequency amplitudes are proportional to the factor

m, the modulation index. This index is usually restricted to a maximum value of 1, which is called 100 per cent modulation. At this value the signal amplitude just reaches zero for the negative peak of the modulation cycle. It will later be shown that higher values of m which produce a phase reversal of the carrier have useful applications. In Fig. 4-3 the appearance of an amplitude-modulated wave is shown. In Fig. 4-4 a vector diagram of the carrier and side-frequency components is given. This type of diagram shows the relative phase positions of the carrier and side-frequency components at a given instant. The carrier vector is held stationary as a reference with the side-frequency vectors rotating counterclockwise to indicate a higher frequency and clockwise to indicate a lower frequency. It will be seen that the side-frequency components combine to form a resultant in phase with the carrier varying in amplitude from $+mA$ to $-mA$.

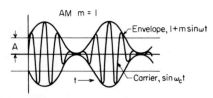

FIG. 4-3. Carrier wave with 100 per cent amplitude modulation by sinusoidal signal.

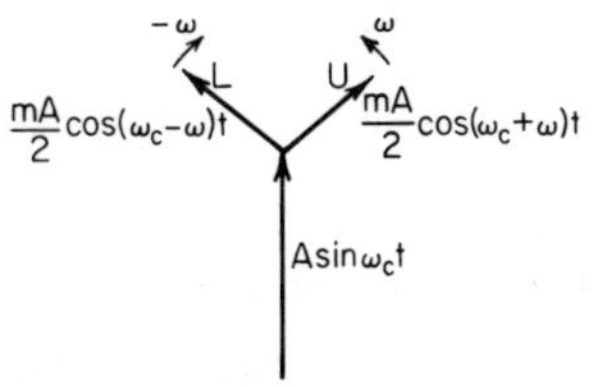

FIG. 4-4. Vector diagram of carrier and side-frequency components in amplitude modulation.

It is evident from Eq. (4-11) that if the modulating wave were complicated but expressible by a series of sine and cosine terms, each term would lead to a pair of side frequencies. Thus a lower and upper sideband of frequencies would result. The upper sideband consists of all the components of the baseband modulating wave translated upward in frequency by an amount equal to the carrier frequency. The lower sideband is identical except for inversion about the carrier frequency. Any given modulating baseband spectrum thus leads to a pair of sidebands having the same relative spectrum shape as the baseband. It is assumed here that the modulating frequency is less than the carrier frequency. Cases where this is not so will be discussed later.

4-3 SQUARE-WAVE AMPLITUDE MODULATION

The spectrum of a baseband on-off dot signal was shown in Eq. (4-9). If such a signal is used to produce 100 per cent modulation of a carrier of frequency $\omega_c/2\pi$ having an unmodulated amplitude $A/2$, we obtain

$$E(t) = A\left\{\frac{1}{2}\sin\omega_c t + \frac{1}{\pi}[\sin(\omega_c t - \omega t) + \sin(\omega_c t + \omega t)]\right.$$

$$-\frac{1}{3\pi}[\sin(\omega_c t - 3\omega t) + \sin(\omega_c t + 3\omega t)]$$

$$\left.+\frac{1}{5\pi}[\sin(\omega_c t - 5\omega t) + \sin(\omega_c t + 5\omega t)] - \cdots\right\} \quad (4\text{-}12)$$

This is seen to be similar to the baseband spectrum of Eq. (4-9) with the d-c term now appearing as a carrier term and with the a-c terms divided between the lower- and upper-sideband terms.

4-4 SINUSOIDAL PHASE AND FREQUENCY MODULATION

A sinusoidal phase-modulated carrier signal can be expressed as

$$E(t) = A\sin(\omega_c t + \Delta\theta\sin\omega t) \quad (4\text{-}13)$$

where $\Delta\theta$ is the maximum phase deviation from that of the unmodulated carrier. The angular velocity of this wave is

$$\frac{d(\omega_c t + \Delta\theta\sin\omega t)}{dt} = \omega_c + \omega\,\Delta\theta\cos\omega t \quad (4\text{-}14)$$

The instantaneous frequency corresponding to this angular velocity is

$$\frac{\omega_c}{2\pi} + \frac{\omega\,\Delta\theta}{2\pi}\cos\omega t = f_c + f\,\Delta\theta\cos\omega t$$

$$= f_c + \Delta f\cos\omega t \quad (4\text{-}15)$$

Thus the instantaneous frequency is the unmodulated carrier frequency f_c, plus a cosine variation in frequency at the modulating frequency $\omega/2\pi = f$. The maximum frequency deviation Δf is equal to the product of the modulating frequency and the peak phase deviation $\Delta\theta$. Going back to Eq. (4-13), we see that it can represent either phase or frequency modulation. If it is written as

$$E(t) = A\sin(\omega_c t + \beta\sin\omega t) \quad (4\text{-}16)$$

$\beta = \Delta\theta$ for phase modulation and $\beta = \Delta f/f$ for frequency modulation. The constant β is called the modulation index and represents the peak phase deviation in radians or the ratio between the peak frequency deviation and the modulating frequency. These relationships hold only for sinusoidal modulation.

The frequency spectrum of the angle modulation expressed by Eq. (4-16) is complicated in structure and depends on both β and ω. It can be expressed as a carrier plus side frequencies by means of Bessel functions as follows:

$$E(t) = A\{J_0(\beta) \sin \omega_c t + J_1(\beta)[\sin (\omega_c + \omega)t - \sin (\omega_c - \omega)t]$$
$$+ J_2(\beta)[\sin (\omega_c + 2\omega)t + \sin (\omega_c - 2\omega)t]$$
$$+ J_3(\beta)[\sin (\omega_c + 3\omega)t - \sin (\omega_c - 3\omega)t] + \cdots$$
$$+ J_n(\beta)[\sin (\omega_c + n\omega)t + (-1)^n \sin (\omega_c - n\omega)t]\} \quad (4\text{-}17)$$

Thus even simple sinusoidal modulation leads to an unlimited number of frequencies on both sides of the carrier, spaced at multiples of the modulating frequency. A graph of Bessel-function values is given in Fig. 4-5. It will be noticed that for very small values of modulation

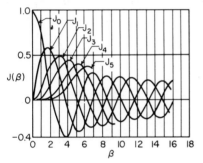

FIG. 4-5. Graphs of Bessel functions.

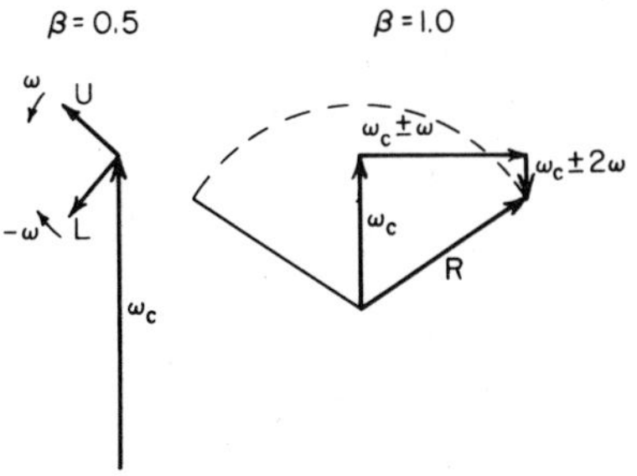

FIG. 4-6. Vector diagrams for angle-modulated waves.

index the amplitudes of the carrier and first-order side frequencies approach those for amplitude modulation, and the higher-order side frequencies become negligible.

Equation (4-17) may also be written as follows:

$$E(t) = A\{J_0(\beta) \sin \omega_c t + [2J_1(\beta) \sin \omega t] \cos \omega_c t$$
$$+ [2J_2(\beta) \cos 2\omega t] \sin \omega_c t + [2J_3(\beta) \sin 3\omega t] \cos \omega_c t + \cdots\}$$
$$(4\text{-}18)$$

Equation (4-18) shows that at any instant the resultant signal vector can be obtained from the sum of a series of amplitude-modulated sine and cosine vectors of the carrier frequency. The even-order components are in phase with the carrier, and the odd-order components are in quadrature with the carrier. For a small modulation index the main difference between amplitude modulation and angle modulation is thus a 90° phase difference of the carrier with respect to the side frequencies. Vector diagrams for angle modulation are shown in Fig. 4-6.

4-5 FREQUENCY MODULATION BY COMPLEX WAVEFORMS

When the FM modulating wave consists of a number of sinusoidal components, the number of side frequencies greatly increases. The side frequencies include, in addition to those which would be present with each component acting separately, all possible cross-modulation frequencies. The amplitude of each resulting side frequency is determined by the product of the Bessel functions of the orders corresponding to the orders of the frequency components involved in the cross modulation.

Frequency modulation by a square-wave dot signal does have a relatively simple spectrum. As shown in Sec. 4-8 it is of the following form:

$$
\begin{aligned}
E(t) = \frac{2Am}{\pi} \bigg\{ &\frac{1}{m^2} \sin \frac{m\pi}{2} \cos \omega_c t \\
&+ \frac{1}{m^2 - 1^2} \cos \frac{m\pi}{2} \left[\cos(\omega_c - \omega)t - \cos(\omega_c + \omega)t \right] \\
&- \frac{1}{m^2 - 2^2} \sin \frac{m\pi}{2} \left[\cos(\omega_c - 2\omega)t + \cos(\omega_c + 2\omega)t \right] \\
&- \frac{1}{m^2 - 3^2} \cos \frac{m\pi}{2} \left[\cos(\omega_c - 3\omega)t - \cos(\omega_c + 3\omega)t \right] + \cdots \bigg\}
\end{aligned}
$$

(4-19)

where m is the deviation ratio equal to the frequency shift between mark and space divided by twice the dotting frequency. Because of the nonsinusoidal modulation, m is not equal to the peak phase deviation. For the case where $m = 1$, which is typical for data transmission, this becomes

$$
\begin{aligned}
E(t) = A \bigg\{ &\frac{2}{\pi} \cos \omega_c t + \frac{1}{2} \left[\cos(\omega_c - \omega)t - \cos(\omega_c + \omega)t \right] \\
&+ \frac{2}{3\pi} \left[\cos(\omega_c - 2\omega)t + \cos(\omega_c + 2\omega)t \right] \\
&- \frac{2}{15\pi} \left[\cos(\omega_c - 4\omega)t + \cos(\omega_c + 4\omega)t \right] - \cdots \bigg\}
\end{aligned}
$$

(4-20)

In comparing this result with the square-wave AM spectrum in (4-12), we observe that the carrier and first-order side frequencies are greater in magnitude and that there is an appreciable second-order side frequency. This is to be expected since the FM wave with its constant amplitude has twice the average power of the on-off wave. It is of interest to note, however, that the higher-order side frequencies die away faster for FM than for AM.

Figure 4-7 shows spectrum diagrams for square-wave FM with various values of deviation ratio. Note that as the ratio increases,

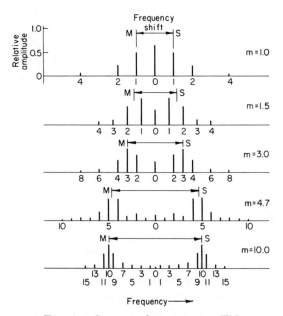

FIG. 4-7. Spectra of square-wave FM.

the energy spreads away from the mid-frequency and concentrates near the steady-state mark and space frequencies. For integer values of the index, the result is the sum of two on-off AM carriers located at the steady-state mark and space frequencies and keyed in phase opposition. This can be illustrated by Eqs. (4-12) and (4-20). This occurs because the integer index preserves the phase of the carrier from one mark interval to the next, and likewise for the space intervals. During a space interval a whole number of cycles will be gained or lost with reference to the mark frequency. For other than integer values of the index, there is no side-frequency component at the steady-state mark and space frequencies, and both even- and odd-order side-frequency components are present. Two such cases are illustrated in Fig. 4-7.

4-6 PHASE MODULATION BY COMPLEX WAVEFORMS

In angle modulation the carrier phase may be expressed as the integral of the instantaneous carrier frequency. Conversely the instantaneous carrier frequency is the derivative of the carrier phase. As previously pointed out, Eq. (4-16), for sinusoidal angle modulation, can represent either phase or frequency modulation. If the phase is represented by a sine function, the frequency is a cosine function with the same argument. For nonsinusoidal modulation the difference is more striking. For instance, the square-wave FM case represents triangular phase modulation as illustrated in Fig. 4-8. On the other hand square-wave phase modulation, except for multiples of 2π, would result in sharp impulses of frequency modulation.

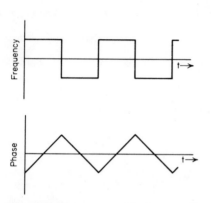

FIG. 4-8. Frequency and phase variations for square-wave FM.

When data are to be transmitted by multilevel square-wave phase modulation, all phase steps are restricted within the range $\pm\pi$ as mentioned in Chap. 3. Such a wave can be considered to be the sum of two amplitude-modulated waves with their carrier phases in quadrature. The signals modulating the individual carriers are multilevel square waves with amplitudes proportional to the cosines and sines of the phase values. The spectra of such phase-modulated waves can thus be considered as the superposition of two AM spectra. For other than square-wave phase modulation the wave can still be resolved into two quadrature AM waves, but the amplitude-modulating functions can differ greatly from the phase function.

4-7 PULSE MODULATION

Examples of binary pulse duration modulation (PDM) and pulse position modulation (PPM) have been previously shown in Figs. 3-12 and 3-13 respectively. In the PDM case the short pulses have a broader frequency spectrum than the long ones and hence determine the bandwidth of the signal. The extreme case is reached in Fig. 3-12 when a long train of 0's is sent leading to a train of regularly spaced short pulses. Figures 4-1 and 4-2 then apply with τ equal to the short pulse duration and T the signaling interval. In the case of International Morse Code this is an all-dot signal with $T = 2\tau$. An infinitely long dot sequence has infinitesimal probability of occurrence, but the ability to transmit very long sequences may be necessary for satisfactory operation. Since the information in a PDM pulse train is actually contained in the starting and stopping times, signal power is used inefficiently. Convenience of instrumentation is the principal reason for which PDM might be chosen in specific situations.

In PPM the pulses all have the same duration, and it is this duration which determines the signal bandwidth. Since the pulse is, in general,

FIG. 4-9. PDM-AM wave.

shorter than would be used in a simple on-off system at the same signaling rate, a PPM signal may be said to require excess bandwidth. In return for the extra bandwidth, a sharp localization of the pulse in time is obtained, which may give protection against disturbance by noise. Pulse position modulation shows an advantage when a fixed amount of average signal power can be concentrated into a short high burst to override momentarily a steady noise background which may have even greater average power.

FIG. 4-10. PPM-AM wave.

Pulse-modulated signals can be used in turn to modulate a carrier in various ways. It is customary to designate such methods by the abbreviations of the modulation schemes in the sequence employed, with hyphens inserted for separation. Thus a binary PDM-AM signal is obtained by using the duration-modulated pulses of Fig. 3-12 to turn a carrier oscillator on and off. The result is the wave shown in Fig. 4-9 made up of short and long spurts of sine waves. Similarly a binary PPM-AM signal (Fig. 4-10) is a sequence of equal-length carrier

spurts governed by a binary PPM wave such as that of Fig. 3-13.   In
a similar manner we can construct PDM-FM, PDM-PM, PPM-FM, and
PPM-PM signals by using the PDM and PPM waves to control the
frequency or phase of the carrier oscillator.   Examples of such "stacked
systems" are most likely to be encountered in telemetry.

The spectral composition of pulse-modulated carrier waves can be
obtained, in general, by the sideband calculations previously illustrated.   Thus in a PPM-AM wave the spectrum of the PPM wave is
translated to upper and lower sidebands on the carrier.   In a PPM-FM
wave higher-order sidebands appear.   The extreme cases which determine the maximum bandwidth required can be constructed from
pulse sequences of maximum frequency spread.   One such case
consisting of an infinite sequence of marks or spaces is included in the
analysis of the following section.

4-8 CALCULATION OF SPECTRAL COMPONENTS IN FM CASE

In this section we apply Fourier analysis to the waves generated by
frequency-modulating a carrier with a periodic baseband signal and
indicate how the results quoted earlier in the chapter are obtained.
We use the conventional definition of instantaneous frequency as time
rate of change of phase.   To calculate spectra, we must specify how
the phase varies with time.   If the instantaneous frequency variation
is known, the phase can be found to within an arbitrary constant by
integration.   When sudden transitions in frequency occur, there are
two cases to consider: (1) continuous phase, such as would be obtained
by shifting the frequency of a single oscillator, and (2) discontinuous
phase, such as would be found if the frequency shift were performed
by switching between two independent oscillators.

We illustrate by working out as an example the case of the frequency-
shift signal produced by a repetition of a mark-space pattern in which
the mark and space are of unequal durations.   The results apply to
the signal generated by periodic keying of an FM transmitter when a
fixed number of spaces is inserted between marks or a fixed number of
marks between spaces.   They also apply to the case of a PPM-FM
signal consisting of uninterrupted marks or spaces.   The square-wave
mark-space frequency-shift sequence of Eq. (4-19) is the special case
in which the mark and space durations are made equal.

Figure 4-11 shows the assumed variation of instantaneous frequency
with time.   The instantaneous angular frequency has the value ω_1
throughout a time interval of duration T_1 and a value ω_2 in an immediately following interval of duration T_2.   This sequence of events

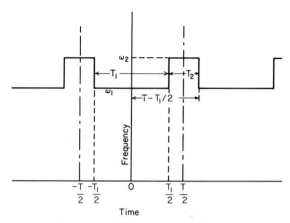

Fɪɢ. 4-11. Periodic frequency-shift sequence.

is repeated periodically with period $T_1 + T_2 = T$. The cases of continuous and discontinuous phase will be treated separately.

Continuous Phase. If the phase $\phi(t)$ is continuous, it is determined to within a single arbitrary constant α by integrating the frequency variation. The result is as shown in Fig. 4-12 in which straight lines of slopes ω_1 and ω_2 and time projections T_1 and T_2 are joined end to end. The constant α is taken as the value of phase at the origin of time. The resulting phase function increases by $\omega_1 T_1 + \omega_2 T_2$ in each period T of frequency variation. Hence, if we subtract

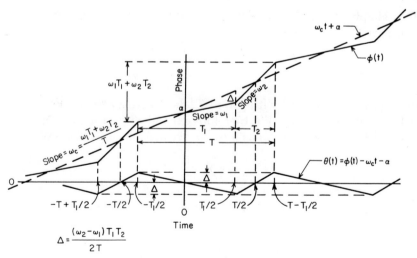

Fɪɢ. 4-12. Continuous-phase function for periodic frequency shift.

the dashed straight line of slope $\omega_c = (\omega_1 T_1 + \omega_2 T_2)/T$, we obtain the residual phase function $\theta(t)$, also shown in Fig. 4-12, which has zero net increment in each period T. We note that ω_c is the average value of carrier frequency, and that

$$\theta(t) = \phi(t) - \omega_c t - \alpha \tag{4-21}$$

The function $\theta(t)$ consists of successive straight lines of alternate slopes $\omega_1 - \omega_c$ and $\omega_2 - \omega_c$ forming a pattern which has the period T along the time scale and which oscillates between Δ and $-\Delta$, where

$$\Delta = \frac{(\omega_c - \omega_1)T_1}{2} = \frac{(\omega_2 - \omega_1)T_1 T_2}{2T} \tag{4-22}$$

Since $\theta(t)$ is periodic it is sufficient to describe it throughout one complete period, which we shall take from $t = -T_1/2$ to $t = T - T_1/2$. The equations of the two straight lines in this interval are

$$\theta(t) = \begin{cases} (\omega_1 - \omega_c)t & -\dfrac{T_1}{2} < t < \dfrac{T_1}{2} \\[2mm] (\omega_2 - \omega_c)\left(t - \dfrac{T}{2}\right) & \dfrac{T_1}{2} < t < T - \dfrac{T_1}{2} \end{cases} \tag{4-23}$$

The actual function of time for which we wish to find the spectral resolution is the wave having the phase $\phi(t)$, that is, the function $E(t)$ defined by

$$E(t) = A \cos \phi(t) \tag{4-24}$$

It is simpler from the computational standpoint to define $E(t)$ as the real part of $F(t)$, where

$$F(t) = Ae^{j\phi(t)} = Ae^{j[\theta(t) + \omega_c t + \alpha]}$$

$$= Ae^{j(\omega_c t + \alpha)}e^{j\theta(t)} \tag{4-25}$$

Since $\theta(t)$ is periodic in t with period T, the function $e^{j\theta(t)}$ is also periodic with the same period. We therefore expand $e^{j\theta(t)}$ in a Fourier series, using the exponential form as more convenient in this case. We write

$$e^{j\theta(t)} = \sum_{n=-\infty}^{\infty} c_n e^{j2n\pi t/T} \tag{4-26}$$

$$c_n = \frac{1}{T} \int_{-T_1/2}^{T-T_1/2} e^{j\theta(t)} e^{-j2n\pi t/T} \, dt \tag{4-27}$$

Let

$$\omega_0 = \frac{2\pi}{T} \tag{4-28}$$

Then

$$c_n = \frac{1}{T} \int_{-T_1/2}^{T_1/2} e^{j(\omega_1 - \omega_c - n\omega_0)t} \, dt$$

$$+ \frac{e^{-j(\omega_2 - \omega_c)T/2}}{T} \int_{T_1/2}^{T - T_1/2} e^{j(\omega_2 - \omega_c - n\omega_0)t} \, dt$$

$$= \frac{2 \sin \left[(\omega_1 - \omega_c - n\omega_0)T_1/2\right]}{(\omega_1 - \omega_c - n\omega_0)T} + \frac{2 \sin \{[(\omega_2 - \omega_c)T_2 + n\omega_0 T_1]/2\}}{(\omega_2 - \omega_c - n\omega_0)T}$$

$$(4\text{-}29)$$

We note that

$$(\omega_2 - \omega_c)T_2 = \frac{(\omega_2 - \omega_1)T_1 T_2}{T} = -(\omega_1 - \omega_c)T_1 \qquad (4\text{-}30)$$

Hence, setting

$$r = \frac{T_1}{T}$$

$$(4\text{-}31)$$

and

$$m = \frac{\omega_2 - \omega_1}{2\omega_0}$$

we find

$$c_n = \frac{2m \sin \{r\pi[2m(1 - r) + n]\}}{\pi(2mr - n)[2m(1 - r) + n]} \qquad (4\text{-}32)$$

From Eqs. (4-25) and (4-26)

$$F(t) = A \sum_{n=-\infty}^{\infty} c_n e^{j[(\omega_c + n\omega_0)t + \alpha]} \qquad (4\text{-}33)$$

Hence

$$E(t) = A \sum_{n=-\infty}^{\infty} c_n \cos \left[(\omega_c + n\omega_0)t + \alpha\right] \qquad (4\text{-}34)$$

In the resolution thus obtained, harmonics of the baseband frequency appear as upper and lower sidebands on the average carrier frequency. The amplitude of the nth-order side-frequency component is Ac_n. In the special case of equal marking and spacing intervals, $r = \frac{1}{2}$, $T_1 = T_2 = T/2 = \pi/\omega_0$, and $\omega_c = (\omega_1 + \omega_2)/2$. We find in this case

$$c_n = \frac{2m \sin \left[(m + n)\pi/2\right]}{\pi(m^2 - {}^2)n} \qquad (4\text{-}35)$$

When this expression is substituted in (4-34), we obtain Eq. (4-19) on replacing ω_0 by ω and setting $\alpha = 0$.

The method of calculation illustrated here has general application to the spectral resolution of waves in which the phase or frequency is shifted periodically. It is to be noted that if a continuous phase function takes on equal increments in equal times, the slope of the straight line which produces that amount of phase increment in the same time becomes the actual carrier frequency about which the signal sidebands occur. In the example just calculated no components appear in the output wave at the frequencies of the oscillator settings; the carrier frequency is in effect moved over to the average position between these settings.

Discontinuous Phase. If the phase changes discontinuously when the frequency is keyed, the spectral analysis depends on the nature of the changes introduced. One case which can be solved in a straightforward manner is that of keying between two independent oscillators set at the mark and space frequencies and adjusted to give equal amplitudes. The waveform transmitted is then of form

$$E(t) = As_1(t) \cos(\omega_1 t + \alpha) + As_2(t) \cos(\omega_2 t + \beta) \qquad (4\text{-}36)$$

Here α and β are fixed angles, and $s_1(t)$ and $s_2(t)$ are periodic switching functions defined by

$$s_1(t) = \begin{cases} 1 & \dfrac{-T_1}{2} < t < \dfrac{T_1}{2} \\[2ex] 0 & \dfrac{T_1}{2} < t < \dfrac{T - T_1}{2} \end{cases} \qquad (4\text{-}37)$$

$$s_2(t) = \begin{cases} 0 & \dfrac{-T_1}{2} < t < \dfrac{T_1}{2} \\[2ex] 1 & \dfrac{T_1}{2} < t < \dfrac{T - T_1}{2} \end{cases} \qquad (4\text{-}38)$$

$$\left.\begin{aligned} s_1(t + lT) &= s_1(t) \\ s_2(t + lT) &= s_2(t) \end{aligned}\right\} \quad l = \pm 1, \pm 2, \ldots \qquad (4\text{-}39)$$

By ordinary Fourier series expansion we calculate

$$s_1(t) = r + 2 \sum_{n=1}^{\infty} \frac{\sin n\pi r}{n\pi} \cos n\omega_0 t \qquad (4\text{-}40)$$

$$s_2(t) = 1 - r - 2 \sum_{n=1}^{\infty} \frac{\sin n\pi r}{n\pi} \cos n\omega_0 t \qquad (4\text{-}41)$$

Then

$$E(t) = rA \cos(\omega_1 t + \alpha) + (1 - r)A \cos(\omega_2 t + \beta)$$

$$+ A \sum_{n=\pm 1}^{\pm\infty} \frac{\sin n\pi r}{n\pi} \{\cos[(\omega_1 + n\omega_0)t + \alpha]$$

$$- \cos[(\omega_2 + n\omega_0)t + \beta]\} \qquad (4\text{-}42)$$

Comparing this result with the continuous-phase case, we see that we now have the superposition of two amplitude-modulated waves on the separate carriers rather than a single FM wave on the average carrier. We also note that in the discontinuous case the high-order side-frequency amplitudes are inversely proportional to n, while in the continuous case they are inversely proportional to n^2. This means that larger components remote from the carrier appear when the phase is not continuous. A band-limited transmission medium does not pass the high-order components and, therefore, might be expected to smooth out the discontinuous-phase transitions.

It is a well-known property[1] of the Fourier series expansion of a discontinuous function that the nth-order terms approach proportionality to $1/n$ when n is large. If the function is itself continuous but has a discontinuous first derivative, proportionality to $1/n^2$ is approached. In general, continuity of the function and its first m derivatives guarantees proportionality to at least the $(m + 1)$ power of $1/n$. Conversely, if we band-limit a time function so as to attenuate the high-order terms, we enforce a certain amount of continuity. However, it is to be noted that these arguments apply to the complete waveform function and not to the phase. In the examples considered it is the continuity of $E(t)$ and not that of $\phi(t)$ which determines how fast the components diminish in amplitude with frequency displacement from midband. It is possible to produce continuous waves with discontinuous-phase transitions, and we cannot say that narrowness of bandwidth insures smooth phase or frequency variations.

In actual experience we find that filtering a wave containing discontinuous transitions does not give an output wave equivalent to one generated directly by continuous-phase transitions. What typically happens is that the band-limited output wave for the case of discontinuous phase shows considerable amplitude variation. Such variation can be removed by subsequent amplitude limiting, but rapid phase changes persist especially in regions where the amplitude is small before limiting. In such regions the instantaneous frequency may undergo a violent change which could be disturbing to the operation of the receiver.

Another case of interest in which the phase may be discontinuous is that of digital phase modulation, i.e., data transmission by PM instead of FM. As an example we might relabel the ordinate scale of Fig. 4-11 as carrier phase instead of instantaneous frequency and replace ω_1 and ω_2 by α and β respectively. This is seen to be a special case of the preceding example in which we do not switch carrier frequencies but only carrier phase. The solution is obtained from (4-42) by setting $\omega_1 = \omega_2 = \omega_c$, where ω_c is the carrier frequency.

A second example of digital phase modulation is that in which the phase is represented by a staircase function; that is, instead of returning to a previous smaller value the phase continues to advance in discrete steps. When this phase function can be resolved into a sum of a straight line and a periodic component, the method used for the continuous-phase case is appropriate. The straight line component indicates a shift in carrier frequency.

REFERENCE

1. Carslaw, H. S.: "Introduction to the Theory of Fourier's Series and Integrals," 3d ed., chap. 8, pp. 270–271, Macmillan & Co., Ltd., London, 1930.

CHAPTER 5

EFFECTS OF RESTRICTED BANDWIDTH

In Chap. 4 the spectral content of various ideal data signals was considered. The data waveforms were expressed by the Fourier series

$$E(t) = \frac{a_0}{2} + \sum_{n=1}^{\infty} (a_n \cos n\omega t + b_n \sin n\omega t) \tag{5-1}$$

where the formulas for a_n and b_n in terms of $E(t)$ were given in Eqs. (4-2) to (4-4). The series can also be written in the form

$$E(t) = \frac{a_0}{2} + \sum_{n=1}^{\infty} A_n \cos (n\omega t + \Phi_n) \tag{5-2}$$

where

$$A_n = (a_n{}^2 + b_n{}^2)^{1/2} \tag{5-3}$$

and

$$\Phi_n = \tan^{-1} \left(-\frac{b_n}{a_n} \right) \tag{5-4}$$

As was previously pointed out, an increase of the pulse repetition period toward infinity crowds the frequencies of the components together and eventually merges them into a continuous spectrum $S(\omega)$. Thus most physically interesting aperiodic real functions of t can be expressed as the integral of the steady-state frequency components of their spectra. This relationship is known as the Fourier integral identity:

$$s(t) = \frac{1}{\pi} \int_0^{\infty} S(\omega) \cos [\omega t + \Phi(\omega)] \, d\omega \tag{5-5}$$

$$S^2(\omega) = a^2(\omega) + b^2(\omega) \tag{5-6}$$

$$\tan \Phi(\omega) = \frac{-b(\omega)}{a(\omega)} \tag{5-7}$$

$$a(\omega) = \int_{-\infty}^{\infty} s(t) \cos \omega t \, dt \tag{5-8}$$

$$b(\omega) = \int_{-\infty}^{\infty} s(t) \sin \omega t \, dt \tag{5-9}$$

49

We can regard $S(\omega)\,d\omega/\pi$ and $\Phi(\omega)$ respectively as the amplitude and phase of the spectral component at frequency ω. The integral is the limit obtained by summing the components over all frequencies.

We note from Eqs. (5-8) and (5-9) that $a(\omega)$ is an even function of ω, and $b(\omega)$ is an odd function of ω. It follows that $S(\omega)$ is an even function of ω, and $\Phi(\omega)$ is an odd function of ω. We also note that if $s(t)$ is an even function of t, the value of $b(\omega)$ is zero. Likewise, if $s(t)$ is an odd function of t, the value of $a(\omega)$ is zero.

5-1 ILLUSTRATIVE EXAMPLES OF PULSES REPRESENTED BY FOURIER INTEGRALS

As a first illustrative example let $s(t)$ be a single rectangular pulse of height h beginning at $t = -T/2$ and ending at $t = T/2$. Then from Eqs. (5-8) and (5-9)

$$a(\omega) = \int_{-T/2}^{T/2} h \cos \omega t\, dt = \frac{2h}{\omega} \sin \frac{\omega T}{2} \qquad (5\text{-}10)$$

$$b(\omega) = \int_{-T/2}^{T/2} h \sin \omega t\, dt = 0 \qquad (5\text{-}11)$$

The amplitude function is thus of form $(\sin x)/x$, similar to the expression obtained in Eq. (4-7) for the harmonic amplitudes in a periodic train of rectangular pulses. Figure 5-1 shows the rectangular pulse and its spectral amplitude function.

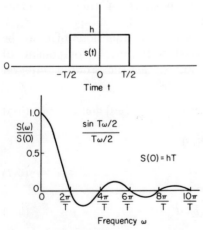

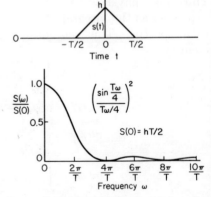

FIG. 5-1. Spectral amplitude function of rectangular pulse.

FIG. 5-2. Spectral amplitude function of triangular pulse.

As a second example (Fig. 5-2), consider a triangular pulse of height h and duration T centered at $t = 0$. The pulse is defined by the set of equations

$$s(t) = \begin{cases} \left(1 - \dfrac{2t}{T}\right)h & 0 \le t \le \dfrac{T}{2} \\[3mm] 0 & t > \dfrac{T}{2} \end{cases} \tag{5-12}$$

$$s(-t) = s(t)$$

It follows that

$$\frac{S(\omega)}{S(0)} = \left[\frac{\sin(\omega T/4)}{\omega T/4}\right]^2 \qquad S(0) = \frac{hT}{2} \qquad \Phi(\omega) = 0 \tag{5-13}$$

Other examples are:
Cosine pulse (Fig. 5-3)

$$s(t) = \begin{cases} h \cos \dfrac{\pi t}{T} & -\dfrac{T}{2} < t < \dfrac{T}{2} \\[3mm] 0 & |t| > \dfrac{T}{2} \end{cases} \tag{5-14}$$

$$\frac{S(\omega)}{S(0)} = \frac{\pi^2 \cos \omega T/2}{\pi^2 - \omega^2 T^2} \qquad S(0) = \frac{2hT}{\pi} \qquad \Phi(\omega) = 0 \tag{5-15}$$

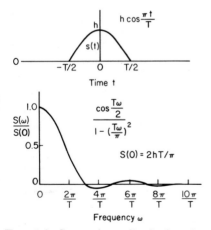

FIG. 5-3. Spectral amplitude function of cosine pulse.

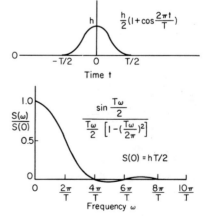

FIG. 5-4. Spectral amplitude function of raised-cosine pulse.

Raised-cosine pulse (Fig. 5-4)

$$s(t) = \begin{cases} \dfrac{h}{2}\left(1 + \cos\dfrac{2\pi t}{T}\right) & -\dfrac{T}{2} < t < \dfrac{T}{2} \\[2ex] 0 & |t| > \dfrac{T}{2} \end{cases} \tag{5-16}$$

$$\frac{S(\omega)}{S(0)} = \frac{8\pi^2 \sin \omega T/2}{\omega T(4\pi^2 - \omega^2 T^2)} \qquad S(0) = \frac{hT}{2} \qquad \Phi(\omega) = 0 \tag{5-17}$$

Exponential pulse (Fig. 5-5)

$$s(t) = \begin{cases} 0 & t < 0 \\ he^{-t/\tau} & t > 0 \end{cases} \tag{5-18}$$

$$a(\omega) = \frac{h\tau}{1 + \omega^2\tau^2} \qquad b(\omega) = \frac{h\omega\tau^2}{1 + \omega^2\tau^2}$$

$$\frac{S(\omega)}{S(0)} = (1 + \omega^2\tau^2)^{-\frac{1}{2}} \qquad S(0) = h\tau \qquad \Phi(\omega) = -\arctan \omega\tau \tag{5-19}$$

Gaussian pulse (Fig. 5-6)

$$s(t) = he^{-(t/\tau)^2} \tag{5-20}$$

$$\frac{S(\omega)}{S(0)} = e^{-\omega^2\tau^2/4} \qquad S(0) = h\tau\pi^{\frac{1}{2}} \qquad \Phi(\omega) = 0 \tag{5-21}$$

The Fourier integral representation of a signal $s(t)$ has an important application in the calculation of the response of a linear transmission

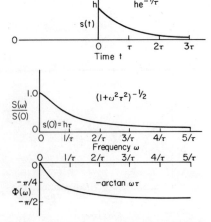

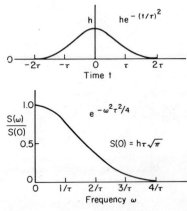

FIG. 5-5. Spectral amplitude and phase functions of exponential pulse.

FIG. 5-6. Spectral amplitude function of gaussian pulse.

system to the signal. If the transmission system has an amplitude-frequency characteristic $A(\omega)$ and a phase-frequency characteristic $B(\omega)$, the output signal $s_1(t)$ is given by

$$s_1(t) = \frac{1}{\pi} \int_0^\infty S(\omega)A(\omega) \cos\left[\omega t + \Phi(\omega) + B(\omega)\right] d\omega \qquad (5\text{-}22)$$

This result is obtained by multiplying the amplitude $S(\omega)\, d\omega/\pi$ of the component at frequency ω by the amplitude function $A(\omega)$, shifting the phase of the component by $B(\omega)$, and summing over all ω.

If, over the frequency range where $S(\omega)$ is of significant value, the transmission has a flat amplitude-frequency characteristic and the phase shift is proportional to frequency, we can set $A(\omega) = K$ and $B(\omega) = -\omega\tau$. The output then becomes

$$s_1(t) = \frac{1}{\pi} \int_0^\infty S(\omega)K \cos\left[\omega(t - \tau) + \Phi(\omega)\right] d\omega$$

$$= Ks(t - \tau) \qquad (5\text{-}23)$$

The resulting output is seen to have the same waveform as the input but with magnitudes multiplied by K and all ordinates delayed in time by τ. The conditions of flat amplitude response and linear phase vs. frequency thus result in distortionless transmission and are sufficient for the preservation of the signal waveform.

We have found that the spectral content of rectangular-shaped data signals extends over an unlimited frequency band. In most practical data transmission systems bandwidth is expensive, and it is not economical to attempt to preserve a rectangular wave shape. Furthermore, it is desirable to exclude components of noise and interference having frequencies outside the band containing the major portion of the signal energy. It is, therefore, important to know to what extent the signal spectrum can be curtailed without undue impairment of the received wave.

5-2 BASEBAND SIGNALS

Some of the limiting conditions in the transmission of baseband signals can be illustrated by considering the impulse response of idealized low-pass filters. As was shown in Chap. 4, if the width of a rectangular pulse is decreased toward an ideal impulse, the spectrum becomes flat. When the origin of time is at the center of the pulse, all the incremental parts of the spectrum have zero phase angle. Thus in the Fourier integral expression, $S(\omega)$ can be considered to be unity and $\Phi(\omega)$ to be zero. In Fig. 5-7 an ideal low-pass filter is shown which has unity transmission up to a cutoff frequency ω_1 and zero transmission beyond ω_1. In addition a phase shift proportional to frequency is assumed. For such conditions the output is given by

$$g(t) = \frac{1}{\pi} \int_0^\infty A(\omega) \cos \omega(t - \tau) \, d\omega \qquad (5\text{-}24)$$

where
$$A(\omega) = 1 \qquad \omega < \omega_1$$
$$A(\omega) = 0 \qquad \omega > \omega_1 \qquad (5\text{-}25)$$
$$\tau = \text{transmission delay}$$

The integral in Eq. (5-24) evaluates to

$$g(t) = \frac{1}{\pi} \left[\frac{\sin \omega(t - \tau)}{t - \tau} \right]_0^{\omega_1} = \frac{1}{\pi} \frac{\sin \omega_1(t - \tau)}{t - \tau} = \frac{\omega_1}{\pi} \frac{\sin \omega_1 t'}{\omega_1 t'} \qquad (5\text{-}26)$$

where t' is measured from the time at which the peak ω_1/π of the received pulse occurs.

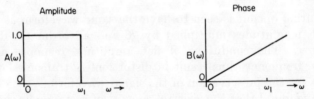

FIG. 5-7. Amplitude and phase functions of ideal low-pass filter.

Comparison of Eq. (5-26) with Eq. (5-10) illustrates the duality of frequency and time in the Fourier integral identity. In Eq. (5-10) we started with a pulse of constant amplitude throughout a finite time interval and obtained a spectral amplitude function of form $(\sin x)/x$ in frequency. In Eq. (5-26) we started with a constant spectral amplitude function in a limited frequency range and found a $(\sin x)/x$ representation in time.

The received wave defined by Eq. (5-26) is shown in Fig. 5-8. The instantaneous response is seen to be zero at $\omega_1 t' = \pm n\pi$, that is, at

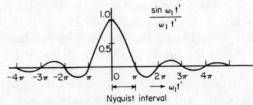

FIG. 5-8. Impulse response of ideal low-pass filter.

$t' = \pm n/2f_1$. Thus impulses can be transmitted at such intervals without interference between the peaks of the received pulses. The reciprocal of $2f_1$ is known as the Nyquist interval and corresponds to a signaling pulse rate of twice the cutoff frequency of the low-pass filter. This is of interest as a limiting case but has no practical application. In the first place, the sharp cutoff of the filter is not attainable since it would involve infinite delay and no phase distortion. It can only be

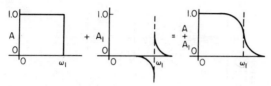

FIG. 5-9. Construction of gradual roll-off which retains nulls of ideal filter response.

approached by use of complicated networks with approximate linearization of a steeply sloped phase characteristic. In the second place, the $(\sin x)/x$ type of response is not desirable because of the precise timing required. Any slight deviations in pulse rate, filter cutoff frequency, or sampling instant would produce failure. This is because the overlapping pulse tails represent a divergent series and can add up to large values which prevent the correct interpretation of the pulse.

With a more gradual cutoff of the low-pass characteristic, the oscillatory nature of the pulse tails is reduced, and it becomes more

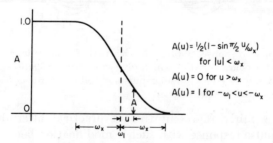

FIG. 5-10. Sinusoidal roll-off which retains nulls of ideal filter response.

practical to equalize to a linear phase characteristic. Such a gradual cutoff is indicated in Fig. 5-9. The original sharp cutoff is modified by an amplitude characteristic having odd symmetry about the cutoff frequency. As will be explained in more detail in Sec. 5-3, Nyquist has shown that such a modification retains the zero points of the $(\sin x)/x$ response and adds certain others. Figure 5-10 shows a practical example of such a case where the shape of the modification is made sinusoidal. In Fig. 5-10, the incremental frequency u relative to the nominal cutoff frequency ω_1 satisfies the equation

$$
\begin{aligned}
A(u) &= \frac{1}{2}\left(1 - \sin \frac{\pi u}{2\omega_x}\right) & |u| &< \omega_x \\
&= 0 & u &> \omega_x \\
&= 1 & -\omega_1 &< u < -\omega_x
\end{aligned}
\tag{5-27}
$$

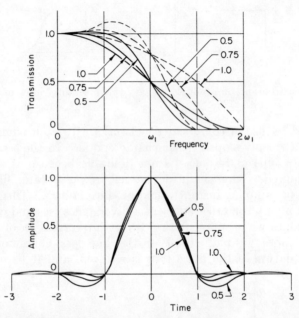

FIG. 5-11. Impulse responses obtainable with various sinusoidal roll-offs. Dashed curves show filter characteristics which give same time responses when impulses are replaced by uncurbed rectangular pulses. Roll-off factor ω_x/ω_1 as defined in Fig. 5-10 is indicated for each curve.

This shape is fairly representative of practical filter designs. The resulting impulse response with such a modification becomes[1]

$$
g(t) = \frac{\omega_1}{\pi} \frac{\sin \omega_1 t'}{\omega_1 t'} \frac{\cos \omega_x t'}{1 - (2\omega_x t'/\pi)^2}
\tag{5-28}
$$

One important change in the nature of overlapping pulse tails of form (5-28) compared with (5-26) is that a converging series is obtained because the denominator of (5-28) increases faster than linearly with t'. This makes possible operation at pulse intervals differing from the exact Nyquist interval. In Fig. 5-11 are shown the resulting pulse shapes for several values of ω_x/ω_1. It will be seen that when $\omega_x = \omega_1$, corresponding to a so-called "full-cosine roll-off," that there are additional zero points at the middle of the intervals brought about by the cosine term in Eq. (5-28). Such an amplitude characteristic is consistent with a nearly linear phase characteristic without the need of phase-equalizing networks.

The impulse response for the full-cosine roll-off characteristic has little oscillation and consequently is not sensitive to variation in the signaling rate. Furthermore, as will be shown in Sec. 5-4, it has a width of one Nyquist interval at the half-amplitude level. Thus if the

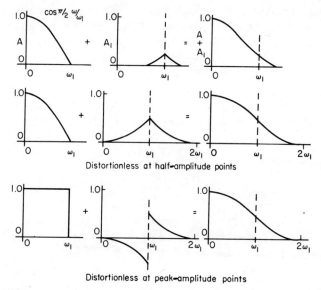

FIG. 5-12. Filter characteristics which permit synchronous signaling with impulses without disturbance of transition times. Full-cosine roll-off shown also preserves sample values.

received signal is squared up or sliced at this half-amplitude level, full-interval pulses are produced. Since the responses to all other pulses at these instants are zero, no interference or distortion of the full-interval pulse occurs. Nyquist has shown (see Sec. 5-4) that this property of no distortion at the half-amplitude point requires a minimum band of width ω_1 with

$$A(\omega) = \cos\frac{\pi}{2}\frac{\omega}{\omega_1} \qquad |\omega| \leq \omega_1 \qquad (5\text{-}29)$$

This characteristic, however, has zero transmission at ω_1, and it is not possible to signal at that rate. The property of no distortion at half amplitude is retained, however, when modified by a factor which has even symmetry about ω_1 as indicated in Fig. 5-12 and derived in Sec. 5-4. It also appears in Fig. 5-12 that the full-cosine roll-off shape meets the conditions of zero distortion both at the peak-amplitude points and at the half-amplitude points. This ideal type of pulse response is obtained, however, by the use of twice the frequency space of the minimum-bandwidth sharp-cutoff filter.

We have thus far been considering the input signal to be a sharp impulse. Usually it is more convenient to start with full-length rectangular pulses. In Chap. 4 it was shown that the spectrum of such a pulse has a $(\sin x)/x$ shape with the first zero point at a frequency equal to the reciprocal of the pulse width. The received pulse spectrum, and consequently the received pulse shape, may be kept the same as for the impulse case considered hitherto by modifying the transmission characteristic of the low-pass filter by the factor $x/(\sin x)$. The modified filter shapes for full-length pulses are shown by the dotted lines in Fig. 5-11.

Another type of amplitude characteristic which produces well-shaped pulses is the gaussian characteristic. It has the general shape,

$$A(\omega) = e^{-\nu\omega^2} \tag{5-30}$$

The impulse response is

$$P(t) = \frac{1}{2(\pi\nu)^{1/2}} e^{-t^2/4\nu} \tag{5-31}$$

To have the response down to 1 per cent of the peak value at $t = \pi/\omega_1$, corresponding to the first zero point of the response shown in Fig. 5-11, $t^2/4\nu$ must be equal to 4.6, or $\nu = 0.54/\omega_1^2$. Thus

$$A(\omega) = e^{-0.54(\omega/\omega_1)^2} \tag{5-32}$$

and
$$P(t) = \frac{\omega_1}{0.83\pi} e^{-0.46(t\omega_1)^2} \tag{5-33}$$

These characteristics are shown in Fig. 5-13. It is seen that although the pulse shape has no overshoot, it is somewhat less ideal than that associated with the full-cosine roll-off shape and furthermore requires more bandwidth.

The response to full-Nyquist-interval pulses was shown in Fig. 5-11. It is often impractical to use pulses of this particular duration, so it is of interest to consider the more general case of a rectangular input pulse. It can be shown that the response of a network to the derivative of a wave $f(t)$ has the same relative waveform as the derivative of its response to the wave $f(t)$. This also applies to the relationship of the integrals. A rectangular pulse of duration T is equivalent to the integral of a positive and a negative impulse separated by time T. The response to the rectangular pulse is, therefore, of the same shape as the integral of the response from the pair of impulses. Each impulse response has a shape dependent on the filter characteristic as previously described. The summation of the two responses, one positive and one negative, is illustrated in Fig. 5-14. The rectangular pulse of duration T can also be viewed as the superposition of two step functions which are the equivalent of the integral of the two impulses.

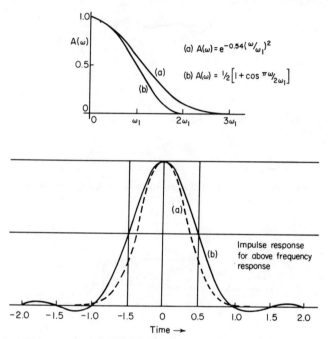

FIG. 5-13. Comparison of impulse responses corresponding to gaussian and raised-cosine spectral amplitude functions.

It is sometimes desirable to pass baseband data signals through circuits which have a low-frequency cutoff in addition to a high-frequency cutoff. Circuits containing transformers are generally of this type. Such a circuit might have a transmission characteristic such as shown in Fig. 5-15. This characteristic can be considered to be the difference between two low-pass characteristics as indicated. The response of each of these to a rectangular pulse is also shown. The difference between the two responses gives the net response. The loss of the low-frequency portion of the spectrum is seen to cause a wandering zero base for the output pulse. A random train of nonreturn-to-zero

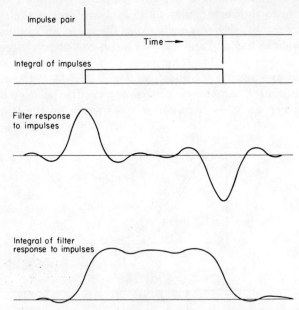

Fig. 5-14. Construction of response to rectangular pulse when impulse response is given.

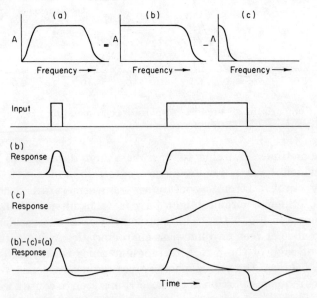

Fig. 5-15. Effect of removing low-frequency components.

data signals passed through such a circuit cannot be correctly interpreted by means of a fixed-level threshold. Means of compensating for this wandering zero effect will be discussed in Chap. 15. The use of signals which have no d-c component, such as those shown in Figs. 3-5 and 3-7, is another way of overcoming the effect of the missing low frequencies.

We have made frequent references to the work of Nyquist in our development of the effect of bandwidth restriction on pulse transmission. Because of the basic importance of Nyquist's contributions, it is desirable at this point to state and derive a number of his principal theorems on suppression of intersymbol interference in a band-limited medium.

5-3 NYQUIST'S FIRST CRITERION: EQUALLY SPACED AXIS CROSSINGS IN THE IMPULSE RESPONSE[2]

At the beginning of Sec. 5-2 we showed that the impulse response of an ideal low-pass filter has equally spaced axis crossings except for a central peak. It follows from Eqs. (5-24) to (5-26) that if impulses are applied to an ideal low-pass filter at instants separated by π/ω_1, the responses to these impulses can be observed independently at these instants. The sampling must take place accurately and instantaneously. Signaling without intersymbol interference is thereby possible at a rate of $\omega_1/\pi = 2f_1$ independent values per second through an ideal low-pass filter cutting off at f_1 cps.

Nyquist proved that, in general, it is impossible to recognize more than $2f_1$ completely arbitrary values per second in the output of such a filter. For suppose that we attempt to send $2(f_1 + \delta)$ values per second where δ is an arbitrarily small positive quantity. Consider the case in which the values sent are alternately $+a$ and $-a$. The resulting wave can be expressed as a Fourier series with period $1/(f_1 + \delta)$ and hence with fundamental frequency $f_1 + \delta$. Since no component of the wave has frequency less than $f_1 + \delta$, the ideal filter gives zero response. The conclusion is that we are not completely free to choose our sequence of symbols when we exceed the Nyquist rate.

Severity of the requirements on a system which samples at axis crossings of the impulse response is lessened by the use of Nyquist's theorem on vestigial symmetry. This shows how the ideal filter can be modified without disturbing the axis crossings. The first modification adds transmission above the cutoff while a symmetrical reduction is made below, as indicated in Fig. 5-10. The theorem is that if a real-valued transmittance function $Y_1(\omega)$ which has skew symmetry about the cutoff frequency is added to the transmittance of an ideal low-pass filter, the same axis crossings of the impulse response persist. That is, we set

$$Y_1(\omega_1 - x) = -Y_1(\omega_1 + x) \qquad 0 < x < \omega_1 \qquad (5\text{-}34)$$

and form a modified filter with the transmittance

$$Y(\omega) = \begin{cases} 1 + Y_1(\omega) & |\omega| < \omega_1 \\ Y_1(\omega) & \omega_1 < |\omega| < 2\omega_1 \end{cases} \qquad (5\text{-}35)$$

We assume that the origin of time is shifted appropriately to remove the delay τ in Eq. (5-26). The impulse response becomes:

$$g(t) = \frac{\sin 2\pi f_1 t}{\pi t} + g_1(t) \qquad (5\text{-}36)$$

$$g_1(t) = \frac{1}{\pi} \int_0^{2\omega_1} Y_1(\omega) \cos \omega t \, d\omega \qquad (5\text{-}37)$$

We divide the integral in two parts, one from 0 to ω_1 and the other from ω_1 to $2\omega_1$. In the first, substitute $\omega = \omega_1 - x$ and in the second, $\omega = \omega_1 + x$. The result is

$$
\begin{aligned}
g_1(t) &= \frac{1}{\pi} \int_0^{\omega_1} [Y_1(\omega_1 - x) \cos t(\omega_1 - x) + Y_1(\omega_1 + x) \cos t(\omega_1 + x)] \, dx \\
&= \frac{\cos \omega_1 t}{\pi} \int_0^{\omega_1} [Y_1(\omega_1 - x) + Y_1(\omega_1 + x)] \cos tx \, dx \\
&\quad + \frac{\sin \omega_1 t}{\pi} \int_0^{\omega_1} [Y_1(\omega_1 - x) - Y_1(\omega_1 + x)] \sin tx \, dx \\
&= \frac{2}{\pi} \sin \omega_1 t \int_0^{\omega_1} Y_1(\omega_1 - x) \sin tx \, dx \qquad (5\text{-}38)
\end{aligned}
$$

The multiplying factor $\sin \omega_1 t$ shows that $g_1(t)$ vanishes for t equal to any multiple of π/ω_1. Hence $g(t)$ also vanishes at these points since it is the sum of two functions individually equal to zero. There may be other nulls as well, but the nulls at $1/(2f_1)$ spacing are guaranteed.

An infinite number of functions for $Y_1(\omega)$ may be found which satisfy the vestigial symmetry requirement. It will be noted that there is, in general, a discontinuity of $2Y_1(\omega_1)$ at $x = 0$. This discontinuity can conveniently be chosen to cancel the discontinuity of unity in the ideal low-pass filter transmittance at $\omega = \omega_1$. To do this we make

$$Y_1(\omega_1 - 0) = -\tfrac{1}{2} \qquad Y_1(\omega_1 + 0) = \tfrac{1}{2} \qquad (5\text{-}39)$$

The complete transmittance function is then continuous and satisfies the condition

$$Y(\omega_1 - x) + Y(\omega_1 + x) = 1 \qquad 0 < x < \omega_1 \qquad (5\text{-}40)$$

An example which satisfies this equation is the raised cosine:

$$Y(\omega) = \frac{1}{2}\left(1 + \cos\frac{\pi\omega}{2\omega_1}\right) \qquad 0 < \omega < 2\omega_1 \qquad (5\text{-}41)$$

It should be stressed that these conditions have been derived for purely real transmittance functions. They can be extended to linear phase functions, in which case a constant shift in the time origin occurs, as illustrated in Eq. (5-26). Nyquist showed also the kind of vestigial symmetry which the imaginary component can have without destroying the equally spaced nulls. If we add $jY_2(\omega)$ with the property

$$Y_2(\omega_1 - x) = Y_2(\omega_1 + x) \qquad 0 < x < \omega_1 \qquad (5\text{-}42)$$

a calculation similar in type to that just given shows that the same nulls occur.

5-4 NYQUIST'S SECOND CRITERION: EQUAL TIMES BETWEEN TRANSITION VALUES

The second of Nyquist's criteria is that of removing intersymbol interference at the instants halfway between adjacent signal impulses. The required transmittance function is:

$$Y(\omega) = \begin{cases} \cos\dfrac{\pi\omega}{2\omega_1} & 0 < \omega < \omega_1 \\ 0 & \omega > \omega_1 \end{cases} \qquad (5\text{-}43)$$

The impulse response is

$$\begin{aligned} g(t) &= \frac{1}{\pi}\int_0^{\omega_1} \cos\omega t \cos\frac{\pi\omega}{2\omega_1}\, d\omega \\ &= \frac{2\omega_1\cos\omega_1 t}{\pi^2(1 - 4\omega_1^2 t^2/\pi^2)} = \frac{4f_1\cos 2\pi f_1 t}{\pi(1 - 16f_1^2 t^2)} \end{aligned} \qquad (5\text{-}44)$$

With two exceptions the response vanishes at odd positive or negative multiples of $\pi/2\omega_1$. The null points are halfway between adjacent null points of the ideal low-pass filter response. The exceptions occur at $t = \pm 1/(4f_1)$, where the simultaneous vanishing of numerator and denominator leads to the nonzero limit:

$$g\left(\pm\frac{1}{4f_1}\right) = \frac{1}{\pi}\int_0^{\omega_1}\cos^2\frac{\pi\omega}{2\omega_1}\, d\omega = f_1 \qquad (5\text{-}45)$$

If the response to any regularly spaced impulse train at rate $2f_1$ per second is measured at instants halfway between adjacent impulses, the response will be f_1 times the sum of the two adjacent impulse weights no matter what the other impulse values are. We may say then that if we sample at these points, we obtain values proportional to the average of adjacent signal values. In the case of binary pulse transmission, the average of adjacent values is either 0, ½, or 1 depending on whether the pairs are two zeros, a zero and 1, or two 1s. A threshold indicator set to respond to ½ multiplied by the constant of proportionality registers the transition instants at which the response goes from either 0 to 1 or 1 to 0. The response function of this section insures that the spacing of such transitions is preserved.

As in the axis-crossing case, transmittance functions of proper symmetry can be added without destroying the desired property. Referring back to Eq. (5-38) we see that since we now wish $g_1(t)$ to vanish for t equal to odd multiples of $1/(4f_1)$, we should insert a factor $\cos 2\pi f_1 t$. This can be done by making

$$Y_1(\omega_1 - x) = Y_1(\omega_1 + x) \qquad Y_1 \text{ real} \qquad (5\text{-}46)$$

Hence, even symmetry about ω_1 is the desired requirement for the added transmittance function. Similarly it may be shown that odd symmetry suffices for an added imaginary term.

An important question to ask at this point is can one obtain simultaneous satisfaction of Nyquist's first and second requirements and thereby preserve the spacing of *both* nulls and transitions? The answer is yes, and it is the raised cosine which furnishes the solution. We have already shown that the raised cosine satisfies the first requirement. To show that it satisfies the second, we examine the difference $Y_1(\omega)$ between the raised cosine (5-41) and the transmittance (5-43).

$$Y_1(\omega) = \begin{cases} \dfrac{1}{2}\left(1 - \cos \dfrac{\pi\omega}{2\omega_1}\right) & \omega < \omega_1 \\[3mm] \dfrac{1}{2}\left(1 + \cos \dfrac{\pi\omega}{2\omega_1}\right) & \omega_1 < \omega < 2\omega_1 \end{cases} \qquad (5\text{-}47)$$

We readily verify that $Y_1(\omega_1 - x) = Y_1(\omega_1 + x)$. The raised-cosine filter thus has a special significance in that it anchors the levels corresponding to zero, one-half, and one at the proper times. Variations are allowed only between these correctly placed points. The cost is a doubling of the minimum band required by the ideal filter, which satisfies only the first criterion. The raised-cosine filter has the additional advantage of tolerating more deviation in the sampling instants than the ideal filter. This follows because the response falls off faster with time, and hence fewer pulse tails contribute significantly.

5-5 NYQUIST'S THIRD CRITERION: PRESERVATION OF PULSE AREAS

A third criterion discussed by Nyquist is that the area under the received wave during a signal time unit should be proportional to the corresponding impressed signal value. A transmittance function which accomplishes this is the truncated reciprocal $(\sin x)/x$ function:

$$Y(\omega) = \begin{cases} \dfrac{\pi\omega}{2\omega_1 \sin{(\pi\omega/2\omega_1)}} & 0 < \omega < \omega_1 \\[2mm] 0 & \omega > \omega_1 \end{cases} \qquad (5\text{-}48)$$

The impulse response is

$$g(t) = \frac{1}{\pi} \int_0^{\omega_1} \frac{\pi\omega \cos \omega t \, d\omega}{2\omega_1 \sin{(\pi\omega/2\omega_1)}} \qquad (5\text{-}49)$$

The criterion applies to the integral of $g(t)$ between adjacent odd multiples of $\pi/2\omega_1$. We form

$$h(t) = \int_{(2m-1)\pi/2\omega_1}^{(2m+1)\pi/2\omega_1} g(t) \, dt \qquad m = 0, 1, \ldots \qquad (5\text{-}50)$$

When the expression for $g(t)$ is inserted and the order of integration interchanged, we find

$$\begin{aligned} h(t) &= \int_0^{\omega_1} \frac{\sin{[(2m+1)\pi\omega/2\omega_1]} - \sin{[(2m-1)\pi\omega/2\omega_1]}}{2\omega_1 \sin{(\pi\omega/2\omega_1)}} \, d\omega \\[2mm] &= \frac{1}{\omega_1} \int_0^{\omega_1} \cos\left(\frac{m\pi\omega}{\omega_1}\right) d\omega = \begin{cases} 1 & m = 0 \\ 0 & m \neq 0 \end{cases} \end{aligned} \qquad (5\text{-}51)$$

The response to each impulse, therefore, has zero area for every signaling interval except its own.

5-6 GENERALIZED SIGNAL PULSE SHAPES

The three criteria have been expressed in terms of signaling with impulses. This is particularly convenient because the spectrum of an impulse is a constant at all frequencies. If any other pulse shape is used, we can satisfy the criteria by inserting a network which changes the given pulse spectrum to a constant and then adding the network previously found for the impulse case. In other words if we are given the pulse spectrum $S(\omega)$ and we wish to satisfy a criterion requiring $Y(\omega)$ as the network appropriate for impulses, we insert a network with transmittance function

$$Y_s(\omega) = \frac{Y(\omega)}{S(\omega)} \qquad (5\text{-}52)$$

instead of $Y(\omega)$.

In summary, signal shaping in the time domain and signal filtering in the frequency domain are interchangeable processes. The frequency functions combine by direct multiplication. The time functions combine by convolution, i.e., if $g(t)$ and $h(t)$ are impulse responses of individual networks, the impulse response of the combined network in which one drives the other is

$$i(t) = \int_{-\infty}^{\infty} g(\lambda)h(t - \lambda)\,d\lambda \qquad (5\text{-}53)$$

5-7 APPLICATION TO AM

Amplitude modulation translates the baseband spectrum to upper and lower sidebands on the carrier. Nyquist's results can be applied

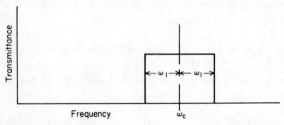

FIG. 5-16. Minimum-bandwidth AM spectrum giving equally spaced nulls in envelope on time axis except for central peak.

to the sidebands separately if we assume a method of detection which translates each sideband back to the original baseband position. One detection method which secures the proper translations of the sidebands back to baseband is the synchronous, or homodyne, detector in which the modulated wave is multiplied by a sine wave having the same frequency and phase as the carrier. The first criterion is then satisfied by a rectangular transmission band extending from ω_1 radians per second below the carrier frequency to ω_1 radians per second above as shown in Fig. 5-16.

Modifications similar to those allowed in the baseband case can be made without violating the criterion. There are now two cutoff frequencies to consider, and vestigial symmetry is permissible for each separately as shown in Fig. 5-17. Furthermore, since the contributions from the two sidebands add to form the recovered baseband signal, arbitrary complementary modifications can be made in the transmission characteristics of the two corresponding frequency ranges. One important example is the so-called vestigial-sideband system (Fig. 5-18), in which partial suppression of one sideband in the neighborhood of the carrier is exactly compensated by partial transmission of the corresponding part of the other sideband. This enables a saving in bandwidth to be obtained compared with sending both sidebands, which contain the signal information in duplicate. A gradual transition

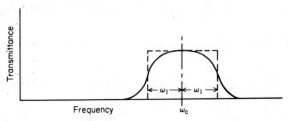

FIG. 5-17. Modification of rectangular AM spectrum retaining nulls in synchronously detected response.

in frequency between full transmission of one sideband and complete suppression of the other sideband is necessary for practical filter realization.

The foregoing concepts are basic to much of carrier data transmission, and for future reference we shall express them here in convenient

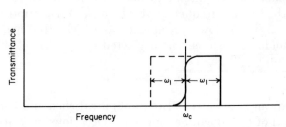

FIG. 5-18. Vestigial-sideband spectrum retaining same nulls in synchronously detected response as rectangular AM spectrum.

mathematical language. Let $s(t)$ be a general signal pulse representable by a Fourier integral as in Eq. (5-5). Consider a carrier pulse $E(t)$ formed by multiplying the output of a sine-wave generator by $s(t)$. We can write $E(t)$ as

$$E(t) = s(t) \cos(\omega_c t + \theta) = \frac{\cos(\omega_c t + \theta)}{\pi} \int_0^\infty S(\omega) \cos[\omega t + \Phi(\omega)] \, d\omega$$

$$= \int_0^\infty \frac{S(\omega)}{2\pi} \{\cos[(\omega_c + \omega)t + \theta + \Phi(\omega)]$$

$$+ \cos[(\omega_c - \omega)t + \theta - \Phi(\omega)]\} \, d\omega \qquad (5\text{-}54)$$

The two cosine terms in the integrand of (5-54) represent the upper- and lower-sideband contributions, respectively. We can calculate the response when $E(t)$ is applied to a linear network with specified transmittance function by inserting the amplitude and phase changes in each component under the integral sign. If the amplitude factor is $A(\omega)$ and the phase shift is $B(\omega)$, the resulting response is

$$I(t) = \frac{1}{2\pi} \int_0^\infty S(\omega)A(\omega_c + \omega) \cos\left[(\omega_c + \omega)t + \theta + \Phi(\omega)\right.$$

$$+ B(\omega_c + \omega)]\,d\omega + \frac{1}{2\pi} \int_0^{\omega_c} S(\omega)A(\omega_c - \omega) \cos\left[(\omega_c - \omega)t + \theta\right.$$

$$- \Phi(\omega) + B(\omega_c - \omega)]\,d\omega + \frac{1}{2\pi} \int_{\omega_c}^\infty S(\omega)A(\omega - \omega_c)$$

$$\cos\left[(\omega - \omega_c)t - \theta + \Phi(\omega) + B(\omega - \omega_c)\right]\,d\omega \qquad (5\text{-}55)$$

The last term represents lower-sideband foldover which occurs when $\omega_c - \omega$ is negative. It is treated separately because physical networks do not distinguish between positive and negative frequencies. It can certainly be eliminated if $S(\omega)$ vanishes for $\omega > \omega_c$, and in practical cases we do not need to consider it if it does not overlap the portion of the lower sideband we intend to use. In mathematical terms if ω_h represents the highest frequency at which $S(\omega)$ has appreciable value, and if $\omega_c - \omega_b$ is the lowest frequency at which $A(\omega)$ has appreciable value, the foldover term can be neglected if $\omega_h - \omega_c < \omega_c - \omega_b$, that is, if

$$\omega_h < 2\omega_e - \omega_b \qquad (5\text{-}56)$$

We assume from here on that Eq. (5-56) is satisfied and hence that the third integral of (5-55) can be omitted. Occasions may arise in which foldover is deliberately inserted to secure a specific pulse shape, but such cases can be treated separately when encountered.

Synchronous detection of the wave (5-55) is accomplished by multiplying by $\cos\left[\omega_c t + \theta + B(\omega_c)\right]$ and accepting only the low-frequency terms in the product. The detected low-frequency output $I_0(t)$ is given by

$$4I_0(t) = \frac{1}{\pi} \int_0^\infty S(\omega)A(\omega_c + \omega) \cos\left[\omega t + \Phi(\omega) + B(\omega_c + \omega)\right.$$

$$- B(\omega_c)]\,d\omega + \frac{1}{\pi} \int_0^{\omega_c} S(\omega)A(\omega_c - \omega) \cos\left[\omega t + \Phi(\omega)\right.$$

$$+ B(\omega_c) - B(\omega_c - \omega)]\,d\omega \qquad (5\text{-}57)$$

Comparing $4I_0(t)$ with the original signal pulse $s(t)$ as specified by (5-5), we see that a transformation into the sum of two components has occurred. The first component, which represents the contribution of the upper sideband, is the response to $s(t)$ of a network having amplitude vs. frequency equal to $A(\omega_c + \omega)$ and phase shift vs. frequency $B(\omega_c + \omega) - B(\omega_c)$. The second component, which represents the contribution of the lower sideband, is the response of a network with amplitude vs. frequency $A(\omega_c - \omega)$ and phase shift $B(\omega_c) - B(\omega_c - \omega)$. We have thus reduced the AM case to an equivalent baseband system with complex transmittance function:

$$Y(\omega) = A(\omega_c + \omega)e^{j[B(\omega_c+\omega)-B(\omega_c)]}$$
$$+ A(\omega_c - \omega)e^{j[B(\omega_c)-B(\omega_c-\omega)]} \quad (5\text{-}58)$$

The required conditions for Nyquist's various criteria of transmission without intersymbol interference can now be applied to the composite signal obtained by transmitting $s(t)$ through the characteristic (5-58). We also note that if Nyquist's conditions are satisfied for the two individual components of (5-58) separately, they will also be satisfied by the sum.

An important simplification results if the phase is symmetrical with respect to the carrier frequency. If we have

$$B(\omega_c + \omega) - B(\omega_c) = B(\omega_c) - B(\omega_c - \omega) \equiv \beta(\omega) \quad (5\text{-}59)$$

the amplitude functions of (5-58) add directly to give

$$Y(\omega) = \alpha(\omega)e^{j\beta(\omega)} \quad (5\text{-}60)$$

where
$$\alpha(\omega) = A(\omega_c + \omega) + A(\omega_c - \omega) \quad (5\text{-}61)$$

If in addition $\beta(\omega)$ is proportional to ω, say

$$\beta(\omega) = -\tau\omega \quad (5\text{-}62)$$

we have
$$Y(\omega) = \alpha(\omega)e^{-j\omega\tau} \quad (5\text{-}63)$$

Here the effect of the phase is to delay the signal by τ and is equivalent to a change in the origin of time. Still further simplification results if the phase function $\Phi(\omega)$ in the Fourier integral representation of $s(t)$ is equal to zero, which means that the signal pulse has even symmetry about the origin. Assuming then that τ is zero, or that the origin of time has been shifted by τ, we obtain

$$4I_0(t) = \frac{1}{\pi}\int_0^\infty S(\omega)[A(\omega_c + \omega) + A(\omega_c - \omega)]\cos t\omega \, d\omega \quad (5\text{-}64)$$

Nyquist's requirements can now be applied either to $S(\omega)A(\omega_c + \omega)$ and $S(\omega)A(\omega_c - \omega)$ separately or to their sum. Figure 5-17 represents a case in which vestigial symmetry is satisfied by each sideband separately. In Fig 5-18, which is the vestigial-sideband case, it is the sum which has the required property.

It is to be noted that the replacement of transmission by an equivalent linear network is valid only for product detection. An envelope detector would not give the response (5-57) unless there were sufficient added carrier to make products of carrier and signal dominate in determining the envelope.

5-8 APPLICATION TO FM

Direct application of Nyquist's results to FM are difficult because the effect of band-limiting on the instantaneous frequency of a wave is not linear. An approximate solution involving a number of restrictive assumptions has been constructed by Sunde[3] to define a band through which Nyquist's first criterion can be satisfied for binary FM transmission. Consider the FM transmitter shown in Fig. 5-19. A switch selects between the output of two oscillators to deliver the spacing or marking frequency to the line in accordance with the binary message. A linear shaping network has the task of converting the switched wave to a band-limited form in which intersymbol interference is suppressed when the instantaneous frequency is sampled at the midpoint of each signaling interval.

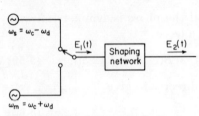

FIG. 5-19. Sunde's method of generating binary FM signals free from intersymbol interference.

Let T be the duration of the signaling interval, and represent the spacing and marking frequencies respectively by $\omega_c + \omega_d$ and $\omega_c - \omega_d$. The midband frequency is ω_c and the frequency shift is $2\omega_d$. In Sunde's minimum-bandwidth solution the condition $\omega_d T = \pi$ is imposed. This is equivalent to making the frequency shift in cycles per second numerically equal to the number of bits per second. When this constraint is imposed, the total phase change during a spacing interval differs from that during a marking interval by exactly $2\omega_d T$ radians or 360°. Therefore, if the phase of the wave is continuous at one transition, it will be continuous at all transitions. In one half of a signaling interval the difference in phase change between spacing and marking is 180°. If the marking and spacing oscillators are 180° out of phase at the midpoint of a signaling interval, they will be in phase at the beginning and end of the interval, thereby insuring continuous phase for the switched wave.

The output of the switch can now be written

$$E_1(t) = \frac{A}{2} \cos \left[(\omega_c - \omega_d)t + \theta\right] - \frac{A}{2} \cos \left[(\omega_c + \omega_d)t + \theta\right]$$

$$+ \frac{A}{2} s(t) \cos \left[(\omega_c - \omega_d)t + \theta\right] + \frac{A}{2} s(t) \cos \left[(\omega_c + \omega_d)t + \theta\right]$$

$$= A \sin \omega_d t \sin (\omega_c t + \theta) + A s(t) \cos \omega_d t \cos (\omega_c t + \theta) \qquad (5\text{-}65)$$

where $s(t)$ has the value $+1$ when the binary message symbol is 1 and has the value -1 when the binary symbol is 0. It is readily verified that $E_1(t)$ as thus defined becomes $A \cos \left[(\omega_c - \omega_d)t + \theta\right]$ when $s(t) = 1$ and becomes $-A \cos \left[(\omega_c + \omega_d)t + \theta\right]$ when $s(t) = -1$. We assume that $t = 0$ at the midpoint of a signaling interval. Conditions are thus established for continuity of phase at the switching instants, which occur when t is an odd multiple of $T/2$. The continuity of phase, however, does not by itself yield a finite bandwidth for $E_1(t)$, since the square wave $s(t)$ appears as a constituent. In Sunde's solution the shaping network in effect changes $s(t) \cos \omega_d t$ to a band-limited function $s_1(t)$ without disturbing the values of instantaneous frequency at the midpoints of the signaling intervals.

To obtain Sunde's result we write

$$E_2(t) = A \sin \omega_d t \sin (\omega_c t + \theta) + A s_1(t) \cos (\omega_c t + \theta)$$

$$= R(t) \cos \left[\omega_c t + \theta + \phi(t)\right] \qquad (5\text{-}66)$$

where
$$R^2(t) = A^2 [s_1^2(t) + \sin^2 \omega_d t] \qquad (5\text{-}67)$$

and
$$\tan \phi(t) = - \frac{\sin \omega_d t}{s_1(t)} \qquad (5\text{-}68)$$

The instantaneous frequency deviation $\omega_i(t)$ from midband is equal to the derivative of $\phi(t)$ with respect to time. Hence

$$\omega_i(t) = - \frac{d}{dt} \arctan \frac{\sin \omega_d t}{s_1(t)}$$

$$= \frac{s_1'(t) \sin \omega_d t - \omega_d s_1(t) \cos \omega_d t}{\sin^2 \omega_d t + s_1^2(t)} \qquad (5\text{-}69)$$

At the sampling instants, $t = nT$. We note that $\sin \omega_d nT = \sin n\pi = 0$ and $\cos \omega_d nT = \cos n\pi = (-)^n$. Hence the nth sample

of instantaneous frequency is given by

$$\omega_i(nT) = (-)^{n+1} \frac{\omega_d}{s_1(nT)} \tag{5-70}$$

Intersymbol interference is absent from the samples if $\omega_i(nT)$ is equal to $-\omega_d$ for marking signals and $+\omega_d$ for spacing signals. Therefore, freedom from intersymbol interference can be obtained if the function $s_1(t)$ assumes the value $(-)^n$ at the midpoints of marking intervals and the value $-(-)^n$ at the midpoints of spacing intervals. Let us write $s_1(t)$ in the form

$$s_1(t) = \sum_{m=-\infty}^{\infty} (-)^m b_m g_1(t - mT) \tag{5-71}$$

where b_m is equal to $+1$ when the mth signal is a mark and -1 if the mth signal is a space. Then if the function $g_1(t)$ satisfies Nyquist's first criterion, i.e., if it has nulls at $t = \pm nT$, $n = 1, 2, 3, \ldots$,

$$s_1(nT) = (-)^n b_n g_1(0) \tag{5-72}$$

Substituting this value in Eq. (5-70) shows that the correct message is received if $g_1(0) = 1$. In particular $g_1(t)$ can be proportional to the impulse response of an ideal low-pass filter cutting off at frequency ω_d

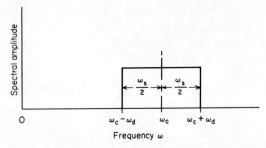

FIG. 5-20. Spectral amplitude function at input to frequency detector when Sunde's binary FM system is operated at minimum bandwidth.

radians per second, or to the impulse response of a low-pass filter with vestigially symmetric cutoff about ω_d. The problem is thereby reduced to finding a transmittance function which will replace $s(t) \cos \omega_d t$ in Eq. (5-65) by an acceptable $s_1(t)$.

Examining the second form of Eq. (5-65), we see that the transmittance function must leave the first term unchanged, while in the second term the amplitude modulation of $A \cos(\omega_c t + \theta)$ must be changed from $s(t) \cos \omega_d t$ to $s_1(t)$. From Eq. (5-71) we note that $s_1(t)$ consists of a sum of pulses of form $\pm g_1(t - nT)$. As discussed in Sec. 5-7, the multiplication of $A \cos(\omega_c t + \theta)$ by $g_1(t)$ translates the spectrum of $g_1(t)$ to upper and lower sidebands on ω_c. In the minimum-bandwidth case, the spectrum of $g_1(t)$ is constant from $\omega = 0$ to

$\omega = \omega_d$ and is zero at higher frequencies. The corresponding minimum bandwidth of the spectrum of $s_1(t) \cos \omega_c t$ extends from $\omega_c - \omega_d$ to $\omega_c + \omega_d$ as shown in Fig. 5-20. A vestigially symmetric case requiring more bandwidth but allowing for a gradual filter cutoff is shown in Fig. 5-21. The upper- and lower-sideband cutoffs must be matched to give even symmetry about ω_c for the complete spectrum.

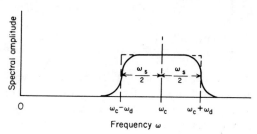

FIG. 5-21. Modification of minimum-bandwidth FM spectrum retaining suppression of intersymbol interference.

It remains to be shown how the transmittance function for the shaping network can be found. For rectangular switching with no lost time, we can write

$$s(t) = \sum_{m=-\infty}^{\infty} b_m g(t - nT) \tag{5-73}$$

where

$$g(t) = \begin{cases} 1 & -\dfrac{T}{2} < t < \dfrac{T}{2} \\ 0 & |t| > \dfrac{T}{2} \end{cases} \tag{5-74}$$

From the Fourier integral representation of a rectangular pulse, calculated at the beginning of the chapter, we have

$$g(t) = \frac{2}{\pi} \int_0^\infty \frac{\sin(\omega T/2)}{\omega} \cos \omega t \, d\omega \tag{5-75}$$

We note that

$$g(t) \cos \omega_d t \cos(\omega_c t + \theta) = \frac{g(t)}{2} \cos[(\omega_c + \omega_d)t + \theta]$$

$$+ \frac{g(t)}{2} \cos[(\omega_c - \omega_d)t + \theta] \tag{5-76}$$

Considering one of these terms, we apply the result of Eq. (5-54) to obtain

$$g(t) \cos [(\omega_c + \omega_d)t + \theta]$$

$$= \frac{1}{\pi} \int_0^\infty \frac{\sin (\omega T/2)}{\omega} \cos [(\omega_c + \omega_d + \omega)t + \theta] \, d\omega$$

$$+ \frac{1}{\pi} \int_0^{\omega_c} \frac{\sin (\omega T/2)}{\omega} \cos [(\omega_c + \omega_d - \omega)t + \theta] \, d\omega$$

$$+ \frac{1}{\pi} \int_{\omega_c}^\infty \frac{\sin (\omega T/2)}{\omega} \cos [(\omega - \omega_c - \omega_d)t - \theta] \, d\omega \qquad (5\text{-}77)$$

The third term represents foldover from the lower sideband. It contains components in the same frequency range as the normal lower sideband and the upper sideband. The way in which the foldover components combine with the others depends on the carrier phase angle θ. Since it would be very difficult to control the value of θ in a practical realization, the midband frequency should be made high enough to reduce the foldover contributions to a negligible amount. The first two terms can then be combined into a single integral by replacing $\omega_c + \omega_d + \omega$ by a new variable in the first integral and $\omega_c + \omega_d - \omega$ by the same variable in the second integral. The result is

$$g(t) \cos [(\omega_c + \omega_d)t + \theta] \approx \frac{1}{\pi} \int_0^\infty \frac{\cos (\omega_c - \omega)T/2}{\omega_d + \omega_c - \omega} \cos (\omega t + \theta) \, d\omega$$

$$(5\text{-}77a)$$

Likewise

$$g(t) \cos [(\omega_c - \omega_d)t + \theta] \approx \frac{1}{\pi} \int_0^\infty \frac{\cos (\omega_c - \omega)T/2}{\omega_d - \omega_c + \omega} \cos (\omega t + \theta) \, d\omega$$

$$(5\text{-}78)$$

Combining, we finally obtain

$$g(t) \cos \omega_d t \cos (\omega_c t + \theta) = \frac{\omega_d}{\pi} \int_0^\infty \frac{\cos (\omega - \omega_c)T/2}{\omega_d{}^2 - (\omega - \omega_c)^2} \cos (\omega t + \theta) \, d\omega$$

$$(5\text{-}79)$$

Returning to the desired output of the shaping network, we write

$$g_1(t) = \frac{k}{\pi} \int_0^{2\omega_d} Y(\omega) \cos \omega t \, d\omega \qquad (5\text{-}80)$$

where, since $Y(\omega)$ must represent the transmittance of a low-pass filter cutoff vestigially symmetric about ω_d, we must have, in accordance with Eq. (5-40),

$$Y(\omega_d - x) + Y(\omega_d + x) = 1 \qquad 0 < x < \omega_d \qquad (5\text{-}81)$$

The value of k is determined from the condition $g_1(0) = 1$. That is,

$$g_1(0) = \frac{k}{\pi} \int_0^{2\omega_d} Y(\omega)\, d\omega$$

$$= \frac{k}{\pi} \int_0^{\omega_d} Y(\omega)\, d\omega + \frac{k}{\pi} \int_{\omega_d}^{2\omega_d} Y(\omega)\, d\omega$$

$$= \frac{k}{\pi} \int_0^{\omega_d} Y(\omega_d - x)\, dx + \frac{k}{\pi} \int_0^{\omega_d} Y(\omega_d + x)\, dx$$

$$= \frac{k\omega_d}{\pi} = 1 \tag{5-82}$$

Therefore, $k = \pi/\omega_d$. Hence

$$g_1(t)\cos(\omega_c t + \theta)$$

$$= \frac{1}{2\omega_d} \int_0^{2\omega_d} Y(\omega)\{\cos[(\omega_c + \omega)t + \theta]$$

$$+ \cos[(\omega_c - \omega)t + \theta]\}\, d\omega$$

$$= \frac{1}{2\omega_d} \int_{\omega_c}^{\omega_c + 2\omega_d} Y(\omega - \omega_c)\cos(\omega t + \theta)\, d\omega$$

$$+ \frac{1}{2\omega_d} \int_{\omega_c - 2\omega_d}^{\omega_c} Y(\omega_c - \omega)\cos(\omega t + \theta)\, d\omega$$

$$= \frac{1}{2\omega_d} \int_{\omega_c - 2\omega_d}^{\omega_c + 2\omega_d} Y(|\omega - \omega_c|)\cos(\omega t + \theta)\, d\omega \tag{5-83}$$

The shaping network must convert the right-hand member of Eq. (5-79) to the right-hand member of Eq. (5-83). Comparing the spectral amplitudes in the two integrals, we see that the required transmittance function for the shaping network is zero outside the range in which ω differs from ω_c by more than $2\omega_d$. Within the range $\omega_c - 2\omega_d < \omega < \omega_c + 2\omega_d$, the required transmittance function is

$$Y_r(\omega) = \frac{\pi[\omega_d{}^2 - (\omega - \omega_c)^2]Y(|\omega - \omega_c|)}{2\omega_d{}^2 \cos[\pi(\omega - \omega_c)/2\omega_d]} \tag{5-84}$$

We recall that a further requirement on the shaping network was found to be that the first part of Eq. (5-65), not involving $s(t)$, must remain unchanged. This means that $Y_r(\omega)$ must have the value unity at $\omega = \omega_c \pm \omega_d$. Substitution of these values in Eq. (5-84) and evaluation of the resulting indeterminate forms show that the requirement is fulfilled.

Graphs of functions $Y_r(\omega)$ which satisfy the required conditions when used with rectangular switching have been given by Sunde in the reference cited. The characteristics differ from those required to satisfy the same criteria with AM because we start with the resultant of two carrier pulses at different frequencies instead of a pulse at one carrier frequency. The FM case does not require as much equalization because the resultant of two pulse spectra is flatter in the middle of the band than the spectrum of one pulse. Figures 5-22 and 5-23 show two

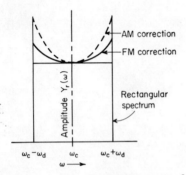

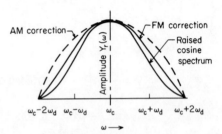

Fig. 5-22. Transmittance of shaping network required to transform from 100 per cent duty-factor rectangular switching to minimum-bandwidth rectangular AM and FM spectra on line.

Fig. 5-23. Transmittance of shaping network required to transform from 100 per cent duty-factor rectangular switching to full raised-cosine roll-off of AM and FM spectra on line.

examples taken from Sunde's paper. The former is the minimum-bandwidth rectangular-spectrum case, and the latter is the raised-cosine case which uses twice the minimum bandwidth.

It might seem at this point that Sunde's example shows that binary FM ideally requires no more bandwidth than binary AM for the same bit rate. However, we must qualify such a conclusion by the observation that while the instantaneous frequency has been controlled, no attempt has been made to obtain a constant-amplitude wave, and hence the solution is not strictly an FM wave—it is a hybrid wave containing both amplitude and frequency modulation. We can produce a pure FM wave from it by limiting the amplitude, but this will change the spectrum and in fact will, in general, widen the range of required frequencies. If the transmission line is tailored to deliver the minimum spectrum and not a wider one, we are forced to conclude that our solution is for a hybrid combination of AM and FM. The signal information is contained in the FM part, but some amplitude modulation is necessary to fit the complete wave into the desired bandwidth. As a matter of fact the resolution of Eq. (5-65) shows that the wave consists of unmodulated sine waves plus suppressed-carrier AM.

With regard to the actual instrumentation of the FM transmitter, it is theoretically essential that there be only two independent frequency sources. One of these is the bit frequency $f_s = \omega_d/\pi$, and the other can be one of the two carrier frequencies or a frequency from which both can be derived. If the marking frequency ω_μ is supplied by an independent oscillator, the spacing frequency can be obtained by generation of the sum frequency $\omega_s + \omega_\mu$ in a multiplier or squarer. Another method is to generate the mark and space frequencies by an n-to-1 step-down from stable independent oscillators accurately set to differ in frequency by n times the bit rate. The phase discontinuities then cannot exceed π/n radians.

It is to be noted that the locked-in relationship between bit rate and shift frequency is not necessarily disturbed by transmission over so-called nonsynchronous carrier channels in which the demodulating carrier is derived from a local oscillator. Slowly varying frequency offset is allowable because the marking and spacing frequencies move together.

In this section we have treated the subject of band-limited FM by strictly analytic methods. It is instructive to consider the same problem from a geometric point of view, making use of the vector representations introduced in Chap. 4. The resulting alternative explanation is given in the next section.

5-9 ANALYSIS OF A FREQUENCY-SHIFT SIGNAL AS AN AM SIGNAL

As was brought out in Chap. 4 and in Sec. 5-8, square-wave frequency-modulation signals can be generated by switching between continuous sources of mark and space frequency. Particularly interesting cases are those in which transitions between the two frequencies always occur when the two sources are at the same phase angle. Once the oscillators are properly phased for the first transition, following transitions avoid phase discontinuities if the pulse lengths are multiples of the reciprocal of the frequency difference. The minimum-bandwidth condition is obtained when the multiple is unity. This results in a difference of one between the number of carrier cycles in a unit mark and the number of carrier cycles in a unit space.

These special cases can be analyzed as examples of amplitude modulation. For instance, consider the spectrum of an isolated

marking pulse.   As indicated in Fig. 5-24, such a signal can be taken
as the sum of three components: (1) a continuous spacing-frequency
wave, (2) a unit pulse of spacing frequency of opposite phase to that of
the first component, and (3) a unit pulse of marking frequency occupying
the same position as the pulse of the second component.   The sum of
the three components results in a unit pulse of marking frequency

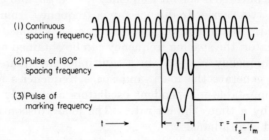

FIG. 5-24. Decomposition of binary FM wave with single mark signal preceded
and followed by long train of space signals.

preceded and succeeded by continuous spacing frequency.   The
spectrum of the first component is a spectral line at the space frequency.
The second and third components give rise to the spectrum of interest.

As described in Chap. 4 the spectrum of a single rectangular pulse
has a $(\sin x)/x$ form.   The rectangular pulses of spacing and marking

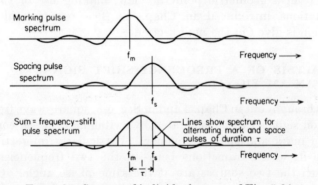

FIG. 5-25. Spectra of individual waves of Fig. 5-24.

carrier thus give rise to two $(\sin x)/x$-shaped spectra centered about
the marking and spacing frequencies as indicated in Fig. 5-25.   The
spectrum of the frequency-shift pulse is thus the sum of these two
spectra.   It will now be shown that components of the two spectra at
a specific frequency are in phase and that the two spectra can be
directly summed.

With no phase discontinuities the marking carrier wave will be in phase with the continuous spacing wave at the beginning and end of the pulse. For the case of minimum frequency shift, there is a difference of one in the number of carrier cycles in a unit mark as compared with that in a unit space. This results in the carrier wave at the center of the marking pulse having a 180° phase relationship with that of the continuous spacing wave. This means that at the center of the reversed-phase spacing pulse the carrier is in phase with the carrier at the center of the marking pulse. Furthermore, at the center of the pulses all the spectral components of the rectangular modulating waves are at their positive or negative peaks as indicated by Eq. (4-8). Since at this same instant the carrier waves have the same phase angle, a specific frequency in the mark pulse spectrum is either in phase or exactly out of phase with the component of the same frequency in the spacing pulse spectrum. The two spectra thus may be added together as indicated in Fig. 5-25.

It will be noticed that this special case of a frequency-shift pulse spectrum is less peaked than for AM and also dies away faster at the higher side frequencies than does AM. The relative amplitude of the spectral lines for alternating mark and space pulses of width τ are given by the spectrum amplitude at intervals $1/(2\tau)$ from midband as indicated in Fig. 5-25. This will be found to agree with Eq. (4-20) of Chap. 4.

We will now proceed to show that it is possible to transmit these frequency-shift pulses through a minimum passband of width $1/\tau$ cps without intersymbol interference as for AM pulses. As was the case for AM pulses this condition calls for a flat received spectrum or a modification thereof according to Nyquist's criteria. To make the frequency-shift pulse spectrum, as shown in Fig. 5-25, flat over a band $\pm 1/(2\tau)$ from midband requires a shaping filter with an amplitude-frequency characteristic as shown in Fig. 5-26. The flat output spectrum will produce a $(\sin x)/x$-shaped envelope having a carrier frequency at midband. In Fig. 5-24 it will be noted that at the middle of the pulse interval the sum of the marking pulse and reversed-phase spacing pulse is 180° out of phase from the continuous spacing wave. On the assumption that the shaping filter of Fig. 5-26 has a linear phase characteristic, the 180° relationship will still hold at the output.

One of the characteristics of the normalized received spectrum at the output of the shaping filter is that it has the value one-half at the marking and spacing frequencies. Consequently the continuous spacing wave at the filter output will have half the amplitude of the $(\sin x)/x$-shaped envelope of the frequency-shift pulse. We can, therefore, represent the filter output as the sum of two vectors as indicated in Fig. 5-27. One of these represents the continuous spacing wave and is taken as the stationary reference. The other represents the pulse of midband frequency which has a $(\sin x)/x$ variation in amplitude. In this example the spacing frequency is the higher frequency so that the second vector rotates clockwise one-half a revolution per pulse interval τ. It also has zero amplitude at intervals τ from the center of the pulse.

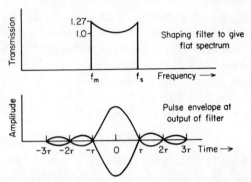

FIG. 5-26. Shaping of FM spectrum to suppress intersymbol interference.

At the center of the pulse the resultant vector will be at position a in Fig. 5-27 and is seen to be rotating clockwise with an angular velocity twice that of the center-frequency pulse vector. It therefore follows that the instantaneous frequency is the full bandwidth away from the spacing frequency and is, therefore, at the marking frequency. At intervals of τ from the center of the pulse, the pulse vector goes through zero amplitude at point b in line with the spacing vector, which makes the instantaneous frequency equal to the spacing value. If a second pulse follows at the interval τ, its vector follows 180° behind that of the first pulse. It will be seen that no pulse can interfere with another at the pulse centers, and that the instantaneous frequency will be either at the marking or spacing value. Hence, it is possible to signal without intersymbol interference.

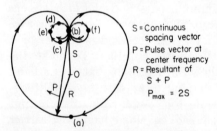

FIG. 5-27. Vector diagram of components in output of minimum rectangular-bandwidth FM shaping filter.

The spectrum can be modified by various symmetrical cutoff shapes at the marking and spacing frequencies in a similar manner as for AM. The case for a raised-cosine spectrum is shown in Fig. 5-28. The resultant vector still passes through points a and b as before but differs at other points. The variation of instantaneous frequency vs. time can be derived from the vector diagram. For instance, points of maximum deviation from the spacing frequency occur at such points as a, c, and d. The instantaneous frequency is equal to the spacing frequency at points such as b, e, and f. The general shape of the instantaneous frequency is shown in Fig. 5-29.

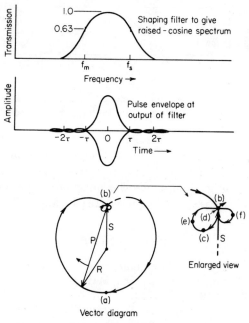

FIG. 5-28. Vector diagram of FM components with full raised-cosine roll-off spectrum.

Frequency-shift signals are usually not generated by switching between continuous sources of mark and space frequency. Phase discontinuities at transitions can more easily be minimized by direct frequency modulation of a single oscillator. However, if the amount of frequency shift between mark and space is equal to the reciprocal of the unit pulse length and occurs abruptly, the resulting signal is the same as analyzed here. If one departs from this particular relation between pulse length and frequency shift, several things change. The frequency-shift pulse spectrum changes shape which in turn changes the envelope shape of the pulse from the shaping filter. The amplitude and phase relationship of the two vectors shown in Figs. 5-27 and 5-28 is thus changed, and the instantaneous frequency will not pass through

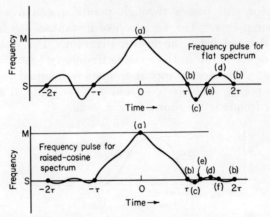

FIG. 5-29. Instantaneous frequency vs. time for rectangular bandwidth and full raised-cosine roll-off. Lettered points indicate corresponding points on vector diagrams, Figs. 5-27 and 5-28.

either the marking or spacing value at the centers of the pulse intervals. The intersymbol interference which results will be less for the gradual cutoff case, as in Fig. 5-28, since the pulse envelope dies away faster and the tails of the response cannot greatly affect the instantaneous frequency.

REFERENCES

1. Sunde, E. D.: Theoretical Fundamentals of Pulse Transmission, I, *Bell System Tech. J.*, vol. 33, pp. 721–788, May, 1954; II, *Bell System Tech. J.*, vol. 33, pp. 987–1010, July, 1954.
2. Nyquist, H.: Certain Topics in Telegraph Transmission Theory, *Trans. AIEE*, vol. 47, pp. 617–644, April, 1928.
3. Sunde, E. D.: Ideal Binary Pulse Transmission by AM and FM, *Bell System Tech. J.*, vol. 38, pp. 1357–1425, November, 1959.
———: Pulse Transmission by AM, FM, and PM in the Presence of Phase Distortion, *Bell System Tech. J.*, vol. 40, pp. 353–422, March, 1961.

CHAPTER 6

TRANSMISSION IMPAIRMENTS

Data transmission channels are subject to several varieties of impairments. Some of these are characteristic of the steady-state response of the channel, some are associated with variations in the channel, and others are extraneous interferences. All of these result in a received signal distorted from that which was transmitted. The various specific types of impairment are discussed in the following sections. Emphasis is given to the characteristics of telephone voice channels because of their importance in providing the bulk of data communication facilities.[1-3]

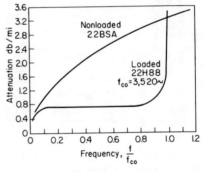

FIG. 6-1. Cable attenuation.

6-1 AMPLITUDE-FREQUENCY DISTORTION

By amplitude-frequency distortion we mean the distortion caused by variation of transmission loss with frequency. The attenuation in decibels of typical cable pairs used in telephone communication is proportional to the square root of the frequency within the voice band. Where runs in excess of about three miles are necessary, it is common practice to add lumped inductance at uniform intervals, which gives both a lower and a more uniform loss. However, this makes the line act as a low-pass filter with an abrupt cutoff. The amplitude-vs.-frequency characteristics of typical loaded and unloaded cable pairs are shown in Fig. 6-1.

Most carrier telephone systems derive a multiplicity of voice channels by frequency-division techniques. The bandpass filters associated with such systems result in a steep cutoff at both the high and the low end of the voice band. Typical attenuation-vs.-frequency characteristics of carrier systems are shown in Fig. 6-2.

83

At the switching points of telephone systems are repeating coils, series capacitors, and shunt inductors used in signaling and supervision. These cause the voice channels to have a low-frequency cutoff even when the connecting facility is capable of transmitting d-c components. The overall attenuation-vs.-frequency characteristic of a typical switched telephone-network connection is exemplified in Fig. 6-3. It has a low-end cutoff of 15 to 25 db per octave starting at about 300 cycles. The range 300 to 1,100 cycles is relatively flat. The range 1,100 to 2,900 cycles usually exhibits a linearly rising loss, which on the average results in the loss at 2,600 cycles being 8 db above that at 1,000 cycles. Above 3,000 cycles the loss rapidly increases at a rate of 80 or 90 db per octave.

The effect of nonuniform attenuation on data communication is to distort the received spectrum and, in turn, the data signal waveform.

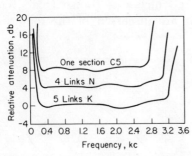

FIG. 6-2. Carrier channel attenuation.

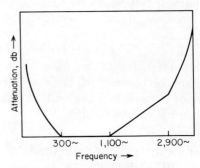

FIG. 6-3. Relative attenuation of typical telephone circuit.

For a particular channel a reasonable amount of such distortion can be allowed for in the design of the over-all transmission characteristic. Provided that the loss is not actually infinite at any important signal frequency, it is theoretically possible to construct linear compensating networks which equalize transmission over the signal band. If the variation in loss is very great, however, there are practical difficulties in supplying sufficient signal power to override noise in the high-loss part of the band. The resultant effect is a fairly definite limitation on useful bandwidth and consequently on rate of signaling.

6-2 PHASE-FREQUENCY DISTORTION

By phase-frequency distortion we mean distortion due to deviation from direct proportionality of phase shift to frequency. Such distortion constitutes the most limiting impairment to data transmission, particularly over telephone voice channels. The reason is that voice communication can tolerate amounts of phase distortion far in excess of that which is severe for high-speed data signals. The ear has the property of resolving signals spatially along the basilar membrane so that components of different frequencies are registered separately with little phase dependence. The main sources of phase distortion are loaded cables and carrier channel filters. The effect is most severe at the band edges where there is a steep rise in attenuation. Phase distortion may also be caused by echoes from nearby imperfect line terminations. Since the effect of phase distortion on data signals is harder to visualize than some other impairments, it will be considered at some length.

As shown mathematically in Chap. 5, a network with phase shift proportional to frequency, such as depicted in Fig. 6-4, causes no distortion of waveform. That this is so can be seen physically by considering a wave made up of harmonically related frequencies. The nth harmonic will suffer a phase shift n times that of the fundamental. However, since the period of the nth harmonic is $1/n$ times that of the fundamental, the time displacement of the nth harmonic will be the same as that of the fundamental. Thus all components and consequently the wave itself are delayed in time by an amount equal to the slope of the phase-vs.-frequency characteristic. Conversely a transmission path exhibiting time delay has a phase-vs.-frequency characteristic with a slope equal to the time delay.

The identification of time delay with the slope of the phase-frequency characteristic is precise only when the system is distortionless, i.e., when the amplitude does not vary with frequency, and the phase shift is proportional to frequency. It has, however, been found convenient in discussing nonideal systems to define the term "envelope delay," or more simply "delay," as the slope of the phase-frequency curve and to speak of the departure of the envelope delay from a constant value as "delay distortion." It should be stressed that the delay defined in this way at a single frequency is only identifiable with true time delay for a narrow-band signal with spectrum centered at that frequency. The range of validity extends only over a frequency interval throughout which the amplitude-frequency characteristic does not vary appreciably, and the phase-frequency characteristic is substantially linear. Hence, the term "envelope delay" is appropriate provided we interpret envelope delay at frequency f as meaning the delay suffered by the detected envelope of a narrow-band AM signal transmitted over the system at carrier frequency f. When we apply a signal having a wide-band spectrum to a system in which the envelope delay is not constant over the band, the distortion suffered depends on the way in which the delay varies with frequency and cannot be determined from the total amount of variation alone.

The phase characteristics of transmission facilities and filter networks used for data communication seldom have the linearity shown in Fig. 6-4. A more general type of shape is given in Fig. 6-5. A baseband signal having a spectrum extending over the nonlinear portion of such a characteristic will experience waveform distortion. Figure 6-6 illustrates the type of distortion which occurs when the frequency components of a baseband wave are unequally delayed by a nonlinear phase characteristic.

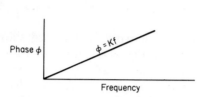

FIG. 6-4. Linear phase characteristic.

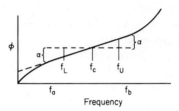

FIG. 6-5. Nonlinear phase characteristic.

In the case of a modulated carrier signal, we are concerned with the effects of the phase characteristic on the wave shape of the modulation. Figure 6-5 shows a phase characteristic which is linear from f_a to f_b but has nonlinearity outside this range. If a sinusoidally modulated AM wave has its carrier and side-frequency components located in the linear region as indicated in Fig. 6-5, it will be seen that the side-frequency components suffer equal but opposite phase shifts with respect to the carrier. The effect of this is to delay the phase of the modulation but not its shape or magnitude. This is illustrated in Fig. 6-7, showing

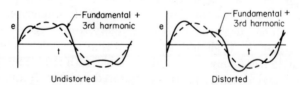

FIG. 6-6. Effect of nonlinear phase on baseband signal.

that the shift in phase of the side-frequency vectors delays the time at which the resultant reaches its peak amplitude. The delay is equal to the phase shift with respect to the carrier divided by the angular velocity of the side-frequency components with respect to the carrier. This is equal to the slope of the phase characteristic.

If the linear portion of the phase characteristic is extended to the zero-frequency axis, the intercept is not necessarily zero phase or a multiple of 2π. When there is a nonzero intercept, the phase shifts of the individual signal components are not proportional to frequency, and a shift in phase of the carrier with respect to the modulation waveform occurs. Fortunately this has no significant effect in the detection of the modulating signal. It is impractical to control the absolute carrier phase over most communication circuits.

With a more complex modulating signal the modulation wave shape is still preserved if all the sideband components fall along a linear phase characteristic. The phase shift of each pair of side-frequency components is proportional to the separation from the carrier and hence to the corresponding modulating frequency which it represents. Consequently all frequency components of the modulation waveform are equally delayed, and the original modulating waveform is preserved.

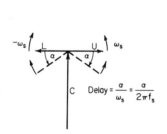

FIG. 6-7. Effect of linear phase characteristic on AM.

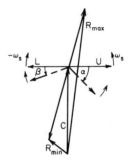

FIG. 6-8. Effect of nonlinear phase characteristic on AM.

If the carrier and side frequencies of an AM signal are situated on a nonlinear portion of the phase characteristic, the envelope shape is distorted as well as delayed. As shown in Fig. 6-8, when the side frequencies are shifted in phase by unequal amounts relative to the carrier, their resultant is no longer in phase with the carrier. This results in a decrease in the peak amplitude of the envelope and in a quadrature component which introduces phase modulation. With some types of detection this quadrature component leads to additional distortion. Nonlinearity of the phase characteristic thus results in the several components of a complex envelope being unequally attenuated and delayed. The envelope shape is thereby distorted.

Similar effects take place for angle modulation. With a linear phase characteristic the relative phase positions of the side-frequency components with respect to the carrier are retained but delayed in time by equal amounts, thus preserving the waveform of the modulation. With a nonlinear phase characteristic the quadrature relationship of the carrier with respect to the odd-order side frequencies is disturbed. This reduces the amount of angle modulation and introduces amplitude modulation. The result is both phase and amplitude distortion of the detected baseband signal.

The measurement of the phase characteristic of a transmission channel is usually done indirectly by a measurement of envelope delay. A low-frequency amplitude modulation, for instance 25 cps, is applied to a carrier which can be varied in frequency over the band of interest. By means of an accurate time base at the receiving end of the channel,

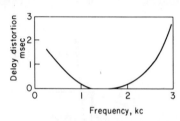

FIG. 6-9. Delay-distortion characteristic.

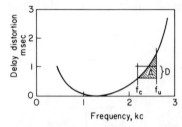

FIG. 6-10. Phase shift and time delay of baseband component. Phase shift of component f_u with respect to carrier $f_c = $ area A. Time delay of component f_u in detected baseband $= D$.

the variation in the phase of the detected low-frequency envelope is measured. As was previously shown the envelope suffers a time delay equal to the slope of the phase-vs.-frequency characteristic. Unless the channel being measured loops back so that the input and output are at the same location, it is seldom practical to measure the absolute delay. Consequently only variations in the phase of the envelope are measured with respect to the phase at some reference frequency. These variations in phase of the low-frequency envelope are expressed in units of time such as milliseconds. A curve, such as shown in Fig. 6-9, is thus obtained which gives the variations in envelope delay as a function of frequency. This is often referred to simply as "delay distortion." Since the phase characteristic can be considered to be linear over the narrow band carrying the low-frequency modulation, the measurement also gives the variations in the slope of the phase characteristic. Specifically the curve represents the deviations in slope from that linear phase corresponding to the unknown reference envelope delay. Integration of the delay-distortion characteristic consequently gives the phase characteristic with respect to the unknown linear reference. It should be noted that the reference is not only unknown in slope but also in zero-frequency intercept. Furthermore, as will be discussed later, the presence of carrier-frequency offset often causes the intercept value to vary continuously with time over a $\pm\pi$ range.

To relate a given delay-distortion characteristic to the waveform distortion it will cause in a specific detected signal, it is necessary to deal with deviations from linear phase. Thus little use can be made directly of the delay-distortion characteristic. To find the phase shift of a particular side frequency with respect to the carrier, it is necessary to integrate the variation in delay distortion between the two frequencies. To find the time delay of the detected baseband component contributed by this particular side frequency, its phase shift must be divided by its frequency separation from the carrier. Thus the amount of time delay of the baseband component is equal to the average value of the variation in delay distortion between the carrier and the side frequency in question. These quantities are illustrated in Fig. 6-10. For a double-sideband type signal with a delay-distortion characteristic which is not symmetrical about the carrier, the upper and lower side-frequency components are delayed unequally so that it is necessary to find their individual delays and then combine them.

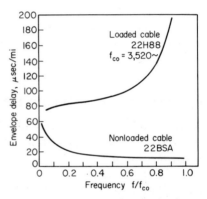

FIG. 6-11. Envelope delay of cable.

It is a common pitfall to think that the delay-distortion curve gives directly the time delay of single-frequency components of a signal.

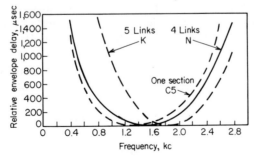

FIG. 6-12. Envelope delay of carrier channels.

A single point on a delay-distortion curve tells only the relative slope of the phase characteristic and the relative envelope delay of a very narrow-band modulated signal whose spectrum is limited to that immediate region of frequency.

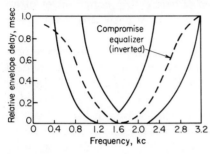

FIG. 6-13. Locus of delay characteristics for 90 per cent of telephone circuits.

As noted in the case of amplitude-frequency distortion, it is possible to compensate phase distortion in an individual channel with linear equalizing networks.

Envelope delay characteristics for cable pairs are shown in Fig. 6-11, and for carrier systems in Fig. 6-12. The locus of a large number of telephone-circuit delay characteristics is shown in Fig. 6-13. The frequency of minimum delay is about 1,700 cycles. The use of a compromise equalization characteristic such as shown dotted in Fig. 6-13 effectively cuts the range of delay distortion by a factor of two.

6-3 NONLINEAR DISTORTION

Amplitude-frequency and phase-frequency distortion as previously described are essentially linear effects. They obey the principle of superposition in that responses to individual signal inputs add directly to form the response when the individual signals are added to form a composite input. It is this property of linearity which makes the resolution of signal waves into components at different frequencies so potent a tool for analysis and measurement. Transmission channels are also subject to nonlinear distortion. While good design tends to make nonlinear effects small, we must consider them in a thorough analysis of the problem.

Nonlinearities in data channels result from many sources, including saturation effects in magnetic cores, nonlinear characteristics of electronic devices, and crowding or limiting in multichannel modulators and amplifiers. These nonlinearities cause harmonic distortion and the creation of spurious frequencies. In general, telephone circuits do not give sufficient harmonic distortion to cause difficulty except in frequency-division systems where large level differences are used between harmonically related channels. The cross-modulation products between two tones of equal amplitude are usually at least 30 db down. Certain types of nonlinearity lead to the "Kendall effect," in which a modulated carrier signal becomes partially demodulated to a baseband signal. If the baseband overlaps the wanted carrier side-bands, it cannot be filtered out and constitutes a form of interference. This phenomenon has not been of much importance in digital transmission, but has been found to be a disturbing factor in telephotography, where small distortions are visible.

Worthy of special mention is a form of nonlinear amplitude distortion which can arise in telephone channels having compandors.[4] A compandor consists of a pair of gain-adjusting circuits which act to maintain a more favorable signal-to-noise ratio over a line facility. At the input of such a channel, one unit compresses the amplitude range of the voice signal. The narrowed range enables transmission through a noisy facility at a relatively high level without overloading. At the channel output a complementary unit expands the amplitude range to that of the original input. The action is not instantaneous but is governed rather by the envelope of the signal wave over a time comparable with the duration of a speech syllable. The variable gain in the two circuits is designed to have equal attack-time characteristics to preserve the original voice waveform. However, the compression and expansion may not be exactly complementary, and the received waveform may, therefore, be different from that originating at the transmitter. Such effects may impair data signals, particularly high-speed AM signals, even though voice signals would not be noticeably affected.

6-4 FREQUENCY OFFSET

It is common practice to use single-sideband suppressed-carrier methods in carrier telephone systems. The demodulating carrier at the receiving end of such a channel may not be locked in frequency with the modulating carrier at the transmitting end. Consequently each component of a signal transmitted over such a channel may suffer a frequency change or offset. Such an offset upsets any harmonic relationship which may have existed between the signal components. To avoid noticeable voice distortion, the amount of offset is usually limited to ± 20 cycles. Most carrier telephone channels meet the CCITT recommendation, which allows ± 2 cycles of offset. This type of impairment is usually not serious in data channels except for those using narrow-band frequency modulation.

The demodulating carriers are sometimes derived from, or controlled by, pilot frequencies transmitted over the carrier telephone system. In such cases no frequency offset occurs, but since the phase of the carrier is not adjusted, the received waveform may be quite different from that transmitted. A phase-angle deviation of the demodulating carrier shifts the phase of all frequency components in the band by a like angle.   Where the carriers are not locked in frequency, any slow drift can be considered as a variation in phase.   This leads to the variable phase-intercept phenomena mentioned previously under phase-distortion effects.

6-5 SUDDEN AMPLITUDE AND PHASE JUMPS

Sudden signal amplitude changes sometimes occur on telephone voice channels.   These may be caused by faulty amplifier components, the substitution of broadband facilities, or operation and maintenance errors.   Such sudden changes are seldom more than 6 db, but changes of this amount can be very disturbing to AM data systems.

Sudden phase changes may also occur on telephone voice channels. These can be caused by switching of carrier supplies not in phase or the substitution of a broadband facility having a different propagation time.   In either case the effect in a voice channel is that of an equal phase-angle change at all frequencies.   Such phase changes are accompanied by amplitude transients during the recovery of steady state in the voice-band channels.

A short-duration loss of signal may occur due to an open circuit or a short circuit.   These are usually the result of accidents, storms, construction work, or maintenance activity.   The intervals are often referred to as "drop outs."   In general, all of the momentary disturbances we have described are called "hits."   They usually cause errrors when the channel is in use for digital transmission.

6-6 ECHOES

Local telephone communication takes place over a pair of wires which handles both directions of signal flow.   For distances beyond a few miles, it is necessary to provide amplification.   Where a small amount of amplification is needed in suburban areas, "negative-resistance" type repeaters are often used.   These inject a negative resistance in series with the two-wire path and thus reduce the attenuation for both directions.   For long distances it is more feasible to introduce the large amounts of necessary amplification in separate paths for the two directions of signal flow.   This conversion between a two-wire two-way circuit and a pair of two-wire one-way circuits is called a two- to four-wire conversion, and is illustrated in Fig. 6-14.

The directions of signal flow are controlled by means of a balancing arrangement.   A network "N" is used which in principle should match the characteristics of the connecting two-wire circuit.   Two multi-winding transformers, $T1$ and $T2$, serve to interconnect the three signal paths and the matching network.   This type of arrangement is known as a "hybrid" circuit. The polings of the windings are such that with a condition of perfect balance no transmission occurs from the output of the receiving line to the input of the sending line. In a telephone switching office the two-wire line may connect to a large variety of trunks and subscriber lines making it impossible to achieve a near perfect balance. A compromise network is possible, which provides a loss between the receiving line and the sending line averaging about 11 db. This is called the "return loss." Some signal is thus allowed to pass back over the four-wire path and become an echo.

In telephone use the echo which returns to the sending end is called "talker echo." When it is sufficiently delayed, it gives the impression of being interrupted. When both ends of a four-wire circuit have poor

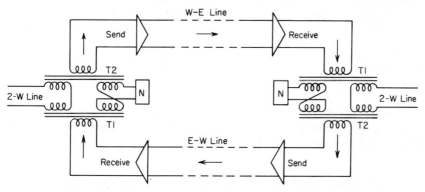

FIG. 6-14. Four-wire circuit with two-wire connections.

balance, the signal can pass completely around the loop and appear as an echo at the receiving end. This is called "listener echo." The longer telephone circuits, which may have long delay times and losses low enough to cause disturbing effects to telephone conversations, usually are equipped with "echo suppressors." These are arrangements placed in a four-wire line which, when voice energy is detected on one line, add high loss to the line in the other direction thus effectively opening the echo path.

In data transmission we are mainly concerned with receiving-end echo. Since signaling rates of 1,000 bits per second or more are commonly used, an echo delay of 1 msec or more appears essentially as an independent interfering signal to the wanted signal. With poor balance at each end of a four-wire circuit, and with a low loss in each direction, a receiving-end echo as strong as 10 db below the main signal may sometimes be encountered.

Sending-end echo may in certain instances be disturbing when a data terminal switches from "send" to "receive" and confuses an echo of what was just sent with a reply from the distant terminal.

6-7 NOISE AND OTHER INTERFERENCE

Noise on telephone voice channels is often thought of as two general types: (1) steady background noise made up of randomly phased components with energy uniformly distributed on the frequency scale, and (2) sharp clicks or bursts termed "impulse noise." The steady type of noise is the most disturbing to voice communication and is usually quite low except for intervals of fading on radio links. Because of the low information rate of speech, impulse noise does not have much effect on voice communication even when its amplitude exceeds that of the signal. Data signals, on the other hand, can stand relatively high steady noise but because of their short symbol intervals are greatly impaired by impulse noise exceeding the signal level.

Impulse noise arises from electrical storms and exposure to other electrical systems. A large part of the impulse noise comes from the contacts which make and break current in telephone switching and signaling equipment.

Interference also results from coupling to other communication channels carrying voice or signaling tones. This is called "crosstalk." Coupling to power transmission lines, electric traction systems, etc., constitutes additional interference.

6-8 VARIABLE CHANNELS

The discussion of transmission impairments has been directed mainly at telephone channels over wire facilities and microwave radio links. Long distance radio circuits in the high-frequency range (3 to 30 Mc) are subject to great variations. Most of these come from reliance on reflected transmission paths which are subject to great daily and seasonal variations. Because of the existence of multiple propagation paths, deep fades and severe phase distortion occur. The difference in propagation times over these paths may be as much as 5 or 6 msec in extreme cases. This leads to selective fading in which several maxima of attenuation may occur across a voice band. These maxima continually move about in frequency. Such effects are consequently much more severe and variable than similar phenomena on the usual continental telephone system.

REFERENCES

1. Horton, A. W., Jr., and H. E. Vaughan: Transmission of Digital Information over Telephone Circuits, *Bell System Tech. J.*, vol. 34, pp. 511–528, May, 1955.

2. Mertz, P., and D. Mitchell: Transmission Aspects of Data Transmission Service Using Private Line Voice Telephone Channels, *Bell System Tech. J.*, vol. 36, pp. 1451–1486, November, 1957.
3. Alexander, A. A., R. M. Gryb, and D. W. Nast: Capabilities of the Telephone Network for Data Transmission, *Bell System Tech. J.*, vol. 39, pp. 431–476, May, 1960.
4. Caruthers, R. S.: The Type N-1 Carrier Telephone System: Objectives and Transmission Features, *Bell System Tech. J.*, vol. 30, pp. 1–32, January, 1951.

CHAPTER 7

BASEBAND SYSTEMS

In this and the next three chapters we shall consider the properties and performance of various idealized types of data transmission systems. Actual methods of instrumentation will be discussed later. Baseband systems will be treated first.

7-1 BASIC FUNCTIONS OF A BASEBAND SYSTEM

The essential parts of a baseband data transmission system are depicted in block diagram form in Fig. 7-1. The signal source in this example is a binary wave made up of on-off non-return-to-zero rectangular pulses as described in Chap. 3. A transmitting low-pass filter is used to limit the signal spectrum applied to the transmission line. The higher-frequency components of the rectangular wave are thus prevented from interfering with other services using the same channel or from crosstalking into other channels. A receiving low-pass filter serves to exclude noise and other interference picked up by the transmission line. The receiver interprets the wave as being one of two

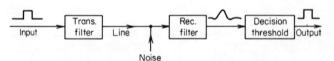

Fig. 7-1. Binary baseband system.

possible values by a binary decision threshold. This process may take either of two forms. In one the received wave is "squared up" by a double-acting limiter or "slicer" as indicated in Fig. 7-2. This gives a restored rectangular wave similar to the original signal source except that the timing of the transitions is subject to displacement by intersymbol interference and transmission impairments. The other form involves sampling the received wave near the center of each pulse interval by means of a local source of timing which for synchronous

96

systems can be derived from, or controlled in phase by, the long time average of the signal transitions. The binary samples thus obtained are used to construct a newly timed or "regenerated" data wave. Thus a nearly perfect replica of the original signal source is obtained.

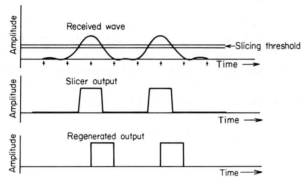

FIG. 7-2. Slicing and regenerating a binary wave.

7-2 ALLOWABLE DISTORTIONS

The restored rectangular wave from the receiver may now serve as the input to another similar transmission link. An intermediate receiver-transmitter for this purpose is called a repeater. If the timing of the wave is also restored it is called a "regenerative repeater." When several transmission links are connected in tandem using ordinary repeaters, the time displacements or distortion of the transitions occurring in each link add together so that a definite limit is placed on the number of links. The transition distortion is commonly expressed in per cent of the unit pulse length. The final receiving device which interprets the data wave does so by a sampling process as in a regenerative repeater. The tolerance to distortion of such a receiving device depends on the accuracy of its timing.

Perfect timing, which samples exactly in the centers of the undistorted pulses, would have a maximum tolerance of ± 50 per cent since if signal transitions were displaced more than one-half a unit pulse, the wrong binary decision would occur. Some devices, such as teletypewriters, operate with start-stop synchronization, and phase their sampling with respect to a particular signal transition in each transmitted character. Distortion of the reference transition subtracts from the tolerance of the sampling. Since the reference transition is subject to the same distorting effects as the other transitions, erroneous decisions are possible with peak distortion of ± 25 per cent based on a fixed time scale. Where start-stop receivers are to be used, the peak distortion in the transmission links should be kept below 20 per cent synchronous distortion (fixed time reference).

7-3 CHANNEL TRANSMISSION CHARACTERISTIC

In Chap. 5 certain minimum-bandwidth low-pass transmission characteristics were considered. In particular a raised-cosine received-pulse spectrum was shown to give a pulse response resulting in a binary pulse train passing through either full or zero amplitude at the centers of the pulse intervals and with the transitions passing through half amplitude at points midway in time between the pulse centers. This is illustrated in Fig. 7-3. A received wave of this form gives the maximum tolerance to interference when sampled at the centers of the intervals. Also,

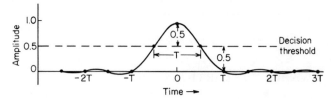

Fig. 7-3. Pulse shape with raised-cosine spectrum.

if the waveform is merely repeated through a slicer set at the half-amplitude level, properly timed transitions will be obtained in the absence of interference.

When the slicing level is not at half amplitude, a type of distortion known as "bias" occurs in which all marking intervals are lengthened or shortened depending on the direction of shift in the slicing level. For example, when the slicing level is nearer to the steady-state mark condition than to that of the spacing condition, the marking intervals are shortened and the signals are said to have "spacing bias." If the slicing threshold at the receiver is fixed, a change in the amplitude of the received wave leads to bias distortion. Changes in received amplitude may occur, for example, because of variations in the attenuation of the transmission line. With a raised-cosine pulse spectrum the transitions are nearly sinusoidal, and a 10 per cent (1 db) decrease in amplitude causes about 7 per cent of spacing bias. This bias effect can be minimized either by applying automatic gain control to keep the received signal amplitude nearly constant or by applying automatic threshold control to maintain the slicing level at the half-amplitude position. When a polar instead of an on-off wave is used, the proper slicing threshold remains at zero for any signal amplitude as long as the mark and space amplitudes are equal. This freedom from bias effects is an outstanding advantage of polar over on-off signals.

A further advantage of the raised-cosine spectrum is that the transient tails of the pulse response die away rapidly. Pulse lengths differing from the exact Nyquist interval are thus subject to only a small amount of intersymbol interference. This is of particular importance when the pulses are repeated without regeneration. The more pronounced pulse tails associated with a more abrupt cutoff lead to greater intersymbol interference for a given departure from Nyquist-interval pulses. When pulses distorted in length by interference in one link are repeated through additional channels, the intersymbol effects build up rapidly if the channels have abrupt cutoffs. For instance, a single pulse once shortened tends to grow still shorter in subsequent transmission links and may fail to reach its destination at all.

We conclude that a sound objective for the combined transmission characteristic of the transmitting and receiving filters plus the transmission line is that the received pulse should have a raised-cosine spectrum. If the transmission lines to be used have some consistent characteristic, this can be allowed for in the filter designs. As previously discussed, the desired pulse reponse also calls for a linear phase-vs.-frequency characteristic. The remaining problem is to find the best division between the transmitting- and receiving-filter characteristics.

7-4 OPTIMUM TRANSMITTING AND RECEIVING FILTERS

Intersymbol interference is determined by the complete channel characteristic including transmitter, line, and receiver. Having set the raised-cosine-vs.-frequency spectrum as a satisfactory goal, we note that there are infinitely many ways of choosing response functions for the individual parts of the channel to obtain the desired overall behavior. We make use of this freedom to combat other sources of trouble as best we can. The two problems of primary importance are noise on the line and mutual interference with other channels sharing the same medium. The latter problem arises when the channels occupy different frequency bands and is more properly treated in the chapter on carrier rather than baseband methods. However, mutual interference between baseband channels on different pairs of wires in the same cable may also have important influence on allocation of filtering.

In the case of noise, we take advantage of differences which may exist between noise and signal at the receiver input. We design the receiving filter to favor acceptance of signal and rejection of noise. The transmitting filter is then determined as that characteristic which when used with the receiving filter will furnish the desired resultant pulse spectrum minimizing intersymbol interference.

The optimum solution evidently depends on the properties of the noise at the receiver input. As stated in Chap. 6, there are two main classifications which are roughly described as steady noise background and infrequent impulses. The steady noise, which is also called thermal noise and gaussian noise, is characterized by its distribution of instantaneous voltages and spectral density. The former follows the gaussian law, which states that the *probability density function $p(E)$*, which when multiplied by the differential voltage range dE gives the probability $p(E) \, dE$ that a random sample of voltage has its value in the range from E to $E + dE$, is

$$p(E) = \frac{1}{\sigma\sqrt{2\pi}} \, e^{-(E-E_0)^2/(2\sigma^2)} \tag{7-1}$$

The quantity σ is the root-mean-square value of noise voltage. The average voltage is E_0 and is typically zero for thermal noise. The *probability distribution function $P(E)$*, which is the probability that the noise voltage is less than E, is obtained by integrating $p(E)$ up to the value E. That is,

$$P(E) = \int_{-\infty}^{E} p(E) \, dE = \frac{1}{2}\left(1 + \operatorname{erf} \frac{E - E_0}{\sigma\sqrt{2}}\right) \tag{7-2}$$

The probability that the noise voltage is greater than E is $1 - P(E)$. The error function appearing in (7-2) is defined by

$$\operatorname{erf} z = \frac{2}{\sqrt{\pi}} \int_0^z e^{-z^2} \, dz \tag{7-3}$$

It is tabulated, for example, in Peirce's *Short Table of Integrals* and in the Jahnke-Emde *Tables of Functions*.[1-3]

Illustrative graphs of the gaussian density function $p(E)$ and the gaussian distribution function $P(E)$ are shown in Figs. 7-4 and 7-5 respectively. Evidently the probability that a voltage sample is in the range from E_1 to E_2 is found by integrating $p(E)$ between these limits. We can write this statement in the form:

$$\text{Prob}\,(E_1 < E < E_2) = \int_{E_1}^{E_2} p(E) \, dE = \frac{1}{2} \operatorname{erf} \frac{E_2 - E_0}{\sigma\sqrt{2}} - \frac{1}{2} \operatorname{erf} \frac{E_1 - E_0}{\sigma\sqrt{2}} \tag{7-4}$$

The probability $P_a(E)$ that the absolute value of noise voltage does not exceed E when the noise is gaussian with zero mean is obtained from

(7-4) by substituting $E_2 = E$, $E_1 = -E$, $E_0 = 0$ and noting that erf $(-z) = -$erf z. The result is

$$P_a(E) = \text{erf } \frac{E}{\sigma\sqrt{2}} \tag{7-5}$$

The other characterizing property of gaussian noise is its spectral density function $w(f)$ which when multiplied by a differential frequency interval df gives the average amount of power in the frequency band from f to $f + df$. Analogous to the probability distribution function, there is a spectral distribution function $W(f)$ defined by

$$W(f) = \int_0^f w(f)\, df \tag{7-6}$$

The function $W(f)$ represents the mean total power in all components of frequency less than f. The mean total power in any band from f_1 to f_2 is obtained by integrating $w(f)$ between these limits. If $w(f)$ is

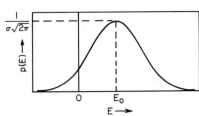

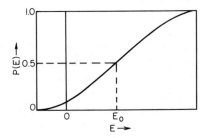

FIG. 7-4. Gaussian probability density function.

FIG. 7-5. Gaussian probability distribution function.

equal to a constant, the noise is said to be *white*. Note that not all gaussian noise is white, but only the special case with constant spectral density.

When gaussian noise is transmitted through a linear system, the output remains gaussian, but the spectral density changes in accordance with the response at individual frequencies. If the complex transmittance function of the system is $Y(f)$, the output spectral density $w_2(f)$ can be calculated from the input spectral density $w_1(f)$ by the formula

$$w_2(f) = |Y(f)|^2 w_1(f) \tag{7-7}$$

By taking the square of the absolute value of $Y(f)$, we ignore the phase-vs.-frequency curve of the system. It is a property of gaussian noise that the phases of its individual components are random with respect to each other. The property of randomness is not affected by any further phase shifts. The probability density and spectral density are related only through the parameter σ. The latter, which is the rms value of E, is determined by the average total power and hence by the integral of $w(f)$ over all frequencies. In other words the probability distribution of voltage samples is not affected by the shape of the spectral density curve but only by its area. The relation between σ and mean total noise power W_n in a circuit with resistance R is

$$W_n = \frac{\sigma^2}{R} \qquad (7\text{-}8)$$

It is convenient to make noise calculations for a circuit of unit resistance since the relative magnitudes of signal and noise are not affected by R.

Impulse noise in contrast to gaussian noise is strongly dependent on the phase of its components. Sharp isolated peaks occur at times when many components of different frequencies add in phase. If the impulsive noise wave is passed through a linear phase filter, the height of any peak is reduced by direct subtraction of the noise components excluded by the filter. If the phase of the filter is not linear with frequency, there is a further reduction because the components passed by the filter suffer relative phase changes which upset the in-phase condition responsible for the high peak. A convenient simplification erring on the pessimistic side is to assume that the impulsive noise components add in phase both before and after filtering. The peak response E_p of a filter with transmittance function $Y(f)$ is then calculated by

$$E_p = c \int_0^\infty |Y(f)|\, w^{1/2}(f)\, df \qquad (7\text{-}9)$$

The model upon which this equation is based is that of a number of in-phase components with specified values of average power. Thus if E_p is the sum of the positive-valued voltages $E_1, E_2, \ldots, E_N$, and if the average power represented by these components individually can be expressed as $W_1 = b^2 E_1{}^2$, $W_2 = b^2 E_2{}^2$, $\ldots$, $W_N = b^2 E_N{}^2$, where b is a constant, then

$$E_p = E_1 + E_2 + \cdots + E_N = \frac{1}{b}(W_1{}^{1/2} + W_2{}^{1/2} + \cdots + W_N{}^{1/2}) \qquad (7\text{-}10)$$

In our case the components may be considered to be the peak voltages in N frequency intervals of width $\Delta f = F/N$ into which the band from 0 to F is divided. If the upper edges of these bands are at F/N, $2F/N, \ldots, NF/N$, then approximately

$$W_1 = w\left(\frac{F}{N}\right)\Delta f,\ W_2 = w\left(\frac{2F}{N}\right)\Delta f,\ \ldots,\ W_N = w\left(\frac{NF}{N}\right)\Delta f \qquad (7\text{-}11)$$

and $\quad E_p = \dfrac{1}{b} (\Delta f)^{\frac{1}{2}} \left[w^{\frac{1}{2}}\!\left(\dfrac{F}{N}\right) + w^{\frac{1}{2}}\!\left(\dfrac{2F}{N}\right) + \cdots + w^{\frac{1}{2}}\!\left(\dfrac{NF}{N}\right) \right]$

$$= \dfrac{1}{b} \left(\dfrac{N}{F}\right)^{\frac{1}{2}} \sum_{n=1}^{N} w^{\frac{1}{2}}\!\left(\dfrac{nF}{N}\right) \Delta f \tag{7-12}$$

If N is not too small or too large, the sum in Eq. (7-12) may be approximated by

$$E_p \approx \dfrac{1}{b} \left(\dfrac{N}{F}\right)^{\frac{1}{2}} \int_0^F w^{\frac{1}{2}}(f)\, df \tag{7-13}$$

Equation (7-9) follows from (7-13) by replacement of $w(f)$ by $|Y(f)|^2 w(f)$, and $b^{-1} (N/F)^{\frac{1}{2}}$ by c. If we attempt to make N approach infinity, the value of E_p approaches infinity, which is indeed what would happen if all the noise components continuously distributed throughout a band of frequencies ever add in phase. This is, in fact, the reason why the peak voltage of gaussian noise is unlimited. Impulse noise must approach gaussian noise if the bandwidth is reduced sufficiently to make transients from successive pulses overlap heavily. We avoid carrying our analysis that far by keeping Δf sufficiently large.

If $Y(f)$ and $w(f)$ are constant throughout a certain band and zero outside, the peak becomes proportional to bandwidth. It is clear that a better suppression of impulse noise peaks relative to signal could be obtained by adjusting the phase of $Y(f)$ to cause out-of-phase addition of impulsive components. The effect of this phasing on signal components could be compensated by preequalization. We shall defer consideration of phase optimization to a later chapter and consider here the more restricted problem of amplitude optimization only.

The description of gaussian and impulsive noise enables us to formulate a solution for an optimum receiving filter in these two cases separately. We follow a general plan similar to that in a paper published by Sunde.[4] Consider first the case of gaussian noise with spectral density $w(f)$ at the receiving-filter input. Let the desired pulse spectrum at the receiving-filter output or detector input be $E_s S(\omega)$ where E_s is the peak value of a signal pulse, and $S(\omega)$ is chosen to minimize intersymbol interference. In terms of our Fourier integral representation of a signal $s(t)$ in Chap. 5, Eqs. (5-5) to (5-9), $s(0) = 1$ and $\Phi(\omega) = 0$. We seek the best transmittance function $Y(f)$ for the receiving filter. The mean total noise power delivered by this filter to the detector input is, by Eq. (7-7),

$$W_n = \int_0^\infty |Y(f)|^2 w(f)\, df \tag{7-14}$$

Some assumptions concerning the detector are necessary to complete the problem. The ultimate criterion of performance is low probability of error, but this must be related to the signal and noise waves. One common type of detector makes a threshold decision based on whether an output magnitude at the time of observation does or does not exceed a critical value. If this output is proportional to the instantaneous sum of the signal and noise waves impressed on the detector, the probability of error can be expressed in terms of the probability that the noise wave exceeds a certain magnitude relative to the peak value of signal E_s at the detector input.

Let kE_s represent the maximum absolute value the noise can have without causing error. Then from Eq. (7-5), the probability that no error occurs is given by

$$P_a(kE_s) = \text{erf} \, \frac{kE_s}{\sigma\sqrt{2}} \tag{7-15}$$

Since the error function increases monotonically with its argument, the probability of error-free detection increases monotonically with E_s/σ. Minimizing the probability of error is achieved by maximizing E_s/σ. Since by Eq. (7-8) σ is proportional to the square root of W_n, we can also express the desired result as a maximization of E_s^2/W_n or as a minimization of W_n/E_s^2. The constraint to be imposed is that the amount of power available for signal transmission is limited, for otherwise we would merely make E_s^2/W_n so large that errors would be practically nonexistent.

We assume that the transmission line is equalized for constant absolute value G_0 of the transmittance and for linear phase over the band of frequencies important to the signal. Let the equalization precede the receiving filter. In order to obtain the desired pulse spectrum $E_s S(\omega)$ at the output of the receiving filter, the transmitting filter must deliver to the line a pulse spectrum $A(\omega)$ defined by

$$A(\omega) = \frac{E_s S(\omega)}{G_0 Y(f)} \tag{7-16}$$

We note that if $Y(f)$ is complex the value of $A(\omega)$ is also complex. We interpret this to mean that the absolute value of $A(\omega)$ represents the spectral amplitude function, and the phase of $A(\omega)$ is the phase function as defined in Chap. 5. By Parseval's theorem[5] the total energy in a pulse with spectrum $A(\omega)$ in a circuit of unit resistance is given by

$$U = 2\int_0^\infty |A(2\pi f)|^2 \, df \tag{7-17}$$

Assume a random sequence containing positive and negative pulses chosen with equal probability is transmitted. Then the average signal power supplied to the line is equal to the energy per pulse multiplied by f_s, the average number of pulses per second. Note that in the example considered f_s is also the signaling rate. If W_s is the average signal power in a unit resistance circuit,

$$W_s = U f_s = \frac{2 f_s E_s^2}{G_0^2} \int_0^\infty \frac{S^2(2\pi f)}{|Y(f)|^2} \, df \qquad (7\text{-}18)$$

From Eqs. (7-14) and (7-18) the expression for the ratio to be minimized is

$$\frac{W_n}{E_s^2} = \frac{2 f_s}{G_0^2 W_s} \int_0^\infty |Y(f_1)|^2 \, w(f_1) \, df_1 \int_0^\infty \frac{S^2(2\pi f_2)}{|Y(f_2)|^2} \, df_2 \qquad (7\text{-}19)$$

The problem thus reduces to the minimization of the product of two integrals I_1 and I_2, which on replacement of $|Y(f)|^2$ by $y(f)$ and $S^2(2\pi f)$ by $x(f)$ become

$$I_1 = \int_0^\infty y(f_1) w(f_1) \, df_1 \qquad (7\text{-}20)$$

$$I_2 = \int_0^\infty \frac{x(f_2)}{y(f_2)} \, df_2 \qquad (7\text{-}21)$$

The functions $w(f)$ and $x(f)$ are given, and we seek the function $y(f)$ which makes the product $I_1 I_2$ smallest. This is a standard problem in the calculus of variations. If we assume $y_0(f)$ is the solution and substitute $y(f) = y_0(f) + \lambda \epsilon(f)$, the first-power term in the expansion of $I_1 I_2$ in powers of λ must vanish for all choices of $\epsilon(f)$. Equating to zero the derivative of $I_1 I_2$ with respect to λ after making this substitution, we find

$$\int_0^\infty \epsilon(f_1) w(f_1) \, df_1 \int_0^\infty \frac{x(f_2)}{y_0(f_2)} \, df_2 = \int_0^\infty y_0(f_1) w(f_1) \, df_1 \int_0^\infty \frac{x(f_2)\epsilon(f_2)}{y_0^2(f_2)} \, df_2 \qquad (7\text{-}22)$$

If we interchange f_1 and f_2 in the integrals on the right-hand side, we obtain

$$\iint\limits_0^\infty \epsilon(f_1) \left[\frac{y_0(f_2) w(f_2) x(f_1)}{y_0^2(f_1)} - \frac{w(f_1) x(f_2)}{y_0(f_2)} \right] df_1 \, df_2 = 0 \qquad (7\text{-}23)$$

The bracketed term must vanish to make the double integral vanish for all $\epsilon(f_1)$. This is seen to require

$$\frac{y_0^2(f_1) w(f_1)}{x(f_1)} = \frac{y_0^2(f_2) w(f_2)}{x(f_2)} \qquad (7\text{-}24)$$

Since the left-hand side depends only on f_1 and the right-hand side only on f_2, neither can vary with either f_1 or f_2. We therefore equate either side to a constant α^4 and find as the solution

$$y_0(f) = \alpha^2 \left[\frac{x(f)}{w(f)}\right]^{1/2} \tag{7-25}$$

In general, it is necessary to verify that the solution obtained actually gives a minimum rather than a maximum or a stationary value which is neither. The verification will be amply covered by presenting families of curves showing the effect of deviations from the solution.

The optimum receiving-filter characteristic we have found requires

$$|Y(f)| = \alpha \frac{S^{1/2}(2\pi f)}{w^{1/4}(f)} \tag{7-26}$$

where α can now be determined by substituting (7-26) in (7-18), giving

$$\alpha^2 = \frac{2f_s E_s^2}{G_0^2 W_s} \int_0^\infty S(2\pi f) w^{1/2}(f)\, df \tag{7-27}$$

Note that the phase angle of $Y(f)$ does not affect the performance and can be allowed to vary in any expedient way.

In the case of white gaussian noise and a raised-cosine spectrum, we set

$$w(f) = w_0 \tag{7-28}$$

and from Eqs. (5-27) and (5-28) with $\omega_x = \omega_1 = \omega_s/2$

$$S(2\pi f) = \frac{1}{f_s} \cos^2 \frac{\pi f}{2f_s} \qquad f < f_s \tag{7-29}$$

Then the optimum receiving-filter characteristic is given by

$$Y(f) = \frac{\alpha}{f_s^{1/2} w_0^{1/4}} \cos \frac{\pi f}{2f_s} \qquad f < f_s \tag{7-30}$$

The constant multiplier is of no importance with regard to relative merit of different filter curves since it is only a gain factor which affects signal and noise components alike. It will be useful later to have the result when the optimum transmittance function Eq. (7-30) is substituted in Eq. (7-19), namely,

$$\frac{W_n}{E_s^2} = \frac{w_0 f_s}{2 G_0^2 W_s} \tag{7-31}$$

Also the corresponding value of α from Eq. (7-27) is

$$\alpha^2 = \frac{E_s^2 w_0^{1/2} f_s}{G_0^2 W_s} \tag{7-32}$$

A particular case of practical interest is that in which the receiving filter has unity gain at frequency zero. From Eq. (7-30) this implies $\alpha^2 = f_s w_0^{1/2}$. Substituting the latter relation in (7-32), we obtain $W_s = E_s^2/G_0^2$, from which $W_s = E_s^2$ if $G_0 = 1$.

In the case of impulse noise, we wish to minimize the ratio E_p/E_s, with E_p given by Eq. (7-9). Again E_s^2 is defined by Eq. (7-18), and we now find

$$\left(\frac{E_p}{E_s}\right)^2 = \frac{2c^2 f_s}{G_0^2 W_s}\left[\int_0^\infty |Y(f_1)|\, w^{1/2}(f_1)\, df_1\right]^2 \int_0^\infty \frac{|S(2\pi f_2)|^2}{|Y(f_2)|^2}\, df_2 \quad (7\text{-}33)$$

Here it is convenient to substitute $y(f) = |Y(f)|$ and $x(f) = S^2(2\pi f)$. We now have a product of integrals $I_1^2 I_2$ to be minimized, with

$$I_1 = \int_0^\infty y(f_1)w^{1/2}(f_1)\, df_1 \tag{7-34}$$

$$I_2 = \int_0^\infty \frac{x(f_2)}{y^2(f_2)}\, df_2 \tag{7-35}$$

The function $y_0(f)$ which gives the minimum value of $I_1^2 I_2$ when substituted for $y(f)$ is found by the same method as used before. We find for the optimum $Y(f)$

$$|Y(f)| = \frac{\beta s^{1/3}(f)}{w^{1/6}(f)} = \frac{\beta\, |S(2\pi f)|^{2/3}}{w^{1/6}(f)} \tag{7-36}$$

In the special case of white noise on the line and a raised-cosine signal spectrum at the detector input Eqs. (7-28) and (7-29) apply, and we find

$$Y(f) = B \cos^{1/3}\frac{\pi f}{2f_s} \qquad 0 < f < f_s \tag{7-37}$$

Here again the value of the multiplying constant B is of no interest in comparing merits of different filter curves.

It is of interest to study the effect of deviating from the optimum curves. Since both optima come out in the form of cosines raised to a power, one convenient comparison is in terms of a family of curves of form $\cos^\nu [\pi f/(2f_s)]$ with ν the parameter to be tested. Our analysis has shown that the best value of ν is unity for gaussian noise and $\frac{1}{3}$ for impulse noise.

Consider first the gaussian case and substitute

$$Y(f) = a \cos^\nu \frac{\pi f}{2f_s} \qquad f < f_s \tag{7-38}$$

along with (7-28) and (7-29) in (7-19). We find that the constant $a = \alpha f_s^{-1/2} w_0^{-1/4}$ cancels out, verifying that its value is immaterial to the

comparison. The result is[6]

$$\frac{W_n}{E_s^2} = \frac{8f_s w_0}{G_0^2 w_s} \int_0^{\pi/2} \cos^{2\nu} \theta \, d\theta \int_0^{\pi/2} \cos^{4-2\nu} \phi \, d\phi$$

$$= \frac{f_s w_0}{8 G_0^2 W_s} \frac{\Gamma(2\nu + 1)\Gamma(5 - 2\nu)}{\Gamma^2(\nu + 1)\Gamma^2(3 - \nu)}$$

$$= \frac{f_s w_0}{2 G_0^2 W_s} \frac{(3 - 2\nu)(1 - 2\nu)}{(2 - \nu)(1 - \nu)} \frac{\tan \nu\pi}{\nu\pi} \tag{7-39}$$

For impulse noise, we substitute Eq. (7-38) with Eqs. (7-28) and (7-29) in (7-33) and, again observing that the constant multiplier cancels, we find

$$\left(\frac{E_p}{E_s}\right)^2 = \frac{16 f_s^2 c^2 w_0}{\pi^3 G_0^2 W_s} \left[\int_0^{\pi/2} \cos^\nu \theta \, d\theta\right]^2 \int_0^{\pi/2} \cos^{4-2\nu} \phi \, d\phi$$

$$= \frac{f_s^2 c^2 w_0}{G_0^2 W_s} \frac{\Gamma^2(\nu + 1)\Gamma(5 - 2\nu)}{8\Gamma^4\left(\dfrac{\nu}{2} + 1\right)\Gamma^2(3 - \nu)}$$

$$= \frac{2 f_s^2 c^2 w_0}{\pi^2 G_0^2 W_s} \frac{2^\nu \tan \pi}{\nu(\nu - 1)(\nu - 2)} \frac{\Gamma^3\left(\dfrac{\nu + 1}{2}\right)}{\Gamma\left(\dfrac{\nu + 2}{2}\right)\Gamma\left(\dfrac{2\nu - 3}{2}\right)} \tag{7-40}$$

We have used Eqs. (7-39) and (7-40) to plot in Fig. 7-6 the deterioration of the signal-to-noise ratio in decibels at the detector input as one departs from the optimum value of ν in the two cases. Both curves have broad minima. Although their best values of ν differ from unity

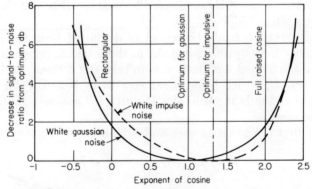

FIG. 7-6. Variation in signal-to-noise ratio with exponent of $\cos(\pi f/2 f_s)$ in receiving-filter characteristic.

in one case to $\frac{2}{3}$ in the other, there is actually not much change throughout this region. If the optimum filter for the other kind of noise is substituted in either case, the loss in signal-to-noise ratio is only 0.15 db. If a compromise filter with $\nu = \frac{7}{6}$ is used for both cases, the loss relative to optimum is 0.05 db for each.

A representative set of filter curves for the various cosine exponents is shown in Fig. 7-7 with their signal-to-noise impairments in decibels when used with gaussian noise. Quite a wide variety of curves show rather small differences in performance. The cosine with exponent zero reduces to an ideal rectangular filter. Its impairment is 1.76 db for gaussian noise and 2.85 db for impulse noise. The exponent two is equivalent to the familiar raised-cosine filter. Its impairment is 1.76 db for gaussian and 1.09 db for impulse noise.

We conclude from this study that receiving filters can indeed be constructed which combat noise in an optimal manner. It appears that the best design in the cases considered is not a critical one since the penalty suffered because of considerable deviation from the ideal filter or from the assumed properties of the noise may be insignificant. The optimum solution does, however, give a basis for apportioning selectivity between the transmitting and receiving filters. A transmittance function

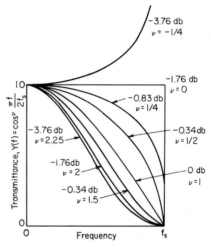

FIG. 7-7. (Cosine)$^{\nu}$-filter curves and their relative effectiveness against white gaussian noise.

$$Y(f) = \cos^{7/6} \frac{\pi f}{2f_s} \qquad (7\text{-}41)$$

appears to be a good compromise between the optima for gaussian and impulse noise with insignificant impairment relative to the best performance for both kinds.

If, as in the representative system of Fig. 7-1, the signal source consists of full Nyquist-interval pulses, the pulse spectrum at the input to the transmitting filter will have a $(\sin x)/x$ shape. The overall characteristic of the transmitting and receiving filters which changes this to the desired raised-cosine spectrum was shown in Fig. 5-11 of Chap. 5. The required transmitting filter selectivity is obtained by the ratio of the characteristic in Fig. 5-11 to the optimum characteristic of the receiving filter.   This is shown in Fig. 7-8 for the gaussian noise case.   In general, we can define:

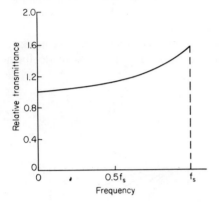

$S_0(\omega) =$ Fourier transform of the pulse generated at the transmitter

$\Upsilon(f) =$ transmittance function of transmitting filter

$Y(f) =$ transmittance function of receiving filter

$S(\omega) =$ Fourier transform of the pulse at the detector input

It follows that

FIG. 7-8. Characteristic of transmitting filter for: (1) uncurbed rectangular pulses, (2) cosine-law receiving filter, and (3) raised-cosine received pulse.

$$S(\omega) = Y(f)\Upsilon(f)S_0(\omega) \quad (7\text{-}42)$$

We have chosen the raised-cosine function of (7-29) as optimum for $S(\omega)$.   Also the optimum $Y(f)$ for gaussian noise only is given by (7-30).   If we further specify full-length rectangular pulses of height E_0 from the transmitter

$$S_0(2\pi f) = 2E_0 \int_{-T/2}^{T/2} \cos 2\pi ft \, dt = \frac{2E_0}{\pi f} \sin \pi fT = \frac{2E_0 \sin \pi f/f_s}{\pi f} \quad (7\text{-}43)$$

Then $\Upsilon(f) = \dfrac{S(\omega)}{Y(f)S_0(\omega)} = \dfrac{\pi f w_0^{1/4}}{4\alpha E_0 f_s^{1/2} \sin(\pi f/2f_s)} \qquad f < f_s \quad (7\text{-}44)$

or $\dfrac{\Upsilon(f)}{\Upsilon(0)} = \dfrac{\pi f}{2f_s \sin(\pi f/2f_s)} \qquad f < f_s \quad (7\text{-}45)$

where $\Upsilon(0) = 1/(2E_0)$.   Note that, except for waste of transmitted power, it is immaterial what the curve for the transmitting filter is like for frequencies above f_s provided that the receiving filter has no response at these frequencies.

7-5   PROBABILITY OF ERROR FOR BINARY SIGNALS

Figures 7-9 and 7-10 show the binary wave at the output of the receiving filter for on-off and plus-and-minus signaling respectively when the spectrum of a single pulse is a raised-cosine function of frequency.   The two waves differ only by a constant $A/2$ equal to half the peak-to-peak variation at the pulse centers.   The on-off

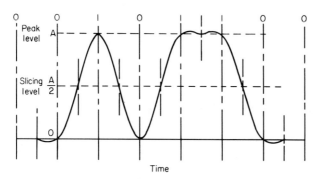

FIG. 7-9. On-off binary pulse train with raised-cosine spectra.

binary wave in the absence of impairment is either full value or zero at the center of pulse intervals. With the decision threshold at the half-amplitude level, the waveform must be distorted in excess of half the full amplitude before the wrong decision is made. If gaussian noise picked up by the transmission line is the only form of impairment, the probability of error is related to the probability of the noise component at the output of the receiving filter exceeding $A/2$ at the pulse centers. If the binary wave is positive with respect to the threshold, the noise component must be negative to produce an error. Thus, at any one sampling instant, we are concerned with only one polarity of noise peaks.

If the signal sample has the value A, the probability that an additive noise sample causes error is equal to the probability p_- that the noise sample is less than $-A/2$. From Eq. (7-2) for gaussian noise with

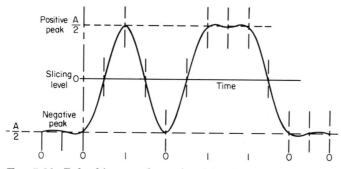

FIG. 7-10. Polar binary pulse train with raised-cosine spectra.

zero mean,

$$p_- = \frac{1}{2}\left(1 - \text{erf}\, \frac{A}{2\sigma\sqrt{2}}\right) \tag{7-46}$$

If the signal sample has the value zero, the probability of error is equal to the probability p_+ that the noise sample is greater than $A/2$. For gaussian noise with zero mean

$$p_+ = 1 - P\left(\frac{A}{2}\right) = p_- \tag{7-47}$$

Hence the probability of making an error at any sampling instant is given by

$$p = p_+ = p_- = \frac{1}{2}\left(1 - \text{erf}\, \frac{A}{2\sigma\sqrt{2}}\right) \tag{7-48}$$

Note that this probability depends on the difference between the two possible signal pulse values at the sampling instant. It holds equally well in the polar binary case of Fig. 7-10, in which the signal values are $+A/2$ and $-A/2$, and the threshold decision occurs at zero voltage.

The curve of error probability vs. signal-to-noise ratio is often used to describe the performance of a digital data transmission system. It is seen from Eq. (7-48) that the error probability in either on-off or polar binary reception in the presence of additive gaussian noise depends only on the ratio of the pulse sample to the rms noise. This ratio can be expressed in terms of a ratio between signal power and noise power in various ways. The value of noise power which governs error probability is the average at the output of the receiving filter. A more convenient reference, however, is the average noise power in a specified bandwidth on the transmission line, since this describes the channel through which we must signal. In the case of white gaussian noise, the mean total noise power is directly proportional to bandwidth, and we can adopt any band we prefer as a standard for defining the noise. One reference we shall use is the average noise power in a bandwidth numerically equal to the bit rate. Another is the noise in the Nyquist bandwidth corresponding to the signaling rate, i.e., the noise in a band of width $f_s/2$. In the case of binary signals the noise in the Nyquist bandwidth is 3 db less than the noise in the bit-rate bandwidth.

A variety of references can be defined for signal power. We can use the average signal power for a random pulse train or the average for some specified signaling sequence. The peak value of signal power may be of interest. In any case it is important to note that it is the values of the pulses at the sampling instants which determine probability of error. To express results in terms of variously defined values of signal power, we must know the relation between these values and the signal samples.

If uncurbed rectangular pulses with no band-limiting are assumed, the peak signal power per ohm of circuit resistance is A^2 for the on-off system and $A^2/4$ for the polar system. This means that 6 db more peak power would be required in the on-off system to obtain the same decision margin. The corresponding average signal power values are $A^2/2$ for the on-off and $A^2/4$ for the polar, showing a difference of 3 db. Such pulses are not very realistic because of the great waste of bandwidth.

A more interesting case is that of the pulses with raised-cosine spectra. Consider the case of a polar random binary sequence with optimum receiving filter for additive white gaussian noise. The value of the ratio $A/2\sigma$ in Eq. (7-48) is equal to $E_s/\sqrt{W_n}$ as defined by Eq. (7-31) with $G_0 = 1$. The expression for probability of error then becomes

$$p = \frac{1}{2}(1 - \mathrm{erf}\, M^{1/2}) \qquad (7\text{-}49)$$

where

$$M = \frac{W_s}{w_0 f_s} \qquad (7\text{-}50)$$

We note that M is the ratio of the average signal output power from the line to the average noise power in a bandwidth equal to the signaling frequency. Also M is twice the ratio of average signal power to the average noise power in the Nyquist bandwidth $f_s/2$.

The on-off binary case differs from the polar only in the presence of transmitted direct current. For a random signal sequence, the average value of the on-off wave at the output of the receiving filter is simply $A/2$, as may be seen by comparing Figs. 7-9 and 7-10. In terms of the previously given solution for optimum polar binary signals, $A/2 = E_s$, the absolute value of the pulse samples. The d-c component received from the line in the random on-off case is given by

$$E_0 = \frac{E_s}{Y(0)} \qquad (7\text{-}51)$$

Making use of the optimized results previously obtained, we substitute $Y(0)$ from Eq. (7-30) and the value of α from (7-32) with $G_0 = 1$ to obtain

$$E_0{}^2 = \frac{f_s w_0{}^{1/2} E_s{}^2}{\alpha^2} = W_s \qquad (7\text{-}52)$$

The d-c component thus represents an amount of power equal to the average signal power in the random polar case. Since the on-off signal is equal to the sum of the d-c component and the polar signal, the average total on-off signal power is twice that of the average polar signal power. Therefore, the random on-off binary case requires 3 db more average power than the random polar.

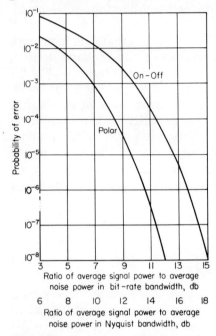

Figure 7-11 shows curves of error probability vs. ratio of average signal power to average noise power for random on-off and polar binary signaling through additive white gaussian noise. Raised-cosine pulse spectra at the output of an optimum receiving filter are assumed. Scales are given for the noise reference taken as either the average power in the bit-rate bandwidth or the Nyquist-rate bandwidth. It will be shown in Chap. 18 that the polar case represents the best possible performance attainable when each binary decision is made independently at the end of the corresponding signaling intervals. In particular the numerical value of 8.4 db representing the ratio of average signal power to average noise power in a bandwidth equal to the number of bits per second with an error rate of one bit in 10^4 is a convenient reference for comparing the performance of digital transmission systems with the ideal.

FIG. 7-11. Error rate of random polar and on-off binary baseband signaling through additive white gaussian noise. Optimum case is assumed with cosine-shaped receiving filter delivering raised-cosine pulse spectrum.

7-6 MULTILEVEL SIGNALS

Some of the properties of multilevel baseband signals can be illustrated by the quaternary case of Fig. 7-12. To make the decision between the four possible levels, it is necessary to establish three thresholds. The margin against noise is consequently reduced so that for the same peak-to-peak signal range the amplitude of noise required to cause an erroneous decision is one-third that required in the binary case. In general, an n-ary signal has a margin against error of $1/(n-1)$ that of the binary case. It will be noticed that the inner signal levels can be disturbed into an error zone by either polarity of noise. Thus these inner levels are twice as likely to be interpreted wrongly as are the outer two levels.

As in the binary case, the most favorable choice of levels for protection against error from noise with a given peak signal is a symmetrical distribution about zero. In the n-ary case, if n is an even number $2m$ with peak-to-peak signal voltage A, the best choice is $\pm A/2$, $\pm(2m-3)$ $A/[2(2m-1)]$, $\pm(2m-5)A/[2(2m-1)], \ldots, \pm A/[2(2m-1)]$. If n is an odd number $2m+1$, the best choice is $\pm A/2$, $\pm(m-1)A/(2m)$, $\pm(m-2)A/(2m), \ldots, \pm A/(2m)$, 0. In either case the separation

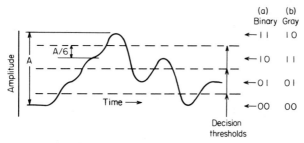

FIG. 7-12. Quaternary signal.

between adjacent levels is $A/(n-1)$. An error will occur whenever the absolute value of the noise wave at the sampling time exceeds half this separation except when the signal sample is $\pm A/2$. When the signal sample is $+A/2$, an error occurs only when the noise sample is less than $-A/[2(n-1)]$; and ˙ ʌen the signal sample is $-A/2$, an error occurs only when the noise sample exceeds $+A/[2(n-1)]$. If all signal levels are equally probable, the probability of any one level is $1/n$. The probability p_n of an error in the detection of any one signal sample in an n-level system containing additive gaussian noise can be written in terms of the gaussian distribution function $P(E)$ defined by Eq. (7-2) as follows:

$$
\begin{aligned}
p_n ={}& \frac{1}{n} P\left[-\frac{A}{2(n-1)}\right] + \frac{1}{n}\left\{1 - P\left[\frac{A}{2(n-1)}\right]\right\} \\
&+ \frac{n-2}{n}\left\{P\left[-\frac{A}{2(n-1)}\right] + 1 - P\left[\frac{A}{2(n-1)}\right]\right\} \\
={}& \frac{n-1}{n}\left[1 - \operatorname{erf}\frac{A}{2(n-1)\sigma\sqrt{2}}\right]
\end{aligned}
\tag{7-53}
$$

Equation (7-53) is the generalization of Eq. (7-48), which is the special case in which $n = 2$. As before, we can compute A in terms of peak and average power values for specific systems. Also since p_n

decreases monotonically with A/σ, the same optimization procedures apply as for the binary case, and the optimum receiving filter is the same. The average signal power output from the line W_{sn}, assuming equal likelihood of positive and negative pulses, is calculated in terms of W_{s2}, the value for the binary case, as follows:

1. Even number of levels, $n = 2m$

$$
\begin{aligned}
W_{sn} &= \frac{W_{s2}}{m}\left[1 + \left(\frac{2m-3}{2m-1}\right)^2 + \left(\frac{2m-5}{2m-1}\right)^2 + \cdots + \frac{1}{(2m-1)^2}\right] \\
&= \frac{W_{s2}}{m(2m-1)^2}[1 + 3^2 + 5^2 + \cdots + (2m-1)^2] \\
&= \frac{(2m+1)W_{s2}}{3(2m-1)} = \frac{(n+1)W_{s2}}{3(n-1)}
\end{aligned} \tag{7-54}
$$

2. Odd number of levels, $n = 2m + 1$

$$
\begin{aligned}
W_{sn} &= \frac{2W_{s2}}{2m+1}\left[1 + \left(\frac{m-1}{m}\right)^2 + \left(\frac{m-2}{m}\right)^2 + \cdots + \frac{1}{m^2}\right] \\
&= \frac{2W_{s2}}{m^2(2m+1)}[1^2 + 2^2 + 3^2 + \cdots + m^2] \\
&= \frac{(m+1)W_{s2}}{3m} = \frac{(n+1)W_{s2}}{3(n-1)}
\end{aligned} \tag{7-55}
$$

The same formula is thus found to hold for both even and odd numbers of levels. The value of W_{s2} is $A^2/4$ in the optimum case for raised-cosine pulse spectra at the detector input providing that the cosine-type receiving filter has unit d-c gain. We observe that the ratio $A/(2\sigma\sqrt{2})$ appearing in Eq. (7-53) is identical with the quantity M of Eqs. (7-49) and (7-50) provided that we replace W_s in the latter equation by W_{s2}. Making this identification and substituting the value of W_{s2} in terms of W_{sn} from (7-54) or (7-55), we obtain

$$
p_n = \frac{n-1}{n}[1 - \text{erf } M_n^{1/2}] \tag{7-56}
$$

where

$$
M_n = \frac{3W_{sn}}{(n^2-1)w_0 f_s} \tag{7-57}
$$

Equations (7-56) and (7-57) show that the probability of error in optimally detecting a random sequence of symmetrical n-ary polar signals with raised-cosine spectra can be obtained from the binary solution by multiplying the signal-to-noise ratio scale by $3/(n^2-1)$. A similar result has been given by Oliver, Pierce, and Shannon[7] for pulses with rectangular spectra cutting off at $f_s/2$.

Figure 7-13 shows the probability of error in multilevel baseband transmission as a function of signal-to-noise ratio for various values of n. In comparing these curves with the binary case, we should note that there are $\log_2 n$ bits of information in an n-ary pulse and hence that for the same bit rate only $1/(\log_2 n)$ times as many pulses per second are required. It, therefore, seems that the number of errors per bit is a more significant quantity than the errors per pulse. To make the conversion for the n-ary case is not straightforward, however, because an error in the n-valued pulse can itself have different values. That is, the transmitted level may be wrongly received as any one of the other $(n - 1)$ levels. When the signal-to-noise ratio is sufficiently high to make the errors rare, it is reasonable to assume that adjacent levels are the ones most likely to be confused.

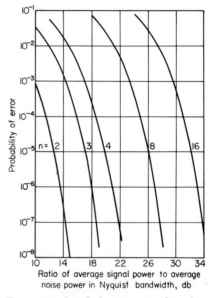

In a data communication link using multilevel signals each level often represents a specific binary sequence. For instance, in the quaternary example each level can represent two binary digits or bits. The input and output of the communication link can be a binary channel with the transmitter and receiver incorporating the necessary translation to and from the multilevel line signal. In such a

Fig. 7-13. Symbol error rate of random polar n-ary baseband signaling through additive white gaussian noise. Optimum case is assumed with cosine-shaped receiving filter delivering raised-cosine pulse spectrum.

case the probability of error in the output binary channel depends in some degree on the specific assignments of binary codes to the various levels. If the most probable error is that of interpreting a particular level as one of the adjacent levels, it is advantageous to have a minimum of difference between the binary codes assigned to adjacent levels. Thus "step-by-step" or "cyclic binary" codes such as the Gray reflected binary code[8] are preferable since adjacent combinations differ by only one digit and, therefore, only one bit is in error in the binary group. In Fig. 7-12 the straight binary assignment shown at a would lead to a higher error rate than the Gray code shown at b. The error rate of a multilevel-type system used to transmit binary data thus depends on more than just the threshold margins. In the particular case in which Gray code is used and only adjacent-level errors are significant, we can approximate the average number of errors per bit by $p_n/(\log_2 n)$ with p_n given by Eqs. (7-56) and (7-57). Because of the extreme steepness of the curves of Fig. 7-13 in the region of very low error probability, a modification to read errors per bit for even $n = 16$, $\log_2 n = 4$, amounts only to a few tenths of a decibel decrease in the signal-to-noise ratio scale.

7-7 EFFECT OF PHASE-FREQUENCY DISTORTION

As discussed in Chap. 6, a transmission line having a phase shift that is not proportional to frequency will distort the signal waveform. A

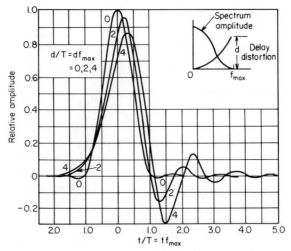

FIG. 7-14. Baseband pulse transmission characteristic for raised-cosine spectrum and quadratic delay distortion. (*From E. D. Sunde, BSTJ, vol. 40, p. 375, March, 1961.*)

typical form of wave distortion which may occur is illustrated in Fig. 7-14, taken from the work of E. D. Sunde. The received waveforms of on-off baseband pulses having a raised-cosine spectrum are shown as they would appear after being subjected to several phase-shift characteristics varying as the cube of the frequency. The corresponding delay distortion for these cases consequently varies as the square of the frequency. Since in physical networks the phase is an odd function of frequency, the most important component of phase-frequency distortion in a baseband system which favors the lowest frequencies is typically cube law. The cube-law term is the lowest-order deviation from linearity obtained by expanding the phase-frequency function in a power series about zero frequency. In Fig. 7-14 the amount of delay distortion has been expressed as the ratio d/T, where d is the delay distortion at the edge of the band and T the Nyquist interval. It will be seen that the received pulse has a reduced amplitude and reaches its peak at a later time. The pulse also develops a pronounced oscillatory tail which no longer passes through zero at half Nyquist intervals and thus causes intersymbol interference.

The reduced noise margin at the sampling point and the distortion of the transitions can be illustrated by considering the range of values which the received binary wave may have over the pulse interval. Curve a of Fig. 7-15 shows a single marking pulse taken from Fig. 7-14 for the case of $d/T = 4$. Curve b of Fig. 7-15 shows the maximum negative value of intersymbol interference which can occur from any sequence of nearby pulses. It does not represent any one particular se-quence. Curve c is the sum of curves a and b and represents the

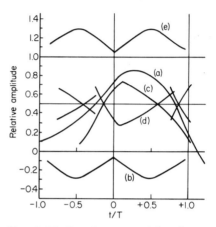

FIG. 7-15. Development of "eye" pattern for delay distortion of $d/T = 4$.

maximum negative location of received waves during a marking interval. A similar consideration for a spacing interval leads to curve d, representing the maximum positive location of received waves during a spacing interval. The opening between curves c and d shows the minimum margins for correct binary decision. The vertical dimension of the opening indicates the minimum margin against noise when sampling the wave. The horizontal dimension indicates the range of correct sampling time and the amount of peak distortion due to inter-symbol interference. Curve b and its corresponding mate, curve e, represent the outer bounds of the received waves during spacing and marking intervals respectively. This type of display is called an "eye" pattern[9] because of the appearance of the center opening. The eye pattern for a random binary data wave can readily be observed on an oscilloscope by using a horizontal sweep, covering one or two pulse intervals, which is synchronized with the pulse rate.

Figure 7-16 shows the minimum eye opening at the nominal pulse center as a function of d/T. The left-hand scale gives the actual opening as a fraction of the undistorted opening. The right-hand scale gives the reduction in opening in decibels and represents the necessary increase in signal level required to obtain a minimum opening equal to the unimpaired opening. The increase in signal level required to regain the same average error rate in the presence of a given noise level will be less, however, than indicated in Fig. 7-16. This is because the condition of minimum margin occurs only for certain pulse sequences. For very low probability of error, where the curve is very steep, the displacement becomes nearly the full amount indicated in Fig. 7-16.

In Fig. 7-15 it will be noted that the maximum eye opening does not occur at the unimpaired pulse center. Consequently, if sampling can

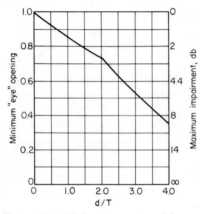

FIG. 7-16. Minimum eye opening at nominal pulse center. (*From E. D. Sunde, BSTJ, vol. 40, p. 377, March, 1961.*)

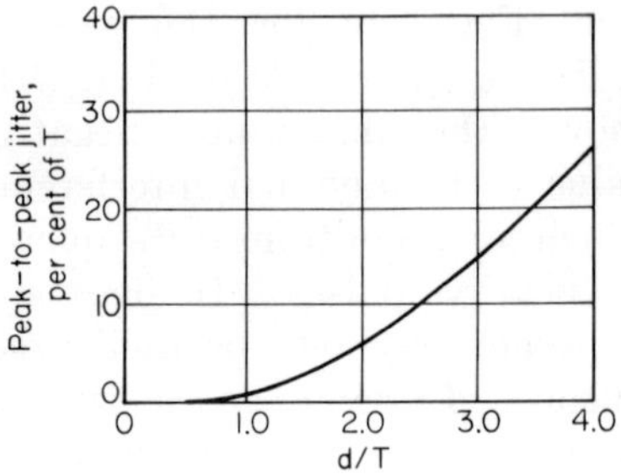

FIG. 7-17. Peak-to-peak time jitter of transitions.

be phased to be at the optimum point, the impairment will be less than that indicated by Fig. 7-16. If the phasing of the sampling is determined from the long time average position of the transitions through the half-amplitude level, the sampling will be held near the center of the eye opening. The peak-to-peak time jitter of the transitions after slicing the wave at the half-amplitude level is shown in Fig. 7-17. The peak synchronous distortion will be half this amount if the nominal transition points are assumed to be at the center of the jitter range.

For a delay-distortion-vs.-frequency variation different from that considered above, the same general procedure holds. The eye pattern can be constructed once the pulse response of the system is known, or, in the case of a physical system, it can be observed on an oscilloscope.

From the eye pattern the signal-to-noise impairment and peak intersymbol distortion can then be determined as previously described.

The distortion caused by the phase-frequency characteristic can be corrected by the use of equalizing networks which have a phase-distortion characteristic complementary to that of the transmission line. Another possible correcting method is to replace the simple rectangular pulse at the transmitter by one of more complicated form so as to produce a pulse spectrum which after distortion by the line will arrive at the receiver as an undistorted raised-cosine spectrum. It is also possible to accomplish nearly the same effect by introducing at the receiver a compensating pulse transient representing the difference between the desired pulse shape and that actually received. These methods are discussed more fully in Chap. 15.

7-8 BINARY SIGNALING ABOVE THE NYQUIST RATE

As previously pointed out in Chap. 5, the use of a square cutoff band requires signaling exactly at the Nyquist rate to avoid the accumulation of large intersymbol interference. With a more gradual cutoff one can signal over a range of rates with only moderate amounts of interference. There does not appear to be any common agreement on what is meant by the Nyquist rate for a band in which the transition is gradual from maximum to zero transmittance. In theory it is possible to equalize a channel for uniform response over any band of frequencies in which the response is not actually zero at any frequency. Therefore, a channel with gradual cutoff could be regarded as having a Nyquist bandwidth extending up to the highest frequency at which there is any significant response. Since a physical system does not have an absolute cutoff frequency above which the response is identically zero, an arbitrary numerical criterion of smallness would have to be specified to define Nyquist rate generally in terms of bandwidth. We could, for example, define $2f_b$ as the "x-db Nyquist rate" if the channel has a loss of more than x db at all frequencies above f_b. Such a definition would seem to be indispensable for any precise discussion of actual signaling performance relative to the Nyquist rate, but there is scant record of such usage.

An alternative definition of the Nyquist rate is the maximum signaling rate at which intersymbol interference vanishes.* This definition coincides with the one based on bandwidth in the special case of

---

* To fit cases in which interchannel interference cannot be made to vanish at any signaling rate, an "x per cent Nyquist rate" could be defined as the maximum rate at which the intersymbol interference does not exceed x per cent.

signaling with impulses through an ideal low-pass filter. Here it is impossible to signal faster than the Nyquist rate because the intersymbol interference which can accrue from nonzero samples of the unwanted $(\sin 2\pi f_b t)/(2\pi f_b t)$ pulse responses is unbounded. The difficulty is associated with the discontinuity in the amplitude-vs.-frequency function, which in turn implies that the pulse response envelopes decay only as $1/t$. Replacement of the perpendicular cutoff of the band by a continuous transition makes the decay at least as fast as $1/t^2$ for large t and insures boundedness of the accumulated interference from any pulse sequence. A modest increase in the pulse rate is then possible at the cost of reduced margin over noise. Inherent system failure does not occur until the upper bound of the intersymbol interference falsifies a decision.

On the basis of freedom from intersymbol interference, the Nyquist rate for a channel with vestigially symmetric cutoff about a frequency f_1 becomes $2f_1$. Thus with the amplitude-frequency characteristic of Fig. 5-10, the Nyquist rate would be defined as $2f_1$ even though there is nonzero response up to a frequency $f_1 + f_x$. We avoid intersymbol interference if we signal with impulses at the rate $2f_1$, but there is no real contradiction of Nyquist's theory if by accepting some intersymbol interference, we signal successfully at a rate up to $2(f_1 + f_x)$. However, if we could surpass the latter rate within the ground rules of Nyquist's treatment, there would be some cause for excitement.

We shall describe several schemes which at first glance appear to send and receive signals at a rate greater than twice the true bandwidth. The loophole by which they escape Nyquist's logic is describable as a mapping of the permitted signal values at the transmitter into a greater number of possible received samples. Furthermore, decoding of the received set is unique only when certain of the other signal values in the sequence can be determined. These operations are not permitted in Nyquist's model, which requires that a choice of one out of n possible signal values is made at the transmitter during each signaling interval and that the received wave during the corresponding interval is characterized by one out of n distinguishable values in one-to-one correspondence with the choices available at the transmitter. If the number of receiving levels which must be distinguished is greater than the number of levels which can be sent, the system should more properly be compared with one of Nyquist type in which the greater number of values is used at both the transmitter and receiver. Thus, if we send binary signals over a system which delivers three possible levels decodable into the original binary values, the resulting information rate should be compared with that of a Nyquist system which sends and receives ternary data.

The systems we shall discuss are basically related to an old telegraph technique called "doubling the dotting speed." The dotting speed of a channel can be loosely defined as the maximum reversal rate at which the received signal is clearly readable. In typical channels it was found that when the reversals were sent approximately twice as fast as this limiting rate, the output wave had insufficient amplitude to operate the receiving relay. This meant that the fundamental frequency of the reversal wave had been pushed above the cutoff frequency of the channel. But it was observed under these conditions that the relay operated when two successive marks or two successive spaces were sent. There were, in fact, three classes of output: positive, negative, and zero. The first indicated a mark, the second a space, and the third a reversal of the previous value. If the message had been correctly received for all previous signaling intervals, the present signal could be correctly identified.

A long sequence of reversals producing no output made a message difficult to read because of the uncertainty in the number of intervals. A remedy was devised by Gulstad[10] in the form of a vibrating relay. This relay had auxiliary windings which when associated with a battery and a capacitor formed an electromechanical relaxation oscillator delivering marks and spaces alternately when no signal was impressed on the line windings. When a departure from the alternating sequence of transmitted signals occurred, the current in the main windings became sufficient to take control of the relay. Note that the phase of the alternate marking and spacing signal could not be determined without knowledge of the previous signal history. The practical performance was limited by differences in frequency and phase between the local oscillations and the incoming signals. An improvement in the form of a synchronous vibrating relay was applied by Clokey[11] to transatlantic submarine cable telegraphy in the mid-twenties. The vibrating relay was operated by pulses delivered from a segmented commutator located on the receiving head of the distributor. To quote Clokey: "The accuracy with which the missing impulses of unit length are reinserted by this means makes it possible to realize the full speed possibilities of the vibrating relay principle and obtain faithful reproduction on a given cable at almost double the speed obtainable through the use of ordinary non-vibrating relays."

A graphical development of the waveforms used in the double-speed method is given in Fig. 7-18. We assume a channel in which full-length Nyquist-interval transmitted pulses deliver raised-cosine pulse spectra at the receiver. The single full-length pulse response of such a channel is shown in Fig. 7-18b. The corresponding step response is shown in a of the same figure. The response to a half-length pulse,

Fig. 7-18c, passes through a value of either 0.0 or 0.5 at instants half a Nyquist interval apart. A random series of double-speed polar binary pulses applied to such a channel produces the type of received wave indicated in Fig. 7-18d. At half intervals this wave has values of -1, 0, or $+1$ and can be considered to deliver three-level samples without intersymbol interference.

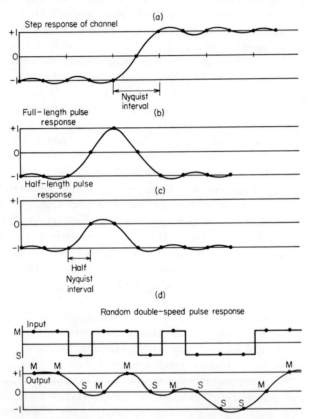

FIG. 7-18. Waveforms in double-speed binary signaling system.

It will be noted that the original binary information can be recovered by sampling the wave and interpreting a full positive value to be mark, a full negative value to be space, and the zero value to be the opposite of the previously determined state. Thus for a 6-db reduction in margin over noise the signaling speed is doubled. This is an improvement over the 9.5-db reduction in margin associated with quaternary signaling at the Nyquist rate illustrated in Fig. 7-12. The technique can be applied to any type of binary channel that is linear or nearly so.

Thus it can be used with AM and FM as well as baseband.

A paper by Lender describes FM data terminals based on an application of this general principle which has been given the name "duobinary."[12] Differential encoding at the transmitter simplifies the interpretation of the received wave. A space is converted to a transition and a mark to no transition. From Fig. 7-18d it is seen that a transition at the channel input always results in a zero-valued sample at the receiver. Consequently after differential encoding, space is represented by the zero value and mark by either $+1$ or -1 value. One method of detection involves full-wave rectification which folds the -1 level over on top of the $+1$ level. The resultant can then be sliced at a $+0.5$ level to recover mark and space intervals without sampling. This results in some pulse distortion which is avoided by sampling the three-level wave. The system also offers error detection since correct reception implies that between successive full-valued samples of the same polarity there must be an even number of zero samples and that between successive full-valued samples of opposite polarity there must be an odd number of zero samples.

Further elucidation of the double-rate signaling method can be obtained by writing the expressions for the full- and half-length pulse responses. Since the full-length pulse response is the Fourier transform of a raised-cosine frequency function, it can be written as

$$g_f(t) = \frac{1}{\pi f_s} \int_0^{\omega_s} \cos^2 \frac{\pi f}{2f_s} \cos \omega t \, d\omega \qquad (7\text{-}58)$$

Here we have made use of the raised-cosine frequency function of Eq. (7-29) which corresponds to a pulse of unit amplitude in the time domain. The Fourier transforms of half-length and full-length rectangular pulses of unit height are given respectively by

$$S_h(\omega) = \int_{-T/4}^{T/4} \cos \omega t \, dt = \frac{2}{\omega} \sin \frac{\omega T}{4} \qquad (7\text{-}59)$$

$$S_f(\omega) = \int_{-T/2}^{T/2} \cos \omega t \, dt = \frac{2}{\omega} \sin \frac{\omega T}{2} \qquad (7\text{-}60)$$

To find the half-length pulse response $g_h(t)$, we multiply the integrand of (7-58) by $S_h(\omega)/S_f(\omega)$. Performing this operation and substituting $T = 1/f_s$, we obtain

$$g_h(t) = \frac{1}{f_s} \int_0^{f_s} \cos \frac{\pi f}{2f_s} \cos 2\pi f t \, df$$

$$= \frac{2 \cos 2\pi f_s t}{\pi(1 - 16f_s^2 t^2)} \qquad (7\text{-}61)$$

Comparing this equation with Eq. (5-43), which gives a Fourier transform satisfying Nyquist's second criterion, we deduce that $g_h(t)$ is a pulse which preserves the spacing of transitions when used for signaling at the rate $2f_s$. This property is apparent from Fig. 7-18c. Intersymbol interference midway between the transitions is not prevented, but sampling takes place at the transition points, at which only three levels are possible.

Since the actual bandwidth of the channel is f_s, signaling at a rate $2f_s$ bits per second does not exceed the speed of a Nyquist-type binary channel in spite of the conversion to a ternary code at the receiver. We note, however, that the ternary values are received with zero intersymbol interference. Since the cutoff of the channel is gradual, the speed can be increased above $2f_s$ without producing immediate failure. As previously stated, this result is not a contradiction of Nyquist's theory, which did not allow use of ternary sequence-dependent decoding of binary signals. It is of interest to compare the speed at which intersymbol interference actually breaks the double-speed system with the speed obtained on a straight ternary channel of the same bandwidth operated at the Nyquist rate.

The response of the channel to an arbitrary sequence of binary signals impressed at a rate $2kf_s$ bits per second can be expressed by

$$s(t) = \sum_{n=-\infty}^{\infty} a_n g_h\left(t - \frac{n}{2kf_s}\right) \tag{7-62}$$

where a_n can be either $+1$ or -1 and $g_h(t)$ is given by (7-61). The wave is sampled at odd multiples of $1/(4kf_s)$. The value of the typical sample can be taken at $1/(4kf_s)$ and is given by

$$\begin{aligned}
s_1 &= \sum_{n=-\infty}^{\infty} a_n g_h\left(\frac{1}{4kf_s} - \frac{n}{2kf_s}\right) \\
&= \frac{2k^2}{\pi} \sum_{n=-\infty}^{\infty} a_n \frac{\cos\left[(2n-1)\pi/2k\right]}{k^2 - (2n-1)^2}
\end{aligned} \tag{7-63}$$

The system fails when the largest possible sample from a mark preceded by a space becomes equal to the smallest possible sample from a mark preceded by a mark. A mark preceded by a space is defined by $a_0 = -1$, $a_1 = 1$, while for two successive marks $a_0 = a_1 = 1$. In the former case the contribution of the terms in the series for $n = 0$ and $n = 1$ cancel, while in the latter case they add an amount

$$c_k = \frac{4k^2}{\pi(k^2 - 1)} \cos\frac{\pi}{2k} \tag{7-64}$$

Then for the space-mark sequence, the value of s_1 is given by

$$s_{11} = \frac{2k^2}{\pi} \sum_{n=1}^{\infty} (a_n + a_{-n}) \frac{\cos\left[(2n+1)\pi/2k\right]}{k^2 - (2n+1)^2} \tag{7-65}$$

For the mark-mark sequence, the value of s_1 is

$$s_{12} = s_{11} + c_k \tag{7-66}$$

The largest possible value of s_{11} is

$$s_u = \frac{4k^2}{\pi} \sum_{n=1}^{\infty} \left| \frac{\cos\left[(2n+1)\pi/2k\right]}{k^2 - (2n+1)^2} \right| \tag{7-67}$$

The smallest possible value of s_{12} is

$$s_l = c_k - s_u \tag{7-68}$$

The two bounds become equal when $s_u = c_k/2$, that is, when

$$2(k^2 - 1) \sum_{n=1}^{\infty} \left| \frac{\cos\left[(2n+1)\pi/2k\right]}{k^2 - (2n+1)^2} \right| = \cos\frac{\pi}{2k} \qquad k > 1 \tag{7-69}$$

The problem of finding the value of k which satisfies Eq. (7-69) was programmed on a digital computer by S. Habib. The result was $1/k = 0.700$, which means that the system fails when the bit rate reaches $2f_s/0.700$ or 2.857 times the bandwidth in cycles per second. Straight ternary signaling at a rate of $2f_s$ three-level choices per second gives $2 \log_2 3 = 3.170 f_s$ bits per second without intersymbol interference. Thus the true Nyquist rate in bits per second is not attainable by the double dotting-speed method.

The question of speed relative to Nyquist rate can also be asked about channels with a low-frequency cutoff. Here there are available the well-known successful methods of low-frequency restoration which date back to early telegraph practice.[13] In the typical example the system contains a high-pass network which impairs transmission of the components at the lower edge of the signal band and completely suppresses the response at zero frequency. The received wave then droops toward zero whenever a long sequence of like pulses is sent, as has been previously illustrated in Fig. 5-15. Correction is obtained by recognizing the slightly impaired initial transitions as they occur and compensating the subsequent response by feeding back a locally generated wave containing the missing part.

As exemplified in a patent issued to MacColl,[14,15] this principle can be extended to enable signaling at an arbitrarily high rate over a linear time-invariant noise-free channel of arbitrarily narrow bandwidth. Nyquist's theory admits the same result by prescribing choice from an arbitrarily large number of signal values in each interval.

It is to be noted that the digital signals can be unambiguously received only if other impairments are small. The margin over noise and interference is reduced as the transmitted band is more severely trimmed. Degradation of performance because of the reduced margin must be balanced against the difficulties associated with transmitting a wider band.

7-9 REGENERATION

Instead of waiting until the digital signal is received at the far end of a system to make decisions, regenerative repeaters can be inserted at intermediate points. Decisions can be made at these repeater points under conditions more favorable than if all the distortion were allowed to accumulate. Transmission of new signals from the repeater points then gives a better chance for correct decisions at the end of the system.

A partial sort of regeneration called "reshaping" sends out new pulses in accordance with the measured times of arrival of pulses from the preceding station. The timing jitter is not corrected and accumulates with the number of links. In the early days of telegraphy, reshaping by means of electromechanical relays was effectively used to extend the distance over which signals could be transmitted. This was, in fact, the only kind of amplification available, and it was necessary to insert repeaters sufficiently close together to allow the attenuated currents to remain above the operating currents of the relays.

With the advent of high gain analog amplifiers, the spacing between repeaters could be lengthened. Reshaping at closer spacing than required by sensitivity of receiving apparatus could still produce a benefit in the presence of certain kinds of line distortion. For example, if we consider the curve of peak-to-peak jitter vs. square-law delay distortion shown in Fig. 7-17, we see that the amount of jitter increases more rapidly than a linear function of delay distortion. It is reasonable to expect that the amount of delay distortion would increase with the length of the transmission line. If the line were broken into a number of segments and a reshaping done at the output of each segment, the increase in jitter per segment would follow a curve similar to the initial part of Fig. 7-17. The curve of Fig. 7-17 would thereby be replaced by a connecting set of initial segments which would not increase as fast with length of line as in the case of no intermediate reshaping. We can say roughly that reshaping n times over a given distance holds the accumulated jitter to n times the jitter in one section. If the reshaping were not done, the jitter could be much greater.

Complete regeneration requires that new pulses be retimed as well as reshaped. In a system equipped with complete regenerators, there is no accumulation of either jitter or pulse distortion with length of the system. The performance of the entire system is the same as that of one regenerative link. Actual regenerators cannot quite attain this ideal performance, but they can come arbitrarily close.

It is instructive to compare the performance of straight analog vs. regenerative links as a function of the number of links. For the analog case we assume that the average noise power increases directly with the number of links and that analog repeaters maintain the same signal power at the output of each link. In the regenerative case we assume that each repeater has an independent probability of error which though very small is not zero. With these assumptions we compute curves of error probability vs. number of links.

In the analog case the noise-to-signal power ratio ν_n for n links satisfies the formula

$$\nu_n = n\nu_1 \qquad (7\text{-}70)$$

The probability of error p_n for any binary symbol detected after transmission over n analog links is then given by

$$p_n = f(\nu_n) = f(n\nu_1) \qquad (7\text{-}71)$$

Hence
$$p_1 = f(\nu_1) \qquad \text{or} \qquad \nu_1 = f^{-1}(p_1) \qquad (7\text{-}72)$$

and the error probability for n links is expressed in terms of that for one link by

$$p_n = f[nf^{-1}(p_1)] \qquad (7\text{-}73)$$

Thus if we know the error probability vs. noise-to-signal ratio for one link, we can plot the error probability vs. number of links.

One case in which we can carry through numerical calculations is that of additive gaussian noise. This is ultimately the most significant case because other sources of error can, in theory, be discovered and eliminated. For an optimum binary channel with additive gaussian noise, it is known that

$$f(\nu_n) = \tfrac{1}{2} \operatorname{erfc} \nu_n^{-\frac{1}{2}} \qquad (7\text{-}74)$$

The abbreviation "erfc" represents the complementary error function which is one minus the error function. It follows that

$$p_n = \tfrac{1}{2} \operatorname{erfc} [n^{-\frac{1}{2}} \operatorname{erfc}^{-1}(2p_1)] \qquad (7\text{-}75)$$

A family of curves for p_n vs. n plotted from this equation for various values of p_1 is designated by "Analog links" in Fig. 7-19.

For the regenerated digital links we assume that any binary symbol transmitted through the system has an independent probability p_1 of being inverted by any link. If p_1 is very small and n is not too large, the probability of error after n links is very nearly equal to np_1. For very large n, the probability of more than one inversion must be taken into account. Let p_n represent the probability that a binary symbol is in error after transmission through n regenerative repeaters. Then p_n is also the probability of an odd number of errors since an even

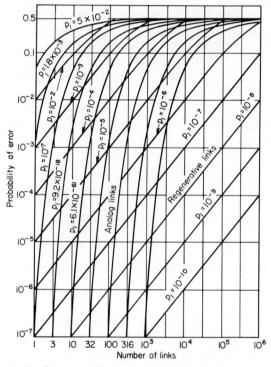

Fig. 7-19. Regenerative vs. analog links for binary data.

number of errors restores the original value. Counting zero as an even number, the probability of an even number of errors is $1 - p_n$. Then

$$p_{n+1} = p_n(1 - p_1) + (1 - p_n)p_1$$
$$= (1 - 2p_1)p_n + p_1 \qquad (7\text{-}76)$$

The solution of this linear first-order difference equation is

$$p_n = \tfrac{1}{2}[1 - (1 - 2p_1)^n] \qquad (7\text{-}77)$$

When p_1 and n are small, the right-hand member of Eq. (7-77) reduces to np_1; while for large n, it approaches one-half asymptotically.

A family of curves plotted for various values of p_1 is designated "Regenerative links" on Fig. 7-19. To violate the regenerative payoff,[7] we must find numbers of links at which the regenerative curves overtake the analog curves and thereafter exhibit a higher probability of error as the number of links is further increased. Such crossovers do in fact occur, but they are in the range of error probability approaching one-half.

The curves of Fig. 7-19 apply specifically to systems designed for binary transmission. One difference between the regenerative and analog cases which does not show in the comparison is that the regenerative system can be used only for binary signals. The analog system on the other hand is available for any type of signal which accepts the bandwidth and signal-to-noise ratio provided. To use the binary regenerative system for analog signals or general n-ary data requires a conversion to binary signal form. This typically increases the required bandwidth and hence, decreases the repeater spacing of the regenerative system relative to that of the analog system. In comparing systems which must transmit either binary data or some analog signal such as voice, the curves of Fig. 7-19 can still be used but with the caution that the numbers of links do not represent the same distances in the two cases.

REFERENCES

1. Peirce, B. O.: "A Short Table of Integrals," Ginn & Co., Boston, 1929.
2. Jahnke-Emde-Losch: "Tables of Higher Functions," 6th ed., McGraw-Hill Book Company, New York, 1960.
3. U.S. Department of Commerce, *National Bureau of Standards, Applied Mathematics Series* 41, Oct. 22, 1954.
4. Sunde, E. D.: Ideal Binary Pulse Transmission by AM and FM, *Bell System Tech. J.*, vol. 38, pp. 1357–1426, November, 1959.
5. Titchmarsh, E. C.: "Introduction to the Theory of Fourier Integrals," Oxford University Press, p. 50, London, 1937.
6. Whittaker and Watson: "Modern Analysis," 3d ed., p. 256, Cambridge University Press, London, 1920.
7. Oliver, B. M., J. R. Pierce, and C. E. Shannon: The Philosophy of PCM, *Proc. IRE*, vol. 36, pp. 1324–1332, November, 1948.
8. Goodall, W. M.: Television by Pulse Code Modulation, *Bell System Tech. J.*, vol. 30, pp. 33–49, January, 1951.
9. Brand, S., and C. W. Carter: A 1,650-bit-per-second Data System for Use over the Switched Telephone Network, *AIEE Trans.*, Part I (Communication and Electronics), vol. 80, pp. 652–661, January, 1962.
10. Gulstad, K.: Vibrating Cable Relay, *Elec. Rev. (London)*, vol. 42, 1898; vol. 51, 1902.

11. Clokey, A. A.: Automatic Printing Equipment for Long Loaded Submarine Telephone Cables, *Bell System Tech. J.*, vol. 6, pp. 402–424, July, 1927.
12. Lender, A.: The Duobinary Technique for High Speed Data Transmission, Conference Paper CP63-283, IEEE Winter General Meeting, 1963.
13. Bennett, W. R.: Synthesis of Active Networks, *Polytech. Inst. Brooklyn Symposium Proc.*, vol. 5, pp. 45–61, 1955.
14. MacColl, L. A.: U.S. Patent 2,056,284, Oct. 6, 1936.
15. Black, H. S.: "Modulation Theory," D. Van Nostrand Company, Inc., Princeton, N.J., 1953.

CHAPTER 8

AMPLITUDE-MODULATION SYSTEMS

The essential parts of an AM data transmission system are shown in Fig. 8-1. The data source typically controls the generation of rectangular on-off pulses. The pulses are passed through a low-pass shaping filter before modulating the carrier. The low-pass filter limits the width of the baseband and thereby restricts the extent of the sidebands

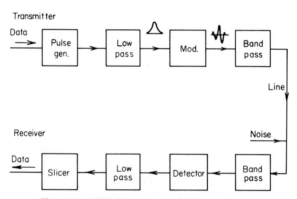

FIG. 8-1. AM data transmission system.

produced by the modulator. The modulator varies the amplitude of the carrier in accordance with the shaped baseband wave. The transmitting bandpass filter further restricts the spectrum applied to the line. As discussed for baseband systems, the transmitting filter serves not only as part of the overall channel characteristic but also controls the interference into other channels. At the receiving location a receiving bandpass filter attenuates noise and interference outside the band of interest. The detector recovers the baseband wave by means of a product modulator or by simple rectification as discussed later. The low-pass filter separates the baseband signal from the higher-frequency components resulting from detection. The resulting baseband wave is then sliced to recover rectangular pulses. If synchronous data are being transmitted, the pulses can be regenerated as discussed for baseband signals in Chap. 7. Certain of these system functions will now be taken up in more detail.

8-1 TRANSMITTING MODULATOR

The modulator performs the function of multiplying the sine wave from the carrier source by the data wave. As covered in Sec. 5-7, if the carrier is $\cos(\omega_c t + \theta)$ and the data wave is $s(t)$, the resulting AM carrier signal may be written

$$E(t) = s(t) \cos(\omega_c t + \theta) \qquad (8\text{-}1)$$

Let $s(t)$ be representable by a Fourier integral as in Eq. (5-5):

$$s(t) = \frac{1}{\pi} \int_0^\infty S(\omega) \cos[\omega t + \phi(\omega)]\, d\omega \qquad (8\text{-}2)$$

Then from Eq. (5-54):

$$E(t) = \frac{1}{2\pi} \int_0^\infty S(\omega) \cos[(\omega_c + \omega)t + \theta + \phi(\omega)]\, d\omega$$

$$+ \frac{1}{2\pi} \int_0^{\omega_c} S(\omega) \cos[(\omega_c - \omega)t + \theta - \phi(\omega)]\, d\omega$$

$$+ \frac{1}{2\pi} \int_{\omega_c}^\infty S(\omega) \cos[(\omega - \omega_c)t - \theta + \phi(\omega)]\, d\omega \qquad (8\text{-}3)$$

The last term of Eq. (8-3) represents foldover of the lower sideband about zero frequency. The term disappears if $S(\omega)$ is negligible for $\omega > \omega_c$. Otherwise the low-pass shaping filter before the modulator should suppress the high-frequency baseband components which would be reflected into the band to be transmitted. The foldover effect is of importance in data systems utilizing a relatively wide band located near zero frequency, as is the case with a whole voice band. If foldover is allowed to occur in the modulation, it cannot be corrected later. Simple AM data systems in which a voice-frequency carrier is modulated by abrupt on-and-off switching have a small amount of fortuitous distortion from foldover which is often called "keying loss." It may also be described as an insufficient number of cycles per bit. The closer the carrier is placed to zero frequency, the greater this distortion becomes. We note that if the baseband is sufficiently limited in width to make the third integral of (8-3) negligible, we can also replace the upper limit of the first integral by ω_c.

In the range where $\omega < \omega_c$, the low-pass shaping filter controls the transmitted spectrum symmetrically about the carrier frequency.

Thus, if a symmetrical spectrum is desired, its shape can be controlled either by the low-pass shaping filter or by the transmitting bandpass filter. Where one sideband is to be attenuated, as for vestigial-sideband transmission, it must be done by the transmitting and receiving bandpass filters. Any d-c component of $S(\omega)$ will appear in the transmitted signal as a carrier-frequency component.

More often than not the modulators used in AM data systems are not true multipliers as considered up to this point but are the so-called "switch-type modulators." One form of switch modulator shown in Fig. 8-2 acts essentially like a reversing switch driven by the source of carrier frequency. The polarity of the modulating wave is thus switched at the carrier-frequency rate. This is equivalent to multiplying the wave by $+1$ during one-half of the carrier cycle and by -1 during the other half. Such a switching function is equivalent to a polar square wave which was shown in Sec. 4-1 to be representable as follows:

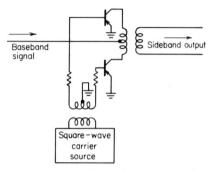

FIG. 8-2. Reversing switch-type modulator.

$$g(t) = \frac{4}{\pi} \cos \omega_c t - \frac{4}{3\pi} \cos 3\omega_c t + \frac{4}{5\pi} \cos 5\omega_c t - \cdots \qquad (8\text{-}4)$$

With such a wave substituted for the sinusoidal carrier in Eq. (8-1), we see that in addition to the $S(\omega)$ sidebands on either side of the carrier frequency ω_c, there will be similar sidebands on either side of the odd harmonics $3\omega_c$, $5\omega_c$, etc. For $\omega < \omega_c$, however, the transmitting bandpass filter can separate out the desired first-order spectrum centered about ω_c. Thus such a switch-type modulator can perform the necessary multiplying function. The output of such a modulator does not contain any of the baseband modulating signal and is termed a balanced modulator. Also no carrier-frequency component appears except that resulting from the d-c component of the modulating signal.

An unbalanced type of modulator is sometimes used in which the carrier-frequency multiplying function alternates between $+1$ and 0. For instance, a series or shunt gating action can be used as illustrated for the latter case in Fig. 8-3. This is equivalent to multiplying by the following series

$$g_0(t) = \frac{1}{2} + \frac{2}{\pi} \cos \omega_c t - \frac{2}{3\pi} \cos 3\omega_c t + \frac{2}{5\pi} \cos 5\omega_c t - \cdots \qquad (8\text{-}5)$$

Here we see that the modulator output will contain, in addition to the components from the balanced version, the baseband modulating signal. For $\omega > \omega_c/2$, there would thus be an overlap of the lower sideband and the baseband. Such a modulator is thus more restrictive in the choice of carrier frequency.

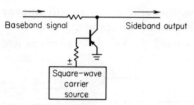

FIG. 8-3. On-off switch-type modulator.

8-2 SYNCHRONOUS DETECTION

The method of synchronous, coherent, or homodyne detection will be considered first. This involves multiplying the amplitude-modulated received signal by a local source of carrier which has the same frequency and phase as that associated with the received signal. As in Sec. 5-7, let the amplitude and phase characteristic of the band-pass filters and the transmission medium be $A(\omega)$ and $B(\omega)$. If the output of the transmitting modulator is restricted to the first two integrals of Eq. (8-3), the input to the detector will then be

$$
\begin{aligned}
E_R(t) = \frac{1}{2\pi} \int_0^{\omega_c} & S(\omega)A(\omega_c + \omega) \cos \left[(\omega_c + \omega)t + \theta + \phi(\omega) \right. \\
& \left. + B(\omega_c + \omega)\right] d\omega \\
+ \frac{1}{2\pi} \int_0^{\omega_c} & S(\omega)A(\omega_c - \omega) \cos \left[(\omega_c - \omega)t + \theta - \phi(\omega) \right. \\
& \left. + B(\omega_c - \omega)\right] d\omega
\end{aligned}
\tag{8-6}
$$

The proper carrier wave for synchronous detection is $\cos \left[\omega_c t + \theta + B(\omega_c)\right]$. The product of this and Eq. (8-6) is

$$
\begin{aligned}
E_D(t) = \frac{1}{4\pi} \int_0^{\omega_c} & S(\omega)A(\omega_c + \omega) \cos \left[(2\omega_c + \omega)t + 2\theta + \phi\omega \right. \\
& \left. + B(\omega_c + \omega) + B(\omega_c)\right] d\omega \\
+ \frac{1}{4\pi} \int_0^{\omega_c} & S(\omega)A(\omega_c + \omega) \cos \left[-\omega t - \phi(\omega) - B(\omega_c + \omega) \right. \\
& \left. + B(\omega_c)\right] d\omega \\
+ \frac{1}{4\pi} \int_0^{\omega_c} & S(\omega)A(\omega_c - \omega) \cos \left[(2\omega_c - \omega)t + 2\theta - \phi(\omega) \right. \\
& \left. + B(\omega_c - \omega) + B(\omega_c)\right] d\omega \\
+ \frac{1}{4\pi} \int_0^{\omega_c} & S(\omega)A(\omega_c - \omega) \cos \left[\omega t + \phi(\omega) - B(\omega_c - \omega) \right. \\
& \left. + B(\omega_c)\right] d\omega
\end{aligned}
\tag{8-7}
$$

The first and third integrals represent new upper and lower sidebands centered around twice the carrier frequency. The second and fourth integrals represent the wanted baseband signal resulting from the contributions of the upper and lower sidebands of the received signal. For $\omega < \omega_c$ there is no overlap, and the low-pass filter after detection can separate the baseband components from the sideband extending below twice the carrier frequency.

If the phase characteristic has odd symmetry about ω_c so that

$$B(\omega_c + \omega) - B(\omega_c) = B(\omega_c) - B(\omega_c - \omega) \equiv \beta(\omega) \qquad (8\text{-}8)$$

then the two baseband contributions add in phase to give

$$E_D(t) = \frac{1}{4\pi} \int_0^{\omega_c} [S(\omega)A(\omega_c + \omega) + S(\omega)A(\omega_c - \omega)]$$
$$\times \cos[\omega t + \phi(\omega) + \beta(\omega)]\,d\omega \qquad (8\text{-}9)$$

Also if the amplitude characteristic has even symmetry about ω_c, that is, if

$$A(\omega_c + \omega) = A(\omega_c - \omega) = \alpha(\omega) \qquad (8\text{-}10)$$

then

$$E_D(t) = \frac{1}{2\pi} \int_0^{\omega_c} S(\omega)\alpha(\omega) \cos[\omega t + \phi(\omega) + \beta(\omega)]\,d\omega \qquad (8\text{-}11)$$

The recovered baseband signal thus becomes the original baseband signal at the input to the transmitting modulator [Eq. (8-2)] modified by the transmission characteristic of the channel. The two conditions of Eqs. (8-8) and (8-10) may be compactly expressed by setting $M(\omega)$ equal to the complex transmittance of the medium and $M^*(\omega)$ equal to the conjugate of $M(\omega)$. Then (8-8) and (8-10) are represented by the single equation

$$\frac{\alpha(\omega)e^{j\beta(\omega)}}{|M(\omega_c)|} = \frac{M(\omega_c + \omega)}{M(\omega_c)} = \frac{M^*(\omega_c - \omega)}{M^*(\omega_c)} \qquad (8\text{-}12)$$

If the demodulating carrier has a square waveform as in Eq. (8-4), the demodulator output will contain additional components consisting of sidebands centered about $2\omega_c$, $4\omega_c$, $6\omega_c$, etc. All of these can be rejected by the low-pass filter. If an unbalanced demodulator is used, some of the received signal appears in the output. Then, as discussed in Sec. 8-1, ω must be less than $\omega_c/2$ to permit separation of the baseband signal.

8-3 ENVELOPE DETECTION

Envelope detection is often accomplished by simple rectification of the received signal. For example, if an ideal full-wave rectifier is used, the received wave effectively becomes multiplied by $+1$ or -1 as determined by the polarity of the wave. The result is easily interpreted when the transmission characteristic has the symmetry prescribed by Eq. (8-12). For this case we note that Eq. (8-6) for the received carrier wave becomes

$$
\begin{aligned}
E_R(t) &= \frac{1}{2\pi} \int_0^{\omega_c} S(\omega)\alpha(\omega) \cos\left[(\omega_c + \omega)t + \theta + \phi(\omega) + \beta(\omega)\right.\\
&\quad + \left. B(\omega_c)\right] d\omega + \frac{1}{2\pi} \int_0^{\omega_c} S(\omega)\alpha(\omega) \cos\left[(\omega_c - \omega)t + \theta\right.\\
&\quad - \phi(\omega) - \beta(\omega) + B(\omega_c)\right] d\omega \\
&= \frac{1}{\pi} \cos\left[\omega_c t + \theta + B(\omega_c)\right] \int_0^{\omega_c} S(\omega)\alpha(\omega) \cos\left[\omega t + \phi(\omega)\right.\\
&\quad + \beta(\omega)\right] d\omega
\end{aligned}
\tag{8-13}
$$

It is seen that this wave certainly has zero crossings coincident with those of the proper demodulating carrier $\cos\left[\omega_c t + \theta + B(\omega_c)\right]$. If, also, the value of the integral in (8-13) never changes sign, there are no additional zero crossings, and in the absence of interference, full-wave rectification gives the same result as synchronous detection. The condition for no zero crossings contributed by the integral is that the received wave must not have more than 100 per cent amplitude modulation. This is the condition which would prevail in on-off signaling except in cases of unusually severe transmission distortion. It would not hold for polar signaling.

If the sidebands are not symmetrically disposed about the carrier, the zero crossings of the received wave depart from those of the proper demodulating carrier and the rectified baseband wave becomes distorted. An AM signal having asymmetrical sidebands can be resolved into two AM signals each with symmetrical sidebands but with one having its carrier in quadrature with that of the other. When synchronous detection is used, only the in-phase component of the signal contributes to the recovered baseband since the contributions of the sidebands of the quadrature component cancel. This may be demonstrated by multiplying Eq. (8-6) by $\sin\left[\omega_c t + \theta + B(\omega_c)\right]$ instead of by $\cos\left[\omega_c t + \theta + B(\omega_c)\right]$. The difference-frequency components will be found to add to zero whereas there will again be sidebands on either side of twice the carrier frequency as in Eq. (8-7). When full-wave rectification is used, the output is determined by the resultant of the in-phase and quadrature components or the envelope of the carrier signal. In single-sideband and vestigial-sideband operation the inevitable presence of the quadrature component leads to an envelope shape which differs from the shape of the modulating signal, and synchronous detection must be used to avoid distortion. However, the presence of a relatively large in-phase carrier component, either transmitted over the line or added at the receiver, minimizes the amount of distortion associated with envelope detection.

Figure 8-4 illustrates geometrically how the presence of a large carrier component causes the amplitude variations of the resultant to approximate more closely that of the component in phase with the carrier. The horizontal vector P represents an in-phase component with small magnitude relative to the vertical vector Q, the quadrature component. The length of the resultant vector E is seen to be principally determined by Q. If we add a vector P_0 in the same direction

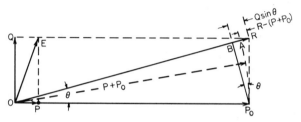

FIG. 8-4. Effect of large carrier component on envelope of modulated wave.

as P, a resultant vector R is obtained making an angle θ with P. The angle θ can be made as small as we please by increasing the magnitude of P_0. Construct an arc centered at the origin with radius equal to the length of $P + P_0$ intersecting R at A, and drop a perpendicular from the terminus of P_0 to R at B. We see that $OB < OA$. Hence, if the letters P, P_0, Q, and R now represent the magnitudes of the corresponding vectors,

$$R - (P + P_0) < Q \sin \theta \qquad (8\text{-}14)$$

Therefore,

$$R = P + P_0 + \epsilon \qquad (8\text{-}15)$$

where

$$\epsilon < Q \sin \theta < Q \tan \theta = \frac{Q^2}{P_0 + P} \qquad (8\text{-}16)$$

If $P_0 > P$,

$$\epsilon < \frac{Q^2}{P_0} \left(1 - \frac{P}{P_0} + \frac{P^2}{P_0{}^2} - \cdots \right) \qquad (8\text{-}17)$$

If both P and Q are small compared with P_0, R differs from $P + P_0$ by less than Q^2/P_0, which can be made arbitrarily small by increasing P_0. The wanted in-phase signal component is P. Since P_0 is in effect a large additive bias on the recovered signal, accurate control of its value is necessary. The increased amount of carrier can also be thought of as reducing the phase modulation of the zero crossings and thus more closely approximating the same result as obtained by synchronous detection.

The quantitative role of the in-phase and quadrature components can be shown in more detail by writing Eq. (8-6) for the received carrier signal in the form

$$E_R(t) = P(t) \cos [\omega_c t + \theta + B(\omega_c)] - Q(t) \sin [\omega_c t + \theta + B(\omega_c)]$$

$$(8\text{-}18)$$

By manipulation of the trigonometric terms in (8-6), we find

$$P(t) = \frac{1}{2\pi} \int_0^{\omega_c} S(\omega) A(\omega_c + \omega) \cos [\omega t + \phi(\omega) + B(\omega_c + \omega)$$

$$- B(\omega_c)] \, d\omega + \frac{1}{2\pi} \int_0^{\omega_c} S(\omega) A(\omega_c - \omega) \cos [\omega t + \phi(\omega)$$

$$- B(\omega_c - \omega) + B(\omega_c)] \, d\omega \qquad (8\text{-}19)$$

$$Q(t) = \frac{1}{2\pi} \int_0^{\omega_c} S(\omega) A(\omega_c + \omega) \sin [\omega t + \phi(\omega) + B(\omega_c + \omega)$$

$$- B(\omega_c)] \, d\omega - \frac{1}{2\pi} \int_0^{\omega_c} S(\omega) A(\omega_c - \omega) \sin [\omega t + \phi(\omega)$$

$$- B(\omega_c - \omega) + B(\omega_c)] \, d\omega \qquad (8\text{-}20)$$

We define $P(t)$ and $Q(t)$ as the in-phase and quadrature terms respectively for the particular choice of carrier phase made in (8-18). It is seen that for the conditions of symmetry of Eq. (8-12), the two components of $P(t)$ add to twice the value of each one, and the two components of $Q(t)$ cancel to give zero. In the general case we can write (8-18) in terms of an envelope function $R(t)$ and a phase function $\Psi(t)$, thus

$$E_R(t) = R(t) \cos [\omega_c t + \theta + B(\omega_c) + \Psi(t)] \qquad (8\text{-}21)$$

where
$$R(t) = [P^2(t) + Q^2(t)]^{\frac{1}{2}} \qquad (8\text{-}22)$$

and
$$\Psi(t) = \arctan \frac{Q(t)}{P(t)} \qquad (8\text{-}23)$$

An envelope detector delivers the wave $R(t)$. A full-wave linear rectifier delivers the wave

$$F(t) = R(t)h(t) \qquad (8\text{-}24)$$

where
$$h(t) = |\cos z| \qquad (8\text{-}25)$$

with
$$z = \omega_c t + \theta + B(\omega_c) + \Psi(t) \qquad (8\text{-}26)$$

But by Fourier series expansion

$$h(t) = \frac{4}{\pi} \left(\frac{1}{2} + \frac{\cos 2z}{2^2 - 1} - \frac{\cos 4z}{4^2 - 1} + \frac{\cos 6z}{6^2 - 1} - \cdots \right) \tag{8-27}$$

If the important frequencies present in $R(t)$ are sufficiently small compared with those in $\cos 2z$, $\cos 4z$, . . . , a low-pass filter can be used to select the term $2R(t)/\pi$ from the output wave $F(t)$. Under these circumstances, the full-wave rectifier with unity as amplitude factor gives a low-frequency output component equal to $2/\pi$ times the envelope.

The effect of adding a large in-phase carrier component is to produce the wave

$$F_R(t) = P_0 \cos z_1 + P(t) \cos z_1 - Q(t) \sin z_1 = R_0(t) \cos (z_1 + \Psi_0) \tag{8-28}$$

where
$$z_1 = \omega_c t + \theta + B(\omega_c) \tag{8-29}$$

$$R_0(t) = \{[P_0 + P(t)]^2 + Q^2(t)\}^{\frac{1}{2}}$$
$$= P_0 \left[1 + \frac{2P(t)}{P_0} + \frac{P^2(t) + Q^2(t)}{P_0^2} \right]^{\frac{1}{2}} \tag{8-30}$$

$$\tan \Psi_0 = \frac{Q(t)}{P_0 + P(t)} \tag{8-31}$$

If P_0 is large compared with $P(t)$ and $Q(t)$, we can expand in power series by the binomial theorem. We thereby find

$$R_0(t) = P_0 + P(t) + \frac{Q^2(t)}{2P_0} + \cdots \tag{8-32}$$

The envelope thus reproduces the in-phase component $P(t)$ to within an error of order $Q^2(t)/(2P_0)$. Note that by adding carrier in any phase, we can detect the in-phase component corresponding to that phase. In particular, if we wish the envelope to represent the quadrature component in the above example, we merely add $P_0 \sin z_1$ instead of $P_0 \cos z_1$. Two independent channels using the same carrier frequency can be detected in this way without mutual interference if their carriers differ in phase by 90° at the transmitter.

8-4 OPTIMUM FILTERS FOR NOISE SUPPRESSION

The relationship between the baseband spectrum and the sideband spectra in AM was covered in Sec. 5-7. The material in Sec. 7-4 on optimum transmitting and receiving filters for a baseband system can be applied to the bandpass filters of an AM system when synchronous detection is used and the noise spectrum is symmetrical about the carrier frequency. As pointed out before, control of the transmitted spectrum is a joint function of the low-pass shaping filter before modulation and of the transmitting bandpass filter. The receiving bandpass filter together with the low-pass filter after detection determine the noise spectrum which is accepted. The optimum receiving-filter characteristics calculated for the baseband system as, for example, the results obtained in Eqs. (7-26), (7-30), (7-36), (7-37), and (7-41) for various noise conditions, can be divided at will between the receiving bandpass filter and the postdetection low-pass filter. That part which is inserted in the bandpass filter must be duplicated symmetrically in the upper- and lower-sideband ranges. That is, if the optimum low-pass receiving filter for the baseband case is $Y(f)$, then an optimum solution for the synchronous AM case with symmetrical noise band is furnished by any combination of a bandpass filter characteristic $Y_b(f)$ satisfying the conditions of symmetry specified by (8-12), and a postdetection low-pass filter $Y_l(f)$ satisfying the relation

$$2\,|Y_b(f_c+f)|\,|Y_l(f)| = |Y(f)| \qquad (8\text{-}33)$$

The mean total noise power W_n received at the slicer input is given by

$$W_n = 2\int_0^{f_c} |Y_l(f)|^2\,|Y_b(f_c+f)|^2\,w(f_c+f)\,df \qquad (8\text{-}34)$$

Similar free choice can be made in the division of the corresponding transmitting filter characteristic between baseband low-pass filter and the postmodulation bandpass filter.

The cases of vestigial-sideband transmission and unsymmetrical noise spectra require some further discussion. Suppose the noise is gaussian with spectral density function $w(f)$ at the receiving bandpass filter input, and that we are using vestigial-sideband transmission with synchronous detection to obtain a detected pulse with Fourier transform $E_s S_D(f)$. We specify that $S_D(f)$ is made up of components $S_U(f)$ and $S_L(f)$ contributed by the upper and lower sidebands respectively. That is,

$$S_D(f) = S_U(f) + S_L(f) \qquad (8\text{-}35)$$

where, in terms of the complex notation introduced in Eq. (5-58),

$$E_s S_U(f) = G_0 Y_l(f) Y_b(f_c+f) e^{-jB(\omega_c)} A(\omega_c+\omega) \qquad (8\text{-}36)$$

$$E_s S_L(f) = G_0 Y_l(f) Y_b{}^*(f_c-f) e^{jB(\omega_c)} A^*(\omega_c-\omega) \qquad (8\text{-}37)$$

The function $A(\omega)$ is the Fourier transform of a pulse applied at the input of a flat loss medium with transmittance G_0. It follows that

$$A(\omega) = \begin{cases} \dfrac{E_s S_U(f - f_c)e^{jB(\omega_c)}}{G_0 Y_i(f - f_c)Y_b(f)} & 2f_c > f > f_c \\[4mm] \dfrac{E_s S_L{}^*(f_c - f)e^{jB(\omega_c)}}{G_0 Y_i{}^*(f_c - f)Y_b(f)} & 0 < f < f_c \end{cases} \tag{8-38}$$

This equation replaces Eq. (7-16) in the analysis for optimum receiving-filter characteristics performed in Chap. 7. When the new value of $A(\omega)$ is substituted in (7-17) and the resulting value of U substituted in (7-18), we obtain the following expression for the average transmitted signal power W_s in a unit-resistance circuit:

$$\begin{aligned} W_s &= \frac{2f_s E_s{}^2}{G_0{}^2}\left[\int_0^{f_c} \frac{|S_L(f_c - f)|^2}{|Y_i(f_c - f)Y_b(f)|^2}\,df + \int_{f_c}^{2f_c} \frac{|S_U(f - f_c)|^2}{|Y_i(f - f_c)Y_b(f)|^2}\,df\right] \\[2mm] &= \frac{2f_s E_s{}^2}{G_0{}^2}\int_0^{f_c} \frac{df}{|Y_i(f)|^2}\left[\frac{|S_L(f)|^2}{|Y_i(f_c - f)|^2} + \frac{|S_U(f)|^2}{|Y_b(f_c + f)|^2}\right] \\[2mm] &\equiv \frac{2f_s E_s{}^2}{G_0{}^2}\,I_2 \end{aligned} \tag{8-39}$$

We also replace (7-14), the equation for mean total gaussian noise power at the slicer input, by

$$\begin{aligned} W_n &= \int_0^{f_c} |Y_i(f)|^2\,[\,|Y_b(f_c - f)|^2\,w(f_c - f) \\ &\quad + |Y_b(f_c + f)|^2\,w(f_c + f)]\,df \equiv I_1 \end{aligned} \tag{8-40}$$

The new version of (7-19) then becomes

$$\frac{W_n}{E_s{}^2} = \frac{2f_s}{G_0{}^2 W_s}\,I_1 I_2 \tag{8-41}$$

where I_1 and I_2 are the integrals appearing in (8-39) and (8-40) respectively. The problem now is to find the functions $Y_i(f)$ and $Y_b(f)$ which minimize the product $I_1 I_2$. The procedure is similar to that employed in Chap. 7 for the baseband except that we now deal with simultaneous minimization with respect to two functions. The optimum baseband receiving-filter characteristic of Eq. (7-26) is found to be replaced by two conditions for optimum, viz.:

$$\begin{aligned} |Y_i(f)|\,|Y_b(f_c - f)| &= \alpha\,\frac{|S_L(f)|^{1/2}}{w^{1/4}(f_c - f)} \\[2mm] |Y_i(f)|\,|Y_b(f_c + f)| &= \alpha\,\frac{|S_U(f)|^{1/2}}{w^{1/4}(f_c + f)} \end{aligned} \tag{8-42}$$

We interpret these results to mean that when the upper- and lower-sideband contributions to signal have been specified, the frequency ranges above and below the carrier frequency can be optimized separately by treating each combination of sideband with the low-pass filter as a composite baseband filter. We can then ask the question as to what is the best resolution of signal spectrum into upper- and lower-sideband contributions. For the case of white noise, all resolutions are equally good as far as signal-to-noise ratio at the slicer input is concerned. The resolution would, therefore, be based on other considerations such as bandwidth conservation and simplicity of filter design. If $w(f)$ varies with frequency, it would be desirable to select sideband contributions from frequency regions of low noise density insofar as the selection does not conflict with other design objectives. For example, if the spectral density of the noise increases with frequency, the lower sideband is preferable to the upper, but we cannot provide a bandpass filter which cuts off abruptly at the carrier frequency. The portion of the upper sideband accepted would be determined by practical filter realization art.

We have restricted the analysis of the optimum bandpass filter so far to the case of synchronous detection. A synchronous detector shifts the spectrum of a noise band on the frequency scale without changing the shape. It follows that filtering before and after the detector can be made interchangeable. The results are not generally applicable to envelope detection because nonlinear effects change the shape of the noise spectrum. One exception in which we can apply our results approximately is the case in which a large in-phase component of carrier is present in the input to the envelope detector. To show this we make use of the following theorem from noise theory:[1]

A gaussian noise wave $v(t)$ with spectral density $w(f)$ equal to zero outside the range $f = 0$ to $f = 2f_c$ can be uniquely represented in the form

$$v(t) = x(t) \cos 2\pi f_c t - y(t) \sin 2\pi f_c t \qquad (8\text{-}43)$$

where $x(t)$ and $y(t)$ are gaussian noise waves with spectral densities each equal to $w(f_c - f) + w(f_c + f)$ in the range $f = 0$ to $f = f_c$ and equal to zero for $f > f_c$.

The theorem can be verified by considering individual noise components in the band as sine waves. A second useful theorem is that values of $x(t)$ and $y(t)$ for the same t are independent.

Making use of the theorem, we can include the noise in the received wave with large in-phase carrier by modifying (8-28) to

$$F_R(t) = [P_0 + P(t) + x(t)] \cos z_1 - [Q(t) + y(t)] \sin z_1 \qquad (8\text{-}44)$$

If P_0 is large compared with $P(t)$, $x(t)$, $Q(t)$, and $y(t)$, the envelope can be written as

$$R_0(t) = P_0\left[1 + 2\frac{P(t) + x(t)}{P_0} + \frac{[P(t) + x(t)]^2 + [Q(t) + y(t)]^2}{P_0{}^2}\right]^{1/2}$$

$$\approx P_0 + P(t) + x(t) \tag{8-45}$$

neglecting terms in $1/P_0{}^2$. In this approximation the noise wave $x(t)$ adds to the in-phase signal component $P(t)$. The problem is thereby reduced to a baseband case in which $P(t)$ is the received signal, and $x(t)$ is additive gaussian noise. Filtering at the receiver can be divided at will between a bandpass filter acting on the modulated wave and a low-pass filter acting on the detected wave as in the previous examples.

The more general case of envelope detection without a large in-phase carrier component cannot be resolved so neatly. Filtering before and after the detector are no longer equivalent processes because the detector itself changes the spectral density function of the noise in a complicated way. We can make a reasonably satisfactory statement if the filter following the detector has only the function of removing the harmonics of the carrier and the associated sidebands. This means the selection of the term $2R(t)/\pi$ in Eqs. (8-24) and (8-27) without discriminatory treatment of any of the frequencies present in the envelope $R(t)$. For this case, as we shall develop in more detail later, all the noise power accompanying the modulated carrier in the receiving bandpass-filter output contributes to the probability of error at the slicer. Hence the minimum probability of error is obtained by minimizing noise-to-signal ratio in the bandpass-filter output. This means in turn that the optimization procedures are to be applied to the bandpass filter only. Previously obtained formulas involving both bandpass and low-pass characteristics can be used by setting the low-pass filter transmittance function equal to unity.

8-5 OPTIMUM FILTERS FOR SUPPRESSION OF MUTUAL INTERFERENCE

It is common practice to divide a band of frequencies among a number of independent AM channels operating on equally spaced carrier frequencies. In such systems the function of the bandpass filters is extended to include prevention of mutual interference between the channels as well as reduction of the noise effects we have previously studied. The transmitting filter is called upon to restrict the band of the modulated wave not only to make efficient use of available power but also to remove components which fall in the band of the other channels. The receiving filter likewise not only operates to reduce the band of accepted noise but also to exclude the signals of the other channels. We accordingly consider the problem of allocating the transmitting- and receiving-filter selectivities to minimize mutual interference between channels.

We assume as before that the raised-cosine pulse spectrum at the slicer input has been adopted to secure freedom from intersymbol interference. In theory this requires no transmission of baseband frequencies greater than f_s, the symbol rate. Hence one solution can be found by (1) stipulating channel filters which do not transmit any frequencies differing from the carrier by more than f_s, and (2) setting the spacing between adjacent carrier frequencies at least as great as $2f_s$. Under these idealized conditions there is no mutual interference between double-sideband channels.

There are at least two reasons why the idealized solution may not be the most desirable one in practical situations. One is that it does not use bandwidth with maximum efficiency. In digital transmission systems a certain amount of interference can exist without actually causing error. By spacing the carrier frequencies closer together than the $2f_s$ interval, we can get more channels in a given band at the cost of some frequency overlap. The overlap may reduce the margin against other disturbances, but the cost of this must be weighed against the advantage of more channels. A second reason for deviating from the ideal is that filters with infinite attenuation outside their passbands are not practically realizable. In any real filter we must take account of a small amount of transmission at frequencies beyond the nominal cutoff. To reduce the resulting frequency overlap between channels to a negligibly small contribution may require an inordinately expensive filter. It is sound engineering practice to assign a tolerance limit for interchannel interference in economic balance with other disturbing sources. It may, of course, turn out in some cases that bandwidth is a minor consideration. The most economic solution is then to space the carriers so far apart that simple filters adequately suppress interchannel interference.

We illustrate by treating a case in which the major interchannel interference comes from adjacent-sideband overlap as indicated in Fig. 8-5. Since the situation is symmetrical with respect to the two flanking channels, we need analyze only the overlap of one pair of sidebands, which we shall take as the interference produced by the lower sideband from the channel with next higher carrier frequency. Referring to Fig. 8-5, we consider transmission by AM on the channel with carrier frequency ω_c in the presence of interference from similar transmission on the channel with carrier frequency $\omega_c + \omega_a$. Let

$\omega_s = 2\pi f_s$ and assume $\omega_s < \omega_a < 2\omega_s$. That is, we allow adjacent sidebands to overlap but never more than two sidebands to have appreciable components at any frequency. It is considered that the effect of overlap of nonadjacent sidebands is negligible compared with that of adjacent ones. Let $s(t)$ be a pulse modulated on the lower carrier frequency and $s(t - \tau)$ an equivalent pulse modulated on the upper. We assume identically shaped symmetrical bandpass-filter characteristics displaced in midband frequency by ω_a in the two channels. The transmitting filters in the two channels have transmittance functions $Y_T(\omega - \omega_c)$ and $Y_T(\omega - \omega_c - \omega_a)$ respectively, and the receiving filters have corresponding transmittance functions $Y_R(\omega - \omega_c)$ and $Y_R(\omega - \omega_c - \omega_a)$. To simplify the analysis, we assume that these functions have real values at all frequencies. Linear phase shifts can be considered to be included by assuming that corresponding shifts in the origin of time are made. We also introduce a low-pass filter with real transmittance $Y_L(\omega)$ following the detector

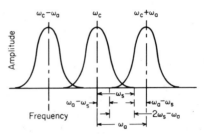

FIG. 8-5. Overlapping channel spectra in frequency-division multiplex.

in each channel and assume that this filter, as well as the corresponding baseband filter at the transmitter, cuts off at $\omega = \omega_s$.

With a distortionless line and synchronous detection, we find an expression for the in-band detected signal in the lower-frequency channel by inserting $A(\omega_c + \omega) = A(\omega_c - \omega) = Y_T(\omega)Y_R(\omega)$ in Eq. (8-10) and by setting $\beta(\omega) = 0$ in Eq. (8-8). We can also insert the effect of the low-pass filter $Y_L(\omega)$ as a multiplying factor in the integrand of Eq. (8-11), giving for the input to the slicer from the wanted signal

$$E_S(t) = \frac{1}{2\pi} \int_0^{\omega_s} S(\omega) Y_T(\omega) Y_R(\omega) Y_L(\omega) \cos \left[\omega t + \phi(\omega) \right] d\omega \quad (8\text{-}46)$$

To find the contribution $F_S(t)$ at the slicer input from the unwanted lower sideband on the upper flanking channel, we first consider what the second or lower-sideband term of (8-6) becomes when ω_c is replaced by $\omega_c + \omega_a$, t by $t - \tau$, θ by θ_a, and $B(\omega)$ by zero. We also insert the condition of no baseband signal components above the frequency ω_s as enforced by the transmitting baseband filter. The amplitude characteristic $A(\omega_c - \omega)$ in Eq. (8-6) becomes $A(\omega_c + \omega_a - \omega)$ and is equal to the product of the two factors $Y_T(\omega_c + \omega_a - \omega - \omega_c - \omega_a) = Y_T(\omega)$ contributed by the transmitting filter of the upper flanking channel, and $Y_R(\omega_c + \omega_a - \omega - \omega_c) = Y_R(\omega_a - \omega)$ contributed by the receiving filter of the channel in which the interference is being studied.   The resulting input to the detector is

$$F_R(t) = \frac{1}{2\pi} \int_0^{\omega_s} S(\omega) Y_T(\omega) Y_R(\omega_a - \omega) \cos\left[(\omega_c + \omega_a - \omega)(t - \tau)\right.$$
$$\left. + \theta_a - \phi(\omega)\right] d\omega \quad (8\text{-}47)$$

The process of synchronous detection in the disturbed channel consists of multiplying $F_R(t)$ by $\cos(\omega_c t + \theta)$.   The low-frequency components in the response are then selected by means of a low-pass filter with transmittance function $Y_L(\omega)$.   The resulting interference in the input to the slicer is

$$F_S(t) = \frac{1}{4\pi} \int_{\omega_a - \omega_s}^{\omega_s} S(\omega) Y_T(\omega) Y_R(\omega_a - \omega) Y_L(\omega_a - \omega) \cos\left[(\omega_a - \omega)\right.$$
$$\times (t - \tau) - \phi(\omega) + \theta_a - \theta - \omega_c\tau\right] d\omega \quad (8\text{-}48)$$

The lower limit becomes $\omega_a - \omega_s$ instead of zero because $Y_L(\omega_a - \omega)$ vanishes for $\omega_a - \omega > \omega_s$, which is equivalent to $\omega < \omega_a - \omega_s$.

One significant quantity affecting the margin over error is the ratio of peaks of wanted and unwanted detected signals.   In other words it would be advantageous to maximize the ratio of peak value of $E_S(t)$ to peak value of $F_S(t)$.   It is not clear that this would always be the best procedure, for it might be possible to stagger the signaling intervals in the different channels to prevent simultaneous occurrence of peak desired signal and peak interchannel interference.   We assume here that such control is not feasible.   To estimate the peaks from Eqs. (8-46) and (8-48), we assume the signal pulse is an even function of time and hence $\phi(\omega) = 0$.   The maximum value of $E_S(t)$ is then obtained at $t = 0$, at which time the cosine function is replaced by its upper bound of unity.   The signal peak E_s at the slicer input is then

$$E_s = \frac{1}{2\pi} \int_0^{\omega_c} S(\omega) Y_T(\omega) Y_R(\omega) Y_L(\omega) \, d\omega \quad (8\text{-}49)$$

For the interference peak we assume pessimistically that at some time the absolute value of the cosine function is unity throughout the entire frequency range, i.e., at time $t = \tau$ if $\theta_a - \theta - \omega_c\tau$ is a multiple of π.   Then the peak interference E_i is given by

$$E_i = \frac{1}{4\pi} \int_{\omega_a - \omega_s}^{\omega_s} S(\omega) Y_T(\omega) Y_R(\omega_a - \omega) Y_L(\omega_a - \omega) \, d\omega \quad (8\text{-}50)$$

We now wish to maximize E_s/E_i subject to the condition:

$$S(\omega) Y_T(\omega) Y_R(\omega) Y_L(\omega) = S_S(\omega) \quad (8\text{-}51)$$

where $S_S(\omega)$ is the desired pulse spectrum at the slicer input.   It appears that the product $Y_R(\omega)Y_L(\omega)$ enters as a single composite function which we define as

$$Y_C(\omega) = Y_R(\omega)Y_L(\omega) \tag{8-52}$$

Substitution of Eq. (8-51) in Eqs. (8-49) and (8-50) then gives

$$E_s = \frac{1}{2\pi}\int_0^{\omega_c} S_S(\omega)\,d\omega \tag{8-53}$$

$$E_i = \frac{1}{4\pi}\int_{\omega_a-\omega_s}^{\omega_s} \frac{S_S(\omega)Y_C(\omega_a - \omega)}{Y_C(\omega)}\,d\omega \tag{8-54}$$

Since E_s is fixed by the specified value of $S_S(\omega)$, the ratio of E_s/E_i is maximized by minimizing E_i with respect to the function $Y_C(\omega)$. Proceeding in the same manner as in the previous examples, we find the best function to be

$$Y_C(\omega) = KS_S^{1/2}(\omega) \tag{8-55}$$

We note by comparison with (7-26) and (8-33) that this is the same solution found for the maximum protection against in-band white gaussian noise. It is reassuring to find that optimum procedures taken toward combating noise within the channel are also effective in protecting against interference from adjacent channels.

In the particular case of a raised-cosine pulse spectrum at the slicer input

$$S_S(\omega) = \frac{4\pi E_s}{\omega_s}\cos^2\frac{\pi\omega}{2\omega_s} \qquad \omega < \omega_s \tag{8-56}$$

$$Y_C(\omega) = K\sqrt{\frac{\pi E_s}{\omega_s}}\cos\frac{\pi\omega}{2\omega_s} \qquad \omega < \omega_s \tag{8-57}$$

$$\frac{E_i}{E_s} = \frac{1}{\omega_s}\int_{\omega_a-\omega_s}^{\omega_s}\cos\frac{\pi\omega}{2\omega_s}\cos\frac{\pi(\omega_a - \omega)}{2\omega_s}\,d\omega$$

$$= \left(1 - \frac{\omega_a}{2\omega_s}\right)\cos\frac{\pi\omega_a}{2\omega_s} + \frac{1}{\pi}\sin\frac{\pi\omega_a}{2\omega_s} \tag{8-58}$$

The interior channels are exposed to flanking channels on each side and hence can suffer interference peaks twice as great as indicated by (8-58). The ratio of maximum peak interference to peak signal therefore becomes

$$\frac{2E_i}{E_s} = \left(2 - \frac{\omega_a}{\omega_s}\right)\cos\frac{\pi\omega_a}{2\omega_s} + \frac{2}{\pi}\sin\frac{\pi\omega_a}{2\omega_s} \tag{8-59}$$

The resulting curve of peak signal pulse to peak interfering pulse, expressed in decibels, is shown in Fig. 8-6 as a function of ω_a/ω_s, the ratio of the carrier-frequency spacing to the baseband width.

Another approach to the optimum filter design for frequency-division multiplex AM channels is to assume a specific type of filter with one or more disposable parameters. One parameter is typically that which determines the bandwidth. All transmitting filters can be assigned the same bandwidth parameter but, of course, must have different midband frequencies. All receiving filters are likewise given a common bandwidth parameter assignment, which, in general, differs from that of the transmitting filters. Such a system typically permits intersymbol interference within the channels as well as interchannel interference. The problem is then to choose the parameter assignments which minimize the sum of the two contributions to interference. The minimization is often done by calculating many cases and comparing the results. We have seen that a rigorously computed optimum filter may be only slightly better in performance than a considerably different filter. Hence, the restriction to one family of filter curves which may not include the best possible characteristic does not necessarily prevent attainment of a very good combination of filters.

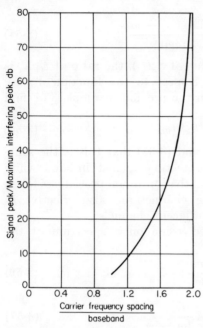

FIG. 8-6. Maximum interference from flanking channels in frequency-division multiplex AM system with optimum filter design.

An example of such a filter study has been published by Marcatili.[2] The filters assumed were either gaussian or an approximation to a three-element maximally flat variety obtained by adding two displaced gaussian curves. In the particular application, the actual filtering was to be accomplished by successive transmissions and reflections in a waveguide structure in which the flanking channels did not contribute equally to interference. There were in effect two equal sources of intersymbol interference, namely—the preceding and succeeding pulses, but there was only one predominant source of interchannel interference. Marcatili's computations therefore allowed 3 db more intersymbol than interchannel interference. His curves are plotted for various interference ratios with abscissas equal to the ratio of transmitting-filter bandwidth to receiving-filter bandwidth and ordinates equal to the ratio of carrier-frequency spacing to receiving-filter bandwidth.   Impulses are assumed as the input pulses to the transmitting filters.

We cannot make an exact comparison of our results with Marcatili's because he always allows a nonzero amount of intersymbol interference, and also because he assumes unsymmetrical filtering of the flanking channels.   In Fig. 3 of his paper, a set of curves is plotted for various fixed values of intersymbol and interchannel interference with approximately 0.8 times the ratio of carrier-frequency spacing to pulse repetition frequency as ordinate and ratio of transmitting to receiving-filter bandwidths as abscissa.   If we consider his curves showing intersymbol interference 30 db down and interchannel interference 27 db down, the minimum ratio of ω_a/ω_s exhibited is 1.35/0.8 or 1.7.   From the curve of Fig. 8-6, it appears that interchannel interference can be made at least 27 db down with $\omega_a = 1.62\omega_s$ and with no intersymbol interference.   Since we have assumed in-phase addition of equal flanking contributions, the individual interfering sidebands are actually 33 db down.   If we had only one interfering sideband, we would read one curve at a 6-db lower ordinate and obtain $\omega_a = 1.52\omega_s$.   Comparison at substantially lower signal-to-intersymbol interference ratios should take into account that if our optimum solution permitted intersymbol interference, the signal pulses could be sent at a faster rate.

8-6 SIGNAL-TO-NOISE RATIO AND ERROR PROBABILITY

When synchronous detection is used, there is a linear relationship between the sideband spectra and the baseband spectrum after demodulation.   Consequently, the signal-to-noise ratio at the input to the slicer, Fig. 8-1, can be calculated by applying the receiving bandpass and postdetection low-pass filter characteristics to the received signal and noise spectra from the line.   The curves previously given in Chap. 7 for probability of error in baseband systems can then be applied.

The relative signal-to-noise performance of three simple types of AM signals is shown in the chart of Fig. 8-7.   The first is a carrier 100 per cent modulated by a sinusoid.   As indicated, the signal consists of full-carrier plus upper- and lower-sideband components.   The second has the carrier suppressed with only the two sideband components remaining.   The third has only one of the sideband components.   By coherent detection the sinusoidal modulation can be recovered from all three of these signals.   The chart indicates the envelope shape of the signal and gives the peak envelope power, the average power, and the peak-to-peak amplitude of the detected signal. The signal is assumed to be coherently detected by multiplication with a ±1 switching function at carrier frequency. The relative noise power in the detected output is also shown, assuming a constant noise density across the band. The last three columns give the relative signal-to-noise ratio of each detected signal and the relative performance under conditions of

Type of AM signal	Signal power		p-p det. signal	Noise Power	Rel. S/N det. signal	Relative S/N performance for equal power	
	Envel. peak	Average				Peak	Average
100 per cent AM signal 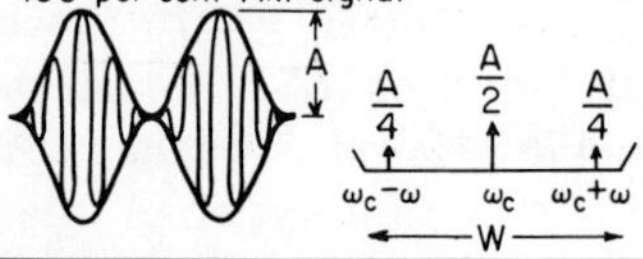 	$A^2/2$	$3A^2/16$	$2A/\pi$	P_N	0.db	0.db	0.db
DSBSC 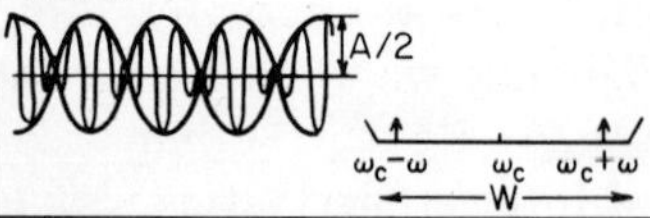 	$A^2/8$	$A^2/16$	$2A/\pi$	P_N	0.db	+6.db	+4.8
SSB 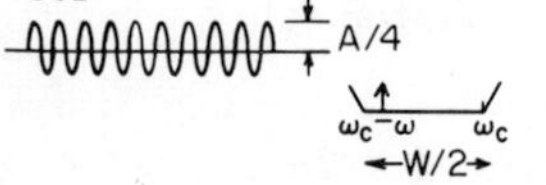 	$A^2/32$	$A^2/32$	A/π	$P_N/2$	−3.db	+9.db	+4.8db
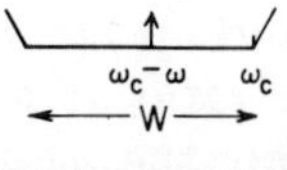	$A^2/32$	$A^2/32$	A/π	P_N	−6.db	+6.db	+1.8db

FIG. 8-7. Relative performance of double-sideband and single-sideband suppressed-carrier AM with respect to 100 per cent AM for sinusoidal modulation.

fixed peak power and of fixed average power. The first-type signal with full carrier is used as the 0 db reference. Two cases of the single-sideband-type signal are given: (1) with the band half the double-sideband width, which reduces the accepted noise power by half, and (2) with the band left the same, which permits the transmission of twice as high a modulating frequency. The comparisons in the last two columns show the significant advantages of suppressing carrier and of using single sideband.

The comparisons of Fig. 8-7 do not apply to a case of random binary signals. In such a case the performance depends on the particular pulse shaping which is used and how the channel shaping is divided between the transmitter and receiver. In the simple examples of Fig. 8-7, no shaping was involved. We shall now discuss the case where random binary signals are transmitted through optimally shaped filters. Specifically we shall consider the case in which cosine filtering of the line signal produces raised-cosine pulse spectra at the detector input. The noise on the line is assumed to be white gaussian.

It is convenient to use the binary polar baseband case as a reference. The simplest modulation system for comparison purposes is ideal single sideband with carrier suppressed. Synchronous detection of the single-sideband wave linearly translates the signal and noise components back to baseband. The ratio of average signal power to average noise power in the baseband must be the same as it would be if straight baseband transmission were used. Hence, the baseband error probability curve for the binary polar case (Fig. 7-11) is also valid for single-sideband suppressed carrier using the same signal pulse shape. The validity can be extended to synchronously detected vestigial-sideband transmission with an optimal receiving filter.

In the double-sideband suppressed-carrier case, the mean total received signal power from the line is twice that for one sideband. Hence, if we specify the same mean total power as for baseband, the mean power in each sideband must be half that of the reference baseband signal. The double-sideband signal occupies twice the baseband width, and hence the receiver must accept twice as much average noise power. The detected contributions from the upper and lower sidebands add in phase to give a baseband signal of twice the amplitude or four times the average power furnished by one sideband. Since each sideband was assumed to have half the mean power of the reference baseband signal, the total mean signal power from the two sidebands is twice that of the baseband signal. Compared with the reference baseband case, the double-sideband case with the same average received power gives twice as much average detected signal power and twice as much average detected noise power. Hence, the baseband signal-to-noise ratio is the same for the two cases. We conclude that the curve of Fig. 7-11 can also be used for double-sideband suppressed carrier.

If the plus and minus carrier pulses are replaced by on-off carrier pulses and synchronous detection is retained, the only change is the added average transmitted power. The effect is the same as that of the d-c component in on-off baseband signaling in that a penalty of 3 db more average signal power is required to obtain the same performance with random data. In the case of AM proper with envelope detection of on-off pulses, however, nonlinear treatment of signal and noise destroys the validity of our previously developed formula for probability of error.   We proceed to give the appropriate modifications.

It will be sufficient here to analyze a simplified version of the problem in which there is no quadrature component.   For the sake of transmission efficiency, we also omit any excess carrier component.   Accordingly, in Eq. (8-44) we set P_0 and $Q(t)$ equal to zero.   In the absence of noise, a threshold decision is made at a time when $P(t)$ reaches a peak value E_s.   The probability of error in the presence of noise is calculated from the probability density function of the envelope ρ defined by

$$\rho^2 = (E_s + x)^2 + y^2 \tag{8-60}$$

where x and y have the independent gaussian probability density functions

$$p(x) = \frac{e^{-x^2/(2\sigma^2)}}{\sigma\sqrt{2\pi}} \qquad p(y) = \frac{e^{-y^2/(2\sigma^2)}}{\sigma\sqrt{2\pi}} \tag{8-61}$$

$$\sigma^2 = 2\int_0^{f_c} w(f + f_c)\, df \tag{8-62}$$

Because of the independence, the joint probability density function of x and y is $p(x)p(y)$.

The form of Eq. (8-60) suggests a transformation from rectangular to polar coordinates setting

$$\begin{aligned} E_s + x &= \rho \cos\phi \\ y &= \rho \sin\phi \end{aligned} \tag{8-63}$$

Then $dx\, dy = \rho\, d\rho\, d\phi$ and the joint probability density function of ρ and ϕ is given by

$$\begin{aligned} q(\rho,\phi) &= \rho p(E_s - \rho \cos\phi) p(\rho \sin\phi) \\ &= \frac{\rho}{2\pi\sigma^2} \exp\left(-\frac{\rho^2 - 2E_s\rho \cos\phi + E_s^2}{2\sigma^2}\right) \qquad \rho > 0 \end{aligned} \tag{8-64}$$

The probability density function $q(\rho)$ for ρ only is found by averaging over all values of ϕ.   We find thus[3]

$$q(\rho) = \int_{-\pi}^{\pi} q(\rho,\phi)\, d\phi = \frac{\rho}{\sigma^2} I_0\left(\frac{E_s\rho}{\sigma^2}\right) \exp\left(-\frac{\rho^2 + E_s^2}{2\sigma^2}\right) \tag{8-65}$$

Here $I_0(z)$ is the zero-order Bessel function of imaginary argument. We note that if no signal is present, we have $E_s = 0$, and the probability density function $q_v(\rho)$ of the envelope of noise alone is thereby found to be

$$q_v(\rho) = \frac{\rho}{\sigma^2} \exp\left(-\frac{\rho^2}{2\sigma^2}\right) \tag{8-66}$$

The probability distribution function $Q_v(\rho)$ for the envelope of noise alone is

$$Q_v(\rho) = \int_0^\rho q_v(\rho)\, d\rho = 1 - e^{-\rho^2/(2\sigma^2)} \tag{8-67}$$

Equations (8-66) and (8-67) define the so-called Rayleigh distribution, which applies to the envelope of symmetrical narrow-band gaussian noise. The distribution function $Q_{vs}(\rho,E_s)$ representing the envelope of the sum of a sine wave and gaussian noise is given by

$$Q_{vs}(\rho,E_s) = \int_0^\rho q(\rho)\, d\rho = \exp\left(-\frac{E_s{}^2}{2\sigma^2}\right) \int_0^{\rho/\sigma} u I_0\left(\frac{E_s u}{\sigma}\right) \exp\left(-\frac{u^2}{2}\right) du \tag{8-68}$$

This distribution function is not simply expressible in terms of tabulated' functions. By successive integration by parts it can be expressed as an infinite series:

$$Q_{vs}(\rho,E_s) = \exp\left(-\frac{E_s{}^2 + \rho^2}{2\sigma^2}\right) \sum_{m=1}^{\infty} \left(\frac{\rho}{E_s}\right)^m I_m\left(\frac{\rho E_s}{\sigma^2}\right) \tag{8-69}$$

The series can be expressed in terms of Lommel's[4] functions of two variables defined by

$$U_n(w,z) = \sum_{m=0}^{\infty} (-)^m \left(\frac{w}{z}\right)^{n+2m} J_{n+2m}(z) \tag{8-70}$$

In this notation

$$Q_{vs}(\rho,E_s) = \exp\left(-\frac{E_s{}^2 + \rho^2}{2\sigma^2}\right)\left[U_2\left(\frac{\rho^2}{j\sigma^2}, \frac{\rho E_s}{\sigma^2}\right) - jU_1\left(\frac{\rho^2}{j\sigma^2}, \frac{\rho E_s}{\sigma^2}\right)\right] \tag{8-71}$$

Bark and Kuznetzov[5] have tabulated the values of the related bivariant cylindrical functions

$$\gamma_1(y,x) = \sum_{n=0}^{\infty} \left(\frac{y}{x}\right)^{2n+1} I_{2n+1}(x) \tag{8-72}$$

$$\gamma_2(y,x) = \sum_{n=0}^{\infty} \left(\frac{y}{x}\right)^{2n+2} I_{2n+2}(x) \tag{8-73}$$

In terms of these functions

$$Q_{vs}(\rho,E_s) = \exp\left(-\frac{E_s{}^2 + \rho^2}{2\sigma^2}\right)\left[\gamma_1\left(\frac{\rho^2}{\sigma^2}, \frac{\rho E_s}{\sigma^2}\right) + \gamma_2\left(\frac{\rho^2}{\sigma^2}, \frac{\rho E_s}{\sigma^2}\right)\right] \tag{8-74}$$

The distribution of the sum of a sine wave and gaussian noise is sometimes called the Rice distribution after S. O. Rice,[6] who studied it extensively. The envelope distribution function $Q_{vs}(\rho,E_s)$ occurs in other statistical problems, and many alternate expressions for it have been found. It can be related to what in radar theory has been called the circular coverage function or Q function[7] defined by

$$Q(a,b) = e^{-a^2/2} \int_b^\infty x e^{-x^2/2} I_0(ax) \, dx \tag{8-75}$$

We establish the relationship from Eq. (8-68) as

$$Q_{vs}(\rho,E_s) = 1 - Q\left(\frac{E_s}{\sigma}, \frac{\rho}{\sigma}\right) \tag{8-76}$$

The Q function has been extensively tabulated and studied. A practical difficulty with the tables is their insufficient coverage in the regions of low probability. Asymptotic expressions are available but their accuracy may be difficult to estimate. For a straightforward numerical evaluation of the Q function, we can replace $I_0(ax)$ by the equivalent integral representation

$$I_0(ax) = \frac{1}{\pi} \int_{-1}^{1} (1 - t^2)^{-1/2} e^{axt} \, dt \tag{8-77}$$

The integration with respect to x can then be performed and the result rearranged to establish the formula

$$Q(a,b) = \exp\left(-\frac{a^2 + b^2}{2}\right) I_0(ab) + \frac{a e^{-a^2/2}}{\sqrt{2\pi}} \int_{-1}^{1} e^{-a^2 z^2/2}$$

$$\text{erfc} \, \frac{b - a\sqrt{1 - z^2}}{\sqrt{2}} \, dz \tag{8-78}$$

Numerical integration to any desired accuracy now presents no difficulty.

The probability of error in the decisions made by a threshold detector following an envelope detector can now be calculated. Suppose the decision threshold is set at kE_s, so that a mark is read if the detector output ρ is greater than kE_s and a space if ρ is less than kE_s. If a space signal is sent, the envelope is that of noise alone with probability distribution function $Q_v(\rho)$ given by (8-67). The signal is erroneously read as a mark if ρ exceeds kE_s. Hence the probability of error in a spacing signal is given by

$$P(M \mid S) = 1 - Q_v(kE_s) = e^{-k^2 E_s^2/(2\sigma^2)} \tag{8-79}$$

If a mark is sent the envelope is that of noise plus signal as specified by the distribution function $Q_{vs}(\rho,E_s)$. The signal is erroneously read as a space if ρ is less than kE_s. Hence the probability of error in a marking signal is

$$P(S \mid M) = Q_{vs}(kE_s,E_s) \tag{8-80}$$

In expressing the signal-to-noise ratio in the input to an envelope detector, it is important to distinguish between "peak instantaneous signal power" and "peak average signal power at the carrier pulse peak." The former is described by a peak signal-to-noise ratio E_s^2/σ^2 and the latter by $E_s^2/(2\sigma^2)$. To avoid confusion we distinguish the two ratios by defining

$$r_1 = \frac{E_s^2}{\sigma^2} \qquad r_2 = \frac{E_s^2}{2\sigma^2} \qquad (8\text{-}81)$$

When these ratios are large compared with unity, the asymptotic expansions for the Bessel functions in (8-69) can be substituted leading to the following approximate result:

$$P(S \mid M) \sim \frac{e^{-(1-k)^2 r_2}}{2(1-k)} \sqrt{\frac{k}{\pi r_2}}$$

$$\times \left[1 - \frac{3 + 6k - k^2}{16k(1-k)^2 r_2} + \cdots \right]$$

$$(8\text{-}82)$$

In contrast to the case of gaussian noise added to a pulse in the input to a threshold device, the two probabilities are not equal when the threshold is set at half the pulse peak. For we observe that if $k = \frac{1}{2}$, the value of $P(M \mid S)$ is greater than $P(S \mid M)$ and hence more errors will occur

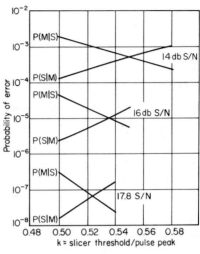

FIG. 8-8. Error rate vs. signal-to-noise ratio at detector input for envelope detection of random binary AM in presence of additive gaussian noise. Abscissa scale also applies to ratio of average signal power on line to average noise power in Nyquist bandwidth on line when optimum receiving filter is used.

$$S/N = 10 \log_{10} E_s^2/(2\sigma^2) = 10 \log_{10} r_2.$$

on spacing signals than on marking signals. If spacing and marking signals are equally likely, the unequal probabilities of error lead to a lowered information rate. The two probabilities can be equalized by increasing the value of k by an amount which depends on the signal-to-noise ratio. In Fig. 8-8 we have plotted $P(M \mid S)$ and $P(S \mid M)$ as functions of k for various fixed values of signal-to-noise ratio. The intersection of the two curves for the same signal-to-noise ratio gives as abscissa the value of k which equalizes the two error rates and as ordinate the actual probability of error when the equalization is attained. Figure 8-9 shows a curve of the required slicer level values vs. signal-to-noise ratio in decibels. The corresponding error probabilities are shown in Fig. 8-10.

We point out that, in general, a nonlinear operation performed on gaussian noise results in a nongaussian noise output. The envelope detector is nonlinear except in limiting special cases. Its response to noise alone has the Rayleigh distribution (8-67), which is the distribution in the radial coordinate for a two-dimensional noise process with independent gaussian distributions of equal variance in two rectangular

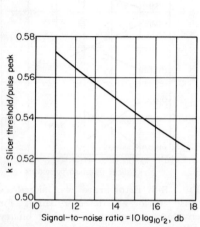

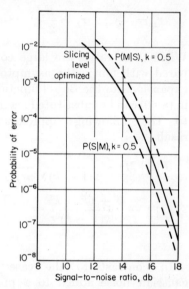

FIG. 8-9. Envelope slicer thresholds for minimum error rate in binary AM with additive gaussian noise. Note: Signal power is defined as average sine-wave power at carrier pulse peak.

FIG. 8-10. Probability of error in envelope detection of binary AM with additive gaussian noise. Note: Signal power is defined as average sine-wave power at carrier pulse peak.

coordinates. The response to noise and signal has the Rice distribution (8-68).

In the results we have obtained so far for the envelope detection of AM, the noise reference is the mean-square value of the noise at the detector input. To compare with the previously given curves for other methods, we should convert to average noise power on the line in a bandwidth equal to either f_s or $f_s/2$. We should also express signal power in terms of average power on the line from a random sequence. As previously pointed out in Sec. 8-4, the monotonic variation of error probability with signal-to-noise ratio makes the same receiving-filter shape optimum for envelope detection as for synchronous detection. Hence on the basis of a raised-cosine spectrum for the carrier pulse envelope at the detector input, the optimum receiving-filter shape is the positive lobe of a cosine function reaching zero at $\omega_c \pm \omega_s$. The exact expression for a raised-cosine spectrum corresponding to a carrier pulse of height E_s is

$$S(\omega) = S_0 \cos^2 \frac{\pi(\omega - \omega_c)}{2\omega_s} \qquad |\omega - \omega_c| < \omega_s \qquad (8\text{-}83)$$

where S_0 is defined by

$$E_s = \frac{1}{\pi} \int_{\omega_c - \omega_s}^{\omega_c + \omega_s} S_0 \cos^2 \frac{\pi(\omega - \omega_c)}{2\omega_s} \, d\omega = 2f_s S_0 \qquad (8\text{-}84)$$

Hence
$$S_0 = \frac{E_s}{2f_s} \qquad (8\text{-}85)$$

The carrier pulse spectrum on the line is then given by

$$A(\omega) = \frac{S(\omega)}{\cos\left[\pi(\omega - \omega_c)/2\omega_s\right]} = \frac{E_s}{2f_s} \cos \frac{\pi(\omega - \omega_c)}{2\omega_0} \qquad (8\text{-}86)$$

The average signal power on the line in a unit resistance circuit is the average square of a random train of on-off carrier pulses having the spectrum $A(\omega)$. Such a pulse train has half as much average power as a random train of plus-and-minus carrier pulses with the same spectrum. The average power in the latter case can be computed by the method used to derive Eqs. (7-17) and (7-18). We thus find for the average signal power in the random on-off carrier pulse sequence

$$W_s = \frac{1}{2} \, 2f_s \frac{E_s^2}{4f_s^2} \int_{f_c - f_s}^{f_c + f_s} \cos^2 \frac{\pi(f - f_c)}{2f_s} \, df = \frac{E_s^2}{4} \qquad (8\text{-}87)$$

If the average noise power in unit bandwidth on the line is w_0, the mean-square noise at the receiving-filter output is given by

$$\sigma^2 = w_0 \int_{f_c - f_s}^{f_c + f_s} \cos^2 \frac{\pi(f - f_c)}{2f_s} \, df = w_0 f_s \qquad (8\text{-}88)$$

The ratio of mean signal power to mean noise power in a bandwidth numerically equal to the bit rate is then

$$M = \frac{W_s}{w_0 f_s} = \frac{E_s^2}{4\sigma^2} = \frac{r_2}{2} \qquad (8\text{-}89)$$

Therefore, if we reduce by 3 db the signal-to-noise ratio scales in terms of r_2, we obtain results in terms of the ratio of average signal power on the line to noise power per bit-rate bandwidth. If the scales in terms of r_2 are left unchanged, the reference becomes the noise power in the Nyquist bandwidth.

Comparing envelope detection with synchronous detection when optimum on-off random binary carrier pulses are transmitted, we see that the envelope detector requires 0.5 db more average signal power to obtain an error probability of 10^{-4}. At higher signal-to-noise ratios and consequently lower probabilities of error, the difference between the two methods becomes smaller.

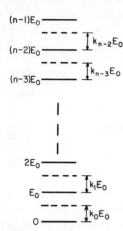

FIG. 8-11. Envelope slicing levels in n-ary AM system.

The considerations of error probability for multilevel baseband signals covered in Chap. 7 apply directly to multilevel AM signals when synchronous detection is used. When envelope detection is used, poorer results are obtained for the lower amplitude levels as may be seen by repeating the analysis which led to Eq. (7-53) with the baseband error probabilities replaced by the appropriate expressions for the envelope case. As shown in Fig. 8-11, let the n signal voltage steps be 0, E_0, $2E_0$, ..., $(n - 1)E_0$, and the slicer threshold levels be set at k_0E_0, $(1 + k_1)E_0$, ..., $(n - 2 + k_{n-2})E_0$, where values of $k_0, k_1, ..., k_{n-2}$ would usually be one-half, but as seen before could be optimized at slightly greater values dependent on the signal-to-noise ratio. Let $P(l \mid m)$ represent the conditional probability that the lth signal level is received given that the mth level is sent. We then calculate:

$$P(0 \mid m) = Q_{vs}(k_0E_0, mE_0)$$
$$P(l \mid m) = Q_{vs}[(l + k_l)E_0, mE_0]$$
$$- Q_{vs}[(l - 1 + k_{l-1})E_0, mE_0] \qquad 1 < l < n - 1$$
$$P(n - 1 \mid m) = 1 - Q_{vs}[(n - 2 + k_{n-2})E_0, mE_0] \qquad (8\text{-}90)$$

The total probability $P_e(m)$ that an error is made in reception when the mth signal is sent is given by

$$P_e(m) = 1 - P(m \mid m) \qquad (8\text{-}91)$$

We note that

$$P_e(0) = 1 - Q_v(k_0E_0) = e^{-k_0^2E_0^2/(2\sigma^2)} \qquad (8\text{-}92)$$

If $k_0 = \frac{1}{2}$ and $E_0 = E_s/(n - 1)$, this reduces to

$$P_e(0) = e^{-E_s^2/[8(n-1)^2\sigma^2]} \qquad (8\text{-}93)$$

The corresponding result for the baseband case with peak voltage range A is

$$P_b(0) = \frac{1}{2}\left[1 - \text{erf}\frac{A}{2(n - 1)\sigma\sqrt{2}}\right] \qquad (8\text{-}94)$$

For small signal-to-noise ratios, $P_e(0)$ approaches unity while $P_b(0)$ approaches one-half.   For large signal-to-noise ratios we can use the asymptotic expansion

$$1 - \operatorname{erf} z \sim \frac{e^{-z^2}}{z\sqrt{\pi}}\left(1 - \frac{1}{2z^2} + \frac{1\cdot 3}{4z^4} - \cdots\right) \tag{8-95}$$

or

$$P_b(0) \sim \frac{(n-1)\sigma\sqrt{\dfrac{2}{\pi}}}{A}e^{-A^2/[8(n-1)^2\sigma^2]} \tag{8-96}$$

If $E_s = A$,

$$P_e(0) \sim \frac{A}{(n-1)\sigma}\sqrt{\frac{\pi}{2}}\,P_b(0) \qquad \text{for } A \gg (n-1)\sigma \tag{8-97}$$

This shows that for high signal-to-noise ratios the probability of error in the envelope detection case becomes much greater for the symbols represented by magnitudes near zero than in the corresponding baseband case.

8-7 EFFECT OF PHASE-FREQUENCY DISTORTION

As discussed in Chap. 6, if the phase characteristic across the transmission band is not linear with respect to frequency, the detected waveform is distorted.   Two general types of nonlinear phase will be considered here, as described by E. D. Sunde.[8]   In one of these the departure from phase linearity has odd symmetry and varies as the cube of the frequency from midband.   The corresponding delay distortion has even symmetry and a square-law variation with frequency.   In the other type it is the departure from phase linearity which has even symmetry and is proportional to the square of the frequency displacement from midband.   This results in the delay distortion having odd symmetry and a linear variation with frequency.   These two types of delay distortion are illustrated in Fig. 8-12.   The ratio of the

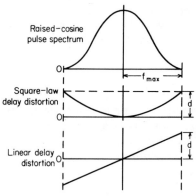

Fig. 8-12. Explanation of notation used in describing delay distortion in bandpass transmission. $d = $ Maximum delay distortion at edge of spectrum, $T = $ Nyquist interval $= 1/f_{\max}$. (*From E. D. Sunde, BSTJ vol. 40, March, 1961, p. 405.*)

delay distortion d at the edge of the band to the Nyquist interval T is taken as a measure of the amount of distortion as indicated in the figure. Figures 8-13 and 8-14 show the effect of these types of delay distortion on double-sideband AM pulses having a raised-cosine spectrum as calculated by Sunde.

The even symmetry of the pulse spectrum about the carrier frequency in the case of double-sideband AM is retained when there is even-symmetry delay distortion. Consequently, the quadrature component

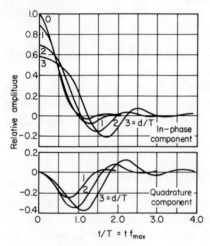

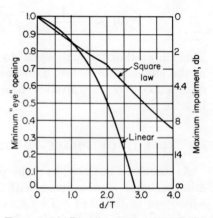

FIG. 8-13. Effect of linear delay distortion on AM pulses with raised-cosine spectrum. (*From E. D. Sunde, BSTJ vol. 40, March, 1961, p. 380.*)

FIG. 8-14. Impairments caused by linear and square-law delay distortion in double-sideband AM system with raised-cosine spectrum and synchronous detection. (*From E. D. Sunde, BSTJ vol. 40, March, 1961, pp. 377 and 381.*)

remains zero. The resulting envelope shapes of pulses subjected to square-law delay distortion are the same as previously shown for baseband pulses in Fig. 7-14. In the case of linear delay distortion, the odd symmetry leads to a quadrature component. The phase of the demodulating carrier can be chosen to make the quadrature component zero at the center of the pulse. Such a choice also gives the maximum amplitude of in-phase component. For this optimum condition the envelope shapes of the in-phase and quadrature components are as shown in Fig. 8-13. The envelope shapes for odd-symmetry delay distortion are symmetrical in time about the nominal pulse peak.

The impairment for both types of delay distortion is shown in Fig. 8-14. The left-hand scale indicates the minimum eye opening as a fraction of the unimpaired opening. The right-hand scale gives the maximum impairment in signal-to-noise ratio in decibels.

REFERENCES

1. Bennett, W. R.: "Electrical Noise," p. 234, McGraw-Hill Book Company, New York, 1960.
2. Marcatili, E. A.: Time and Frequency Crosstalk in Pulse-modulated Systems, *Bell System Tech. J.*, vol. 40, pp. 951–970, May, 1961.
3. Watson, G. N.: "Theory of Bessel Functions," p. 79, Cambridge University Press, London, 1922.
4. *Ibid.*, p. 537.
5. Bark, L. S., and P. E. Kuznetzov: "Tables of Cylindrical Functions of Two Imaginary Arguments," Moscow, 1962.
6. Rice, S. O.: Properties of a Sine Wave plus Random Noise, *Bell System Tech. J.*, vol. 27, pp. 109–157, January, 1948.
7. Marcum, J. I., and P. Swerling: Studies of Target Detection by Pulsed Radar, *IRE Trans. Inform. Theory*, vol. IT-6, pp. 59–267, April, 1960.
8. Sunde, E. D.: Pulse Transmission by AM, FM, and PM in the Presence of Phase Distortion, *Bell System Tech. J.*, vol. 40, pp. 353–422, March, 1961.

CHAPTER 9

FREQUENCY-MODULATION SYSTEMS

In Fig. 9-1 we show the essential parts of an FM data transmission system. The data source typically controls the generation of rectangular on-off pulses. The sharp transitions are rounded off by a low-pass shaping filter, which thereby restricts the extent of the sidebands produced by the modulator. As in AM systems, shaping of the modulating wave is particularly important in controlling foldover about zero frequency. The output of the frequency-modulated

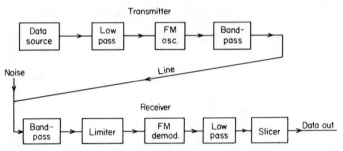

FIG. 9-1. FM data system.

oscillator is a carrier wave varying in frequency in accordance with the ordinates of the baseband modulating wave. The resulting spectrum is trimmed by the transmitting bandpass filter to fit the band allotted to the channel on the line. Line noise and interference outside the band of interest are removed by the receiving bandpass filter. Residual amplitude modulation, which can be caused by band restriction as well as by in-band noise, is removed by a limiter. The resulting constant-amplitude signal applied to the demodulator produces a baseband signal proportional to the instantaneous frequency of the received wave. A receiving low-pass filter removes the out-of-band modulation products and noise. The restored baseband wave is then sliced or sampled as discussed for baseband and AM systems. Certain of these system functions will now be discussed more fully.

164

9-1 FREQUENCY MODULATORS

The function of the frequency modulator is to generate a carrier wave with instantaneous frequency varying linearly with the baseband signal.   If the latter is represented by $s(t)$, the ideal result is generation of a wave

$$E(t) = A_0 \cos \left[\omega_c t + \theta + \lambda \int_{t_0}^{t} s(t) \, dt \right] \qquad (9\text{-}1)$$

where A_0 is the amplitude, ω_c is the unmodulated carrier frequency, θ is the carrier phase with respect to a particular origin of time, t_0 is an arbitrary reference time, and λ is a constant of proportionality. The instantaneous frequency ω_i is defined as the time rate of change of phase and is given by

$$\omega_i = \omega_c + \lambda s(t) \qquad (9\text{-}2)$$

One of the advantages of FM is the independence of recovered signal relative to any reference carrier amplitude or phase.

In the case of amplitude modulation, it was found possible to obtain a relatively simple Fourier-integral representation of the line signal in terms of the Fourier transform of the baseband pulse.   In the case of frequency modulation, there is, in general, no correspondingly simple way of going from the baseband signal to the spectrum of the transmitted FM wave.

The reason for the difficulty is that the wave $E(t)$ of Eq. (9-1) is a nonlinear function of the signal $s(t)$.   Nonlinear operations tend to destroy not only the simplicity but also the usefulness of representations based on decomposition of a signal into additive components.   In a linear case calculations can be facilitated by treating individual components separately and adding the results.   In the nonlinear case such superposition is not valid, and the analytical operations must be performed on the entire signal.

A partially successful way of circumventing the nonlinear problem can be evolved for the particular species of FM transmitters operated by "frequency-shift keying" (FSK).   For example, in the ideal binary FM case in which a switch changes the oscillator frequency abruptly from one value to the other, the output can be synthesized as the sum of two on-off AM waves, one at each carrier frequency.   The response of a linear transmission system can then be evaluated as in AM, the only difference being that there are two sets of sidebands and two carriers to consider instead of a single carrier with its single pair of sidebands.

The AM synthesis method of analyzing FM has been extensively used by Sunde[1] and was illustrated in Chap. 5 as a means of realizing an idealized minimum-bandwidth binary FM system. The method can be extended to a gradual kind of keying in which the two carrier-oscillator outputs are multiplied separately by independent baseband signal waves before being added. To make the results meaningful for FM, the composite wave should exhibit the mark and space frequencies at the proper instants of time.

Sunde analyzed a somewhat different representation of shaped frequency transition in which he added to a steady spacing signal $-\cos[(\omega_c - \omega_d)t + \phi_c]$, a marking pulse of form $\cos[\omega_c t + \phi_c - \phi(t)] + \cos[\omega_c t + \phi_c + \phi(t)]$ confined to a limited time interval. The phase function $\phi(t)$ was so chosen as to achieve the marking frequency $\omega_c + \omega_d$ as the value of the instantaneous frequency of the composite wave at the midpoint of the pulse. Several forms of the function $\phi(t)$ were investigated, and in particular it was shown that if $\phi(t)$ was the integral of a raised-cosine function in time, the requirements for suppression of intersymbol interference could almost be satisfied. It is to be noted that this is a very special kind of shaping which cannot be represented by applying a shaped baseband signal to frequency modulate a single oscillator.

One shortcoming of the synthesis method is that it does not yield a true FM wave as described by Eq. (9-1). When two AM waves are added, the amplitude of the sum is, in general, not constant with time. The resultant is, therefore, a hybrid-modulated wave exhibiting both AM and FM. The amplitude modulation can be suppressed by passing the wave through a limiter, but this is a nonlinear operation bringing in the analytical difficulty previously mentioned. Sunde's analysis assumes that no amplitude limiting exists at the transmitter. He is then able to calculate the effect of a linear combination of transmitting filter, transmission line, and receiving filter by applying the steady-state response-vs.-frequency characteristics to the individual components of the switched AM waves. Amplitude limiting cannot conveniently be inserted in the analysis at any of these steps because the resulting rearrangement of the spectrum is difficult to compute by a straightforward frequency-domain attack.

This is not to say that exact computation with both amplitude limiting and frequency selectivity is impossible. All the necessary calculations are in fact straightforward in concept but typically require machine methods for practical completion in a reasonable amount of time. Given a description of the frequency modulator in the form of a differential equation, for example, we can determine the output wave for a specified baseband signal by either an analog or digital computer.

Such calculations are most conveniently done in the time domain. The nonlinear operation involved in amplitude limiting is readily computed when done numerically. The effect of line filters and transmission media can also be evaluated in the time domain, since these elements can be specified in terms of impulse response just as well as steady-state amplitude and phase vs. frequency. The response is expressed as a convolution integral containing the applied waveform and the impulse response.

Instead of actually keying two oscillators the data signal of most FM transmitters acts on a variable frequency-determining element of a single oscillator. When the carrier frequency is high compared with the modulating frequency, rectangular modulation can be used with negligible foldover effects. Such modulation is easily produced by abruptly changing the value of a reactive element in an oscillating circuit. For instance, an ordinary LC oscillator can have its value of L or C abruptly switched by the data signal. However, an abrupt change in one of these energy-storing elements can result in amplitude and phase changes which lead to distortion. When there are as many as 10 cycles of carrier per bit interval, the distortion is usually acceptable. For very few cycles per bit the frequency modulation can be carried out at a higher frequency and afterward translated down to the desired frequency location. It is possible to devise circuits which switch the frequency of an oscillator without distortion.[2] One of these makes use of a free-running multivibrator with period controlled by biasing voltages or currents without switching of energy-storing elements. The output of the transmitting baseband filter can be inserted as a control bias to produce a gradual transition providing phase continuity and avoiding sideband foldover.

As previously pointed out and as illustrated by example in Chap. 4, the sideband spectra associated with frequency modulation are not linearly related to the modulating baseband spectrum. Analysts tend to seek linearizing approximations for practical operating conditions. One method is the previously described synthesis from amplitude modulation explained by Sunde. Another approach begins with the observations that in binary data transmission the amount of frequency shift between mark and space is usually about equal to the maximum bit rate, and that under these conditions only the carrier and one pair of sidebands have major importance. It would be convenient if these sidebands were linearly related to the signal, for then an analysis could be performed similar to that of AM except for a shift of 90° in the carrier phase. Referring to Eq. (9-1), we observe that a linear relationship between sidebands and signal will approximately hold if the term containing the signal represents a small deviation in phase angle.   This is not the same thing as small frequency deviation, for even if the term $\lambda s(t)$ in Eq. (9-2) is small, a continued repetition of either mark or space frequency integrates to a large phase deviation.   The so-called "low-index" FM case, in which small frequency deviation leads to a single pair of sidebands linearly related to the signal, is not applicable unless the baseband signal reverses polarity often enough to keep the area of the frequency-deviation curve from accumulating to a large value.

In analog transmission systems it has been found advantageous in certain situations to make the frequency deviation much larger than the bandwidth occupied by the baseband signal.   Provided that the required additional bandwidth is available in the transmission medium and provided also that the noise peaks in the wide band are rarely large enough to overload the detector input, an improvement can be obtained in the form of an increased signal-to-noise ratio in the detected analog output wave.   That is, if the amplitude of the FM wave is definitely larger than that of the noise in the transmission medium almost all of the time, an increase in the frequency deviation is practically equivalent to an increase in the carrier amplitude by the same ratio. For binary signals this would be useless because (1) if the carrier amplitude exceeds the noise peaks in a bandwidth sufficient to control intersymbol interference, no errors occur and further noise suppression is unnecessary, and (2) if the noise peaks exceed the carrier amplitude, the increased noise from a widened band would be still more destructive. For n-ary digital signals with $n > 2$, some trade-off between frequency deviation and carrier amplitude becomes possible because of the higher signal-to-noise ratios required.   In the limit as n approaches infinity, the digital and analog signals approach equivalence.

Except for Sunde's special case described in Chap. 5 and the severely restricted low-index case, there is no idealized analytical solution to the shaping problem for FM signals.   In practice the transmitting baseband filter has a gradual roll-off comparable with what would be employed in the corresponding AM situation.   We recall that in AM the highest important baseband frequency was constrained to be less than the carrier frequency in order to avoid sideband foldover.   In the FSK case the synthesis in terms of two AM waves indicates that a similar restriction should apply with the lower of the two carrier frequencies determining the highest baseband frequency to be used. However, Sunde's special case, in which bit rate and peak-to-peak swing are made equal, establishes an effective carrier frequency equal to the average of the two oscillator frequencies.   It is this intermediate value then which governs the permissible baseband width.

9-2 THE LIMITER

The limiter effectively passes only a narrow amplitude slice of the received signal centered about zero amplitude. Thus only the zero-crossing information is preserved. If the carrier frequency is high compared with the modulating frequency, the zero crossings are sufficient to specify the instantaneous frequency of the received signal. For binary data transmission it is sufficient to have at least one zero crossing per signal element.

The limiter output is essentially a square wave and consequently contains odd harmonics as well as the fundamental. The harmonics suffer phase swings and frequency deviations proportional to their order. Thus, in order to separate the fundamental from the third harmonic by filter networks, the frequency deviation of the fundamental from midband must be less than one-half the center frequency. If the limiting does not take place symmetrically about zero, the output also contains some even harmonics. To allow separation of the fundamental from the second harmonic, the frequency deviation of the fundamental from midband must be less than one-third the center frequency. The frequency-modulation detector is usually amplitude sensitive to some degree. The main function of the limiter is to remove the amplitude variations so that the detector can respond only to the frequency variations.

A general mathematical description of an amplitude limiter can be obtained by defining a function

$$y(z) = \begin{cases} K & \cos z > 0 \\ -K & \cos z < 0 \end{cases} \tag{9-3}$$

This function can be represented by a Fourier series in z. It is, in fact, the symmetrical square-wave function previously shown, e.g., Eq. (4-9) with the d-c term subtracted, to be expressible as

$$y(z) = \frac{4K}{\pi} \left[\cos z - \frac{1}{3} \cos 3z + \frac{1}{5} \cos 5z - \cdots \right] \tag{9-4}$$

The resolution is valid for any real variable z. Hence, it holds if we substitute $z = \omega_c t + \phi(t)$. The response of an amplitude limiter to the wave $E(t) = y[\omega_c t + \phi(t)]$ is therefore

$$E_L(t) = \frac{4K}{\pi} \left\{ \cos [\omega_c t + \phi(t)] - \frac{1}{3} \cos 3[\omega_c t + \phi(t)] \right.$$
$$\left. + \frac{1}{5} \cos 5[\omega_c t + \phi(t)] - \cdots \right\} \tag{9-5}$$

The principal restriction necessary to make the amplitude limiter useful in FM detection is that the important frequencies contained in $\cos 3[\omega_c t + \phi(t)]$ must be sufficiently above those in $\cos [\omega_c t + \phi(t)]$ to enable a filter to select the latter component and give the filtered response

$$E_l(t) = \frac{4K}{\pi} \cos [\omega_c t + \phi(t)] \tag{9-6}$$

9-3 IDEAL FREQUENCY DETECTORS

An ideal frequency detector gives a response proportional to the time derivative of the phase of a carrier wave. That is, if the applied wave is represented by

$$E(t) = R(t) \cos [\omega_c t + \phi(t)] \tag{9-7}$$

with $R(t) \geq 0$, the response of an ideal frequency detector is

$$\omega_i(t) = \omega_c + d\phi(t)/dt = \omega_c + \dot{\phi} \tag{9-8}$$

Here we have adopted the customary notation in which the derivative with respect to time is indicated by a dot over the symbol. The constant term equal to the "rest frequency" represents a d-c component of the output not usually of interest. The signal information is contained in the varying component $\dot{\phi}$. It is to be noted, however, that ω_c should be sufficiently large to prevent $\omega_i(t)$ from changing sign and thereby introducing a foldover effect in the recovered signal. If $E(t)$ is of the form (9-1), the ideal detector reproduces the signal $s(t)$.

It is often convenient to resolve the received wave into in-phase and quadrature components relative to some reference carrier frequency ω_c and phase ϕ_c. The resolution is of form

$$E(t) = P(t) \cos (\omega_c t + \phi_c) - Q(t) \sin (\omega_c t + \phi_c) \tag{9-9}$$

By trigonometric manipulation, we can also write

$$E(t) = R(t) \cos [\omega_c t + \phi_c + \phi(t)] \tag{9-10}$$

$$R^2(t) = P^2(t) + Q^2(t) \tag{9-11}$$

$$\tan \phi(t) = \frac{Q(t)}{P(t)} \tag{9-12}$$

An ideal frequency detector then delivers the response

$$\omega_i(t) = \frac{d}{dt} [\omega_c t + \phi_c + \phi(t)]$$

$$= \omega_c + \dot{\phi} = \omega_c + \frac{P\dot{Q} - Q\dot{P}}{P^2 + Q^2} \tag{9-13}$$

Since it is not obvious that practical circuits for frequency detection are in fact phase differentiators, it is important to establish relations between ideal and real models. Also since actual frequency detectors are commonly sensitive to amplitude variations, it will be assumed that all are preceded by an amplitude limiter converting the input to the constant-amplitude form of Eq. (9-6).

9-4 ACTUAL FREQUENCY DETECTORS

There are two general types of circuits used for frequency detection. One of these, known as a zero-crossing, axis-crossing, or cycle-counting detector, derives a baseband component directly from the time rate

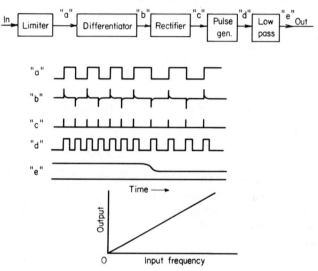

FIG. 9-2. Zero-crossing type demodulator.

of zero crossings. This is done by generating a pulse of fixed length and height at each zero crossing and integrating the pulse train in a low-pass filter to remove those components centered about the pulse-repetition frequency and its harmonics. This method is simple and particularly attractive when the frequency shift is relatively large, since the output is directly proportional to the frequency of the signal. Satisfactory performance of the low-pass filtering requires restriction of the baseband to less than twice the minimum frequency of the FM signal. The zero-crossing type detector is illustrated in Fig. 9-2.

To analyze the zero-crossing detector, let the pulses be of duration τ and height h. The train of pulses is then representable by $x(t)$

defined by

$$x(t) = \begin{cases} h & t_n < t < t_n + \tau \\ 0 & t_n + \tau < t < t_{n+1} \end{cases} \tag{9-14}$$

where t_n represents the values of t such that

$$\omega_c t_n + \phi(t_n) = \frac{(2n + 1)\pi}{2} \tag{9-15}$$

We note that the $(n + 1)$st pulse occurs at t_{n+1} defined by

$$\omega_c t_{n+1} + \phi(t_{n+1}) = \frac{(2n + 3)\pi}{2} \tag{9-16}$$

By subtracting (9-15) from (9-16), we find that

$$\omega_c(t_{n+1} - t_n) + \phi(t_{n+1}) - \phi(t_n) = \pi \tag{9-17}$$

If the phase function $\phi(t)$ can be approximated by a straight line between successive nulls, we can replace $\phi(t_{n+1})$ to within small error by

$$\phi(t_{n+1}) \approx \phi(t_n) + \dot{\phi}(t_n)(t_{n+1} - t_n) \tag{9-18}$$

We then find by substituting this approximation in (9-17)

$$t_{n+1} - t_n \approx \frac{\pi}{\omega_c + \dot{\phi}(t_n)} \tag{9-19}$$

The average value E_D of the pulse train in the detector output over the interval between the beginning points of successive pulses is found by dividing the area τh of one pulse by the length of the interval $t_{n+1} - t_n$. Hence, for the nth interval,

$$E_D \approx \frac{\tau h}{\pi} [\omega_c + \dot{\phi}(t_n)] \tag{9-20}$$

Thus the short-term average value of the detector output tends to follow the derivative of the phase of the input wave. A low-pass filter cutting off between the highest important baseband frequencies and the lower sidebands on the lowest pulse rate gives a short-term average response and hence approximately recovers the original signal. A more exact study of the axis-crossing detector can be done by machine computation. It is evident that the difficulty of recognizing the intended signal frequency must increase as the number of axis crossings per bit decreases, but it is not clear where the onset of failure begins.

The other detection method involves passing the limited signal through a frequency-selective network which introduces an amplitude variation proportional to the instantaneous frequency. The output can then be rectified and filtered to recover the baseband signal. The ideal frequency-selective circuit necessary to recover the instantaneous frequency from $E_1(t)$ is a perfect differentiator followed by an envelope detector or full-wave rectifier. The differentiator yields the wave

$$\frac{d}{dt} E_1(t) = -\frac{4K}{\pi} [\omega_c + \dot{\phi}] \sin (\omega_c t + \phi) \qquad (9\text{-}21)$$

The envelope of this wave is proportional to $\omega_c + \dot{\phi}$ and as explained in Chap. 8 can be separated from other components in the output of a full-wave rectifier by a low-pass filter if the frequencies contained in $\dot{\phi}$ are low compared with those in $\dot{\phi} \cos 2(\omega_c t + \phi)$.

In practical circuits the differentiator is replaced by a tuned circuit with the "rest carrier frequency" ω_c placed in the center of an approximately linear portion of one side of the steady-state response peak. If the instantaneous frequency of the impressed signal changes slowly, we would expect the amplitude of the output to follow the steady-state response amplitude. An amplitude linearly related to the instantaneous frequency is thus approximated. Calculation of the actual response is theoretically straightforward but tends to be laborious without machine computing aids.

One form of such a frequency-discriminating circuit is illustrated in Fig. 9-3. It consists of two tuned circuits which acting in push-pull fashion produce a net detected output which varies nearly linearly with frequency over the band of interest. With perfect matching of the two circuits, the contributions from even-order curvature terms cancel and no d-c response occurs when the carrier frequency is unmodulated. Such an arrangement has response to frequencies well outside the useful linear range and consequently, unless preceded by a bandpass filter, will not be able to attenuate the harmonics in the output of the limiter properly when the frequency swing is relatively large. This restriction can be overcome by translating the signal to a higher frequency before detection. However, the use of the zero-crossing detector in such cases is usually simpler.

The operation of a linear discriminator network at the higher modulation frequencies can be visualized as indicated by the vector diagrams in Fig. 9-3. The sloping characteristic causes the upper- and lower-sideband components to become unequal. This causes amplitude modulation of the envelope. The amount of amplitude variation caused by a specific pair of side frequencies is shown to be proportional to their original amplitudes U and L and to their separation from the carrier ω. Their contribution to the instantaneous frequency variation is also proportional to their original amplitudes and separation from

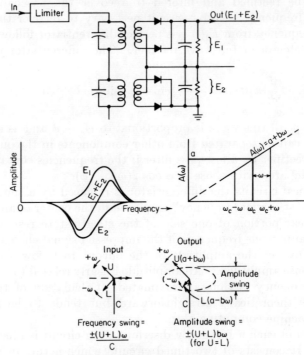

Fig. 9-3. Linear-discriminator-type demodulator.

the carrier. Consequently, the amplitude variation is proportional to the instantaneous frequency.

9-5 ADDITIVE GAUSSIAN NOISE

Since the process of frequency detection is nonlinear, the superposition of gaussian noise on the received FM signal leads, in general, to nongaussian noise in the detector output. In the analysis of FM transmission of analog signals, it is usually considered sufficient to evaluate the ratio of average detected signal power to average detected noise power without much concern over the way the noise magnitudes are distributed. For digital transmission on the other hand, the distribution is all-important because it determines error probability, and the latter is the ultimate criterion of performance. We encountered a similar problem in Sec. 8-6 with envelope detection, which is also nonlinear. There we found that additive gaussian noise in the transmission medium led to a Rayleigh distribution of detected noise samples in the absence of signal and a Rice distribution of resultant samples of signal and noise. Probabilities of error in reading marks and spaces from instantaneous threshold decisions were calculated from these distributions.

Detecting the frequency of the sum of an FM signal wave and gaussian noise can be analyzed in a manner somewhat parallel to our solution for envelope detection of a noisy AM signal. We shall represent the signal wave at the FM detector input in terms of in-phase and quadrature components $P(t)$ and $Q(t)$ with respect to a midband sine wave $\cos \omega_c t$. The gaussian noise is also expressed in terms of in-phase and quadrature components $x(t)$ and $y(t)$ as previously introduced in Eq. (8-43). The complete input to the detector is then of form

$$E_R(t) = [P(t) + x(t)] \cos \omega_c t - [Q(t) + y(t)] \sin \omega_c t \qquad (9\text{-}22)$$

The functions $P(t)$ and $Q(t)$ include the effect of signal pulse shaping, sending filter, transmission line, and receiving filter. As remarked in Sec. 8-4, $x(t)$ and $y(t)$ are gaussian noise waves with spectral densities given by

$$w_x(f) = w_y(f) = w(f_c - f) + w(f_c + f) \qquad (9\text{-}23)$$

where $w(f)$ is the spectral density of the gaussian noise wave received with the signal. By making the reasonable assumption that the function $w(f)$ has even symmetry about the midband frequency f_c, we further simplify the problem because it can be shown that x, y, $\dot{x}$, and $\dot{y}$ are then mutually independent.

Assume an ideal frequency detector which recovers the wave

$$\dot{\phi} = \frac{d}{dt} \arctan \frac{Q + y}{P + x} = \frac{(P + x)(\dot{Q} + \dot{y}) - (Q + y)(\dot{P} + \dot{x})}{(P + x)^2 + (Q + y)^2} \qquad (9\text{-}24)$$

To obtain this result requires good separation between the frequencies contained in $\dot{\phi}$ and those in $\dot{\phi} \cos 2(\omega_c t + \phi)$, as explained in the discussion of Eq. (9-21). Normally P and Q are band-limited to less than ω_c in order to avoid foldover effects. The receiving bandpass filter should perform a similar limiting for x and y. If this amount of limiting is not sufficient to enable isolation of $\dot{\phi}$, a heterodyne process can be used to shift the value of ω_c upward before detecting the frequency. Experience has shown that heterodyning does not usually produce a significant change in practical results.

In binary FM our ultimate interest is only in whether the frequency deviation from ω_c is positive or negative at the sampling instants. To evaluate probability of error, we require the probability that the sign of $\dot{\phi}$ as given by Eq. (9-24) is negative when the original signal called for a positive frequency shift, and also the probability that the sign is positive when a negative shift is intended. We assume that the noise-free wave has not suffered sufficient distortion to falsify the detection and hence that the intended sign of $\dot{\phi}$ is that obtained by removing x, y, $\dot{x}$, and $\dot{y}$ in (9-24). We further note that since the denominator is a sum of squared real quantities it cannot assume negative values. The sign is, therefore, determined by the numerator only.

Let $\qquad x_1 = P + x \qquad$ and $\qquad y_1 = Q + y \qquad$ (9-25)

Then $\qquad \dot{x}_1 = \dot{P} + \dot{x} \qquad\qquad \dot{y}_1 = \dot{Q} + \dot{y} \qquad$ (9-26)

Let $\qquad z = x_1\dot{y}_1 - y_1\dot{x}_1 \qquad$ (9-27)

Our problem is to determine the two probabilities

$$P_1 = \text{Prob } (z < 0 \qquad \text{when} \qquad P\dot{Q} > Q\dot{P}) \qquad (9\text{-}28)$$

$$P_2 = \text{Prob } (z > 0 \qquad \text{when} \qquad P\dot{Q} < Q\dot{P}) \qquad (9\text{-}29)$$

If m_1 is the probability of a positive signal-frequency deviation, the net probability of error in a decision is

$$P_e = m_1 P_1 + (1 - m_1) P_2 \qquad (9\text{-}30)$$

When marking and spacing signals are equally probable, m_1 is equal to one-half and P_e is the average of P_1 and P_2.

The joint distribution of x and y is the product of two independent gaussian distributions. The variance σ_0^2 of each is obtained by integrating the noise spectrum over the band accepted by the detector, which we shall assume to be $f_c - f_0$ to $f_c + f_0$, that is,

$$\sigma_0^2 = 2\int_0^{f_0} w(f_c + f)\,df \qquad (9\text{-}31)$$

When x and y are independent of each other it follows that their derivatives $\dot{x}$ and $\dot{y}$ are also independent of each other. We can also show that x and $\dot{x}$ as well as y and $\dot{y}$ are independent of each other when evaluated at the same instant of time. Independence of x and $\dot{y}$ and of $\dot{x}$ and y follow from our assumed symmetrical spectral density of the received noise. These matters are discussed in the reference previously cited and also in Rice's classic paper on noise.[3] The joint probability density function of x, y, $\dot{x}$, and $\dot{y}$ can therefore be written as the product of four independent gaussian functions, thus

$$p(x,y,\dot{x},\dot{y}) = \frac{1}{4\pi^2\sigma_0{}^2\sigma_1{}^2}\, e^{-(x^2+y^2)/(2\sigma_0{}^2)-(\dot{x}^2+\dot{y}^2)/(2\sigma_1{}^2)} \qquad (9\text{-}32)$$

In Eq. (9-32) σ_1^2 is the variance or mean-square value of either $\dot{x}$ or $\dot{y}$. Since differentiation of a wave with respect to time is equivalent to passing it through a linear network with transmittance $j\omega$, we deduce from Eq. (7-7) that the spectral density of $\dot{x}$ is $4\pi^2 f^2$ times that of x. Hence

$$\sigma_1{}^2 = 8\pi^2 \int_0^{f_0} f^2 w(f_c + f)\, df \qquad (9\text{-}33)$$

The parameters in Eq. (9-32) are thus expressible in terms of the area and moment of inertia of the spectral density of the noise. By substituting the relations (9-25) and (9-26), we obtain the joint probability density function of x_1, y_1, $\dot{x}_1$, and $\dot{y}_1$. The new variables are gaussian with the same variances but with nonzero means P, Q, $\dot{P}$, and $\dot{Q}$ respectively.

Evaluation of the probability of error in terms of a single definite integral can be performed in various ways.[4,5] It turns out that the problem thereby solved is sufficiently general to include many important cases in the binary detection of both frequency- and phase-modulated waves. For economy of future efforts, we formulate the solution in general terms at this point. We can then apply the results to the present problem and to the others as they arise.

9-6 A GENERAL EVALUATION OF ERROR PROBABILITIES IN BINARY ANGLE MODULATION

Let u_1, u_2, u_3, and u_4 represent four independent gaussian variables with average values a_1, a_2, a_3, and a_4 respectively. Let u_1 and u_2 have equal standard deviations σ_a and likewise let u_3 and u_4 have equal standard deviations σ_b. We wish to calculate the probability that the quadratic form $z = u_1 u_4 + u_2 u_3$ has a sign opposite to that of $a_1 a_4 + a_2 a_3$. The solution of this problem applies to the FM case of present interest if we make the following identifications: $u_1 = x_1$, $u_2 = y_1$, $u_3 = -\dot{x}_1$, $u_4 = \dot{y}_1$, $a_1 = P$, $a_2 = Q$, $a_3 = -\dot{P}$, $a_4 = \dot{Q}$, $\sigma_a = \sigma_0$, and $\sigma_b = \sigma_1$.

We note that if u_1 and u_2 are held constant, we can regard z as defined by a linear operation on two independent gaussian variables u_4 and u_3. We can therefore obtain the conditional probability density function $p(z \mid u_1, u_2)$, which is the probability density function for z when u_1 and u_2 are known, by the following properties of gaussian processes:

1. Multiplication of a gaussian variable by a constant results in a new gaussian variable with mean value and standard deviation multiplied by the same constant.

2. Addition of two independent gaussian variables results in a new gaussian variable with mean equal to the sum of the original means and variance equal to the sum of the original variances.

That is, with u_1 and u_2 fixed, z is a gaussian variable with mean value $u_1 a_4 + u_2 a_3$ and variance $(u_1{}^2 + u_2{}^2)\sigma_b{}^2$.   Therefore

$$p(z \mid u_1, u_2) = \frac{1}{\sigma_b[2\pi(u_1{}^2 + u_2{}^2)]^{1/2}} \exp\left[-\frac{(z - a_4 u_1 - a_3 u_2)^2}{2(u_1{}^2 + u_2{}^2)\sigma_b{}^2}\right] \quad (9\text{-}34)$$

The unconditional probability density function of z is found by averaging over all values of u_1 and u_2, thus

$$p(z) = \iint\limits_{-\infty}^{\infty} p(z \mid u_1, u_2)\, p(u_1, u_2)\, du_1\, du_2 \quad (9\text{-}35)$$

where

$$p(u_1, u_2) = \frac{1}{2\pi\sigma_a{}^2} \exp\left[-\frac{(u_1 - a_1)^2 + (u_2 - a_2)^2}{2\sigma_a{}^2}\right] \quad (9\text{-}36)$$

Then if $a_1 a_4 + a_2 a_3$ is positive, the conditional probability of a negative sign for z is

$$P_1 = \int_{-\infty}^{0} p(z)\, dz = \int_{0}^{\infty} p(-z)\, dz \quad (9\text{-}37)$$

The conditional probability P_2 of the opposite kind of crossover in signs is obtained by integrating $p(z)$ from zero to infinity when $a_1 a_4 + a_2 a_3$ is negative. The same formulas are found to apply in both cases, and hence we can identify either P_1 or P_2 with the net probability of error P_e.

The only place in which z occurs in the integration is in the conditional probability density function $p(z \mid u_1, u_2)$. The integration with respect to z is therefore completed by the following step, making the substitution $(z + a_4 u_1 + a_3 u_2)^2 = 2\sigma_b{}^2(u_1{}^2 + u_2{}^2)\lambda^2$.

$$\int_{0}^{\infty} p(-z \mid u_1, u_2)\, dz = \pi^{-1/2} \int_{U(u_1, u_2)}^{\infty} e^{-\lambda^2} d\lambda$$

$$= \tfrac{1}{2} - \tfrac{1}{2}\operatorname{erf} U(u_1, u_2) \quad (9\text{-}38)$$

where

$$U(u_1, u_2) = \frac{a_4 u_1 + a_3 u_2}{\sqrt{2}\,\sigma_b(u_1{}^2 + u_2{}^2)^{1/2}} \quad (9\text{-}39)$$

Substituting these results in the complete integral for P_e and noting that when $p(u_1, u_2)$ is integrated over all values of u_1 and u_2 the result must be unity, because all eventualities are included, we find

$$P_e = \tfrac{1}{2} - \tfrac{1}{2}\iint\limits_{-\infty}^{\infty} p(u_1, u_2)\operatorname{erf} U(u_1, u_2)\, du_1\, du_2 \quad (9\text{-}40)$$

Now transforming to polar coordinates by setting $u_1 = r \cos \phi$, $u_2 = r \sin \phi$, $du_1\, du_2 = r\, dr\, d\phi$, we obtain

$$
1 - 2P_e = \frac{1}{2\pi\sigma_a^2} \exp\left(-\frac{a_1^2 + a_2^2}{2\sigma_a^2}\right)
$$

$$
\int_0^{2\pi} \operatorname{erf} \frac{a_4 \cos \phi + a_3 \sin \phi}{\sqrt{2}\, \sigma_b}\, d\phi
$$

$$
\int_0^\infty \exp\left[-\frac{r^2 - 2r(a_1 \cos \phi + a_2 \sin \phi)}{2\sigma_a^2}\right] r\, dr \qquad (9\text{-}41)
$$

We express the integral with respect to r as the sum of two integrals by subtracting and adding $a_1 \cos \phi + a_2 \sin \phi$ to the linear term in r. One integrand can then be made into a perfect differential giving the value σ_a^2 for its integral. The other integral is expressed in terms of the error function by completing the square in the argument of the exponential. We observe that since the error function is an odd function of its argument, and since the values of both $\cos \phi$ and $\sin \phi$ change sign when ϕ is increased by π, it follows that

$$
\int_0^{2\pi} \operatorname{erf} \frac{a_4 \cos \phi + a_3 \sin \phi}{\sqrt{2}\, \sigma_b}\, d\phi = 0 \qquad (9\text{-}42)
$$

We thereby find

$$
1 - 2P_e = \frac{1}{2\sigma_a\sqrt{2\pi}} \exp\left(-\frac{a_1^2 + a_2^2}{2\sigma_a^2}\right) \int_0^{2\pi} (a_1 \cos \phi + a_2 \sin \phi)
$$

$$
\times \exp \frac{(a_1 \cos \phi + a_2 \sin \phi)^2}{2\sigma_a^2}
$$

$$
\times \operatorname{erf} \frac{a_4 \cos \phi + a_3 \sin \phi}{\sqrt{2}\, \sigma_b}
$$

$$
\times \left(1 - \operatorname{erf} \frac{a_1 \cos \phi + a_2 \sin \phi}{\sqrt{2}\, \sigma_a}\right) d\phi \qquad (9\text{-}43)
$$

The error function in the last bracket does not contribute anything to the value of the integral because it becomes part of a product which changes sign when ϕ is increased by π. The remainder of the integrand repeats its value when ϕ is increased by π, and the limits of integration can be changed to the range $-\pi/2$ to $\pi/2$ by inserting a multiplying factor of 2.

It is convenient at this point to adopt the following notation:

$$
\rho_a^2 = \frac{a_1^2 + a_2^2}{2\sigma_a^2} \qquad\qquad \rho_b^2 = \frac{a_3^2 + a_4^2}{2\sigma_b^2} \qquad (9\text{-}44)
$$

$$
\tan \theta_a = \frac{a_2}{a_1} \qquad\qquad \tan \theta_b = \frac{a_3}{a_4} \qquad (9\text{-}45)
$$

The substitution $\phi = \theta + \theta_a$ now gives the result

$$1 - 2P_e = \frac{\rho_a}{\sqrt{\pi}} \int_{-\pi/2}^{\pi/2} \exp\left(-\rho_a^2 \sin^2 \theta\right) \cos \theta \operatorname{erf}\left[\rho_b \cos\left(\theta + \theta_a - \theta_b\right)\right] d\theta$$

(9-46)

Substituting $x = \sin \theta$ and reducing, we obtain

$$P_e = \frac{1}{2} - \frac{\rho}{2\sqrt{\pi}} \int_{-1}^{1} e^{-\rho^2 x^2} \operatorname{erf}\left[\rho(a\sqrt{1 - x^2} - kx)\right] dx$$

(9-47)

where

$$\rho = \rho_a$$

$$a = \frac{a_1 a_4 + a_2 a_3}{a_1^2 + a_2^2} \frac{\sigma_a}{\sigma_b}$$

(9-48)

$$k = \frac{a_2 a_4 - a_1 a_3}{a_1^2 + a_2^2} \frac{\sigma_a}{\sigma_b}$$

Equation (9-47) has been found to be satisfactory in itself for numerical computations by a digital computer, but further transformation is helpful for studying the limiting form approached for large signal-to-noise ratio. We substitute $\rho x = x'$, drop the prime, replace the error function by its definition as an integral, and obtain

$$P_e = \frac{1}{2} - \frac{1}{\pi} \int_{-\rho}^{\rho} dx \int_{0}^{a\sqrt{\rho^2 - x^2} - kx} \exp\left[-(x^2 + y^2)\right] dy$$

(9-49)

The region of integration in the xy plane is shown in Fig. 9-4. A transformation to polar coordinates gives the equivalent form

$$P_e = \frac{1}{2} - \frac{1}{\pi} \int_{0}^{-\arctan k} d\phi \int_{F(\phi)}^{\rho/\cos \phi} re^{-r^2} dr$$

$$- \frac{1}{\pi} \int_{0}^{\pi - \arctan k} d\phi \int_{0}^{F(\phi)} re^{-r^2} dr$$

$$- \frac{1}{\pi} \int_{\pi - \arctan k}^{\pi} d\phi \int_{0}^{-\rho/\cos \phi} re^{-r^2} dr$$

(9-50)

where

$$F(\phi) = a\rho[(\sin \phi + k \cos \phi)^2 + a^2 \cos^2 \phi]^{-\frac{1}{2}}$$

(9-51)

The integrations with respect to r can be performed, giving the result

$$P_e = \frac{1}{2\pi} \int_{0}^{\pi} \exp\left[-\frac{a^2 \rho^2}{(\sin \phi + k \cos \phi)^2 + a^2 \cos^2 \phi}\right] d\phi$$

$$= \frac{1}{2\pi} \int_{0}^{\pi} \exp\left[-\frac{c^2 \rho^2}{1 + d^2 \cos \theta}\right] d\theta$$

(9-52)

where
$$c^2 = \frac{2a^2}{1 + a^2 + k^2}$$

$$d^2 = \frac{[(a^2 + k^2 - 1)^2 + 4k^2]^{\frac{1}{2}}}{1 + a^2 + k^2}$$

(9-53)

An asymptotic expansion for the value P_e can now be found for the case of ρ large and the values of a and k fixed. We employ the method of steepest descents and write

$$P_e = \frac{1}{2\pi} \int_0^\pi \exp\left[-c^2\rho^2 f(\theta)\right] d\theta$$

(9-54)

where
$$f(\theta) = (1 + d^2 \cos \theta)^{-1}$$

(9-55)

We calculate $f'(\theta) = d^2 f^2(\theta) \sin \theta$, $f'(\theta_0) = 0$ for $\theta_0 = 0$ or π, and $f''(\theta_0) = d^2 f^2(\theta_0) \cos \theta_0$. The proper sign for a decaying exponential is obtained for $\theta_0 = 0$. Expanding the argument of the exponential about this point, we have

$$P_e = \frac{1}{2\pi} \int_0^\pi \exp\left[-\frac{c^2\rho^2}{1 + d^2}\right.$$
$$\left. - \frac{d^2 c^2 \rho^2 \theta^2}{2(1 + d^2)^2} - \cdots\right] d\theta$$

$$\sim \frac{1 + d^2}{2cd\rho\sqrt{2\pi}} \exp\left(-\frac{c^2\rho^2}{1 + d^2}\right)$$

(9-56)

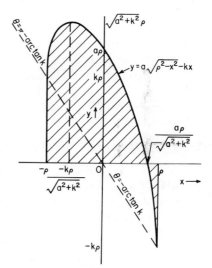

FIG. 9-4. Region of integration in Eq. (9-49).

Equation (9-56) has been found to give a satisfactory approximation for the probability of error in the range of practical interest. In comparing different schemes of detection, it turns out that the coefficient of ρ^2 in the argument of the exponential plays a dominant role. The value of this coefficient in terms of a and k is

$$\frac{c^2}{1 + d^2} = \frac{2a^2}{1 + a^2 + k^2 + [(a^2 + k^2 - 1)^2 + 4k^2]^{\frac{1}{2}}}$$

(9-57)

The exact expression of Eq. (9-52) can be related to various other functions which have been used in noise problems. For example, it is possible to give an evaluation in terms of the Ie function introduced by Rice,[6] thus

$$P_e = \frac{1}{2} - \frac{\sqrt{1-d^2}}{2} \, Ie\left(d^2, \frac{c^2\rho^2}{1-d^4}\right) \tag{9-58}$$

where
$$Ie(y,z) = \int_0^z e^{-x} I_0(yx) \, dx \tag{9-59}$$

The Ie function can in turn be expressed as the difference between two Q functions as follows:

$$\sqrt{\frac{1-y}{1+y}} \, Ie(y,z)$$

$$= Q\left[\sqrt{\frac{z}{2}} \, (\sqrt{1+y} + \sqrt{1-y}), \sqrt{\frac{z}{2}} \, (\sqrt{1+y} - \sqrt{1-y})\right]$$

$$- Q\left[\sqrt{\frac{z}{2}} \, (\sqrt{1+y} - \sqrt{1-y}), \sqrt{\frac{z}{2}} \, (\sqrt{1+y} + \sqrt{1-y})\right] \tag{9-60}$$

The Q function is the one defined by Eq. (8-75). Available tables of the Ie and Q functions do not usually give sufficient coverage for calculation of error rates under conditions of practical interest. Machine calculations from Eq. (9-47) or (9-54) and use of the asymptotic approximation of Eq. (9-56) have been found preferable.

9-7 PROBABILITY OF ERROR IN BINARY FM

We can now apply the general results of the previous section to calculate the probability of error in the detection of a binary FM signal perturbed by additive gaussian noise. The solution is given by P_e of Eq. (9-52) where the parameters have the following values

$$\rho^2 = \frac{P^2 + Q^2}{2\sigma_0{}^2} = \frac{R^2}{2\sigma_0{}^2}$$

$$a = \frac{\sigma_0(P\dot{Q} - \dot{P}Q)}{\sigma_1 R^2} = \frac{\sigma_0 \dot{\phi}}{\sigma_1} \tag{9-61}$$

$$k = \frac{\sigma_0(P\dot{P} + Q\dot{Q})}{\sigma_1 R} = \frac{\sigma_0 \dot{R}}{\sigma_1 R}$$

The parameters have direct physical significance in terms of the signal and noise waves. Since $R^2/2$ is the mean-square value of the carrier wave over a cycle including the sampling instant, the value of ρ^2 can be regarded as the signal-to-noise power ratio at the time of sampling. The value of a is the instantaneous signal frequency deviation from midband multiplied by σ_0/σ_1, the ratio of the rms noise voltage to the rms value of the differentiated noise voltage. The parameter k is obtained by multiplying σ_0/σ_1 by the ratio of the derivative of the signal envelope to the envelope itself at the sampling instant. If the signal envelope is constant, the value of k is zero.

The calculation can be made for any set of samples of P, $\dot{P}$, Q, and $\dot{Q}$. The average error rate for a given sequence depends on the sets of samples which occur. A computer can be programmed to calculate the samples for a specified sequence transmitted over a specified channel and to determine the corresponding error probabilities. In accordance with whatever results are of most interest, we can instruct the computer to average the probabilities or to print out the highest and lowest values. In theory the computations should be made for all sequences to obtain a complete evaluation. Practically a pseudo-random test word of moderate length is sufficient to exhibit all significantly different behavior with weighting corresponding to likelihood of occurrence.

The reason why the expected error rate varies from message to message as well as internally within any one message is that the intersymbol interference produces a variable pedestal for the noise. It is advantageous to keep the intersymbol interference low, but some compromise may be necessary if minimum channel bandwidth is also an objective. Chapter 5 pointed out the difficulties encountered in controlling the overlap of pulse responses in an FM system with restricted bandwidth. As described there Sunde offered a notable exception in the form of a band-limited binary FM channel which achieves freedom from intersymbol interference at the sampling instants. It is instructive to apply the equations for binary FM error probability to a channel such as Sunde proposed.

We recall from Eqs. (5-66), (5-71), and (5-72) that the signal at the detector input of Sunde's FM channel could be expressed by

$$E_2(t) = A \sin \omega_d t \sin \omega_c t + A s_1(t) \cos \omega_c t$$

$$s_1(t) = \sum_{m=-\infty}^{\infty} (-)^m b_m g_1(t - mT)$$

$$g_1(nT) = \delta_{n0} = \begin{cases} 1 & n = 0 \\ 0 & n \neq 0 \end{cases} \tag{9-62}$$

$$\omega_d T = \pi$$

$$T = 1/f_s$$

The first term of $E_2(t)$ can be written in the alternate form

$$A \sin \omega_d t \sin \omega_c t = \frac{A}{2} \cos (\omega_c - \omega_d)t - \frac{A}{2} \cos (\omega_c + \omega_d)t \tag{9-63}$$

There are, therefore, steady-state sine-wave components of the signal with frequencies $\omega_c - \omega_d$ and $\omega_c + \omega_d$ corresponding to the marking and spacing frequencies respectively. The amplitudes of the sine-wave components are each equal to $A/2$. Since sine waves contain no information, their presence constitutes a penalty in average power which the system pays for a useless purpose in the strict information-theoretic sense. Actually these waves are necessary to enable a noncoherent frequency detector to perform its function at the receiver. In theory they could be transmitted at arbitrarily low amplitude over the line. Sharply tuned circuits could then extract the low-level components without accepting appreciable noise. After amplification to the proper strength, they could be reinserted in the signal wave. Such operations are difficult to carry out in practice and tend to destroy the advantage of simplicity, which is one of the strongest reasons for using binary FM. It appears more realistic to regard the sine waves as an inherent part of the FM signal and charge the system for the average power they consume. The advantage attainable by suppressing them will be evaluated and stated separately as a matter of theoretical interest.

The second term of $E_2(t)$ can be regarded as either a binary phase-modulated wave or a polar binary suppressed-carrier AM wave. We could in fact generate binary PM in this manner by removing the mark and space frequency components from the output of a binary FM transmitter. Coherent detection would then be required. The steady-state components play the role of transmitted carrier and enable a noncoherent detector to recover the signal.

We note from Eqs. (9-9) and (9-62)

$$P(t) = As_1(t) \qquad Q(t) = -A \sin \omega_d t$$
$$\dot{P} = A\dot{s}_1 \qquad \dot{Q} = -A\omega_d \cos \omega_d t \tag{9-64}$$

For a sample taken at $t = nT$, the values become

$$P = As_1(nT) = A \sum_{m=-\infty}^{\infty} (-)^m b_m \delta_{n-m,0} = (-)^n b_n A$$

$$\dot{P} = A \sum_{m=-\infty}^{\infty} (-)^m b_m [\dot{g}_1]_{t=(n-m)T}$$

$$Q = -A \sin n\omega_d T = 0$$

$$\dot{Q} = -\omega_d A \cos n\omega_d T = -(-)^n \omega_d A$$

$$\dot{\phi} = \frac{P\dot{Q} - Q\dot{P}}{P^2 + Q^2} = \frac{\dot{Q}}{P} = -\omega_d b_n \tag{9-65}$$

$$\dot{\phi}^2 = \omega_d{}^2$$

$$R^2 = P^2 = A^2$$

$$\dot{R} = \dot{P}$$

The parameters of Eq. (9-61) then assume the following values

$$\rho^2 = \frac{A^2}{2\sigma_0^2}$$

$$a^2 = \frac{\sigma_0^2 \omega_d^2}{\sigma_1^2} \tag{9-66}$$

$$k^2 = \frac{\sigma_0^2 \dot{P}^2}{\sigma_1^2 A^2}$$

It will be noted from Eq. (9-65) that $\dot{P}$ depends on the entire data sequence. Hence the parameter k, which is one of the factors affecting the error probability, is not memory-free in spite of the freedom attained from intersymbol interference in the absence of noise. The nonlinear detection process introduces an interaction between signal and noise which causes the signal history to exert influence on the perturbation of the samples of instantaneous frequency by noise.

Inspection of the asymptotic expansion as exhibited by Eqs. (9-56) and (9-57) for the probability of error at large signal-to-noise ratios shows that the exponent decreases monotonically with k^2. Hence, with the other two parameters fixed, the larger the value of k^2 the larger the error probability becomes. Since ρ^2 and a^2 are independent of the data sequence, we can say that the sequence most vulnerable to error is the one which produces the largest value of $\dot{P}^2$. We proceed to find this largest value for one particular realization of Sunde's system, namely, that in which $g_1(t)$ is the impulse response of a full raised-cosine filter. For this case we set $\omega_x = \omega_1 = \omega_d$ in Eq. (5-28) and apply a constant multiplier to make $g_1(0) = 1$. Then

$$g_1(t) = \frac{\pi^2 \sin 2\omega_d t}{2\omega_d t(\pi^2 - 4\omega_d^2 t^2)} \tag{9-67}$$

$$\frac{d}{dt} g_1(t) = \frac{2\pi^2 \omega_d t(\pi^2 - 4\omega_d^2 t^2) \cos 2\omega_d t - \pi^2(\pi^2 - 12\omega_d^2 t^2) \sin 2\omega_d t}{2\omega_d t^2(\pi^2 - 4\omega_d^2 t^2)^2} \tag{9-68}$$

It follows that

$$\dot{g}_1 = \begin{cases} 0 & \text{at } t = 0 \\ \dfrac{\omega_d}{n\pi(1 - 4n^2)} & \text{at } t = nT, \ n = \pm 1, \pm 2, \ldots \end{cases} \tag{9-69}$$

$$\dot{P} = \frac{(-)^n \omega_d A}{\pi} \sum_{m=1}^{\infty} (-)^m \frac{b_{n-m} - b_{n+m}}{m(1 - 4m^2)} \tag{9-70}$$

The minimum value of $\dot{P}^2$ is obviously zero, which occurs when $b_{n-m} = b_{n+m}$. This is the case in which data symbols equally spaced before and after the one being detected are the same. The largest value of $\dot{P}^2$ occurs when $b_{n+m} = -b_{n-m} = (-)^m$. All the terms in the series then have the same sign. The resulting series can be summed,[7] and we obtain

$$|\dot{P}_{max}| = \frac{2}{\pi} \omega_d A \sum_{m=1}^{\infty} \frac{1}{m(4m^2 - 1)} = \frac{2}{\pi} \omega_d A (\log_e 4 - 1)$$

$$= 2f_s A(\log_e 4 - 1) = 0.7726 f_s A \qquad (9\text{-}71)$$

The upper and lower bounds corresponding to the error rates for the most and least vulnerable data sequence can now be calculated when A, ω_d, σ_0, and σ_1 are given. Averaging over all data sequences is a more formidable task and is not of much practical interest if the two bounds for the error rate are reasonably close together.

The next problem to consider is the design of the receiving filter to minimize the error rate. We note that the situation differs from the previously solved cases in which the detection was linear. We cannot make a simple identification of minimum error rate with minimum ratio of average noise power to average signal power. There are in fact two noise-to-signal ratios to consider since both the incident noise and its derivative enter into the evaluation. Direct optimization procedures lead to considerable complication.

A somewhat roundabout but effective approach can be established by observing that after the value of k^2 corresponding to Eq. (9-71) is substituted, the exponent in (9-56) increases monotonically with either A^2/σ_0^2 or A^2/σ_1^2. Maximization of the exponent is equivalent to minimizing the error rate. Since it is difficult to evaluate the effect of varying σ_0^2 and σ_1^2 simultaneously, we adopt the less direct procedure of optimizing with respect to one of these parameters with the other held constant. The resulting solution can then be subjected to a second optimization by a numerical search for the best value of the parameter held fixed in the first step.

Assume that the receiving filter has the symmetrical transmittance function $Y(f_c + f) = Y^*(f_c - f)$, and let

$$\zeta(f) = |Y(f_c + f)|^2 = |Y(f_c - f)|^2 \qquad (9\text{-}72)$$

Represent the spectral density of the noise on the line by $\xi(f - f_c) = \xi(f_c - f)$. Then noting that in Sunde's system the signal components on the line cannot extend outside the frequency range $f_c - f_s$ to

$f_c + f_s$, we rewrite (9-31) and (9-33) as

$$\sigma_0{}^2 = 2 \int_0^{f_s} \xi(f)\,\zeta(f)\,df$$

$$\sigma_1{}^2 = 8\pi^2 \int_0^{f_s} f^2 \xi(f)\,\zeta(f)\,df \tag{9-73}$$

Adopting a constraint of fixed average signal power on the line, we set

$$A^2 \int_0^{f_s} \frac{|G_1(2\pi f)|^2}{\zeta(f)}\,df = K \tag{9-74}$$

where $G_1(\omega)$ is the Fourier transform of $g_1(t)$. The problem of minimizing $\sigma_0{}^2/A^2$ when $\sigma_1{}^2/A^2$ is given and Eq. (9-74) holds is equivalent to finding the function $\zeta(f)$ which minimizes the value of

$$U = \int_0^{f_s} \xi(f)\,\zeta(f)\,df + \lambda^2 \int_0^{f_s} f^2 \xi(f)\,\zeta(f)\,df + \mu^2 \int_0^{f_s} \frac{|G_1(2\pi f)|^2}{\zeta(f)}\,df \tag{9-75}$$

where λ^2 and μ^2 are Lagrange multipliers. The standard procedures of the calculus of variations give the solution

$$\zeta(f) = \mu\,|G_1(2\pi f)|\,\xi^{-\frac{1}{2}}(f)(1 + \lambda^2 f^2)^{-\frac{1}{2}} \tag{9-76}$$

We then obtain

$$\sigma_0{}^2 = 2\mu \int_0^{f_s} \frac{|G_1(2\pi f)|\,\xi^{\frac{1}{2}}(f)}{(1 + \lambda^2 f^2)^{\frac{1}{2}}}\,df \tag{9-77}$$

$$\sigma_1{}^2 = 8\pi^2 \mu \int_0^{f_s} \frac{f^2\,|G_1(2\pi f)|\,\xi^{\frac{1}{2}}(f)}{(1 + \lambda^2 f^2)^{\frac{1}{2}}}\,df \tag{9-78}$$

The problem is now reduced to finding the value of λ which gives a minimum value for the error probability.

We note from Eq. (9-66) that the value of σ_1 enters only in the parameters a and k, while the parameter ρ is determined by σ_0 only. In the special case of white gaussian noise on the line and a raised-cosine signal spectrum at the detector input, it has been found by computer trial that the error probability is principally sensitive to the value of ρ. To within the limits of practical significance, minimization of σ_0 is then optimum. This means setting $\lambda = 0$. We then obtain the same solution as in the corresponding baseband and AM problems. The transmittance function of the optimum receiving filter becomes a full positive lobe of a cosine function centered at f_c and decreasing to zero at $f_c \pm f_s$. The equations for this near optimum case are

$$\xi(f) = \xi_0 \qquad\qquad \zeta(f) = \mu\xi_0^{-\frac{1}{2}} |G_1(2\pi f)|$$

$$G_1(2\pi f) = \frac{1}{f_s} \cos^2 \frac{\pi f}{2f_s} \tag{9-79}$$

$$\sigma_0^2 = \mu\xi_0^{\frac{1}{2}} \qquad\qquad \sigma_1^2 = \frac{4\mu\xi_0^{\frac{1}{2}} f_s^2}{3} (\pi^2 - 6)$$

As in the previous optimal solutions of Chap. 7, we set M equal to the ratio of average signal power on the line to the average noise power in a band of width numerically equal to the bit rate, that is

$$M = \frac{W_s}{\xi_0 f_s} \tag{9-80}$$

We first calculate the value of W_s contributed by the phase-modulated component of the FM wave. On the assumption that the two steady-state components are transmitted with negligibly small amplitude, we have by extension of Eq. (7-18)

$$W_s = 2f_s A^2 \text{ av } (\cos \omega_c t)^2 \int_0^{f_s} \frac{|G_1(2\pi f)|^2}{\zeta(f)} \, df$$

$$= \frac{f_s A^2 \xi_0^{\frac{1}{2}}}{\mu} \int_0^{f_s} |G_1(2\pi f)| \, df = \frac{f_s A^2 \xi_0^{\frac{1}{2}}}{2\mu} \tag{9-81}$$

Substituting this value of W_s in Eq. (9-80), we obtain

$$\mu = \frac{A^2}{2M\xi_0^{\frac{1}{2}}} \tag{9-82}$$

We thereby deduce the following results

$$\sigma_0^2 = \frac{A^2}{2M} \qquad\qquad \sigma_1^2 = \frac{2A^2}{3M} (\pi^2 - 6)f_s^2$$

$$\rho^2 = M \qquad\qquad a^2 = \frac{3\pi^2}{4(\pi^2 - 6)} = 1.913 \tag{9-83}$$

$$k_{max}^2 = \frac{3(\log_e 4 - 1)^2}{\pi^2 - 6} = 0.1157$$

$$k_{min}^2 = 0$$

The parameters obtained in Eq. (9-83) enable the calculation of the upper and lower bounds of the error probability as a function of M in the somewhat unnatural case in which the steady-state components are not transmitted. To make the solution applicable to true FM detection the average signal power in the steady-state components must be added. At the detector input the sine waves are of amplitude $A/2$ and frequencies $f_c \pm f_s/2$. The required amplitude at the input to the filter is $(A/2)\zeta^{-1/2}(f_s/2)$. Therefore, the mean-square value of the steady-state components on the line is

$$W_{s0} = \frac{2A^2}{8\zeta(f_s/2)} = \frac{A^2 f_s \xi_0^{1/2}}{4\mu \cos^2 \pi/4} = \frac{A^2 f_s \xi_0^{1/2}}{2\mu} \qquad (9\text{-}84)$$

By comparison with Eq. (9-81) we see that the average power in the steady-state components is equal to the average power of the phase-modulated component on the line. Therefore, to include all the power transmitted on the line we should double the value of W_s in (9-81) with the result that we then have

$$\rho^2 = \frac{M}{2} \qquad (9\text{-}85)$$

The penalty in average power ascribable to the steady-state components is 3 db.

Figure 9-5 shows curves of error probability for the system just described. The curve marked "Ideal" holds for synchronous detection of binary AM with carrier suppressed. It is, in fact, the same curve shown for polar baseband transmission in Fig. 7-11. It is also the curve which would be obtained if the steady-state components of the FM wave were suppressed at the transmitter and the remaining part of the wave were then detected synchronously by a local carrier having the midband frequency. The pair of

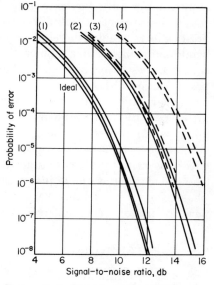

Fig. 9-5. Error probabilities for Sunde's binary FM system with additive gaussian noise. Bounds are for most and least vulnerable sequences. Noise reference is mean noise power in bandwidth equal to bit rate. (1) Optimum filter with suppressed mark and space frequencies. (2) Optimum filter without suppression. (3) Rectangular filter with suppression. (4) Rectangular filter without suppression.

curves designated (1) were calculated by S. Habib on a digital computer for the parameters of (9-83). They show the error rates for the least and most vulnerable data sequences as a function of a signal-to-noise ratio scale appropriate when the steady-state components are suppressed. In the more normal case in which the complete FM wave is transmitted, the signal-to-noise ratio values are increased by 3 db giving the error bounds designated by (2). Curves (3) and (4) show a nonoptimum case in which the receiving band filter has a rectangular characteristic cutting off at $f_c \pm f_s$. The corresponding parameters with all components transmitted are $\rho^2 = 2M/5$, $a^2 = \frac{3}{4}$, and $k_{max}^2 = 3(\log_e 4 - 1)^2/\pi^2$. The penalty for transmitting the sine waves in this case turns out to be 2.2 db instead of 3 db.

In the analysis so far the low-pass postdetection filter has performed no other function than to separate the instantaneous-frequency wave from the higher-frequency components in the output of the frequency demodulator. By further restricting the band of this filter, we can shape the response to obtain a wave different from $\dot\phi$. Some of the noise effects would thereby be removed but the signal component would suffer distortion. Since there are both beneficial and harmful consequences of narrowing the band, it is possible that an optimum postdetection filter which shapes as well as selects $\dot\phi$ could be found in particular cases. Analytical determination of such an optimum runs into a very difficult problem—the probability distribution of a filtered nongaussian process. There is reason to believe that the practical advantage attainable by optimum postdetection shaping compared with observing the instantaneous frequency intact must be small. The calculations we have just presented indicate that detection of the phase derivative attains very nearly the theoretically best possible performance of a coherent receiver.

9-8 IMPULSE NOISE

A general formulation of the effect of impulse noise on an FM signal is complicated because of the great variety of conditions which can occur. The simplest case is that of a single isolated impulse arriving at the detector input through a path with specified amplitude and phase vs. frequency. The path does not necessarily have the same properties as the complete signal channel, since the impulse could enter at various intermediate points. The receiving bandpass filter should always be a part of the path, for there would be an unnecessary penalty incurred if the detector were exposed to interfering components outside the band used for signaling. In general, the interfering input to the detector caused by an impulse of original weight I at time t can be written in the form

$$E_I(t) = Ih(t) = I[h_1(t) \cos \omega_c t - h_2(t) \sin \omega_c t] \qquad (9\text{-}86)$$

where $h(t)$ is the impulse response of the coupling path. The resolution of $h(t)$ into in-phase and quadrature components is obtained from the amplitude function $A(\omega)$ and phase function $B(\omega)$ of the coupling path by writing

$$h(t) = \frac{1}{\pi} \int_0^\infty A(\omega) \cos [t\omega + B(\omega)] \, d\omega$$

$$= \frac{1}{\pi} \int_0^\infty A(\omega) \cos [\omega_c t + t(\omega - \omega_c) + B(\omega)] \, d\omega \qquad (9\text{-}87)$$

from which

$$h_1(t) = \frac{1}{\pi} \int_0^\infty A(\omega) \cos [(\omega - \omega_c)t + B(\omega)] \, d\omega \qquad (9\text{-}88)$$

$$h_2(t) = \frac{1}{\pi} \int_0^\infty A(\omega) \sin [(\omega - \omega_c)t + B(\omega)] \, d\omega \qquad (9\text{-}89)$$

The complete input to the detector from the signal wave and a single impulse at time $t = \tau$ can then be written

$$\begin{aligned} E_r(t) &= P(t) \cos (\omega_c t + \theta) - Q(t) \sin (\omega_c t + \theta) \\ &\quad + I h_1(t - \tau) \cos \omega_c(t - \tau) \\ &\quad - I h_2(t - \tau) \sin \omega_c(t - \tau) \\ &= [P(t) + I h_x(t)] \cos (\omega_c t + \theta) \\ &\quad - [Q(t) + I h_y(t)] \sin (\omega_c t + \theta) \end{aligned} \qquad (9\text{-}90)$$

where

$$h_x(t) = h_1(t - \tau) \cos \psi + h_2(t - \tau) \sin \psi \qquad (9\text{-}91)$$

$$h_y(t) = h_2(t - \tau) \cos \psi - h_1(t - \tau) \sin \psi \qquad (9\text{-}92)$$

$$\psi = \omega_c \tau + \theta \qquad (9\text{-}93)$$

The various possible phase relations have been inserted by assuming that the origin of time is chosen with respect to the data wave. The carrier phase angle θ is a property of the frequency-modulation process. The phase of the impulse response is determined by the time of occurrence τ, which is a uniformly distributed random variable. It follows that the angle ψ is uniformly distributed throughout the range 0 to 2π.

The distribution of the impulse weight I requires experimental determination. It has been found in many cases that the probability density function decreases rapidly with increasing I in the region of interest and can be satisfactorily approximated there by a high inverse power law such as $(I/I_0)^{-5}$. The form of the distribution for small I is not of much interest because of the corresponding insignificant threat to the signal. A good fit with experimental data is often furnished by Pareto's distribution:[8,9]

$$1 - P_I(I) = \left(\frac{I_0}{I}\right)^\alpha$$

$$p_I(I) = \frac{\alpha}{I_0} \left[\frac{I_0}{I}\right]^{\alpha+1} \qquad I > I_0, \, \alpha > 0 \qquad (9\text{-}94)$$

Error in binary detection of the instantaneous frequency occurs if the sign of z is opposite to that of $P\dot{Q} - Q\dot{P}$ where

$$
\begin{aligned}
z &= (P + Ih_1 \cos \psi + Ih_2 \sin \psi)(\dot{Q} - I\dot{h}_1 \sin \psi + I\dot{h}_2 \cos \psi) \\
&\quad - (\dot{P} + I\dot{h}_1 \cos \psi + I\dot{h}_2 \sin \psi)(Q - Ih_1 \sin \psi + Ih_2 \cos \psi) \\
&= P\dot{Q} - Q\dot{P} - PI(\dot{h}_1 \sin \psi - \dot{h}_2 \cos \psi) - QI(\dot{h}_1 \cos \psi + \dot{h}_2 \sin \psi) \\
&\quad + \dot{P}I(h_1 \sin \psi + h_2 \cos \psi) + \dot{Q}I(h_1 \cos \psi + h_2 \sin \psi) \\
&\quad + (h_1\dot{h}_2 - h_2\dot{h}_1)I^2
\end{aligned}
\tag{9-95}
$$

A considerable simplification results if the impulse coupling path has even symmetry in its amplitude response and odd symmetry in its phase response referred to the midband frequency. Under these conditions $h_2 = 0$, $h = h_1$, and z reduces to

$$
z = P\dot{Q} - Q\dot{P} + Ir \cos \beta
\tag{9-96}
$$

where
$$
r^2 = (h\dot{Q} - \dot{h}Q)^2 + (\dot{h}P - h\dot{P})^2
\tag{9-97}
$$

$$
\beta = \psi - \arctan \frac{\dot{h}P - h\dot{P}}{h\dot{Q} - \dot{h}Q}
\tag{9-98}
$$

The angle β has the same uniform distribution as ψ.

The probability of error in binary FM detection when the data value calls for a positive frequency deviation is given by

$$
P_e = \frac{1}{2\pi} \int_{\pi/2}^{3\pi/2} d\beta \int_{(Q\dot{P}-P\dot{Q})/(r \cos \beta)}^{\infty} p_I(I) \, dI
\tag{9-99}
$$

If the Pareto distribution is assumed for I and if $Q\dot{P} - P\dot{Q} > rI_0$,

$$
P_e = \frac{\alpha\Gamma(\alpha + 1)}{2^{\alpha+1}(\alpha + 1)\Gamma^2\left(\dfrac{\alpha}{2} + 1\right)} \left(\frac{rI_0}{P\dot{Q} - Q\dot{P}}\right)^{\alpha}
\tag{9-100}
$$

The probability of error increases monotonically with the ratio $rI_0/(P\dot{Q} - Q\dot{P})$. We note that a similar calculation for a synchronously detected polar binary AM signal leads to the same result except that the ratio just cited is replaced by hI_0/P. To compare vulnerability of the two systems to impulse noise, we need only compare the two ratios. The larger-valued ratio indicates poorer performance. The maximum sampled response of the FM detector in the absence of noise is obtained by sampling when $Q = 0$, leading to the result

$$
\frac{rI_0}{P\dot{Q} - Q\dot{P}} = \frac{h}{P} \left[1 + \left(\frac{\dot{P}}{\dot{Q}} - \frac{\dot{h}P}{\dot{Q}h}\right)^2\right]^{1/2}
\tag{9-101}
$$

Under these conditions and with the same value of P for both systems, the FM case can certainly be no better than the synchronous polar

AM and will generally be worse. If both systems are constrained to the same average power on the line the value of P must be smaller in the FM case because of the power wasted in the steady marking and spacing components.

We conclude that the error rate of binary FM is, in general, higher than that of coherent binary AM when the two systems are exposed to the same impulse noise environment and are equivalent in terms of average signal power and bit rate. This is illustrative of a generally applicable rule that the error rates of data transmission systems which make independent threshold decisions can be rank-ordered for nearly all noise environments by comparing performances in the presence of additive gaussian noise. Validity of the rule is intuitively credible on the basis that if an error is directly attributable to the size of an individual noise peak, it does not matter to what distribution the noise peak belongs.

If isolated impulses actually contribute an important disturbing factor, it is possible to obtain benefits by methods which do neither good nor harm against gaussian noise. A technique which is often proposed but seldom instrumented is based on dispersing the signal wave in time at the transmitter and reassembling the components in proper order at the receiver. The names "smear-desmear," "chirp," and "sweep-frequency modulation" have been applied to various forms of realization. In a smear-desmear system the sending and receiving terminals are equipped with complementary members of a pair of all-pass networks individually having large variations in envelope delay over the signal band. The signal passes through both networks and in theory should suffer no distortion from their use. An impulse originating on the line passes through only one of the networks and is, therefore, prolonged in duration and reduced in height. If the increase in duration is not so great as to overlap prolonged responses to other impulses, an advantage is obtained in the ratio of peak signal to peak impulse noise at the input to the detector. The distribution of peaks in gaussian noise would be wholly unaffected by an all-pass network since the phases remain random and the spectral density is unchanged.

A possible disadvantage is that the signal waveform on the line is drastically altered. The heavy overlap of responses over a range of signaling intervals generates a wave resembling random noise. The resulting high ratio of peak-to-rms value causes a penalty if the channel is peak-limited since the rms value must be reduced to a lower level than would be allowed for the undistorted signal wave on the line. An alternative available in FM is to use a peak clipper at the cost of some waveform distortion in the restored signal.

Some quantitative experimental results obtained by R. R. Anderson and V. G. Koll on the application of the smear-desmear technique to binary FM data transmission are summarized in Figs. 9-6 to 9-8. Each network contained seventeen all-pass sections producing a total delay variation of 10 msec in the band from 500 to 2,500 cps. The FM data set was operated at 800 and 1,200 bits per second with the marking and spacing frequencies at 1,200 and 2,200 cps respectively. Figure 9-6 shows test runs with and without the networks when gaussian noise was added on the line. If the networks had complemented each other

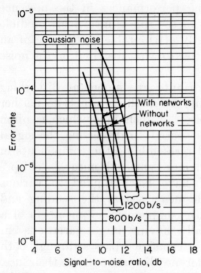

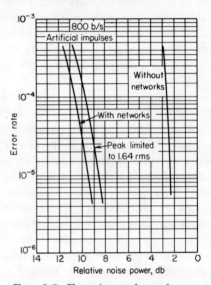

FIG. 9-6. Experimental results in smear-desmear method applied to binary FM with additive gaussian noise.

FIG. 9-7. Experimental results on smear-desmear method applied to binary FM with added artificial impulse noise.

perfectly, their insertion would not have affected the error rate. Residual departures in the actual networks in the band of signal frequencies used produced about 1-db degradation in performance. This is a penalty chargeable to practical instrumentation and could be reduced by a more precise network design. The effect is equivalent to that of added delay distortion in the channel.

The error performance in the presence of artificial impulse noise generated by a relay circuit is shown in Fig. 9-7. The circumstances were favorable to the method in that the repetition rate of the impulses was below that which would cause appreciable overlap of the responses in the output in one of the delay networks. An improvement in the form of an 8-db reduction in signal-to-noise ratio for the same error rate is indicated when the average signal power on the line is the reference. A peak-limiter inserted to maintain the same peak-to-rms signal voltage ratio with and without the smear network reduced the improvement by 1 db. The steepness of these curves results from the use of artificial impulses with uniform height. Figure 9-8 shows curves obtained when a tape recording of noise from an actual telephone channel furnished the added interference. The advantage of the networks was reduced to about 5 db without peak clipping and 4 db with peak clipping. The curves are much less steep than for the artificial impulses. The error rate at fixed signal power shows a reduction by about a factor of 10. The results are consistent with the nature of the actual impulses, which vary in height and spacing.

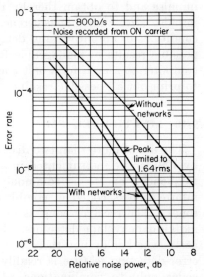

FIG. 9-8. Experimental results on smear-desmear method applied to binary FM with added tape-recorded noise from voice channel.

9-9 TIME JITTER

Quality of an FSK wave is sometimes expressed in terms of variations in the transition instants at which the value of instantaneous frequency crosses the decision threshold. In the binary case the transition instants are those at which the instantaneous frequency deviation from midband is zero. They should occur halfway between sampling times. The amount of departure from the correct crossing times is called "time jitter" or "data distortion." The ratio of departure to the sampling interval represents the jitter as a fraction d. A value of d equal to one-half implies that errors occur in a synchronous system. In a start-stop system a value of one-fourth could cause an error. Jitter furnishes a useful criterion of merit which can be applied under conditions not actually leading to errors. When data transmission links are cascaded without regenerating the timing, the jitter in individual links must be kept sufficiently low to prevent the sum from getting out of bounds.

Both noise and intersymbol interference contribute to jitter. The effects of separate sources are, in general, not directly additive. Jitter in binary FSK systems is determined by the variations in the axis-crossing times of the numerator in the expression previously given for instantaneous frequency. Equating to zero to determine the axis-crossing times leads to a transcendental equation. A more practical approach is to program a computer to calculate the numerator as a function of time with sufficient accuracy to locate the axis crossings. The contribution of intersymbol interference to jitter for various kinds of delay distortion can be evaluated in this way with the signal generated from a representative data sequence. It is also feasible to add an impulse and to obtain thereby the amount of jitter as a function of impulse size, time of occurrence, and carrier phase under specified conditions of amplitude and delay distortion. To keep the volume of possible results in manageable form, it is expeditious to instruct the computer to search for worst combinations of parameters rather than to print out all possible results.

9-10 MULTILEVEL FM

The use of more than two discrete frequencies in digital transmission by FM can be instrumented in a variety of ways. The term "multi-frequency" or MF is commonly applied to a system in which the information is coded in combinations of simultaneously transmitted tones. The receiver consists of parallel bandpass filters followed by individual envelope detectors. Each detector makes a binary decision as to whether or not there is a signal component in its band. An error-detecting feature is readily attainable by assigning information codes only to combinations which contain some fixed number of simultaneous frequencies. Then if the number of detectors giving positive responses in any signaling interval is greater or less than the legitimate number, the receiver does not deliver an accepted symbol for that interval. The frequencies used are sometimes arranged in subgroups as, for example, a so-called 4×4 system in which one frequency is chosen from each of two groups of four. This particular arrangement gives 16 choices in each selection or 4 bits of information.

Since the MF system is equivalent to a number of AM channels in parallel, the various analyses of AM previously given are applicable. The only new features are the constraints imposed on the individual signals. These are the common timing on all channels and the exclusion of some combinations of transmitted signals. The common timing confines the transient splashover among the channels to a segment of time near the transitions. The decisions can then be made under nearly steady-state conditions in all channels, and a resulting relaxation in severity of necessary band filtering can be attained. The restriction on signal combinations sacrifices potential information rate to reduce the risk of accepting wrong information.

Sequential n-ary FM, in which one out of n discrete frequencies is sent during each signaling interval, is the natural extension of binary FM. Figure 9-1 represents a sequential n-ary system if the number of settings on the FM oscillator is increased from two to n. The binary slicer at the receiver is replaced by a multilevel slicer which distinguishes n possible signals. If the data source is binary, translation from binary to n-ary is required ahead of the transmitter and from n-ary to binary after the receiver.

Since frequency detection is inherently a nonlinear process applied to the incident wave, the properties of n-ary FM are not readily deducible from those of the binary case. In the calculation of error probabilities, for example, it is no longer sufficient to distinguish merely between positive and negative values of the detector output. Instead of the probability that the quadratic form $u_1u_4 + u_2u_3$ is negative when the average is positive, we now require the probability that z defined by

$$z = \frac{u_1u_4 + u_2u_3}{u_1{}^2 + u_2{}^2} \tag{9-102}$$

has a value outside the range $z = z_m$ to $z = z_{m+1}$, where z_m and z_{m+1} represent the boundaries allotted to the mth signaling frequency. To evaluate the general n-ary case we require the complete probability distribution $F(z)$.

Balakrishnan and Abrams[4] have given the value of $F(z)$ in terms of an integral for the special case in which the derivative of the signal envelope vanishes at the sampling instants. Their method, which is based on an inverse Fourier transformation applied to the characteristic function of the quadratic form $u_1u_4 + u_2u_3 - zu_1{}^2 - zu_2{}^2$, can presumably be extended to the general case, but not without considerable complication of detail. A general solution in terms of Q functions has recently been found by Salz and Stein.

Stein[10] pointed out that the probability distribution of the quadratic form $u_1u_4 + u_2u_3$ can be reduced to the probability distribution of the difference between two envelopes by the identity

$$u_1u_4 + u_2u_3 = R_1{}^2 - R_2{}^2 \tag{9-103}$$

where
$$R_1{}^2 = \left(\frac{u_1 + u_4}{2}\right)^2 + \left(\frac{u_2 + u_3}{2}\right)^2 \tag{9-104}$$

$$R_2{}^2 = \left(\frac{u_1 - u_4}{2}\right)^2 + \left(\frac{u_2 - u_3}{2}\right)^2 \tag{9-105}$$

The distribution functions of R_1 and R_2 taken separately are known from the results of Chap. 8. This does not immediately solve the problem of finding the probability that $R_1{}^2$ is less than $R_2{}^2$, however, because R_1 and R_2 are not independent. Stein found linear transformations which removed the dependence while retaining the invariance of $u_1u_4 + u_2u_3$. He thereby obtained a solution for the binary FM case in terms of a difference of Q functions.

Salz[11] extended Stein's method to obtain the complete probability distribution of z. The extension is based on first noting that the desired function $F(z)$ can equivalently be expressed as

$$F(z) = \text{prob } [K(u_4 - zu_1)u_1 + K(u_3 - zu_2)u_2 \le 0] \quad (9\text{-}106)$$

where $K > 0$. Let

$$v_1 = K(u_4 - zu_1) \qquad v_2 = K(u_3 - zu_2) \quad (9\text{-}107)$$

Then

$$F(z) = \text{prob } (u_1v_1 + u_2v_2 \le 0) \quad (9\text{-}108)$$

Introduce new variables:

$$\lambda_1 = u_1 + v_1 \qquad \lambda_3 = u_1 - v_1$$
$$\lambda_2 = u_2 + v_2 \qquad \lambda_4 = u_2 - v_2 \quad (9\text{-}109)$$

Then

$$2u_1 = \lambda_1 + \lambda_3 \qquad 2v_1 = \lambda_1 - \lambda_3$$
$$2u_2 = \lambda_2 + \lambda_4 \qquad 2v_2 = \lambda_2 - \lambda_4 \quad (9\text{-}110)$$

and

$$F(z) = \text{prob } (E_1 \le E_2) \quad (9\text{-}111)$$

where

$$E_1 = (\lambda_1{}^2 + \lambda_2{}^2)^{\frac{1}{2}} \qquad E_2 = (\lambda_3{}^2 + \lambda_4{}^2)^{\frac{1}{2}} \quad (9\text{-}112)$$

The λ-variables are gaussian with mean values

$$\text{av } \lambda_1 = (1 - Kz) \text{ av } u_1 + K \text{ av } u_4$$
$$\text{av } \lambda_2 = (1 - Kz) \text{ av } u_2 + K \text{ av } u_3$$
$$\text{av } \lambda_3 = (1 + Kz) \text{ av } u_1 - K \text{ av } u_4$$
$$\text{av } \lambda_4 = (1 + Kz) \text{ av } u_2 - K \text{ av } u_3 \quad (9\text{-}113)$$

It will be found convenient to set

$$a_1{}^2 = (\text{av } \lambda_1)^2 + (\text{av } \lambda_2)^2 \qquad a_2{}^2 = (\text{av } \lambda_3)^2 + (\text{av } \lambda_4)^2 \quad (9\text{-}114)$$

The covariance matrix completing the description of the distribution of the λ-variables is defined by the typical element

$$\text{cov } (\lambda_m, \lambda_n) = \text{av } [(\lambda_m - \text{av } \lambda_m)(\lambda_n - \text{av } \lambda_n)] \quad (9\text{-}115)$$

We have

$$\operatorname{cov}(\lambda_1,\lambda_1) = \operatorname{cov}(\lambda_2,\lambda_2) = (1 - Kz)^2\sigma_0^2 + K^2\sigma_1^2 = s_1^2 \qquad (9\text{-}116)$$

$$\operatorname{cov}(\lambda_3,\lambda_3) = \operatorname{cov}(\lambda_4,\lambda_4) = (1 + Kz)^2\sigma_0^2 + K^2\sigma_1^2 = s_2^2 \qquad (9\text{-}117)$$

$$\operatorname{cov}(\lambda_1,\lambda_2) = \operatorname{cov}(\lambda_1,\lambda_4) = \operatorname{cov}(\lambda_2,\lambda_3) = \operatorname{cov}(\lambda_3,\lambda_4) = 0 \qquad (9\text{-}118)$$

$$\operatorname{cov}(\lambda_1,\lambda_3) = \operatorname{cov}(\lambda_2,\lambda_4) = (1 - K^2z^2)\sigma_0^2 - K^2\sigma_1^2 \qquad (9\text{-}119)$$

It is convenient to let

$$\sigma_s^2 = s_1^2 + s_2^2 \qquad (9\text{-}120)$$

We observe that if we set

$$K^2 = \frac{\sigma_0^2}{\sigma_1^2 + \sigma_0^2 z^2} \qquad (9\text{-}121)$$

the covariances of unlike variables vanish and the λ's become independent gaussian variables. The remainder of the solution is theoretically straightforward since E_1 and E_2 are envelopes of independent processes with distributions expressible by Q functions, that is

$$\operatorname{prob}(E_k < E) = 1 - Q\left(a_k, \frac{E_k}{s_k}\right) \qquad k = 1, 2 \qquad (9\text{-}122)$$

The details are given in the paper by Salz and Stein. The final result is

$$F(z) = \frac{s_2^2}{\sigma_s^2} Q\left(\frac{a_2}{2\sigma_0}, \frac{a_1}{2\sigma_0}\right) + \frac{s_1^2}{\sigma_s^2}\left[1 - Q\left(\frac{a_1}{2\sigma_0}, \frac{a_2}{2\sigma_0}\right)\right] \qquad (9\text{-}123)$$

The result can also be expressed in terms of the Ie function as follows:

$$2F(z) = 1 + Kz \exp\left(-\frac{a_1^2 + a_2^2}{8\sigma_0^2}\right) I_0\left(\frac{a_2}{2\sigma_0}, \frac{a_1}{2\sigma_0}\right)$$

$$+ \frac{a_2 - a_1}{a_2 + a_1} Ie\left(\frac{2a_1a_2}{a_1^2 + a_2^2}, \frac{a_1^2 + a_2^2}{8\sigma_0^2}\right) \qquad (9\text{-}124)$$

REFERENCES

1. Sunde, E. D.: Ideal Binary Pulse Transmission by AM and FM, *Bell System Tech. J.*, vol. 38, pp. 1357–1426, November, 1959.
2. Bowyer, L. R., and W. H. Highleyman: An Analysis of Inherent Distortion in Asynchronous Frequency-shift Modulators, *Bell System Tech. J.*, vol. 41, pp. 1695–1736, November, 1962.
3. Rice, S. O.: Mathematical Theory of Random Noise, *Bell System Tech. J.*, vol. 23, pp. 282–332, July, 1944; vol. 24, pp. 46–156, January, 1945.
4. Balakrishnan, A. V., and I. J. Abrams: Detection Levels and Error Rates in PCM Telemetry Systems, *IRE Intern. Conv. Record*, part 5, pp. 37–55, 1960.

5. Bennett, W. R., and J. Salz: Binary Data Transmission by FM over a Real Channel, *Bell System Tech. J.*, vol. 42, pp. 2387–2426, September, 1963.

6. Rice, S. O.: Properties of a Sine Wave plus Random Noise, *Bell System Tech. J.*, vol. 27, pp. 109–157, January, 1948.

7. Knopp, K.: "Theory and Applications of Infinite Series," Blackie & Son, Ltd., p. 269, London, 1928.

8. Cramér, H.: "Mathematical Methods of Statistics," p. 248, Princeton University Press, Princeton, N.J., 1946.

9. Berger, J. M., and B. Mandelbrot: A New Model for Error Clustering in Telephone Circuits, *IBM J. Res. Develop.*, vol. 7, pp. 224–236, July, 1963.

10. Stein, S.: Unified Analysis of Certain Coherent and Noncoherent Binary Communication Systems, *IEEE Trans. Inform. Theory*, vol. IT-10, pp. 43–51, January, 1964.

11. Salz, J., and S. Stein: Distribution of Instantaneous Frequency for Signal Plus Noise, *IEEE Trans. Inform. Theory*, vol. IT–10, pp. 272–274, October, 1964.

CHAPTER 10

PHASE-MODULATION SYSTEMS

Phase-modulation systems for transmission of digital data usually show more resemblance to AM systems than to FM systems. As previously mentioned, a phase change of $+180°$ cannot be differentiated from a change of $-180°$ unless it takes place slowly enough to indicate the direction of change. For the transmission of a continuous analog quantity, phase changes of any amount could conceivably be used. The signal would be equivalent to an FM wave having an instantaneous frequency equal to the time derivative of the phase. The modulating wave could be recovered by integrating the output of a frequency detector. For digital data, where it is desirable to handle a baseband extending to zero frequency, a direct phase detector is preferable, and only the phase at particular instants of time is of importance. The useful range of phase change then becomes $\pm180°$. Such a signal can be expressed as two double-sideband AM signals at quadrature carrier phase. Indeed such signals are often generated and detected as composite AM signals.

As brought out before, amplitude modulation of a carrier by a polar baseband wave results in plus and minus amplitudes which are the same as carrier phase reversals. Binary phase modulation for optimum results would employ 180° changes and thus would be identical to the case of binary AM with carrier suppressed as covered in Chap. 8. Consequently, we will mainly consider here the case in which there are more than two states and hence more than one bit of information in each Nyquist interval. Since the input and output of a multiphase data system are commonly binary data, it is usual to have the number of phase conditions equal to an integral power of two, such as four or eight to keep the translation simple. With four phases, each interval or symbol carries two bits of information; and with eight phases, each interval carries three bits. Complementary serial-to-parallel and parallel-to-serial conversions are performed at the transmitter and receiver respectively. As in the case of multilevel amplitudes, the Gray code is usually chosen because of fewer bit errors than with natural binary code.

10-1 GENERATION OF PHASE-MODULATION SIGNALS

Figure 10-1 shows how a four-phase signal can be generated by combining two AM waves in quadrature. The binary digits to be transmitted are grouped in pairs. We will designate the first digit in a pair by A and the second digit by B. These A and B digits in polar form are applied simultaneously to linear amplitude modulators.

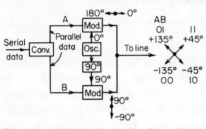

FIG. 10-1. Generation of a four-phase signal.

The A modulator is fed with $0°$ carrier and the B modulator with $90°$ carrier. The A modulator output consists of $0°$ carrier when the A digit is a "1" and $180°$ carrier when the A digit is a "0." Similarly the output of modulator B is a plus or minus $90°$ carrier depending upon whether B is 1 or 0. The modulator outputs are summed to give a four-phase signal. The four possible output phases and their AB-digit combinations are shown in Fig. 10-1. It will be noticed that the two-digit combinations are arranged in a cyclic code so that adjacent steps differ in but one digit. Adjacent codes are separated by $90°$.

In Fig. 10-2 the same general technique is shown expanded to produce an eight-phase signal. In this case the binary digits are grouped in threes, A, B, and C. The third digit C is used to modulate the polar

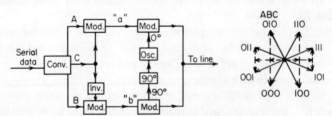

FIG. 10-2. Generation of an eight-phase signal.

A and B digits differentially. The baseband waves at points a and b have four levels, two positive and two negative. When C is a 1, the amplitude of a is greater than that of b. For C a 0, the opposite is true. The four-level polar signals at a and b are used to modulate quadrature carriers as in the four-phase case. The effect of the differential modulation by digit C is of such magnitude as to cause a $\pm22.5°$ shift in the phase of the combined output thus giving a total of eight phases spaced $45°$ apart. The phase positions and their three binary digit designations are shown in the right-hand part of Fig. 10-2. Here again a cyclic code is obtained.

Another possible method of generating a multiphase signal uses phase-shifting networks to obtain sources of each desired phase. Appropriate digital logic and gating circuitry then selects the phase according to the binary combinations of the input data. Still another method generates the various phases by frequency dividing the output of an oscillator running at a multiple of the desired carrier frequency. For example, 45° phase intervals can be obtained by dividing by eight. Proper presetting of the dividing circuitry enables selection of any specific 45° phase.

The signal waves produced by the arrangements of Figs. 10-1 and 10-2 do not have constant amplitude and therefore are not pure phase-modulated signals. However, all restricted-bandwidth angle-modulated signals exhibit AM.

10-2 FIXED-REFERENCE PHASE DETECTION

The changing phase pattern of the signals described in Sec. 10-1 can be detected by comparing the received phase with that of a fixed

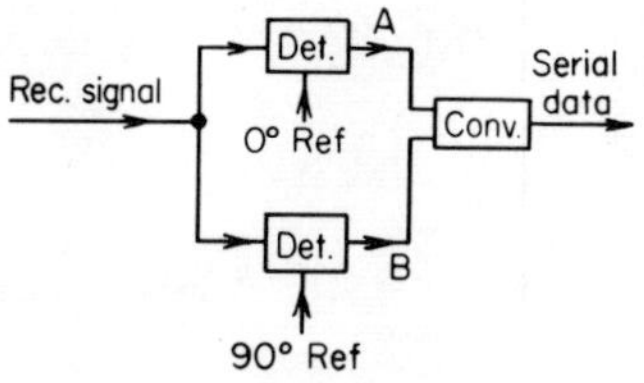

Input phase	Binary code (AB)	A 0° detection	B 90° detection
$+45°$	11	$+$	$+$
$-45°$	10	$+$	$-$
$+135°$	01	$-$	$+$
$-135°$	00	$-$	$-$

Fig. 10-3. Fixed reference detection of a four-phase signal.

reference phase. We will assume for the present that such a reference is available. In Chap. 8 the use of a product modulator was described for detecting AM signals. It was shown to give an output proportional to the signal component in phase with the reference carrier. The output thus varies as the cosine of the angle between the input and the reference carrier and can therefore be used as a phase detector.

Figure 10-3 illustrates a receiver for four-phase signals utilizing a fixed reference. The incoming phases are $\pm45°$ and $\pm135°$. The received signal is applied to two product modulators driven by reference phases of 0° and 90°. The table in Fig. 10-3 shows the relationship between the input phases, their digital assignments, and the polarity of the detector outputs. The 0° reference is seen to detect the A digit, and the 90° reference to detect the B digit. Such a four-phase system as described here is identical to two AM channels operating at quadrature phase to avoid mutual interference. The reference carrier phases correspond to the original carrier phases used in the modulators at the transmitter.

A similar receiving arrangement for eight phases is shown in Fig. 10-4. Here the received signal is assumed to be as generated in Fig. 10-2. It is applied to four product modulators fed with reference carrier at $0°$, $90°$, and $\pm 45°$. The table again shows the relationship

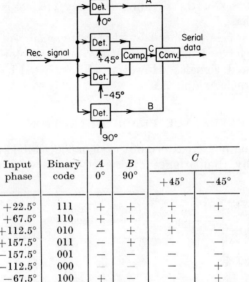

Input phase	Binary code	A $0°$	B $90°$	C	
				$+45°$	$-45°$
$+22.5°$	111	+	+	+	+
$+67.5°$	110	+	+	+	−
$+112.5°$	010	−	+	+	−
$+157.5°$	011	−	+	−	−
$-157.5°$	001	−	−	−	−
$-112.5°$	000	−	−	−	+
$-67.5°$	100	+	−	−	+
$-22.5°$	101	+	−	+	+

FIG. 10-4. Fixed reference detection of an eight-phase signal.

between the input phases, their binary assignment, and the polarity of the modulator outputs. The $0°$ reference detects the A digit. The $90°$ reference detects the B digit. The C digit can be determined by comparing the results obtained with the $\pm 45°$ references. Like polarities indicate a "1" and unlike polarities a "0." The C digit could also be determined from the relative amplitudes of the $0°$ and $90°$ detectors, but the use of the $\pm 45°$ detectors enables the decision to be made by polarity only and is thus insensitive to amplitude variation.

10-3 DIFFERENTIAL PHASE DETECTION

As will be described later, a fixed reference can under certain conditions be maintained from a random sequence of phase-modulated symbols. The receiver has no sense of absolute phase, however, and must be given some initial indication of the correct reference. Because of the difficulties of establishing and maintaining the correct reference phase, it is common practice to encode the information in terms of phase changes and to detect the signal by comparing phases of adjacent symbols. This is often called differential phase detection. For optimum margin against noise, the changes are chosen to space the choices of symbol phase evenly over 360°. In the case of a binary system, the choices should be 180° apart. Phase changes of 0° and 180° or of +90° and −90° are possible choices. In the case of a

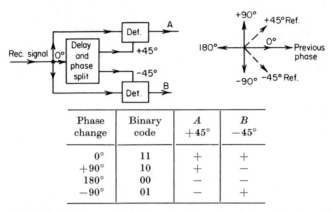

Phase change	Binary code	A +45°	B −45°
0°	11	+	+
+90°	10	+	−
180°	00	−	−
−90°	01	−	+

FIG. 10-5. Differential phase detection of a four-phase signal having changes of 0°, ±90°, and 180°.

quaternary system, the phase changes can be 0°, +90°, −90°, and 180°. The arrangement of Fig. 10-1 together with the proper digital logic to feed the modulators can be used to generate such a signal. It is sometimes desirable to avoid a 0° change by employing phase shifts of ±45° and ±135° for the four possible changes. A total of eight line phases are produced with such changes. Such a signal could be produced by the arrangement of Fig. 10-2 with the proper logical control.

A method of differential phase detection for phase changes of 0°, ±90°, and 180° is shown in Fig. 10-5. The received signal is applied to a broadband delay and phase-splitting network having two outputs with one shifted +45° and the other −45° in phase relative to the input at the carrier frequency. In addition the network has a time delay of one symbol interval. Product demodulators or phase detectors compare the phase at the outputs of the network with that at the input. A vector diagram is given in Fig. 10-5 showing the phase relationships of the previous symbol, the four possible states of the present symbol,

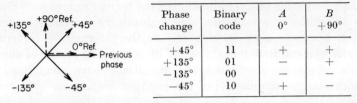

Phase change	Binary code	A 0°	B +90°
+45°	11	+	+
+135°	01	−	+
−135°	00	−	−
−45°	10	+	−

FIG. 10-6. Differential phase detection of a four-phase signal having changes of ±45° and ±135°.

and the two references from the delay network. The table gives the polarities of the demodulator outputs for the four possible phase changes. Also shown are possible binary designations for these changes which result in the demodulator outputs directly representing the A and B digits, thus eliminating the need of any code translation. The vector diagram and table of Fig. 10-6 show how phase changes of ±45° and ±135° can be detected in a similar manner by having the delay network references at 0° and +90°.

The same technique as applied to an octonary signal is shown in Fig. 10-7. Here phase changes of 0°, ±45°, ±90°, ±135°, and 180°

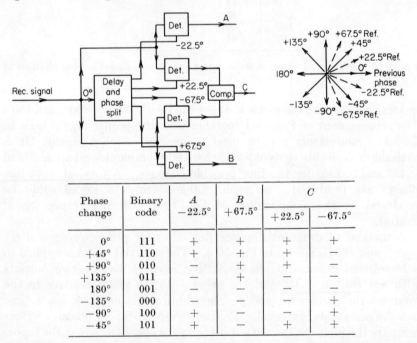

Phase change	Binary code	A −22.5°	B +67.5°	C	
				+22.5°	−67.5°
0°	111	+	+	+	+
+45°	110	+	+	+	−
+90°	010	−	+	+	−
+135°	011	−	+	−	−
180°	001	−	−	−	−
−135°	000	−	−	−	+
−90°	100	+	−	−	+
−45°	101	+	−	+	+

FIG. 10-7. Differential phase detection of an eight-phase signal having changes of 0°, ±45°, ±135°, and 180°.

are assumed. The delay and phase-splitting network provides references at $\pm 22.5°$ and $\pm 67.5°$. Four product demodulators are used.
The table gives the demodulator output polarities for each of the eight
possible phase changes. For the binary designations indicated, it is
seen that the $-22.5°$ reference selects the A digit, the $+67.5°$ reference
the B digit, and a comparison of the likeness of the outputs from the
$-67.5°$ and $+22.5°$ detectors gives the C digit. If phase changes of

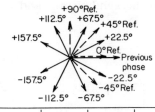

Phase change	Binary code	A $0°$	B $+90°$	C	
				$+45°$	$-45°$
$+22.5°$	111	+	+	+	+
$+67.5°$	110	+	+	+	−
$+112.5°$	010	−	+	+	−
$+157.5°$	011	−	+	−	−
$-157.5°$	001	−	−	−	−
$-112.5°$	000	−	−	−	+
$-67.5°$	100	+	−	−	+
$-22.5°$	101	+	−	+	+

FIG. 10-8. Differential phase detection of an eight-phase signal having changes
of $\pm 22.5°$, $\pm 67.5°$, $\pm 112.5°$, and $\pm 157.5°$.

$\pm 22.5°$, $\pm 67.5°$, $\pm 112.5°$, and $\pm 157.5°$ were used for the eight possibilities, references at $-45°$, $0°$, $+45°$, and $+90°$ would give the same
results as shown by the vector diagram and table of Fig. 10-8.

The four reference phases used in the eight-phase receivers just
described can be derived from a delay network with two outputs
having a quadrature relationship. Figure 10-9 shows a method of
doing this with resistance summing networks. This method also
provides a simple means of adapting a receiver to operate at a different
carrier frequency without redesign of the basic delay and phase-
splitting network. Any desired reference phase can be obtained by the
proper choice of summing resistors.

A shift in carrier frequency at the receiver results in a phase rotation
of the delay-network references. The amount of phase rotation is
determined by the slope of the phase-frequency characteristic, which is
directly related to the network delay. If this rotation is not corrected,

it results in decreased tolerance to interference for some symbols and increases the probability of error. For the amount of frequency offset encountered over telephone voice channels, this effect is relatively small at symbol rates as high as 1,000 per second. For instance, with a delay of 1 msec, a shift of 10 cycles gives a phase shift of 3.6°.

The delay network type of reference has the disadvantage of being somewhat more difficult to adapt to different symbol rates than other methods. However, all phase-modulation systems are usually operated synchronously at a specific symbol rate and consequently are never simple to change.

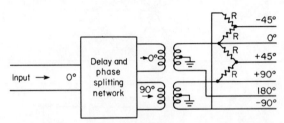

FIG. 10-9. Use of resistance summing networks to derive additional reference phases.

Detection of differential encoding can also be carried out by the receiver arrangements of Figs. 10-3 and 10-4, where fixed phase references are derived from the received signal. In such a case the demodulator outputs need to be processed by digital logic for proper interpretation. Coding of the information in phase change removes the necessity of having the derived phase references start in any specific phase. Also, if they should slip in phase because of interference or a phase jump in the transmission characteristic, the system recovers without aid. Such a fixed reference system also has better margin against noise than a differential detector since the phase references can be heavily filtered to remove noise.

10-4 FILTERING CONSIDERATIONS

The phase-modulation systems previously described use the basic AM techniques which were described in Chap. 8. In the transmitting arrangements of Figs. 10-1 and 10-2, low-pass filters may be placed in the polar baseband inputs to the modulators to control the spectrum and to avoid foldover about zero frequency. A transmitting bandpass filter may also be used, although it is not necessary since the low-pass filters can fully control the desired symmetrical double-sideband spectrum. At the receiver a bandpass filter before demodulation, and low-pass filters after demodulation exclude out-of-band noise and determine the final pulse spectrum. In a fixed-reference system the receiver transmission characteristic can be divided as desired between the bandpass and low-pass filters. As will presently be described, when differential detection is used, the receiver transmission should be determined by the predetection bandpass filter. The optimum filter shapes derived for AM signals based on a raised-cosine spectrum at the demodulator input also apply to these systems.

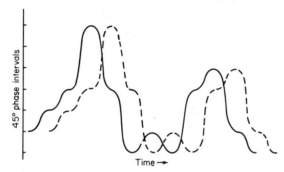

FIG. 10-10. Phase variation with time of a four-phase signal with changes of ±45° and ±135°.

In Chap. 8 it was pointed out in connection with the synchronous detection of AM signals that the carrier frequency must exceed the maximum modulating frequency in order to permit the separation of the desired baseband signal from the higher-frequency products. This is similarly the case for those phase-detection arrangements in which the received signal is synchronously detected by means of a local fixed phase reference. However, in a receiver which compares the phase of adjacent symbol intervals in a product modulator, the carrier frequency should exceed twice the maximum modulating frequency. This comes about because each input to the phase detector consists of an upper and lower sideband about the carrier, and the output contains the sum and difference of these components. Thus for a carrier frequency f_c and a maximum modulation frequency f_s, the maximum difference frequency is $(f_c + f_s) - (f_c - f_s) = 2f_s$, and the minimum sum frequency is $(f_c - f_s) + (f_c - f_s) = 2f_c - 2f_s$. To permit the separation of the sum and difference terms, it is necessary that $(2f_c - 2f_s) > 2f_s$ or $f_c > 2f_s$. The reason for having the postdetection filter accept a frequency of $2f_s$ requires some explanation. The solid curve of Fig. 10-10 shows the phase variation vs. time of a quaternary phase-modulation signal which uses phase changes of ±45° and ±135°.

The dotted curve shows the same phase pattern delayed one symbol interval. The difference in phase between the two curves passes through zero whenever there is a reversal in polarity of the phase change. Figure 10-11 shows the shapes of the possible transitions of differential phase. A linear phase detector preceded by an amplitude limiter would give an eye pattern having transitions as shown in Fig. 10-11. Such severe asymmetry does not occur when limiting is not used, since the signal has amplitude dips which occur simultaneously with the phase changes. The phase detector usually gives zero response for a phase difference of 90°. The amplitude dips result in the curves of Fig. 10-11 being attenuated toward the 90° line in the central region of the figure. The peaking effect at the 0° phase relation is also reduced when the phase detector has a cosine rather than a linear-shaped characteristic. The post-detection filter smoothes out and further reduces the amplitude of these peaks. This variation includes a component of twice the fundamental signaling frequency. If removed by the postdetection filter, it subtracts from the signal amplitude at the sampling points

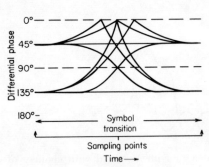

FIG. 10-11. Differential phase transitions of the four-phase signal shown in Fig. 10-10.

and reduces the margin against noise. Consequently, the postdetection filter for differential phase detection should be flat to a frequency equal to $2f_s$.

10-5 NOISE MARGINS

The noise appearing at the output of the low-pass filters in the receiving arrangements of Figs. 10-3 and 10-4 is the same as described for synchronous detection of AM signals in Chap. 8. For a given received peak envelope power, the level of the demodulated signal at the center of the symbol interval can be determined by the phase relationship of the received signal to the reference carrier. All the phase-modulated signals described previously have equal peak envelopes at the center of the symbol intervals. For the four-phase case of Fig. 10-3, there is always a 45° difference between the signal and the reference at the center of the symbol. The demodulated signal has an amplitude proportional to the cosine of the angle and, therefore, has an amplitude of 0.707 times that for a two-phase or suppressed-carrier binary AM system. A four-phase system thus has 3 db less margin to noise than a two-phase system utilizing the same bandwidth and symbol rate. The four-phase system, however, transmits at twice the bit rate of the two-phase system. The probability of bit error is shown in Fig. 10-12. It is assumed that the demodulated signal is sampled at the center of the symbol interval as previously discussed.

In the eight-phase system of Fig. 10-4, the phase angle between the signal and the reference is either $22.5°$ or $67.5°$. Thus the $67.5°$ angle gives a minimum demodulated signal at the center of the symbol of 0.383 times that for the two-phase case. This corresponds to a maximum loss in noise margin of 8.3 db from that of the two-phase system or of 5.3 db from that of the four-phase system. Corresponding comparisons of two-, four-, and eight-level suppressed-carrier AM systems result in a 9.5 db maximum loss in going from two to four levels and 16.9 db maximum loss in going from two to eight levels. The incremental loss upon doubling the number of states approaches 6 db for both systems as the number of states becomes large. For four or eight states, however, there is considerable

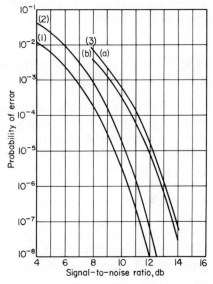

FIG. 10-12. Probability of error in PM systems with additive gaussian noise. Noise reference for f_b transmitted bits per second is mean noise power in bandwidth f_b cps. (1) Coherent binary or quaternary. (2) Differential binary. (3) Differential quaternary: (a) symbol error rate; (b) bit error rate for binary message with Gray code translation.

advantage in multiphase over multi-amplitude encoding. The average loss in noise margin with random signaling is somewhat less than the maximum values just given. The comparison in probability of bit error is shown in Fig. 10-12.

In the receiving methods of Figs. 10-5 and 10-8, where the delay network is used to obtain a reference, the tolerance to noise is lower. This is because of the noise on the reference. As will be shown in the next section, the added loss is only about 1 db for a binary phase-modulation system under typical operating conditions and becomes vanishingly small at very large signal-to-noise ratios. For eight or more phases the loss approaches 3 db. In spite of this impairment, such systems are relatively simple and have the advantage that the reference is available in one symbol interval. A filtered fixed-reference system requires a number of symbol intervals to reach steady state. The probability of bit error with differential phase detection is also given in Fig. 10-12.

10-6 CALCULATION OF ERROR PROBABILITIES IN PM SYSTEMS WITH ADDITIVE GAUSSIAN NOISE

We shall derive here the results previously quoted for probability of error in the presence of gaussian noise. A binary two-phase system with synchronous detection is the same as a polar AM or binary DSBSC-AM system. Hence, the calculations of Chap. 7 suffice. Likewise the case of two binary two-phase signals on quadrature carriers presents no new analytical problem. The cases of differentially detected binary and quaternary PM do, however, require additional study.

The differential binary PM problem can be solved as a special case of the results developed in Chap. 9 for binary angle modulation. The input wave to the detector can be written as

$$V_r(t) = [P(t) + x(t)] \cos \omega_c t - y(t) \sin \omega_c t \qquad (10\text{-}1)$$

The detector operates by multiplying $V_r(t)$ by $V_r(t - T)$, selecting the low-frequency components of the product, and sampling the output at intervals T apart. If we assume $\omega_c T$ is a multiple of 2π and identify quantities evaluated at t-T by the subscript d, the binary decisions are based on the sign of the wave

$$V_a(t) = (P + x)(P_d + x_d) + yy_d \qquad (10\text{-}2)$$

When the correct binary decision is 1, the signs of P and P_d are the same, and an error occurs if the sampled value V_a is negative. When the correct binary decision is 0, the signs of P and P_d are opposite, and an error occurs if the sampled value of V_a is positive. The two cases are symmetric, and an analysis of either suffices. For the case of the symbol 1, $P = P_d$ while for the case of 0, $P = -P_d$.

In calculating the signal-to-noise ratio for the case of a symbol 1, we write

$$V_a = P\left(P + x + x_d + \frac{xx_d + yy_d}{P}\right) \qquad (10\text{-}3)$$

Then if P is large compared with x, x_d, y, and y_d, we approach a condition in which the decisions are based on the sign of $P + x + x_d$. If x and x_d are independent, the sum $x + x_d$ represents samples from random noise with twice as much average power as the samples of either x or x_d alone. This argument appears to indicate a 3-db penalty against differential binary PM compared with synchronous binary PM.

In a direct calculation of error probability, we recognize that the influence of xx_d and yy_d cannot be ignored at the tails of the noise distribution where the errors occur. In particular if x and x_d are both very negative tending to cause an error in a symbol 1, the value of xx_d is large and positive, tending to prevent the threatened damage.

To find the error probability, we compare (10-2) with the quadratic form $z = u_1 u_4 + u_2 u_3$ studied in Sec. 9-6. We note that we have a special case of the previous solution if we make the following identification:

$$z \equiv V_a \qquad u_1 \equiv P + x \qquad u_4 \equiv P_d + x_d$$
$$u_2 \equiv y \qquad u_3 \equiv y_d \tag{10-4}$$

The remainder of the solution proceeds as before if x, y, x_d, and y_d are independent gaussian variables. The independence is guaranteed if the second-order correlation functions vanish at lag time T. A simplification can be made in the present case because the variables x, y, x_d, and y_d all have the same variance. This specialization enables us to set $\sigma_a = \sigma_b = \sigma$. We also have $a_1 = P$, $a_2 = a_3 = 0$, and $a_4 = P_d$. Therefore, from Eqs. (9-44) and (9-48)

$$\rho^2 = \frac{P^2}{2\sigma^2} \qquad a = 1 \qquad k = 0 \tag{10-5}$$

Substituting in Eq. (9-53), we find $c = 1$, $d = 0$. Hence, Eq. (9-52) reduces to

$$P_e = \frac{1}{2} e^{-\rho^2} = \frac{1}{2} \exp\left(-\frac{P^2}{2\sigma^2}\right) \tag{10-6}$$

In the ideal case a bandwidth f_s is sufficient to send signals by binary PM at a rate f_s bits per second without intersymbol interference. This allows for upper and lower sidebands with widths $f_s/2$. If the spectral density of the noise is ξ_0 watts/cps it follows that $\sigma^2 = \xi_0 f_s$. Then M, the ratio of average signal power to the average noise power in a band of width equal to the bit rate, is equal to the ratio of $P^2/2$ to $\xi_0 f_s$, which means $M = \rho^2$. The formula for error probability is thus found to agree with the one given by Lawton.[1,2] Curves for the differential and synchronous cases are given in Fig. 10-12. The former requires average signal power 0.9 db greater than the latter for an error probability of 10^{-4}. The difference in performance between the two cases approaches zero at very high signal-to-noise ratios.

In the differential quaternary PM case we represent the present signal by

$$V_r(t) = (P + x) \cos \omega_c t - (Q + y) \sin \omega_c t \qquad (10\text{-}7)$$

The delayed signal is given by

$$V_d(t) = (P_d + x_d) \cos \omega_c t - (Q_d + y_d) \sin \omega_c t \qquad (10\text{-}8)$$

If these two expressions are multiplied together and only the low-frequency components are retained, we find for the input wave to the slicer:

$$z_1 = (P + x)(P_d + x_d) + (Q + y)(Q_d + y_d) \qquad (10\text{-}9)$$

One set of decisions is made on the basis of the sign of z_1 at the sampling instants.

To complete the determination of the quaternary signal values, the present signal wave is also multiplied by the Hilbert transform of the delayed wave, i.e., by the wave in which all the phases of the components in the delayed wave are shifted 90°. It can be proved that if $x(t)$ and $y(t)$ are band-limited to frequencies of absolute value less than ω_c, the Hilbert transform of $x(t) \cos \omega_c t$ is $x(t) \sin \omega_c t$ and the Hilbert transform of $y(t) \sin \omega_c t$ is $-y(t) \cos \omega_c t$. Hence, the Hilbert transform of $V_d(t)$ is given by

$$\hat{V}_d(t) = (P_d + x_d) \sin \omega_c t + (Q_d + y_d) \cos \omega_c t \qquad (10\text{-}10)$$

By multiplying $V_r(t)$ by $\hat{V}_d(t)$ and selecting the low-frequency components, we obtain the wave

$$z_2 = (P + x)(Q_d + y_d) - (Q + y)(P_d + x_d) \qquad (10\text{-}11)$$

The choice between the four possible values of phase difference—namely $\pm \pi/4$ and $\pm 3\pi/4$—is made from simultaneous determinations of the signs of z_1 and z_2.

The problem now is to calculate the probability that the noise samples x, y, x_d, and y_d cause either or both of the signs of z_1 and z_2 to be reversed from those intended by the data values P, Q, P_d, and Q_d. We assume that the noise samples are mutually independent. By extension of the method employed in Sec. 9-6, we note that if x and y are held fixed, z_1 and z_2 are obtained by a linear transformation of the independent gaussian variables x_d and y_d. Hence the conditional joint probability density function $p(z_1, z_2 \mid x, y)$ is that of a two-dimensional gaussian distribution in z_1 and z_2. The parameters defining this distribution can be obtained from the first- and second-order moments of z_1 and z_2.

With x and y fixed, we calculate

$$\text{av } z_1 = (P + x)P_d + (Q + y)Q_d \qquad (10\text{-}12)$$

$$\text{av } z_2 = (P + x)Q_d - (Q + y)P_d \qquad (10\text{-}13)$$

Let $\qquad u = z_1 - \text{av } z_1 \qquad v = z_2 - \text{av } z_2 \qquad (10\text{-}14)$

Then u and v are gaussian variables with zero mean values. We find

$$u = (P + x)x_d + (Q + y)y_d \qquad (10\text{-}15)$$

$$v = (P + x)y_d - (Q + y)x_d \qquad (10\text{-}16)$$

$$\text{av } u^2 = [(P + x)^2 + (Q + y)^2]\sigma^2 = \text{av } v^2 \qquad (10\text{-}17)$$

where $\qquad \sigma^2 = \text{av } x^2 = \text{av } y^2 = \text{av } x_d{}^2 = \text{av } y_d{}^2 \qquad (10\text{-}18)$

Also since x_d and y_d are independent and both have mean value zero, the average value of $x_d y_d$ is zero. Hence

$$\text{av } (uv) = (P + x)(Q + y)(\text{av } y_d{}^2 - \text{av } x_d{}^2) = 0 \qquad (10\text{-}19)$$

Since there is no term coupling u and v in the probability density function, we can write the desired conditional probability from the standard expression for the joint distribution of two independent gaussian variables. The result can be expressed in the form

$$p(z_1, z_2 \mid x, y) = p_1(z_1 \mid x, y)p_2(z_2 \mid x, y) \qquad (10\text{-}20)$$

$$p_1(z_1 \mid x, y) = \frac{1}{\sigma_{xy}\sqrt{2\pi}} \exp\left[-\frac{(z_1 - \text{av } z_1)^2}{2\sigma_{xy}{}^2}\right] \qquad (10\text{-}21)$$

$$p_2(z_2 \mid x, y) = \frac{1}{\sigma_{xy}\sqrt{2\pi}} \exp\left[-\frac{(z_2 - \text{av } z_2)^2}{2\sigma_{xy}{}^2}\right] \qquad (10\text{-}22)$$

where $\qquad \sigma_{xy}{}^2 = \sigma^2[(P + x)^2 + (Q + y)^2] \qquad (10\text{-}23)$

A complete evaluation of the error probabilities for the four-phase channel requires calculation of all the elements of a 4×4 matrix. The typical element represents the probability that phase m is transmitted and phase n is received. The computation proceeds by inserting the appropriate signal values in the conditional probability density function for z_1 and z_2, averaging over all x and y, and integrating over the values of z_1 and z_2 which define the particular matrix element.

Instead of calculating individual probabilities of the various kinds of errors, we shall evaluate the total probability of error in a choice from the four possible phase differences. We consider the case in which $P = A$, $Q = 0$, $P_d = A/\sqrt{2}$, and $Q_d = A/\sqrt{2}$. This corresponds to a signal phase difference of $\pi/4$, and a correct decision requires the samples of both z_1 and z_2 to be positive. By symmetry the other cases must give the same result. The probability that an erroneous decision is made can be found by subtracting from unity the probability that both z_1 and z_2 are positive. The formula for probability of error therefore becomes

$$P_e = 1 - \frac{1}{2\pi\sigma^2} \iint\limits_{-\infty}^{\infty} \exp\left(-\frac{x^2 + y^2}{2\sigma^2}\right) dx\, dy \int_0^\infty p_1(z_1 \mid x,y)\, dz_1$$

$$\times \int_0^\infty p_2(z_2 \mid x,y)\, dz_2 \quad (10\text{-}24)$$

Inserting the proper expressions for the conditional probabilities and performing the integrations with respect to z_1 and z_2, we obtain

$$P_e = 1 - \frac{1}{8\pi\sigma^2} \iint\limits_{-\infty}^{\infty} \left\{1 + \operatorname{erf} \frac{A(A + x + y)}{2\sigma[(A + x)^2 + y^2]^{1/2}}\right\}$$

$$\times \left\{1 + \operatorname{erf} \frac{A(A + x - y)}{2\sigma[(A + x)^2 + y^2]^{1/2}}\right\} \exp\left(-\frac{x^2 + y^2}{2\sigma^2}\right) dx\, dy \quad (10\text{-}25)$$

Transforming to polar coordinates and performing the integration with respect to the radial coordinate, we find

$$P_e = 1 - \frac{1}{8\pi} \int_{-\pi}^{\pi} \left[1 + \operatorname{erf} \frac{A \cos(\theta - \pi/4)}{\sigma\sqrt{2}}\right]\left[1 + \operatorname{erf} \frac{A \cos(\theta + \pi/4)}{\sigma\sqrt{2}}\right]$$

$$\times \left[\exp\left(-\frac{A^2}{2\sigma^2}\right) + \left(\frac{\pi}{2}\right)^{1/2} \frac{A}{\sigma} \exp\left(-\frac{A^2 \sin^2\theta}{2\sigma^2}\right)\right]$$

$$\times \left(1 + \operatorname{erf} \frac{A \cos\theta}{\sigma\sqrt{2}}\right) \cos\theta\right] d\theta \quad (10\text{-}26)$$

The procedure in going from (10-25) to (10-26) is similar to that used in obtaining (9-43) from (9-40).

To evaluate (10-26) it is convenient to let

$$\rho^2 = A^2/(2\sigma^2) \quad (10\text{-}27)$$

$$f_1(\theta) = \operatorname{erf}\left[\rho \cos(\theta - \pi/4)\right] \quad (10\text{-}28)$$

$$f_2(\theta) = \operatorname{erf}\left[\rho \cos(\theta + \pi/4)\right] \quad (10\text{-}29)$$

$$f_3(\theta) = \operatorname{erf}(\rho \cos\theta) \quad (10\text{-}30)$$

$$f_4(\theta) = \sqrt{\pi}\, \rho \cos\theta \exp(-\rho^2 \sin^2\theta) \quad (10\text{-}31)$$

Then

$$P_e = 1 - \frac{1}{8\pi} \int_{-\pi}^{\pi} [1 + f_1(\theta)][1 + f_2(\theta)]$$

$$\times [e^{-\rho^2} + f_3(\theta)f_4(\theta) + f_4(\theta)]\, d\theta \quad (10\text{-}32)$$

We note that

$$f_k(\theta + \pi) = -f_k(\theta) \qquad k = 1, 2, 3, 4 \tag{10-33}$$

Hence, picking out the factors which contain an even number of sign changes in the two halves of the integration interval, we have

$$P_e = 1 - \tfrac{1}{4} e^{-\rho^2} - \frac{1}{4\pi} \int_0^\pi \{e^{-\rho^2} f_1(\theta) f_2(\theta) + f_3(\theta) f_4(\theta)$$

$$\times [1 + f_1(\theta) f_2(\theta)] + f_4(\theta)[f_1(\theta) + f_2(\theta)]\} \, d\theta \tag{10-34}$$

By the successive substitutions $\theta = \phi + \pi/4$ and $\phi = \lambda + \pi/2$, we find

$$\int_0^\pi f_1(\theta) f_2(\theta) \, d\theta = - \int_{-\pi/4}^{3\pi/4} \mathrm{erf}\,(\rho \cos \phi) \, \mathrm{erf}\,(\rho \sin \phi) \, d\phi$$

$$= - \int_{\pi/4}^{3\pi/4} \mathrm{erf}\,(\rho \cos \phi) \, \mathrm{erf}\,(\rho \sin \phi) \, d\phi$$

$$= \int_{-\pi/4}^{\pi/4} \mathrm{erf}\,(\rho \sin \lambda) \, \mathrm{erf}\,(\rho \cos \lambda) \, d\lambda = 0 \tag{10-35}$$

Also

$$\int_0^\pi f_3(\theta) f_4(\theta) \, d\theta = 2\sqrt{\pi}\rho \int_0^{\pi/2} \mathrm{erf}\,(\rho \sin \theta) \sin \theta \exp\,(-\rho^2 \cos^2\theta) \, d\theta$$

$$= 2\sqrt{\pi}\rho \int_0^1 e^{-\rho^2 x^2} \mathrm{erf}\,[\rho(1 - x^2)^{1/2}] \, dx$$

$$= \pi(1 - e^{-\rho^2}) \tag{10-36}$$

by the result of (9-47) and (9-52) for $a = 1$ and $k = 0$.

Recapitulating,

$$P_e = \frac{3}{4} - \frac{1}{4\pi} \int_0^\pi f_4(\theta)[f_1(\theta) + f_2(\theta) + f_1(\theta) f_2(\theta) f_3(\theta)] \, d\theta$$

$$= \frac{3}{4} - \frac{\rho}{2\sqrt{\pi}} \int_0^1 e^{-\rho^2 x^2} [F_1(x) + F_2(x) + F_1(x) F_2(x) F_3(x)] \, dx$$

$$\tag{10-37}$$

where

$$F_1(x) = \mathrm{erf}\left[\frac{\rho}{\sqrt{2}} (\sqrt{1 - x^2} - x)\right] \tag{10-38}$$

$$F_2(x) = \mathrm{erf}\left[\frac{\rho}{\sqrt{2}} (\sqrt{1 - x^2} + x)\right] \tag{10-39}$$

$$F_3(x) = \mathrm{erf}\,(\rho\sqrt{1 - x^2}) \tag{10-40}$$

For purposes of actual computation it is better to express F_1 and F_2 in terms of the complementary error function erfc $z = 1 - \text{erf } z$. In this notation

$$P_e = \tfrac{1}{2} \text{erfc } \rho + \tfrac{1}{4} e^{-\rho^2}$$

$$+ \frac{\rho}{2\sqrt{\pi}} \int_0^1 e^{-\rho^2 x^2} [(G_1 + G_2)(1 + F_3) - G_1 G_2 F_3] \, dx \quad (10\text{-}41)$$

where

$$G_1 = \text{erfc} \left[\frac{\rho}{\sqrt{2}} \left(\sqrt{1 - x^2} - x \right) \right] \quad (10\text{-}42)$$

$$G_2 = \text{erfc} \left[\frac{\rho}{\sqrt{2}} \left(\sqrt{1 - x^2} + x \right) \right] \quad (10\text{-}43)$$

To express the results in terms of M, we note that it is ideally possible to send a choice of one out of four phases in a time interval equal to the reciprocal of the bandwidth B. Each choice represents two bits of information and hence the bit rate is $2B$. We then have

$$\sigma^2 = \nu_0 B \qquad M = \frac{A^2/2}{2\nu_0 B} \quad (10\text{-}44)$$

Hence

$$A^2 = 4\nu_0 B M \qquad \rho^2 = 2M \quad (10\text{-}45)$$

The error-probability curve calculated from Eq. (10-41) is shown as curve 3 of Fig. 10-12. Signal power 2.8 db greater than for the coherent case is found to be necessary at a symbol error rate of 10^{-4}. To find the asymptotic expression at very large signal-to-noise ratio, we observe that all of the terms of (10-41) are ultimately governed by factors of form $\exp(-z^2)$ with z proportional to ρ. In particular the function erfc z becomes asymptotically equal to $\exp(-z^2)/(z\sqrt{\pi})$. It can be verified that the term $G_1 G_2 F_3$ becomes negligibly small compared with $(G_1 + G_2)(1 + F_3)$ and that $1 + F_3$ approaches the value 2 throughout the important part of the integration. We thus find in the limit

$$P_e \sim \frac{e^{-\rho^2}}{4} \left(1 + \frac{2}{\rho\sqrt{\pi}} \right) + \frac{\rho}{\sqrt{\pi}} \int_0^1 e^{-\rho^2 x^2} (G_1 + G_2) \, dx$$

$$= \frac{e^{-\rho^2}}{4} \left(1 + \frac{2}{\rho\sqrt{\pi}} \right) + \frac{\rho}{\sqrt{\pi}} \int_0^1 e^{-\rho^2 x^2} (2 - F_1 - F_2) \, dx$$

$$= \frac{e^{-\rho^2}}{4} \left(1 + \frac{2}{\rho\sqrt{\pi}} \right) + \text{erf } \rho - \frac{\rho}{\sqrt{\pi}} \int_0^1 e^{-\rho^2 x^2} (F_1 + F_2) \, dx$$

$$\sim \frac{e^{-\rho^2}}{4} \left(1 - \frac{2}{\rho\sqrt{\pi}} \right) + 2P_{0e} \quad (10\text{-}46)$$

where

$$P_{0e} = \frac{1}{2} - \frac{\rho}{2\sqrt{\pi}} \int_{-1}^{+1} e^{-\rho^2 x^2} \operatorname{erf}\left[\frac{\rho}{\sqrt{2}}(\sqrt{1 - x^2} - x)\right] dx \quad (10\text{-}47)$$

The value of P_{0e} is equal to that of the right-hand member of Eq. (9-47) with $a = k = 1/\sqrt{2}$. Hence from (9-53) and (9-56)

$$2P_{0e} \sim \frac{1 + \sqrt{2}}{\rho(\pi\sqrt{2})^{\frac{1}{2}}} \exp\left(-\frac{\rho^2}{2 + \sqrt{2}}\right) \quad (10\text{-}48)$$

When ρ is large this term is dominant over the other term in (10-46) because of the less negative argument in the exponential. Hence

$$P_e \sim \frac{1 + \sqrt{2}}{(2\pi M\sqrt{2})^{\frac{1}{2}}} e^{-(2-\sqrt{2})M} \quad (10\text{-}49)$$

Recalling that coherent detection gives the asymptotic result

$$P_e \sim \frac{\exp(-M)}{2(\pi M)^{\frac{1}{2}}} \quad (10\text{-}50)$$

we conclude that differential four-phase transmission at very large signal-to-noise ratios requires approximately $1 + \sqrt{2}/2 = 1.707$ times as much signal power to achieve the same error rate as the ideal. The penalty in decibels is $10 \log_{10} 1.707$ or 2.3 db. This is in agreement with the result obtained by Cahn.[3]

The error probability P_e represents a symbol error rate. To transform to bit error rate it is necessary to specify a coding scheme relating the quaternary symbols to the binary message and also to evaluate the individual elements of the error probability matrix previously mentioned. The most effective plan is the cyclic or Gray code in which the pairs of bits assigned to adjacent phases differ in only one of the two positions. The following table of error probabilities is appropriate for this case:

Table 10-1. Matrix of Error Probabilities Applicable to Four-phase Transmission of Binary Data by Gray Code

Bit pair transmitted	Probability of detected bit pair			
	00	01	10	11
00	$1 - P_e$	ϵ_1	ϵ_1	ϵ_2
01	ϵ_1	$1 - P_e$	ϵ_2	ϵ_1
10	ϵ_1	ϵ_2	$1 - P_e$	ϵ_1
11	ϵ_2	ϵ_1	ϵ_1	$1 - P_e$

The probability of detecting the adjacent phase is represented by ϵ_1 and the probability of the nonadjacent phase by ϵ_2. When ϵ_1 is small, ϵ_2 is much smaller than ϵ_1.

Since the sum of the probabilities in any row must be unity, we must have

$$P_e = 2\epsilon_1 + \epsilon_2 \tag{10-51}$$

The expected number of bit errors in a pair is $1 \cdot \epsilon_1 + 1 \cdot \epsilon_1 + 2 \cdot \epsilon_2$ or $2(\epsilon_1 + \epsilon_2)$. The probability P_b that a single bit is in error is half this value. Hence

$$P_b = \epsilon_1 + \epsilon_2 = P_e - \epsilon_1 \tag{10-52}$$

We can calculate ϵ_1 by the methods previously developed. In the case of low error rate, however, it is sufficiently exact to assume ϵ_2 is negligible relative to ϵ_1. Then ϵ_1 is approximately half of P_e and

$$P_b \sim \frac{P_e}{2} \tag{10-53}$$

The resulting curve for bit error rate is included in Fig. 10-12.

If we use the natural binary code instead of the Gray code, the pairs 10 and 11 are interchanged in the table, leading to an expected number of bit errors per pair of $1 \cdot \epsilon_1 + 2 \cdot \epsilon_1 + 1 \cdot \epsilon_2$ or $3\epsilon_1 + \epsilon_2$. This gives

$$P_b \sim \frac{3\epsilon_1}{2} \sim \frac{3P_e}{4} \tag{10-54}$$

10-7   AVERAGE SIGNAL POWER IN PM SYSTEMS

In our calculations of the preceding section we have tacitly assumed that the mean square of the signal voltage is equal to half the square of the peak value. This is the relation which would hold if the PM wave had constant amplitude. In a band-limited system it is not possible to maintain constant amplitude when the phase varies with time. Evaluation of the average signal power from the statistics of the data sequence therefore requires a further investigation. The analysis of this section is a special case of a more general treatment given in Chap. 19.

We first consider the case of a binary PM system in which the amplitude-frequency response is symmetrical about the carrier frequency and phase distortion is absent. Then the signal voltage on the line can be represented by

$$V_1(t) = A \sum_{n=-\infty}^{\infty} b_n s_1(t - nT) \cos \omega_c t \tag{10-55}$$

We assume that we have a random data sequence with independent values of b_n. We further assume that any b_n is equally likely to have the value 1 or -1. The function $s_1(t)$ is the envelope response on the line for a signal pulse applied at $t = 0$. We also assume that there is white gaussian noise on the line with spectral density N_0.

A receiving bandpass filter is inserted between the output of the line and the input to the phase detector. Represent the transmittance function of this filter by $Y(\omega)$ where ω is the frequency displacement from midband. Assume that $Y(\omega)$ is a purely real even function of ω. Then the input signal voltage to the phase detector can be written as

$$V_2(t) = A \sum_{n=-\infty}^{\infty} b_n s_2(t - nT) \cos \omega_c t \qquad (10\text{-}56)$$

If $s_1(t)$ is expressed as a Fourier integral by

$$s_1(t) = \frac{1}{\pi} \int_0^{\infty} S_1(\omega) \cos t\omega \, d\omega \qquad (10\text{-}57)$$

it follows that

$$s_2(t) = \frac{1}{\pi} \int_0^{\infty} Y(\omega) S_1(\omega) \cos t\omega \, d\omega \qquad (10\text{-}58)$$

The spectral density of the noise at the input to the phase detector is $|Y(\omega)|^2 N_0$. We assume that $s_2(0)$ is equal to unity. In the notation of the previous section we now have in the absence of intersymbol interference

$$\rho^2 = \frac{A^2}{2\sigma^2} \qquad \sigma^2 = 2N_0 \int_0^{\infty} |Y(\omega)|^2 \, d\omega \qquad (10\text{-}59)$$

The average signal power on the line per mho of circuit conductance is given by

$$W_s = \text{av } V_1^2(t) \qquad (10\text{-}60)$$

To evaluate this average, we first average over the ensemble of data sequences with t fixed. We find

$$\langle V_1^2(t) \rangle = A^2 \cos^2 \omega_c t \left\langle \left[\sum_{n=-\infty}^{\infty} b_n s_1(t - nT) \right]^2 \right\rangle$$

$$= \frac{A^2}{2} (1 + \cos 2\omega_c t) \sum_{m=-\infty}^{\infty} \sum_{n=-\infty}^{\infty} \langle b_m b_n \rangle s_1(t - mT) s_1(t - nT)$$

$$= \frac{A^2}{2} (1 + \cos 2\omega_c t) \sum_{n=-\infty}^{\infty} s_1^2(t - nT) \qquad (10\text{-}61)$$

We now wish to average this result over all values of t. Let

$$F(t) = \sum_{m=-\infty}^{\infty} s_1^2(t - mT) \qquad (10\text{-}62)$$

We verify by substitution that $F(t - T)$ is equal to $F(t)$ and hence that $F(t)$ is periodic in t with period T. We also observe that $F(-t) = F(t)$. Hence $F(t)$ can be expanded in a Fourier series as follows:

$$F(t) = \frac{a_0}{2} + \sum_{n=1}^{\infty} a_n \cos n\omega_0 t \qquad (10\text{-}63)$$

where
$$\begin{aligned} a_n &= \frac{2}{T} \int_0^T F(t) \cos n\omega_0 t \, dt \\ &= \frac{2}{T} \sum_{m=-\infty}^{\infty} \int_0^T s_1{}^2(t - mT) \cos n\omega_0 t \, dt \\ &= \frac{2}{T} \sum_{m=-\infty}^{\infty} \int_{-mT}^{-(m-1)T} s_1{}^2(u) \cos n\omega_0 u \, du \\ &= \frac{2}{T} \int_{-\infty}^{\infty} s_1{}^2(u) \cos n\omega_0 u \, du \end{aligned} \qquad (10\text{-}64)$$

Comparing with Eqs. (10-60) and (10-61) we now have

$$W_s = \text{av} \left\{ \frac{A^2}{2} (1 + \cos 2\omega_c t) \left[\frac{a_0}{2} + \sum_{n=1}^{\infty} a_n \cos n\omega_0 t \right] \right\} \qquad (10\text{-}65)$$

In the case of differential PM, we assumed that $\omega_c T$ was a multiple of 2π. If we write $\omega_c T = 2r\pi$ where r is an integer and recall that $\omega_0 T = 2\pi$, we deduce that $\omega_c = r\omega_0$. The averaging process over t in (10-65) gives nonzero contributions only for the terms a_0 and a_{2r}. The result is

$$W_s = \frac{A^2}{4} (a_0 + a_{2r}) \qquad (10\text{-}66)$$

From Eq. (10-64) applying Parseval's theorem

$$a_0 = \frac{2}{T} \int_{-\infty}^{\infty} s_1{}^2(u) \, du = \frac{\omega_0}{\pi^2} \int_0^{\infty} |S_1(\omega)|^2 \, d\omega \qquad (10\text{-}67)$$

To evaluate a_n in general we observe that $C(\omega)$, the Fourier transform of $s_1{}^2(t)$, is defined by

$$C(\omega) = \int_{-\infty}^{\infty} s_1{}^2(t) \cos \omega t \, dt \qquad (10\text{-}68)$$

Hence
$$a_n = \frac{T}{2} C(n\omega_0) \qquad (10\text{-}69)$$

If $s_1(t)$ is band-limited to frequencies less than ω_0, the square of $s_1(t)$ is band-limited to frequencies less than $2\omega_0$. In this case a_n vanishes for $n > 1$. The value of a_{2r} is therefore zero for such cases, and we obtain the result

$$W_s = \frac{A^2 \omega_0}{4\pi^2} \int_0^{\omega_0} |S_1(\omega)|^2 \, d\omega \qquad (10\text{-}70)$$

To illustrate we consider the case of a raised-cosine signal spectrum at the input to the phase detector and the corresponding optimum receiving filter which, as demonstrated in Chap. 7, is a cosine characteristic. Accordingly

$$Y(\omega) = \cos \frac{\pi \omega}{2\omega_0}$$

$$Y(\omega)S_1(\omega) = \frac{2\pi}{\omega_0} \cos^2 \frac{\pi \omega}{2\omega_0} \qquad |\omega| < \omega_0 \qquad (10\text{-}71)$$

$$S_1(\omega) = \frac{2\pi}{\omega_0} \cos \frac{\pi \omega}{2\omega_0}$$

We then calculate $a_0 = 2$, $W_s = A^2/2$, $\sigma^2 = N_0\omega_0$, and $\rho^2 = M$ as stated in the previous section.

Verification of the corresponding formulas for the differential four-phase system proceeds in a similar manner. Consider the case in which the phase difference between the successive choices is an odd multiple of $\pi/4$. We can then write for the wave received from the line

$$V_1(t) = A \sum_{n=-\infty}^{\infty} s_1(t - 2nT) \cos \left(\omega_c t + c_{2n} \frac{\pi}{2} \right)$$

$$+ A \sum_{n=-\infty}^{\infty} s_1[t - (2n+1)T] \cos \left(\omega_c t + c_{2n+1} \frac{\pi}{2} + \frac{\pi}{4} \right) \qquad (10\text{-}72)$$

The values of c_n are independent and are equally likely to have any one of the four possible choices 0, 1, 2, and 3. When we average the square of $V_1(t)$ over the ensemble of values for c_n with t fixed, we find

$$\langle V_1{}^2(t) \rangle = A^2 \sum_{n=-\infty}^{\infty} s_1{}^2(t - 2nT) \left\langle \cos^2 \left(\omega_c t + \frac{\pi c_{2n}}{2} \right) \right\rangle$$

$$+ A^2 \sum_{n=-\infty}^{\infty} s_1{}^2[t - (2n+1)T] \left\langle \cos^2 \left(\omega_c t + \frac{\pi c_{2n+1}}{2} + \frac{\pi}{4} \right) \right\rangle$$

$$(10\text{-}73)$$

The two ensemble averages on the right are special cases of the following computation

$$\left\langle \cos^2 \left(\frac{\pi c_n}{2} + \theta \right) \right\rangle = \tfrac{1}{2} + \tfrac{1}{2} \langle \cos (\pi c_n + 2\theta) \rangle$$

$$= \tfrac{1}{2} + \tfrac{1}{8} \cos 2\theta + \tfrac{1}{8} \cos (\pi + 2\theta)$$

$$+ \tfrac{1}{8} \cos (2\pi + 2\theta) + \tfrac{1}{8} \cos (3\pi + 2\theta) = \tfrac{1}{2}$$

$$(10\text{-}74)$$

Hence $$\langle V_1{}^2(t) \rangle = \frac{A^2}{2} \sum_{n=-\infty}^{\infty} s_1{}^2(t - nT) \qquad (10\text{-}75)$$

This is seen to be the same as Eq. (10-61) except that the term $\cos 2\omega_c t$ is missing. Since we found before that the latter term did not contribute anything to the average power, we conclude that the average signal power for the four-phase system is the same as that of the two-phase system under the assumed conditions.

REFERENCES

1. Lawton, John G.: Theoretical Error Rates of "Differentially Coherent" Binary and "Kineplex" Data Transmission Systems, *Proc. IRE*, vol. 47, pp. 333–334, February, 1959.
2. Cahn, Charles R.: Performance of Digital Phase-modulation Communication Systems, *IRE Trans. Commun. Systems*, vol. CS–7, pp. 3–6, May, 1959.
3. Cahn, Charles R.: Combined Digital Phase and Amplitude Modulation Communication Systems, *IRE Trans. Commun. Systems*, vol. CS–8, pp. 150–155, September, 1960.

CHAPTER 11

COMPARISONS OF MODULATION METHODS

The preceding chapters have described the characteristics of various modulation methods that are used for data communication. The decision as to which method is best depends on the specific circumstances of use. For example, the choice may be based on simplicity of instrumentation or on tolerance to specific transmission impairments rather than signal-to-noise performance. Interaction with other services sharing the same facility may also be an important consideration. The more important advantages and disadvantages of the various methods will be discussed.

11-1 PERFORMANCE IN PRESENCE OF GAUSSIAN NOISE

We have shown that for fixed average transmitter power the error rate in the presence of flat gaussian noise is minimized by the use of a cosine-shaped receiving filter with a transmitted signal shaped to give a raised-cosine spectrum at the detector input. We have also shown that the same optimum results are obtained when the spectrum has a sharper cutoff provided the cutoff is shaped as illustrated in Fig. 11-1. For double-sideband carrier systems the shapings shown apply to both sidebands. In each example the spectrum at the detector input retains the symmetry condition for no intersymbol interference. With a flat noise spectrum the same noise power is accepted by each of the receiving filters. Also the signal amplitude at the detector input is the same in each case. Consequently, the same optimum performance is obtained for the various shapings shown in Fig. 11-1.

A good measure of performance is the required ratio of average transmitted power to the noise power in the Nyquist band to achieve a given probability of bit error such as 10^{-4}. Another measure of performance is the speed of transmission in bits per second per cycle of this band. For double-sideband systems where the maximum number of symbols per second is equal to the nominal band in cycles per second, the signal-to-noise ratio described is sometimes stated as

225

the average signal energy per symbol to the noise power per cycle of bandwidth.

Table 11-1 compares various systems on a fixed bandwidth basis as just described. For the multilevel cases it is assumed that the symbols are assigned binary designations in a cyclic or Gray code so

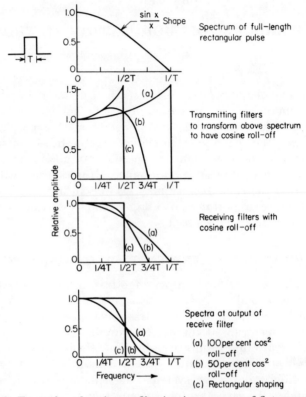

FIG. 11-1. Examples of optimum filtering in presence of flat gaussian noise.

that adjacent states differ by only one bit, as discussed in Sec. 7-6. The limitation on transmitted power in some cases may be set by peak power rather than average power. Table 11-1 also gives the signal-to-noise ratio on the basis of fixed maximum steady-state power. This might apply for systems which in an idle condition remain in the maximum-amplitude state.

The data of Table 11-1, based on average power, are plotted as points in Fig. 11-2. The horizontal coordinate gives the signal-to-noise ratio for a bit error rate of 10^{-4} and the vertical coordinate the transmission speed in bits per second per cycle of bandwidth. Such a diagram displays the various ways in which a channel with a given signal-to-noise ratio can be used. If one is interested in comparing on a fixed bit-speed basis, the signal-to-noise figures need to be corrected according to the bandwidth ratio. For instance, in comparing a quaternary phase-modulation system with a binary phase-modulation

Table 11-1. Comparisons of Various Data Systems Under Limitations of Average and Maximum Steady-state Signal Power

System	Number of states	Speed in bits per second per cycle of bandwidth	Signal-to-noise ratio for 10^{-4} bit error rate	
			Average signal power	Maximum steady-state signal power
Unipolar baseband.........	2	2	14.4	17.4
	4	4	22.8	26.9
Bipolar baseband..........	2	2	14.4	17.4
Polar baseband............	2	2	11.4	11.4
	4	4	18.3	20.8
	8	6	24.3	28.0
	16	8	30.2	34.4
Full carrier AM:				
envelope detection.......	2	1	11.9	14.9
coherent detection.......	2	1	11.4	14.4
	4	2	19.8	23.8
	8	3	26.5	31.0
Suppressed carrier AM,				
coherent detection	2	1	8.4	8.4
	4	2	15.3	17.8
	8	3	21.3	25.0
	16	4	27.2	31.4
PM, coherent detection.....	2	1	8.4	8.4
	4	2	11.4	11.4
	8	3	16.5	16.5
	16	4	22.1	22.1
	32	5	28.1	28.1
	64	6	34.1	34.1
PM, diff. detection.........	2	1	9.3	9.3
	4	2	13.7	13.7
	8	3	19.5	19.5
FM	2	1	11.7	11.7
	4	2	21.1	21.1
	8	3	28.3	28.3
VSB, 50% modulation	2	2	16.2	17.9

VSB, suppressed carrier, coherent detection (see polar baseband)
Quadrature AM, suppressed carrier, coherent detection (see polar baseband)

system at equal bit rates, the quaternary system would require but half as much bandwidth. With coherent detection the two systems become equal when the 3-db correction is made, and each requires a signal-to-noise ratio of 8.4 db for an error rate of 10^{-4}.

It must be pointed out that Fig. 11-2 indicates the theoretical performance of perfectly implemented systems with optimum signal shaping and filtering. Actual systems might well be poorer by one or more decibels. Also where synchronous or coherent detection is assumed at the receiver, a practical system would usually devote some signal power to maintain the coherent reference carrier.

It will be seen that vestigial sideband and quadrature AM with carrier suppressed give the same result as polar baseband and have the best signal-to-noise performance, particularly if more than 2 bits

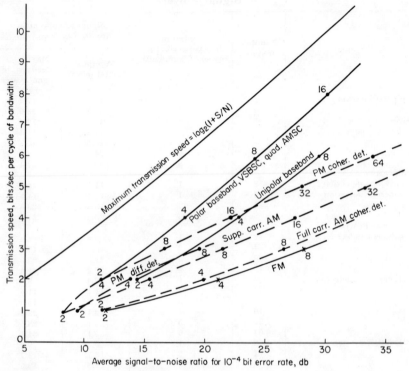

FIG. 11-2. Comparisons of various data systems under an average signal power limitation.

per cycle of bandwidth are to be obtained. It will be noted that they approach within about 7 db of the Shannon limit shown in the figure and discussed more fully in Chap. 18. The binary phase-modulation system can stand the most noise but achieves a capacity of only one-third of the limit. On the other hand, an 8-level VSB system, making use of a high signal-to-noise ratio, achieves a capacity of about three-fourths of the limit. Binary vestigial sideband, two binary AM channels in quadrature, and quaternary phase modulation give equal results. For a greater number of phases than four, the phase-modulation systems are seen to fall along a line that diverges

considerably from vestigial sideband and quadrature AM.   This difference indicates the advantage of utilizing both phase and amplitude.[1]
Phase-modulation systems using differential phase detection suffer an
additional loss of 1 to 3 db.

Two-level suppressed-carrier AM is equivalent to binary phase
modulation.   For larger numbers of levels, the suppressed-carrier AM
systems fall along a line which becomes displaced from the PM systems

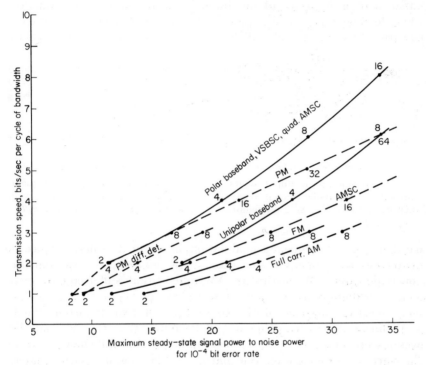

FIG. 11-3. Comparisons of various data systems under a maximum steady-state
power limitation.

toward higher signal-to-noise ratios by about 5 db.   For AM systems
which transmit the full carrier, the line is moved from 3 to 6 db more
toward higher signal-to-noise ratios.   If envelope detection is employed,
an additional loss occurs which for the binary case is 0.5 db.   FM
systems are seen to fall close to the full-carrier AM systems.

The data of Table 11-1 based on maximum steady-state power are
shown in a similar manner in Fig. 11-3.   The FM and PM systems
remain as before.   The variable-amplitude systems are shifted toward
higher signal-to-noise ratios because of the reduced average power.
Consequently, the constant-power signals show to better advantage.

11-2 PERFORMANCE IN PRESENCE OF DELAY DISTORTION

Performance in presence of delay distortion is one of the most important characteristics of a data transmission system, particularly if it is to operate over telephone voice channels.   Figures 11-4 and 11-5, taken from the work of E. D. Sunde,[2] summarize the impairment caused by idealized parabolic and linear delay distortion.   The impairment is in terms of maximum signal-to-noise ratio reduction, which for linear systems is equivalent to the relative closing of the eye pattern of the demodulated signal.   For the case of symmetrical

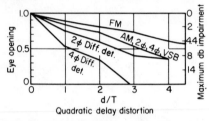

FIG. 11-4. Maximum impairments caused by parabolic-shaped delay distortion.   See Fig. 8-12 for definition of d/T.

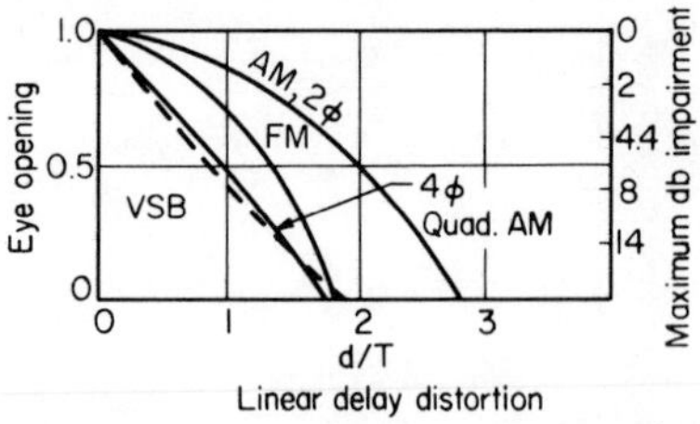

FIG. 11-5. Maximum impairments caused by linear delay distortion. See Fig. 8-12 for definition of d/T.

parabolic delay, frequency modulation shows up the best.   Since no quadrature component is generated with parabolic delays, synchronously detected AM, quadrature AM, and VSB all suffer equal impairments.   Differential detection of two-phase and four-phase signals is more sensitive because of the comparison of two distorted signals. With linear delay distortion it will be noted that the AM and FM systems are in reverse order.   This indicates the difficulty in rating the various systems when the nature of the channel varies widely. The presence of a quadrature component with linear delay distortion leads to more degradation of quadrature AM and VSB than of binary AM.

The impairments shown in Figs. 11-4 and 11-5 for synchronous detection assume that the reference carrier is adjusted in phase to give no quadrature component at the time the received pulse is sampled. If such an adjustment is not made in the actual system, poorer performance will be obtained.

11-3 PERFORMANCE WITH LEVEL VARIATIONS

Systems using frequency or phase modulation are inherently insensitive to variations in the loss of the transmission medium.   If amplitude limiters are used, only the angle-modulation information reaches the detector. A symmetrical binary system such as polar baseband or two-phase modulation is also immune from level variations provided the decision threshold has sufficient sensitivity. An on-off binary baseband or AM system is quite sensitive to level variation. With the decision threshold at half the marking amplitude, complete failure occurs with a decrease in level of 6 db. With more than two levels all AM systems are sensitive to level. Automatic gain control is usually a necessity in such cases to maintain accurate decision thresholds. Level variations occurring rapidly with respect to the gain-control response time are, of course, still detrimental. One of the outstanding advantages of frequency and phase modulation is the relative simplicity of maintaining amplitude stability of the demodulated signal by use of limiters.

11-4 PERFORMANCE WITH FREQUENCY OFFSET

As might be expected, the AM systems are the most tolerant of frequency offset. If the channel has a gentle roll-off and has some excess speed capability, the envelope shape is not materially affected by small changes in carrier frequency. Where synchronous detection is used, the reference carrier must, of course, follow the frequency variations. Phase-modulation systems with synchronous detection are likewise tolerant of carrier-frequency variation. In the case of frequency-modulation systems, however, carrier-frequency variation results in a d-c displacement of the entire demodulated wave, and consequently all decision thresholds are equally affected. For a narrow-band channel having a relatively small frequency swing an offset of 10 cycles may cause severe bias distortion, whereas for a wide-swing high-speed channel the effect would be negligible. Differential phase systems are also somewhat affected by frequency offset, since the amount of phase change between symbols varies with carrier frequency.

11-5 EFFECTS OF SUDDEN PHASE JUMPS

A sudden change of carrier phase will cause some disturbance to all types of data systems. In a band-limited system the sudden phase change causes a change in signal amplitude so that even an AM envelope detector is affected during the transient. For AM or PM systems where a coherent reference is established, the effect can be of considerable duration depending upon the response speed of the carrier-recovery method. A PM system using differential phase detection, or an FM system, has no hangover effect and consequently recovers immediately.

11-6 SIGNAL SPACE DIAGRAMS[3]

All the various types of data signals that we have considered in the previous chapters can be expressed in the general form $A(t) \cos [\omega_c t + \phi(t)]$ representing a carrier signal $\cos \omega_c t$ modulated both in amplitude and in phase. A polar plot of A and ϕ shows the path of the signal vector with respect to $\omega_c t$ as a reference. If the reference ω_c is chosen as the center of the pulse spectrum, a single isolated pulse

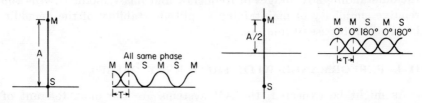

FIG. 11-6. Signal space diagram for on-off AM.

FIG. 11-7. Signal space diagram for suppressed-carrier AM or binary PM.

is represented by a simple pattern. With an undistorted symmetrical pulse spectrum an isolated pulse will appear as a radial line. When pulses of various phases overlap, more complicated patterns are formed. Transmitting at the Nyquist rate forms a stationary pattern which shows a number of interesting comparisons of the various modulation methods. It will be seen that each type of data signal can be considered as a sequence of carrier pulses. The pulse envelope is a characteristic of the channel as previously discussed. The differences among the various modulation methods are due only to the number of pulse amplitudes and phases which are used, the particular phase sequences which can occur, and the spacing between pulses. In the examples to be presented a raised-cosine pulse spectrum has been assumed, and for simplification of the diagrams the pulse envelope has been taken to have a raised-cosine shape in time.

Amplitude Modulation. The first example is for on-off AM where mark is represented by a pulse and space by no pulse. The carrier phase remains the same from pulse to pulse thus resulting in a straight line pattern as shown in Fig. 11-6. The signal positions at the midsymbol sampling instants are indicated by points M and S. The half-envelope shape of the pulses is indicated at the right in the figure.

The diagram for suppressed-carrier AM or two-phase signals is shown in Fig. 11-7. In this case a pulse is sent for both mark and space, but the carrier phase for space is opposite to that for mark. Again the diagram is a straight line, but the mark and space conditions are separated by twice the pulse amplitude. A minimum separation of A is obtained with a pulse amplitude of $A/2$.

Phase Modulation.   Diagrams for two cases of quaternary phase modulation are presented.   When the phase change between symbols is $0°$, $\pm 90°$, or $180°$, the signal is equivalent to two binary suppressed-carrier signals at quadrature phase.   The diagram for such a case is a square with diagonals as shown in Fig. 11-8.   The signal can progress around the square in either direction, go across a diagonal, or remain at one corner with no restrictions.   The four possible positions at the

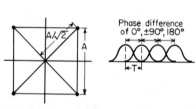

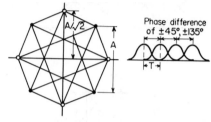

FIG. 11-8. Signal space diagram for quaternary PM using phase changes of $0°$, $\pm 90°$, and $180°$.

FIG. 11-9. Signal space diagrams for quaternary PM using phase changes of $\pm 45°$, $\pm 135°$.

centers of the symbols are indicated by dots.   For a minimum separation A between states, the pulse peak becomes $A/\sqrt{2}$.   This indicates that for this quaternary system to have the same noise margin as the two-phase signal of Fig. 11-7 the power must be increased by 3 db.

When phase changes of $\pm 45°$ or $\pm 135°$ are used between symbols, there are eight possible phases for the pulses.   The possible positions of the signal vector at the center of the symbols are shown as dots and small circles on the diagram of Fig. 11-9.   In this case there is always a phase change between symbols and the signal must alternate between dot positions and circle positions.   For a peak pulse amplitude of $A/\sqrt{2}$ the minimum separation between dots or between circles is again A as in the previous case.

Vestigial Sideband.   It is assumed that the pulse spectrum for vestigial sideband has the same raised-cosine shape used in the previous examples.   It is also assumed that the pulse rate is twice the Nyquist rate for double-sideband operation, and that the pulses originate from the modulation of a suppressed carrier higher in frequency than midband by an amount equal to one-quarter of the pulse rate.   This means that the signal pulses change phase between symbols by

$\pm 90°$. As shown in Fig. 11-10 the pulses overlap to the extent that at the peak of one pulse the adjacent pulses are each at half amplitude. This severe interference is at quadrature to the wanted pulse and is eliminated by the use of coherent detection. The signal phase at the center of a symbol is not affected if the two adjacent pulses are of opposite phase but is perturbed by $\pm 45°$ if the adjacent pulses are of the same quadrature phase. For example, in the diagram of Fig. 11-10 the center of a marking symbol can occur at any of the three dot positions at the top of the diagram, depending on the adjacent symbols as indicated. The phase of the coherent carrier used for detection advances around the diagram by 90°

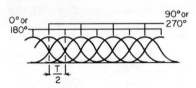

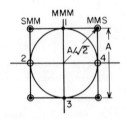

FIG. 11-10. Signal space diagrams for suppressed-carrier vestigial-sideband AM.

for each symbol in the point sequence 1, 2, 3, and 4. A continuous marking signal consequently follows this same sequence. A continuous spacing signal likewise advances 90° during each symbol but remains opposite in phase to the coherent reference.

For continuous mark-space alternations each symbol pulse is retarded by 90° from the preceding pulse, and the signal moves around the circle in the opposite direction from steady mark or space. The signal always alternates between dot and small circle points. The corners of the square portion of the diagram are both dot and circle points, and the signal may rest at such a point continuously and represents an $MMSSMMSS$-type sequence. All changes in direction of rotation about the diagram occur at the corners of the square; otherwise, the only restriction is for the alternating of the dot and small circle positions. Here again with a peak signal of $A/\sqrt{2}$, a minimum separation of A between mark and space dots or mark and space circles is obtained. Thus the speed is doubled at a cost of 3 db more power as in the case of quaternary phase modulation. Note that the individual pulse amplitudes are $A/2$ as for the two-phase case but that twice as many pulses are sent. For vestigial-sideband operation these pulses are sent serially while for the quaternary-phase case of Fig. 11-8, the pulses can be considered to be of amplitude $A/2$ sent two at a time.

Frequency Modulation. The binary frequency-modulation case to be presented here is the ideal one where the bit rate is equal to the frequency shift between mark and space. For a continuous mark or space signal this results in the signal changing phase 180° between successive symbols. Again it is assumed that the signal is shaped to give a raised-cosine pulse spectrum. Such an FM signal can be resolved into two components, a two-phase signal carrying the binary information and a quadrature component consisting of steady mark and space. This quadrature component can be considered to consist of alternating ±90° carrier pulses located between the 0° and 180° pulses carrying the information. The diagram for such an FM signal is shown in Fig. 11-11. A continuous mark condition (lower frequency) causes the signal to move around the circle clockwise. A continuous space causes a counterclockwise rotation. At the center of the symbols

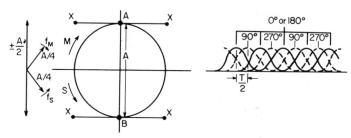

Fig. 11-11. Signal space diagram for binary FM.

the signal is at either point A or B. A frequency transition causes the signal to swing out to one of the points x and reverse the direction of rotation. For continuous reversals the signal swings back and forth through point A or B along a horizontal line. For such a sequence of reversals the phase swing is ±45°.

Although the steady mark and space frequency components which impart the horizontal component of motion in the diagram carry no information, they do permit the detection of the signal on a frequency basis. The mark and space conditions are indicated by the direction of rotation at points A and B. The quadrature component of the signal represents half of its power. Consequently an FM signal requires twice the power of a two-phase signal to produce the same minimum separation of the points A and B. The two-phase component of the FM wave can be detected by a coherent carrier to determine whether the signal is at point A or B. It will be seen, however, that this leads to a polarity ambiguity because of the nature of the encoding. Reversals of either phase can be represented by the signal being at point A or at point B for successive symbols. A change from point A to point B indicates no transition of the information wave.

Duobinary Frequency Modulation. The duobinary technique,[4] described in Sec. 7-8, is a means of doubling the rate of sending binary information.   The data are first differentially encoded so that a transition is made for a space symbol and no transition for a mark symbol. The resulting double-speed binary signal is then passed through a frequency-shift channel as described for ordinary binary operation with no change in frequency shift or channel shaping.   During these half-length pulses the phase can change a maximum of $\pm 90°$.   This results in both the in-phase and quadrature pulses carrying information. The diagram of Fig. 11-11 applies in part, but because of the double rate we are interested in more points of the pattern.   For instance, for steady mark the signal moves around the circle in either direction,

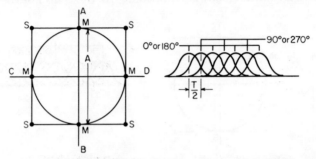

Fig. 11-12. Signal space diagram for duobinary FM.

and the receiver samples the signal not only at points A and B of Fig. 11-11 but also at points C and D as shown in Fig. 11-12.   The occurrence of a space symbol causes a frequency transition, and the signal leaves the circle and reverses direction at one of the points labeled S.   If there are two successive space symbols causing two frequency transitions, the signal pauses at point S for one symbol interval and then continues on in the same direction of rotation.   An odd number of successive space symbols leads to a reversal of rotation, while an even number does not.   The signal can thus proceed around the circle clockwise or counterclockwise or pause at one of the S points.   The rotating conditions represent the high- and low-frequency states, while the pausing represents the midband frequency.   When the signal is detected on a frequency basis, a three-level baseband output is obtained with the outer levels representing mark and the center level space.

The complete duobinary diagram of Fig. 11-12 is seen to be the same as that of Fig. 11-10 for a vestigial-sideband signal.   This indicates that the line signals are of the same form although the encoding is different.   Experimental verification of this identity has been demonstrated by transmitting a vestigial-sideband signal to an FM receiver and obtaining a three-level baseband signal such as received in duo-binary FM.

The foregoing diagrams illustrate that quaternary PM, binary FM, and binary VSB signals all give the same margin against noise for a given transmitted power. This margin is 3 db less than that obtained with binary PM. The quaternary PM and binary VSB systems, however, operate at twice the bit rate of the binary PM or FM systems. It has also been shown that a duobinary FM signal is essentially the same as a binary VSB signal except for its interpretation at the receiver. The relative simplicity afforded by FM detection of such a signal is accomplished at a cost of 6-db margin against noise.

Signal space diagrams as illustrated in the figures can be displayed on an oscilloscope by coherently detecting the in-phase and quadrature components of a data signal with respect to midband and applying them to the X and Y deflection circuits.

11-7 FACTORS AFFECTING CHOICE OF DATA SYSTEMS

Making a choice among the various types of data transmission systems depends on many factors. Of primary importance is the performance under the expected channel characteristics. Economic considerations, however, may swing the choice toward the simpler or more reliable terminal rather than the ultimate in performance. The several modulation and detection methods also differ in their ability to handle a variety of codes and speeds of transmission. Some of the characteristics to be considered in choosing a system are given relative weighting in Table 11-2. In all columns except the second and third, the systems are given numbers indicating the order of preference under each characteristic. The same number given to more than one system indicates either that the systems are equal or that there is insufficient basis for a choice.

A few general remarks can be made summarizing Table 11-2. The baseband system is the simplest and is also high in performance. It would be the obvious choice provided a suitable baseband channel is available. Where carrier methods are necessary, the simple AM method gives satisfactory results if the channel amplitude characteristic is stable and there is little noise and interference. The FM system is reasonably simple, provides stable operation over a wide variety of channels, and permits asynchronous operation. The combination of simplicity, good performance, and versatility has made FM the most widely used form of data transmission. Binary PM provides the best tolerance to noise but when detected differentially is limited to fixed-speed synchronous operation. When coherent detection is used,

Table 11-2. Characteristics to be Considered in Choosing a Data System

System	Complexity of instrumentation	Bits per cycle of nominal band	Variable speed asynchronous operation	Signal-to-noise performance — Equal bit rate	Signal-to-noise performance — Equal bandwidth	Tolerance to parabolic delay distortion	Tolerance to linear delay distortion	Tolerance to amplitude change	Tolerance to frequency offset	Tolerance to phase jumps
Binary polar baseband ..	1	2	Yes	1	3	2	—	1	—	—
Binary on-off AM...	2	1	Yes	5	5	2	1	3	1	1
Binary FM	3	1	Yes	4	4	1	2	1	3	2
Binary PM differentially coherent	4	1	No	2	2	3	3	2	3	2
Binary PM coherent	5	1	Yes	1	1	2	1	1	1	4
VSB AM suppressed carrier	6	2	Yes	1	3	2	5	1	2	4
Quaternary PM differentially coherent	7	2	No	3	5	4	4	2	4	3

variable speed asynchronous operation is possible, but the problems of carrier recovery and polarity ambiguity lead to increased complexity. Suppressed-carrier VSB is attractive because it combines double-speed capability with optimum tolerance to noise. However, the carrier recovery problem again leads to complexity, and also there is less tolerance to unsymmetrical delay distortion because the carrier frequency is near the edge of the band. Differential quaternary PM provides the double-speed capability without the problems of carrier recovery but is limited to fixed-speed synchronous operation and is also fairly complex. All the various systems are thus seen to have their strong and weak characteristics. Those that are controlling depend on the specific application at hand.

REFERENCES

1. Hancock, J. C. and R. W. Lucky: Performance of Combined Amplitude- and Phase-modulated Communication Systems, *IRE Trans. Commun. Systems*, vol. CS-8, pp. 232–237, December, 1960.
2. Sunde, E. D.: Pulse Transmission by AM, FM, and PM in the Presence of Phase Distortion, *Bell System Tech. J.*, vol. 40, pp. 353–422, March, 1961.
3. Davey, J. R.: Digital Data Signal Space Diagrams, *Bell System Tech. J.*, vol. 43, pp. 2973–2983, November, 1964.
4. Lender, A.: The Duobinary Technique for High Speed Data Transmission, *IEEE Trans. Commun. and Elect.*, vol. 82, pp. 214–218, May, 1963.

CHAPTER 12

PAST AND PRESENT DATA COMMUNICATION SYSTEMS

The previous chapters have presented material on the various fundamental methods of modulation and detection and on their performance capabilities. We shall now discuss some of the more useful systems which have been developed through the years. It will become evident that the course of digital communication has been affected to a major extent by the types of line facilities developed for telephone communication.

12-1 EARLY TELEGRAPH SYSTEMS

As pointed out in Chap. 1, telegraph communication developed rapidly after the general adoption of the Morse electromechanical system. The early lines consisted of a single wire with ground as the return path. Figure 12-1 shows a simple closed-circuit type system

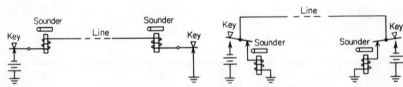

FIG. 12-1. Closed-circuit telegraph system.

FIG. 12-2. Open-circuit telegraph system.

in which the keys and sounders of the terminal and intermediate stations form a single series circuit in which a single battery is sufficient. In the idle condition all keys are closed and current flows in the line. Any station can signal to all others by opening the circuit. Figure 12-2 shows a simple open-circuit system which was popular in Europe. In this arrangement each key can apply battery to the line. Operation of a key disconnects the home sounder. Each station requires a battery, but there is no current during the idle condition.

An improvement was obtained by inserting a main line relay to repeat the line signals into a local battery circuit containing the sounder. This permitted operation with much weaker currents and greatly increased the possible line lengths. The line relay could be made much more sensitive than a sounder, since it did not need to be heavy enough to make readily audible clicks. The development of the relay also enabled weak signals from one telegraph line circuit to be repeated as full-strength signals into another line circuit. Several line sections could then be connected in tandem to span great distances. Branch lines could also be established to form a whole network of stations having a community of interest. A telegraph repeater for open-and-close signals is shown in Fig. 12-3.

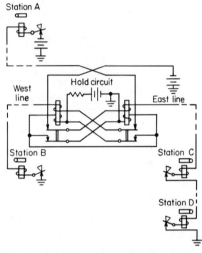

Fig. 12-3. Repeater for open-close signals.

The simple early systems which signaled by open-and-close, or current and no-current, are termed neutral circuits since the signals can be received by a nonpolarized, or neutral, relay or sounder. The change in circuit impedance from the open to close condition causes the signal transitions to be asymmetrical. The asymmetry leads to severe bias distortion on long circuits if the receiving device has an

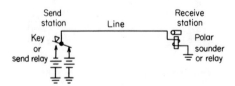

Fig. 12-4. One-way polar telegraph system.

operating threshold near the half marking-current value. Later systems utilized polar or effective polar transmission to keep the sending impedance constant. A one-way polar telegraph system is shown in Fig. 12-4. Where two-way communication is required, two such circuits must be provided.

12-2 DUPLEX TELEGRAPH SYSTEMS

As noted in Chap. 1, means were soon devised which permitted signaling in both directions simultaneously over a single-wire ground-return telegraph system.   This duplex operation was brought about by the use of double-winding differential relays together with a balancing artificial line circuit as shown in Fig. 12-5.   With proper

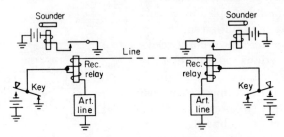

Fig. 12-5. Differential duplex telegraph system.

poling of the two windings and with the artificial line circuit matching the real line, the differential relay responds only to signals from the distant transmitting contacts.

Examples of duplex circuits utilizing polarized relays are the bridge polar duplex (Fig. 12-6) and the differential duplex (Fig. 12-7).   Here again the receiving relay responds only to the distant transmitting

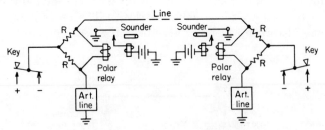

Fig. 12-6. Bridge polar duplex telegraph system.

contacts.   To keep the interference between the two directions of transmission low over long lines, the artificial line must present a reactive impedance like that of the line.   Usually an RC network suffices.

Edison developed the quadruplex system, which consisted of a combination of polar and neutral differential duplex.   This allowed two messages to be transmitted in each direction simultaneously.

The principle of operation is shown in Fig. 12-8.   The four key-and-sounder pairs forming the four independent channels are labeled A, B, C, and D.   Keys A and C are of the pole-changing type and serve to reverse the polarity of the battery applied to the line.   Keys B and D change the value of the battery voltage.   The differentially wound polar relays respond only to the polarity of battery applied at the distant end.   The differentially wound neutral relays are not sensitive to polarity.   They are biased to operate on only the higher value of

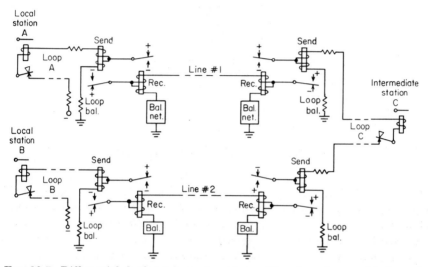

FIG. 12-7. Differential duplex telegraph system with polar relays and balanced station loops.

differential current which results when the larger battery voltage is applied at the distant end.   Since there are four different values of potential available at each end of the line, there are sixteen possible line states.   The quadruplex system represented the practical limit of complexity attained by d-c telegraph methods.

The duplex systems not only provided for two-way simultaneous operation but also furnished much higher quality of transmission than the simple neutral-type systems.   They are, however, point-to-point systems and require additional arrangements for building up a network of several stations.   For multistation operation the lines usually transmit in only one direction at a time.   The ability to transmit both ways at once, however, provides a quick and rapid means of interrupting the sender when necessary.   This is termed half-duplex operation.   A common way of arranging the local termination

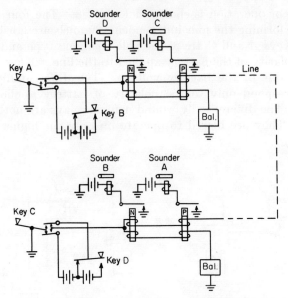

FIG. 12-8. Edison's quadruplex telegraph system.

of a differential duplex system is shown in Fig. 12-7. Means are shown for terminating in a local loop when sending is done on an open-and-close basis, and also for interconnecting two line sections with an intermediate station loop. It will be noted that the sending relays are connected differentially between the local loop and a loop-balancing resistor to prevent operation from the associated receiving relay. This arrangement is known as a balanced loop.

12-3 LINE FACILITIES FOR D-C TELEGRAPHY

As mentioned before, the early lines were single wires with ground return. After the advent of the telephone, means were developed to share the same wires. Where the telephone line circuit consists of two wires forming a balanced circuit, the arrangement of Fig. 12-9, called simplex, can be used. A phantom telephone circuit can also be simplexed for telegraph as indicated in Fig. 12-10. Another method

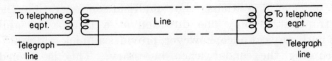

FIG. 12-9. Simplex telegraph line.

uses a filter network called a composite set to provide a baseband telegraph channel below the voice band as indicated in Fig. 12-11. A bandwidth of about 80 cps is commonly obtained.

The need for more telephone circuits led to the multipair cable. This, too, was composited and simplexed to provide telegraph lines.

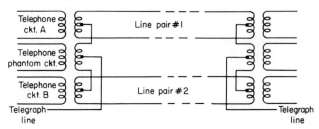

Fig. 12-10. Simplex-phantom telegraph line.

An ungrounded or metallic-type telegraph system was sometimes used on composited telephone cables. Such a system could use weaker currents because of freedom from ground potential differences, and therefore produced less interference in the telephone circuits.

In the course of telephone development more and more telephone channels were derived by carrier multiplex techniques. The carrier

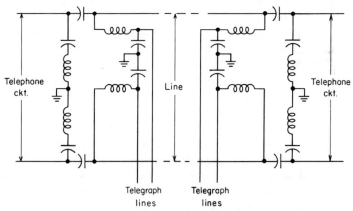

Fig. 12-11. Composited telegraph circuit.

channels had no baseband to be utilized by telegraph. This fact together with the advantages of carrier methods has gradually relegated d-c telegraph to local area use where cable pairs are more readily available. Even here the trend is toward carrier telegraph because of the ease in obtaining voice channel facilities directly to the ultimate destination, and because of the need for higher transmission speeds.

12-4 CARRIER TELEGRAPH SYSTEMS

The early carrier telephone systems were used on open wire lines and provided additional voice channels in the frequency range above the voice-frequency band. The early carrier telegraph systems utilized this same frequency range to derive a number of telegraph channels. These open wire systems were commonly two-wire with separate frequency assignments given to the two directions of transmission. Simple on-off keying was used at the sending end, and envelope detectors with manual gain control at the receiving end.

It soon became apparent that voice-frequency carrier telegraph deriving several telegraph channels from a voice channel would be more flexible since it could be used over voice channels built up of various types of facilities. One type of early AM voice-frequency carrier telegraph furnished twelve channels spaced 170 cps apart, centered from 425 cps to 2,295 cps. The signaling rate rarely exceeded 50 bits per second. The sending relay keyed a source of voice frequency obtained from a motor-driven tone-wheel type generator. The receiver utilized two triode electron tubes, one for amplification and one as a grid-leak type detector operating a polar receiving relay. Later improvements gave some degree of automatic gain control (AGC) by changing the value of grid-leak resistance between the received mark and space condition. The development of the screen-grid and variable-gain electron tubes permitted a much improved AM telegraph system which had a flat bias characteristic over 20 db or more of receive level variation. With the same 170-cps spacing, the number of channels was extended to 18, using the range from 255 cps to 3,145 cps. This was possible since the newer carrier telephone channels had a wider bandwidth.

The work of Armstrong in FM broadcast service aroused interest in FM telegraph possibilities. Early FM voice-frequency telegraph systems were developed by the Western Union Telegraph Company. The use of FM for radiotelegraph and radio picture transmission was pioneered by the Press Wireless Corporation. Frequency modulation has now become practically the standard means of transmitting narrow-band voice-frequency telegraph signals and is also widely used in radiotelegraphy.

12-5 HIGHER-SPEED VOICE-BAND DATA TRANSMISSION

The need to transmit digital data at faster rates than could be handled by the usual telegraph channels has led to numerous systems utilizing a full voice channel. Depending upon the quality of the voice channel, speeds of 1,200 to 2,400 bits per second are obtained. It is interesting to note that speeds as high as 1,000 words per minute (about 500 bits per second) were demonstrated over early open wire telegraph lines back in 1874 by Edison. The signals were sent from punched paper tape and received on paper tape by electrochemical action. It was found, however, that the time and manpower required to punch the tape at the transmitter and transcribe the recorded message at the receiver was about the same as required with several key-and-sounder channels having equal capacity. Thus no real need for such point-to-point single-channel speeds developed until recent years with the coming of modern data processing systems.

All types of modulation methods have been utilized in transmitting digital data in a full voice channel. The various methods differ in relative performance, flexibility, and complexity. As time passes certain types will probably tend to be standardized for worldwide connections, but at present it is not clear which these will be. The salient features of a number of voice-band data transmission systems are given in the following sections.

12-6 DATA TERMINALS USING AMPLITUDE MODULATION

AN/TSQ Data System.[1] One of the earliest voice-band data systems was the AN/TSQ using full-carrier double-sideband AM. It was intended for use over untreated telephone voice channels and was designed for operation at 750 bits per second. The carrier frequency was 1,500 cps, and full-wave envelope detection was used at the receiver. The data were organized in blocks, and a 600-cps ready signal was used to aid the framing of these blocks as described in Chap. 14, Fig. 14-4.

A1 Data System.[2] In connection with the development of the SAGE (Semiautomatic Ground Environment) system for continental air defense, the need arose for data channels operating at speeds of 1,300 and 1,600 bits per second. A vestigial-sideband AM system was developed by the Bell System to furnish such a data service. A carrier of 2,000 cps is modulated by a ternary signal having relative amplitudes of 1.0, 0.73, and 0.27. The maximum level is used only as a framing signal, and the two lower levels carry the binary information. Envelope detection is used in the receiver. The low modulation index keeps the quadrature distortion of the envelope small. The system is operated synchronously, and the receiving clock is controlled in phase by the framing signal.

Rixon Sebit.[3] This is a vestigal-sideband AM system with envelope detection and about 50 per cent modulation. One of the unique features is a binary-type AGC which operates on both the mark and space levels. Synchronous operation at 2,500 bits per second is provided with a precision-type receive clock which is phase adjusted, in accordance with the signal, by a servomotor. The terminal also incorporates adjustable delay-correcting networks. A small oscilloscope is provided to observe the eye pattern as a measure of signal quality. An improved version using enhanced carrier detection and increased modulation operates up to 3,600 bits per second on high-quality voice channels.

ACF Data Terminal.[4] A vestigal-sideband AM system designed by ACF suppresses the carrier and uses synchronous detection. The carrier is recovered at the receiver by the method of modulating the received signal with the demodulated signal as described in Chap. 13. The system operates synchronously at 2,400 bits per second. Equalization of the received signal is accomplished by transversal filter techniques.

12-7 DATA TERMINALS USING FREQUENCY MODULATION

Bell System 202-type Data Sets.[5] The 202-type data set uses FM at speeds up to 1,200 bits per second. A multivibrator type of frequency-modulated oscillator permits shaping of the modulated wave to minimize foldover. The marking and spacing frequencies are 1,200 cps and 2,200 cps respectively. The demodulator is a zero-crossing detector. Asynchronous operation with start-stop codes is possible at any speed up to the maximum. Synchronous operation requires that bit synchronization be provided by the data processing equipment. A compromise delay and amplitude equalizer is added for operation over the switched telephone network.

Lenkurt Quaternary FM Data Set. The Lenkurt Electric Company has developed a four-level FM data set of the heterodyne type in which the modulation and detection is carried out in the range from 8 to 10 kc. For transmission over a voice channel the signal is translated to the range from 1 to 3 kc. This simplifies the generation of a wide-frequency swing signal and also makes it easier to filter out carrier ripple after detection. Terminals of this type have been arranged for operation up to 3,400 bits per second over a high-quality voice channel. A recent version uses the duobinary technique, described in Chap. 7, instead of four levels and operates at 2,400 bits per second.

12-8 DATA TERMINALS USING PHASE MODULATION

Collins Data Terminals.[6] The Collins Radio Company has developed a number of quaternary phase-modulation systems which use differential phase detection.   A unique feature of these systems is the use of gated high-Q carrier-frequency resonators to sample and store the signal phase.   During the sampling interval the received signal is impressed on a resonator causing a linear buildup of oscillation having the average phase of the interval.   At the end of the sampling interval the resonator is allowed to continue oscillating, thus storing the phase information.   Differential phase detection is accomplished by using a pair of resonators which alternately sample the incoming phase intervals.   While one is sampling, the other is storing the previous interval.   At the end of each sampling period, a comparison of the phases of the two resonators gives a measure of the phase change between intervals.   The resonator holding the older sample is then quickly quenched and allowed to sample again.   An important property of such a sampling method is that the response of the resonator to carrier frequencies other than its own is zero when the spacing of the carrier frequencies is a multiple of the sampling frequency.   This permits multichannel operation with efficient channel spacing without the use of transmitting channel filters.

The Collins 202 system uses 20 quaternary-phase channels with 110-cps spacing from 605 cps to 2,695 cps.   Each of these carries the information of two 75-bit-per-second channels giving a total capacity of 3,000 bits per second.   An auxiliary channel provides synchronizing information for proper phasing of the sampling intervals.   The Collins 206 system uses four channels with 440-cps spacing.   Each of these is equivalent to two 300-bit-per-second channels.   Synchronization is obtained by amplitude modulating the composite signal with 150 cps. This system can be used in a parallel mode at 300 eight-bit characters per second or serially at 2,400 bits per second.   Several other variations of the same general method have been developed.

Bell System 201-type Data Sets.[7]   This is a quaternary phase-modulation system using differential phase detection.   Phase changes of $\pm 45°$ or $\pm 135°$ are transmitted.   The line signal, therefore, has continual phase changes.   The transmitter contains an oscillator running at eight times the carrier frequency, and generates any of the eight possible carrier phases by properly presetting an 8-to-1 binary frequency-dividing chain.   The differential phase detection is performed by the use of a delay and phase-splitting network as described in Chap. 10.   Continuous bit timing for all data sequences is recovered by splitting the received signal spectrum into upper and lower sidebands which are then multiplied together.   One version of this set operates at 2,000 bits per second and another at 2,400 bits per second.

Lincoln Laboratories Phase-modulation Terminal.[8]   A binary phase-modulation system using differential phase detection has been developed by Lincoln Laboratories.   Code translation is employed as a part of the synchronization process.   Each group of four bits of incoming serial data is encoded into a five-bit sequence.   The required sixteen sequences are chosen from the 32 possible five-bit sequences in such a way as to assure a generous number of signal transitions from which to recover bit timing at the receiver.   In addition one of the five-bit sequences is reserved as a unique framing code.   The system was designed to operate at 1,625 bits per second on line giving a net bit rate of 1,300 plus a framing signal.   This is compatible with the requirements for SAGE data links.

Hughes Quaternary Phase-modulation Terminal.[9]   Hughes Aircraft has developed a quaternary phase-modulation system employing differential phase detection.   The unique feature of this system is the use of a nonsynchronous reference oscillator in the receiver.   The oscillator runs at a frequency close to the expected received carrier signal and is used to resolve each incoming interval into in-phase and quadrature components which are stored in analog form as voltages on capacitors.   By using two sets of storage capacitors which alternately sample the received signal, the amount of phase change is determined from the difference in the stored components from adjacent intervals.   The reference oscillator changes phase a sufficiently small amount in one symbol interval to make negligible error in the measurement of phase change.

Robertshaw-Fulton Multi-Lok Terminal.[10]   This binary phase-modulation system uses a phase change of 120° between the two states instead of 180°.   A reference phase is generated at the receiver by multiplying and dividing the received carrier frequency by three. The recovered carrier may thus have an error of $\pm 120°$.   If this should occur the receiver detects the presence of the unused or forbidden 120° phase position.   It then advances the divide-by-three counter until only the two permitted phases are received.

12-9   DATA TERMINALS FOR WIDER THAN VOICE-BAND FACILITIES

The need for remote access to high-speed digital computers has called for the development of high-speed data terminals requiring wider than voice-band facilities.   Recently developed high-speed black-and-white facsimile systems also require a high-speed binary channel.   A commonly available wide band is the group band which occurs in multiplex-telephony systems.   This band normally accommodates a group of 12 single-sideband voice channels spaced 4 kc apart. Special terminations have been developed to make these group bands available for high-speed data transmission.   For example, the Bell System 301B data set operates at 40,800 bits per second over such circuits using the same quaternary phase-modulation technique as the 201-type data set described in Sec. 12-8.

The next widest band commonly available in broadband carrier telephone systems is the 240-kc supergroup band which normally accommodates five group bands.   This band permits speeds of over 200,000 bits per second.   Speeds of several million bits per second can be obtained by employing a television channel.

The Bell System T1 carrier system[11] utilizes binary baseband transmission over cable pairs at about 1.5 million bits per second.   Where these high-speed transmission channels are available, they can be adapted to handle a variety of bit rates and numbers of data channels by the use of time-division techniques.

REFERENCES

1. Koenig, W.: Coordinate Data Sets for Military Use, *Bell Lab. Record*, vol. 36, pp. 166–170, May, 1958.
2. Soffel, R. O., and E. G. Spack: Sage Data Terminals, *AIEE Trans.*, part I (Communication and Electronics), vol. 77, pp. 872–879, 1958.
3. Hollis, J. L.: Digital Data Fundamentals and the Two-level Vestigial-sideband System for Voice Bandwidth Circuits, *IRE WESCON Conv. Record*, part 5, vol. 4, pp. 132–145, 1960.
4. Digital Data Communications, Technical Papers, Report No. 9201, vol. 3, ACF Industries Inc., Riverdale, Md.
5. Meyers, S. T.: An FM Data Set for Voiceband Data Transmission, *Bell Lab. Record*, vol. 41, pp. 2–7, January, 1963.
6. Mosier, R. R.: A Data Transmission System Using Pulse Phase Modulation, *IRE Convention Record of First National Convention on Military Electronics*, June 17–19, 1957, Washington, D.C.
7. Baker, P. A.: Phase-modulation Data Sets for Serial Transmission at 2000 and 2400 Bits per Second, *AIEE Trans.*, part I (Communication and Electronics), No. 61, pp. 166–171, July, 1962.
8. Hofman, E. J.: Specifications for a COBI Data Transmission Modem, Lincoln Lab., Report 25G-0035, p. 47, February, 1961.
9. Toeffler, J. E., and J. N. Buterbaugh: *IRE WESCON*, Paper 36/1, p. 6, 1961.
10. Crafts, C. A.: Phase Multilock Communication, *Conference Proc., IRE-PGMIL Second National Convention*, 1958.
11. Cravis, H., and T. V. Crater: Engineering of T1 Carrier System Repeatered Lines, *Bell System Tech. J.*, vol. 42, pp. 431–486, March, 1963.

CHAPTER 13

METHODS OF ESTABLISHING
A REFERENCE CARRIER FOR
SYNCHRONOUS DETECTION

The merits of synchronous or coherent detection of AM and PM signals have been established in Chaps. 8 and 10. We will consider here methods of establishing and maintaining a suitable carrier for this purpose. Because of the frequency offset occurring in single-sideband carrier telephone systems, the reference carrier required at the receiver will often differ in frequency from the carrier at the transmitter by several cycles. Furthermore, the phase stability of the channels is such that essentially continuous control is required to maintain a coherent carrier. This means that carrier frequency and phase information must either be conveyed by the data signal itself or by some auxiliary signal which accompanies it. To achieve maximum performance it is desirable to transmit this carrier information with as little power as possible.

13-1 REFERENCE CARRIER FOR BINARY DOUBLE-SIDEBAND AM

Synchronous detection of on-off AM is seldom undertaken since the improvement attainable over simple envelope detection is small. It is, however, easy to obtain a reference carrier from such a signal because there is a strong carrier component of constant phase. It can be separated from the sidebands by a narrow bandpass filter or the equivalent in the form of a phase-locked oscillator.

Of more interest is the case of suppressed-carrier AM, where there is no carrier component in the signal during a random sequence. Here the carrier phase during marking intervals is opposite to that during spacing intervals. A narrow filter in this case would give no output if the signal consisted of equal numbers of mark and space symbols. If, however, the received wave is full-wave rectified, a strong second harmonic of the carrier is formed which does not reverse phase between mark and space. This double carrier frequency can then be divided by two to obtain the desired reference.[1] Such an arrangement is shown in Fig. 13-1. The reference thus obtained may be either in phase or out of phase with the suppressed carrier, giving an ambiguity in the polarity of the detected signal. If the receiver can detect in

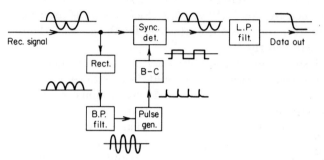

FIG. 13-1. Carrier recovery by generation of second harmonic of suppressed carrier.

some way that the polarity is reversed, steps can be taken to reverse the phase of the reference. Another way of avoiding this trouble is to encode the information in terms of signal transitions. For instance, a mark may be represented by a transition and a space by no transition. It then makes no difference in which phase the reference is established. If the reference should reverse phase during a transmission, errors

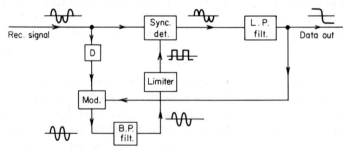

FIG. 13-2. Carrier recovery by modulating received signal with detected data wave.

would be formed only momentarily. It is necessary, however, to operate the channel synchronously.

A second method of recovering a reference carrier is shown in Fig. 13-2. Here the received signal is passed through a phase-reversing modulator controlled by the polarity of the detector output. The output of the modulator is a constant-phase signal since a compensating phase reversal is introduced at each phase reversal of the received wave.[2] The delay shown at D in Fig. 13-2 compensates for the delay of the low-pass postdetection filter so that the compensating phase reversals occur in synchronism with those of the received signal. The constant-phase signal is passed through a narrow filter to remove amplitude variations and noise. Here again there is a phase ambiguity of 180°. A method giving similar performance to that of Fig. 13-2 has been described by Costas.[3] A phase-locked loop is used instead of the bandpass filter, and the phase-reversal feedback from the data output is introduced into the loop.

A less desirable method involves adding some in-phase carrier to the signal at the transmitter. This could, for instance, cause the marking level to exceed the spacing level. If restrictions were placed on the length of spacing intervals, the output of a narrow-band carrier detection filter might never reverse its phase. Such a restriction on the signal sequence together with the diversion of considerable signal power to the carrier makes this an unattractive method in spite of its freedom from polarity ambiguity. The decision threshold would also have to be offset from zero, and the advantage of a balanced system against level variations would be partially lost.

13-2 REFERENCE CARRIER FOR BINARY VESTIGIAL-SIDEBAND AM WITH SUPPRESSED CARRIER

As previously described, vestigial-sideband operation with synchronous detection affords an attractive method of doubling the signaling speed capability of a given channel over that possible with double-sideband operation. When low modulating frequencies are present in such a system, a double-sideband spectrum exists in the neighborhood of the carrier frequency. This can be used to derive a reference carrier with a phase ambiguity of 180° as discussed in the previous section. However, when only higher modulating frequencies are present, a single-sideband spectrum exists which contains no information from which to derive a reference carrier. Consequently, if it is desired to maintain the reference during periods of no low-frequency modulation, it is necessary to add some carrier information to the signal. This could take the form of an added low-level marking-phase carrier, but it would be necessary to accept a 180° ambiguity since a long spacing interval would cause a phase reversal. Furthermore, a signal sequence could exist with just the right amount of carrier component of spacing phase to cancel the added marking carrier and prevent its detection.

The required carrier information could also be inserted as a low-frequency modulation such as to place a pair of spectral lines in the double-sideband portion of the spectrum. The detection methods of Figs. 13-1 and 13-2 could then be applied. The added low-frequency modulation would be superimposed on the detected data wave at the receiver. It could be canceled out by selecting the low-frequency modulation with a narrow filter and subtracting it in proper amplitude from the data wave. The frequency of the modulation should be one not likely to occur in the data wave with any significant strength,

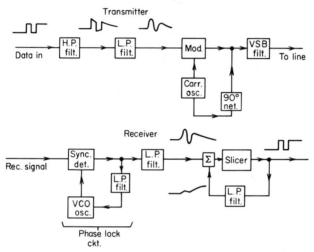

FIG. 13-3. Carrier-recovery method using removal and restoration of low-frequency components of data signal.

since this would interfere with both the carrier recovery and the cancellation process at the receiver.

One method which avoids both the 180° ambiguity and the need for any data-sequence restriction confines the data signal and a reference carrier to separate frequency bands.[4]   Such an arrangement is shown in Fig. 13-3. At the transmitter the very low data frequencies are removed by a high-pass network before modulation. Consequently, no data spectrum is formed in a narrow band adjacent to the carrier frequency. This permits the detection of a reference carrier at the receiver without interference from the data signal. If the added reference carrier is in quadrature with the suppressed data carrier, no d-c component is added to the demodulated data signal at the receiver. At the receiver the missing low frequencies of the data signal are reinserted by a method of quantized feedback* through a

* Described more fully in Sec. 15-4.

low-pass network complementary to the high-pass network at the transmitter. In the absence of noise and delay distortion, the signal transitions are received with accurate timing and the low frequencies are accurately restored. When the received data transitions are displaced by delay distortion and other impairments, the reinserted low-frequency component is in error, and the distortion becomes magnified. Consequently, this method leads to greater sensitivity to distorting influences. This effect can be made small by making the low-frequency cutoff near zero. However, the phase-lock circuit of Fig. 13-3 would then be perturbed by data components near the carrier.

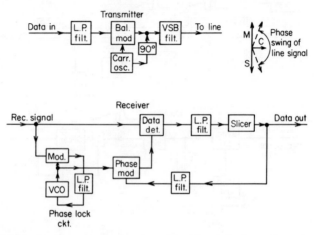

FIG. 13-4. Method of compensating for phase modulation of carrier by low-frequency components of data signal.

The bandwidth of the carrier-recovery circuit must be kept sufficiently wide to allow for frequency offset and to achieve lock-on within a reasonable time.

A more desirable system would permit the transmission of the complete data spectrum and avoid the shortcomings of reinserting the low frequencies. A method which has this desirable feature is shown in Fig. 13-4. A transmitter like that of Fig. 13-3 is used except that the high-pass filter is omitted. Again the receiver employs a phase-locked loop to detect the added quadrature carrier. The now present low-frequency data components perturb the phase of the detected carrier as indicated in the vector diagram. For example, if the added quadrature carrier has half the amplitude of a steady mark or space data condition, the maximum range of perturbation is about $\pm 60°$. Since the effective bandwidth of the phase-locked loop is small, the range of phase swing during most data sequences is considerably less.   Over this normal range of variation, the departure from the desired in-phase condition is approximately in linear relation to the average value of the binary data sequence.   As shown in Fig. 13-4, a portion of the data output from the slicer is smoothed by a low-pass filter.   The smoothed wave phase modulates the carrier recovered from the phase-locked loop to remove most of the phase variation.   The phase-corrected carrier is then used to demodulate the received signal.

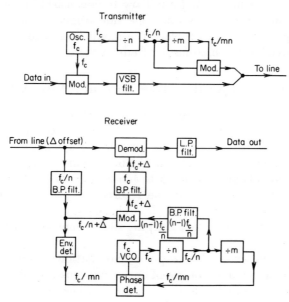

FIG. 13-5. Transmission of carrier by means of a modulated auxiliary tone outside of data band.

The time constant of the phase correction is matched approximately to that of the phase-locked loop.   In the quantized feedback scheme of Fig. 13-3, the time constant of the low-frequency reinsertion must be materially shorter than that of the phase-locked loop.   Consequently, the phase-correction method can be made less sensitive to the distorting effects of delay variation.

   Still another method of transmitting reference carrier information employs a sinusoidally modulated tone outside of the data signal band. The frequency of this auxiliary tone and also the frequency of its modulation are chosen to be harmonically related to the frequency of the data carrier.   At the receiver both the original carrier frequency and the amount of frequency offset of the channel can be obtained from such a signal.   Figure 13-5 shows an example of this method applied to a vestigial-sideband system. The modulated tone in this example is at the lower edge of the channel. The disadvantage of such a method is that the phase of the recovered carrier may require adjustment for optimum detection. The auxiliary signal is outside the data band and hence can suffer a different amount of phase shift from that of the data signal spectrum. The advantage of the method is the complete isolation of the reference carrier information from the data signal. Consequently, any type of digital or analog data can be transmitted. The modulated auxiliary tone consists of a carrier plus two side frequencies. Since only one side frequency is required, an alternative procedure is to replace the modulated tone with a pair of tones separated by the modulating frequency.

13-3 REFERENCE CARRIER FOR QUADRATURE AM

For a quadrature AM system there is no phase of reference carrier which will not be detected by one or both of the data channels. However, the method of removing the low data frequencies at the transmitter, as described for vestigial sideband, can be applied. If the individual channels are restricted to binary signaling, the missing low frequencies can be restored at the receiver as previously discussed.[5] The d-c component added to the data channel by the reference carrier can be blocked from the data output, since there are no transmitted low frequencies.

For the special case of four-phase modulation where the symbol intervals consist of carrier pulses of one of four possible phases with 90° spacing, carrier could be derived from the signal under certain conditions. For instance, if the pulse shapes were nearly rectangular and there were relatively many carrier cycles per symbol, the second harmonic of the rate of zero crossings would give a reference of four times the carrier. This could be divided by four to obtain a recovered carrier with a phase ambiguity of 0°, ±90°, or 180°. In a practical system, however, with restricted bandwidth, the phase change between symbols is not abrupt. With repeated 90° changes in the same direction, the carrier frequency appears to shift, and carrier recovery becomes impossible.

Another method of separating the reference carrier and data information is the use of time-division techniques. For example, the data can be organized into blocks of symbols, each preceded by a short burst of reference carrier. The receiver detects and stores this reference information for the detection of the following symbols. Such a procedure involves giving up a smooth continuous flow of symbols, but with suitable buffer storage the channel can be made to appear continuous. The possible length of block depends on the phase stability of the transmission path and the accuracy with which the receiver detects and remembers the reference burst.

Carrier for quadrature AM can also be derived from an auxiliary out-of-band reference signal as described in Sec. 13-2.

REFERENCES

1. Rieke, J. W. and R. S. Graham: The L-3 Coaxial System: Television Terminals, *Bell System Tech. J.*, vol. 32, pp. 915–942, July, 1953.
2. Hopner, E.: Phase Reversal Data Transmission System for Switched and Private Telephone Line Applications, *IBM J. Res. Develop.*, vol. 5, pp. 93–105, April, 1961.
3. Costas, J. P.: Synchronous Communications, *Proc. IRE*, vol. 44, pp. 1713–1718, December, 1956.
4. Becker, F. K., J. R. Davey, and B. R. Saltzberg: An AM Vestigial Sideband Data Transmission Set Using Synchronous Detection for Serial Transmission up to 3000 Bits per Second, *AIEE Trans.*, part I (Communications and Electronics), No. 60, pp. 97–101, May, 1962.
5. de Jager, F., and P. J. van Gerwen: Co-modulation, A New Method for High-speed Data Transmission, *IRE Trans. Inform. Theory*, vol. IT-8, pp. 285–290, September, 1962.

CHAPTER 14

METHODS OF SYNCHRONIZATION

A digital receiver requires timing information in order to interpret the received signal sequence properly. Each symbol in the sequence must be sampled at a time when its value has become fully established and it is not in a condition of transition. The timing necessary to accomplish this will be designated here as symbol timing, or in the special case of binary symbols as bit timing. In a serial-type system where groups of symbols are used to represent a character, it is also necessary to determine the boundaries of such groups. We shall call this requirement group or character timing. The characters are in turn organized into some sort of message. It is, therefore, necessary to recognize the start and end or framing of these messages. These various types of timing information must either be conveyed by the data channel itself or by an auxiliary timing channel. This chapter considers various means of providing the timing information.

14-1 SYMBOL TIMING FOR A SYNCHRONOUS BINARY SYSTEM

In a synchronous binary channel, the signal transitions occur at integral multiples of the unit symbol length. If the transitions occur fairly frequently, the symbol timing, or bit timing in this case, can be established from the transitions. For example, if an impulse is generated at each transition, the resulting spectrum has a line at the symbol rate which can be detected by a resonant circuit or other narrow bandpass circuit. The amplitude of the sinusoidal signal thus obtained is proportional to the density of the transitions. Means can be provided for adjusting the phase and limiting the signal to produce a timing wave which has the proper orientation with respect to the data signal. Usually the objective is to have either the positive- or the negative-going transitions of the timing wave coincide with the centers of the received bit intervals.

When it is desirable to maintain the bit timing wave during periods of few or no transitions, better results are obtained by having the transitions control the phase of a local oscillator. An indication can be obtained of the required correction by comparing the phase of the transitions with that of the timing wave. The form of the correction may be of several varieties. For instance, a sawtooth timing wave can be sampled at the transition times to derive an error signal which is proportional to the amount of correction required. The error signal can then act on the phase or frequency of the timing oscillator to bring about the correction. It is usually desirable to have the correction take place slowly so that the phase of the timing wave follows the long-time average phase of the transitions. In the absence of transitions, no correction is made; consequently, the period of time during which synchronism is maintained depends on how close the natural frequency of the oscillator is to the transmitter timing.

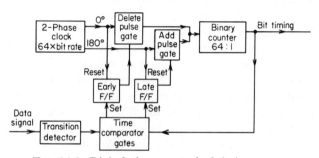

Fig. 14-1. Digital phase control of timing wave.

To form the error signal for controlling the timing phase, the transitions need not be weighted proportionally to their deviations from the timing wave. In fact, it is sufficient and perhaps desirable to classify the transitions only as early or late and to control the timing phase so as to have about equal numbers of each. A convenient digital method of phase control is shown in Fig. 14-1. A timing wave is obtained by frequency-dividing the output of a crystal oscillator running, for example, at 64 times the bit rate. If the timing wave is found to be leading in phase at a transition, one of the count pulses from the oscillator is deleted, thus retarding the phase by 1/64 of a bit interval. On the other hand, when the timing wave is lagging in phase, an extra count pulse is fed to the count-down circuit, thus advancing the phase by 1/64 of a bit interval. For the highest degree of accuracy, it is desirable to control the frequency of the timing wave by a method including memory. Then, in the absence of transitions, the last setting is maintained instead of reverting to a fixed natural frequency. The memory can be in the form of a servomechanism or a digital storage.

The symbol timing can also be carried by some form of modulation of the data signal itself. For example, if a return-to-zero polar binary signal is transmitted, there will be a component of bit rate frequency in the received signal for all signaling conditions. This is obtained, however, at the expense of additional bandwidth, since frequencies in excess of half the bit rate are not required to transmit the data information. The symbol timing for quaternary phase modulation can be transmitted in much the same way. For instance, if in a quaternary differential phase-modulation system, phase changes of $\pm 45°$ and $\pm 135°$ are used, and if sufficient bandwidth is used to permit the rate of phase change to approach zero at the centers of the symbol intervals, then there will be a detectable component at the symbol rate. Various other approaches could also be used, such as combinations of AM and FM or AM and PM, to obtain effectively a second channel to convey the symbol timing. Extra bandwidth could be avoided in these dual modulation methods by transmitting a half-symbol-rate frequency.

Where the transmission medium does not introduce phase distortion or frequency offset, the symbol timing of an AM or PM system can be integrally related to the carrier frequency. The latter can then be used to maintain synchronism during periods of no symbol transitions. This method could also be used for FM by having all steady-state frequencies integrally related to the symbol rate. Such methods are seldom employed, however, because few communication channels have the necessary phase stability.

Still another method of transmitting continuous bit timing employs a pilot carrier separated from the data signal carrier by a frequency equal to the bit rate. This frequency difference can then be detected at the receiver to establish a bit timing signal. In the case of vestigial-sideband operation, the frequency separation can be made some submultiple of the bit rate. Alternatively two pilot carriers separated by the bit rate or a submultiple thereof can be used. The main problem in the use of such pilot carriers is the difference in phase shift between the detected difference frequency and the received data wave. A phase adjustment is required for optimum results. A modulated pilot carrier, as previously discussed in Sec. 13-2, can also be used to transmit a subharmonic of the bit timing.

14-2 SYMBOL TIMING FOR A SYNCHRONOUS MULTILEVEL SYSTEM

In a multilevel receiver more than one decision threshold is established. Symbol timing can be derived from the transitions across these thresholds. Since a symbol transition can cause several threshold transitions that are spread in time, there is potentially more jitter than in a binary system. A local oscillator can be controlled in phase by the average phase of the threshold transitions. To obtain a true average, it is necessary to employ equal weighting. When several are grouped together at a symbol transition, no one of them can be allowed to have the major effect. This general technique can be applied to AM, FM, or PM systems. Symbol rate information can also be transmitted by the means discussed for binary signals in Sec. 14-1.

14-3 SYMBOL AND CHARACTER TIMING IN START-STOP SYSTEMS

Start-stop operation is widely used in printing telegraph systems. Each character begins with a mark-to-space transition followed by the code pulses after one unit of space. The initial mark-to-space transition serves to phase the sampling of the code pulses. Each character

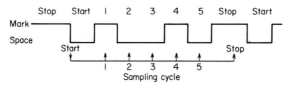

FIG. 14-2. Bit and character timing in start-stop system.

is terminated by a minimum of one to two units of mark, thus providing a pause or stop before the start of the next character. The character timing is thus asynchronous while the bit timing is synchronous in spurts. These features of a start-stop signal are shown in Fig. 14-2. If the receiving selector is falsely started, or if the signal is mutilated, there may be no marking interval to pause on at the end of the normal sampling cycle. In such a case some selectors proceed to run through additional sampling cycles without pausing until a marking interval is found at the end of a cycle. Other selectors are arranged to stop even if no marking interval is found and to wait for the next mark-to-space transition before recycling. Depending upon what the received signal is at the time, the selector usually regains synchronization quickly unless some repeated combination is transmitted which causes the selector to synchronize on some mark-to-space transition other than the normal start.

The outstanding advantages of start-stop synchronization are its simplicity and its ability to accept irregular character spacing such as sent from a keyboard transmitting machine. Since no preparatory synchronization procedure is required, it is ideal for to-and-fro or chit-chat type communication and for use in large multistation networks. Also, because simple binary channels are used, the individual links making up a network can be interconnected in a simple manner without synchronization problems. As discussed in Chap. 16 start-stop operation has less tolerance to signal distortion than a purely synchronous system and is also more likely to lose character synchronization. The tolerance to distortion becomes equal to that of a synchronous system if the length of the stop period is always an integral number of unit marking intervals and a synchronous regenerator is inserted ahead of the start-stop receiver. This requires sufficient transitions or other means to maintain bit timing for the regenerator and, of course, sacrifices much of the flexibility of start-stop operation.

14-4 CHARACTER TIMING FOR A SYNCHRONOUS BINARY SYSTEM

In a synchronous system the successive characters are usually made up of a fixed number of bits. The frequency of the character timing can thus easily be obtained by dividing the bit timing. The problem then becomes that of properly phasing the character timing. This is usually accomplished by reserving one of the code combinations or words for character synchronization. If this word is unique in that it never occurs in any normal data sequence, it can be used to rephase the character timing whenever it is recognized. More often a combination is used which may occur in certain data sequences. In order to indicate the character phasing, the word is repeated several times together with other specific combinations which indicate when the system is in the character synchronizing mode. An error-detecting code is useful in indicating a loss of character synchronization and a consequent need for the system to revert to the synchronizing mode.

Some systems provide a third signal condition used only for framing of the words or characters. This enables the framing to be accomplished faster at the expense of channel complexity. An entirely separate channel is sometimes devoted to the character timing and phasing function.

14-5 METHODS OF IMPROVING RELIABILITY OF SYNCHRONIZATION

The synchronization methods discussed in the previous sections are usually satisfactory for two-way types of data systems. In such systems a loss of synchronization can be made known to the transmitting station and the missed portion of the message repeated. In one-way systems any missed message can only be supplied after some delay by some other communication means. For timely information such delay may render the information useless. It is often desirable in such systems to use a more rugged synchronization method to minimize the loss of messages. For synchronous systems this means strengthening the framing or character phasing since the bit timing can readily be made as rugged as necessary. For start-stop systems this means improved phasing of both characters and bits.

A special type of binary sequence useful for a framing indication has been described by R. H. Barker.[1] Such a sequence is designed to have the autocorrelation coefficient as small as possible except for zero time

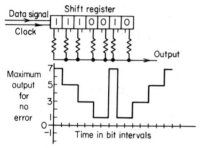

FIG. 14-3. Detection of framing sequence.

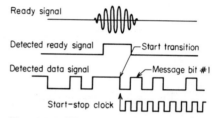

FIG. 14-4. Use of auxiliary channel "ready" signal.

lag. Figure 14-3 shows a method for detecting such a seven-bit sequence by use of a shift register and suitable summing network. Considering the contribution of each digit to the output as ± 1, it is seen that the maximum output for exact match is $+7$. When the sequence is received without error and is preceded and followed by the most unfavorable combination of bits, the output of the detector is as shown in Fig. 14-3. It will be noted that the exact match is indicated by a pronounced rise in output. It will also be seen that sufficient margin exists to allow one bit to be in error without missing the correct phasing.

In start-stop synchronization the three functions "ready," "phasing," and "start" are required. The "ready" alerts the receiver as to when to look for the start and phasing information. The "phasing" indicates the proper orientation of the sampling. The "start" indicates the location of the first information bit. In the simple teletypewriter code the receiver assumes the "ready" condition as soon as it completes the sampling of a character. The initial mark-to-space transition of the following character carries both the "phasing" and the "start" information. Improvements can be obtained by designing the synchronizing signal to perform these three functions more specifically. Figure 14-4 shows a method in which a ready signal is transmitted over an auxiliary channel. The particular time interval is thereby identified in which the data channel transitions indicating the phasing and start signals are to be found. The latter can employ one or more transitions. Use of more than one transition offers the possibility of averaging the transition times to lessen the effect of noise and distortion. Use of the separate ready signal greatly lessens the possibility of false starts.

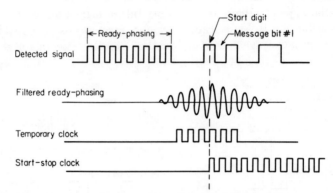

FIG. 14-5. Method of combining "ready" and "phasing" functions.

Figure 14-5 shows a method of combining the ready and phasing functions. At the expense of some extra bandwidth, a burst of double-speed reversals is used as a ready signal. The data signal spectrum has a null at this frequency, and the ready signal can easily be separated by a narrow bandpass filter. The double-bit-rate signal from the filter has a phase representing the average phase of the burst and consequently gives an accurate indication of the proper phasing for the bit sampling. It can also be used as a temporary receiving clock to sample for the start pattern instead of depending on signal transitions. The start may consist of an isolated marking bit or a more complex pattern. Once the start is located the regular receive clock is started in the same phase as that of the temporary clock signal. In quite long messages the receive clock can be phase corrected during the message by the average transition times if desired. Such an arrangement is able to operate start-stop with nearly the same sampling margin as a purely synchronous system.

These more rugged start-stop systems are often used when a data terminal is to receive a sequence of short messages from a number of different transmitters. With the transmitters located at various distances, the messages arrive with different phasings of bit timing. Thus the receiver must be capable of rephasing its receive clock for each message.

14-6 CHARACTER TIMING IN PARALLEL SYSTEMS

In a parallel-type system, the several individual bits making up a character are transmitted over separate channels. The timing of bits and characters thus becomes one and the same. An auxiliary channel is often provided for timing and enables either synchronous or asynchronous operation. In the case of synchronous operation, the timing can be derived from the transitions in the individual channels as discussed for a single binary channel. Return-to-zero-type signaling may also be used to indicate the timing at the expense of bandwidth or speed.

REFERENCE

1. Barker, R. H.: Group Synchronization of Binary Digital Systems, "Communication Theory," W. Jackson (ed.), pp. 273–278, Butterworth Scientific Publications, London, 1953.

CHAPTER 15

EQUALIZATION OF DATA CHANNELS

In Chap. 4 it was shown that certain pulse spectrum shapes are desirable to minimize intersymbol interference. In Chap. 6 it was shown that departure from a linear phase-vs.-frequency characteristic distorts the received pulse and causes intersymbol interference. When it is desirable to transmit over a number of channels which vary considerably in their amplitude and phase characteristics, it may be necessary to apply corrective means or equalization to keep the pulse distortion within reasonable limits. In this chapter we consider methods of bringing about this correction.

15-1 EQUALIZATION NETWORKS

The most common approach to equalizing a data channel is to place a network at the receiver which has attenuation and phase characteristics equal to the differences between the desired and actual ones.[1,2]

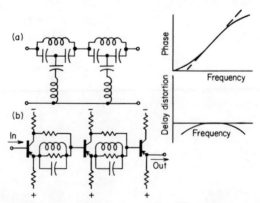

FIG. 15-1. Network sections for correction of delay distortion.

As brought out in Chap. 6, in the use of telephone voice channels for high-speed data communication, pulse distortion is more likely to arise from nonlinear phase than from variations in attenuation. One type of network section which is useful for correction of nonlinear phase or delay

268

distortion is shown in Fig. 15-1a. With a number of such sections in tandem, almost any phase characteristic superimposed on a straight line of sufficiently large positive slope can be obtained. Envelope delay is kept constant across the band of interest by making the variations from linear phase equal but opposite to that of the line. Additional flat delay is added in bringing about the corrections. Figure 15-1b shows an equivalent type of circuit using one transistor per stage and only half the number of reactive elements. A compromise delay equalizer suitable for use with switched telephone network channels typically requires two or three sections of the type in Fig. 15-1.

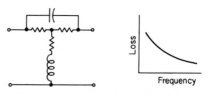

FIG. 15-2. Attenuation equalizer.

Attenuation variations over the useful portion of a telephone channel are usually of the type termed "slope" in which the loss increases toward the upper end of the channel. Such a slope may be compensated by making the gain of the receiver rise toward the higher frequencies. This can usually be accomplished by simple RC networks in the coupling between stages of the normally required amplification. Where a constant-resistance network is required, the bridged-T configuration of Fig. 15-2 can be used.

15-2 USE OF TRANSVERSAL-TYPE FILTERS

Where it is necessary to select among or to adjust several attenuation and phase characteristics, the use of a transversal filter offers great flexibility.[3] A transversal-type filter is shown in Fig. 15-3. The signal is applied to a tapped delay line and the output is obtained from a summation of signals from the several taps. Each tap is provided with a means of effectively multiplying its contribution by any value between $+1$ and -1. The action of such a filter on the amplitude-frequency characteristic may be visualized by considering the summation of the three middle taps, a_0, a_{-1}, and a_{+1}. The multiplier for a_0 is set at $+1$ and those for a_{-1} and a_{+1} at equal but smaller positive values. A vector diagram of these three components is shown in Fig. 15-4. As the frequency of the input signal is raised, the a_{+1} component increasingly lags a_0 in phase while a_{-1} increasingly leads a_0. The sum of the three remains in phase with a_0 but varies in amplitude.

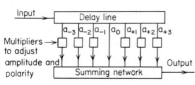

FIG. 15-3. Transversal filter.

Figure 15-4 indicates the resulting cosine variation in amplitude vs. frequency. At a frequency equal to the reciprocal of the tap spacing, the vectors are in the same position as at zero frequency, and the amplitude pattern starts to repeat. If now taps a_{-2} and a_{+2} are also included with small equal positive multiplier values, an added variation in amplitude is obtained with half the period obtained before. Thus any variation representable by a summation of harmonically related cosine terms can be obtained from a set of symmetrically located pairs of taps with equal multiplier settings. This includes any

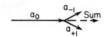

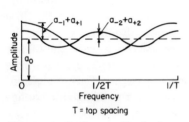

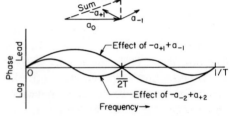

FIG. 15-4. Cosine amplitude characteristic of a transversal filter.

FIG. 15-5. Approximate sinusoidal phase characteristic of a transversal filter.

shape with even symmetry about a frequency equal to one-half the reciprocal of the tap spacing or any shape between zero and half the reciprocal of the tap spacing. The even symmetry of the pairs of components introduces no change in the phase characteristic.

Now consider the case where the multiplier settings for each pair are made to be opposite in sign. Figure 15-5 shows the summation of a_{-1}, a_0, and a_{+1} under such a condition. The major effect as the frequency is increased is an approximately sinusoidal variation in phase with minor changes in amplitude as indicated in Fig. 15-5. Thus any shaped variation in phase obtainable from a summation of harmonically related sine terms is possible. These will all start from zero at zero frequency and have odd symmetry about half the frequency of the reciprocal of the tap spacing. Large phase variations will involve amplitude changes, but these in turn can be corrected by even symmetry multiplier adjustments. Consequently, any correction of both phase and amplitude characteristics can be brought about by such a transversal filter. If the adjustable components from the taps are considered as echoes of the original signal, it will be seen that the transversal filter is a method of summing pairs of echoes having either even or odd symmetry.[4]

Having considered the functioning of the transversal filter in the frequency domain, let us now consider it purely in the time domain.

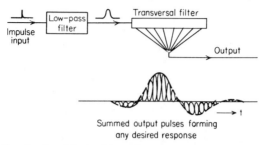

Summed output pulses forming
any desired response

FIG. 15-6. Synthesis of desired impulse response by a transversal filter.

In Fig. 15-6 a transversal filter is shown with a low-pass filter at its input. The filter has the indicated impulse response, which is passed by the delay line with little distortion. If the taps are spaced no farther apart than the width of this input pulse, the summed output can be made to have any shape desired over a period equal to the total delay of the line. Thus the transversal filter can be adjusted to have any desired transmission characteristic from a knowledge of the impulse response of the desired characteristic. This is illustrated in Fig. 15-6.

Although it is relatively easy to adjust a transversal equalizer to have a particular impulse response, it is often not practical to calculate the desired impulse response. Fortunately a transversal equalizer can usually be adjusted as part of the channel to give the desired over-all pulse response. A single data pulse distorted by a parabolic-shaped delay characteristic is shown as wave a in Fig. 15-7. Sampling instants are indicated along the time axis oriented with respect to the pulse peak. Considerable intersymbol interference is evidenced by the

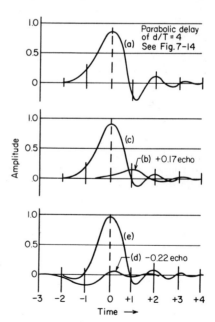

FIG. 15-7. Improvement of pulse response by addition of echoes.

nonzero values of the wave at the sampling instants of nearby bits. The interference at any one sampling instant can be reduced to zero by the addition of an echo of the distorted pulse. This is illustrated in Fig. 15-7 by the echo wave b having a peak value at $t = +1$ which just cancels the value of the main pulse a at $t = +1$. The resultant wave after addition of the echo is shown as wave c. The addition of the echo also changes the value of the wave at other sampling instants but to a lesser extent. The pulse can then be further corrected by addition of an echo as shown by wave d which has a peak value at $t = -1$ such as to produce a zero in the resultant e at that point. In so doing, the value at $t = +1$ is moved from its previous zero adjustment. However, the intersymbol interference is seen to be considerably reduced by the addition of the two echoes. If the main pulse peak is large compared with the other sample values, the output wave can be made to approach zero rapidly at both $t = +1$ and $t = -1$ by successive adjustments of the echo amplitudes. Additional echoes spaced at the sampling intervals can be added to reduce the total intersymbol interferences to nearly zero.

Instead of adjusting the response at each sample point away from the main pulse to be zero by successive adjustments of the corresponding echo amplitudes, the adjustments can be made to give the maximum eye opening with a random pulse train applied. This tends to result in compromise adjustments which minimize the total intersymbol interference rather than making it zero at one particular sample point. Here again if the initial distortion is not too great, the successive adjustments rapidly converge to optimum settings. With very high distortion such that the eye opening cannot be seen, the effect of any one adjustment may not be apparent. Usually trial adjustments of the echoes spaced one or two bits on either side of the main response initiate an eye opening. If corrections approaching the amplitude of the pulse peak are required, many echo taps are necessary and the adjustments are so interdependent that a manual solution becomes difficult and tedious.

Spacing the echoes at bit-length intervals as described corresponds to controlling the transmission characteristic up to a frequency equal to half the bit rate. With echoes spaced at half-bit intervals, the characteristic can be controlled up to a frequency equal to the bit rate as would be required to correct a full raised-cosine pulse spectrum.

For a linear AM or PM system the equalization can be carried out at baseband either before modulation or after detection. This has the advantage that the delay line need be effective only up to a frequency equal to the bit rate. If the equalization is done at carrier frequencies, the delay line must be effective over the wider frequency range occupied by the useful sidebands. This requires a delay line with more taps as well as more bandwidth. Performing the equalization at line frequencies will thus tend to be more costly and complex.

15-3 EQUALIZATION BY PREDISTORTION

Equalization of a channel can be accomplished by predistorting the transmitted pulses in such a way that the pulses have the desired shape after transmission through the channel. A simple way of performing the required predistortion of binary signals is shown in Fig. 15-8. A shift register is used in the same manner as the analog delay line of Fig. 15-3. If each register stage consists of a symmetrical

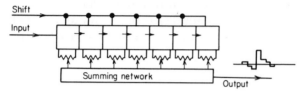

FIG. 15-8. Predistortion of binary signals by use of shift register.

transistor flip-flop, a potentiometer connected across the two collectors can provide adjustment of the amplitude and polarity of the contribution from each stage. The summed output constitutes the signal to be transmitted. If the shift register is advanced once per bit interval, the result is equivalent to that obtained in Fig. 15-3 with a tap spacing of one-bit interval. The advance of a single isolated marking bit down the shift register might generate a wave as shown in Fig. 15-8. One of the center stages contributes the main signal while the other stages contribute adjustable echoes. Finer control of the waveform can be obtained by advancing the shift register twice per bit interval. This is equivalent to using a delay line with taps at half-bit-length intervals. With a random signal passing down the shift register, the summed output is a multilevel-type signal. With n stages in the register there can be 2^n levels.

Since a four-level signal can be formed by the addition of two binary signals, a pair of shift registers could generate a predistorted four-level signal. Generally, the use of an analog-type delay line would be more suitable for multilevel-type signals since it can handle any number of levels.

The predistortion method using a shift register is attractive for binary signals because of its simplicity compared with the use of a tapped analog delay line at the receiver. The main disadvantage is that it is remote from the receiver, where the received signal quality is known. This can be overcome either by sending a measure of signal quality back to the transmitter or by controlling the adjustments of predistortion remotely from the receiver. A second disadvantage is that it would not be of use when transmitting to a number of receivers simultaneously.   On the other hand, predistortion could be attractive when several transmitters send to a single receiver.

15-4   EQUALIZATION BY QUANTIZED FEEDBACK

Quantized feedback can be used to perform certain types of equalization.   It can be applied when the difference between the actual and desired step response of the channel is negligible until after the transition is detected.   This is often true when the low-frequency portion of the signal spectrum needs correction.   As an example Fig. 15-9 shows the circuit diagram and step response of a baseband channel

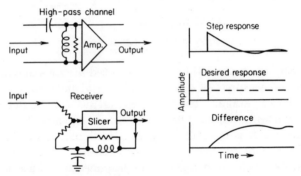

Fig. 15-9. Correction of low-frequency deficiencies by quantized feedback.

containing a high-pass filter.   In this case, the desired step response is that which would be obtained with the high-pass filter removed.   The difference between the two begins after the initial transition and can therefore be generated locally and added to the received signal, thereby effectively equalizing the response. Figure 15-9 shows how the compensating waveform can be generated by passing the detected step through a low-pass filter with a response complementary to that of the high-pass filter in the channel.   Since the compensating transient is of fixed amplitude, the received signal must be of a matching amplitude if the compensation is to be correct.   This general form of equalization is usually restricted to binary signaling when a missing d-c component is to be inserted.   If more than two levels are attempted, the output can get out of step with the transmitted signal.   If full transmission occurs at zero frequency, but some other low-frequency deficiency is to be compensated, multilevel feedback becomes feasible. The simple slicer in the binary example must then be replaced by a multilevel decision and regeneration process.

Quantized feedback can also be used to increase the binary signaling speed capability of a channel at the expense of margin against noise. Figure 15-10 shows how the effective step response of a channel can be made sharper by controlling the shape of the step beyond the detection of the transition. It will be noted in the example that the effective amplitude of the signal is reduced and that the decision threshold is moved closer to the steady-state condition. Since the compensated wave reaches steady state much earlier, the signaling speed can be increased without severe intersymbol interference. Equalization of this type was first used in d-c telegraph systems, where it was easily implemented by connecting a suitable network from the armature of

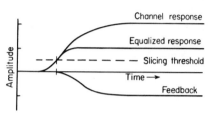

FIG. 15-10. Increasing binary signaling speed by quantized feedback.

the receiving relay to an auxiliary winding on the same relay. Because of the positive feedback action the relay could be made to oscillate in the absence of line current and was consequently known as a "vibrating relay circuit." Such arrangements were also of use in increasing the speed capabilities of transoceanic cables as described in Sec. 7-8. As illustrated in Fig. 15-10, the speed can be approximately doubled for a 6-db decrease in tolerance to noise.

Quantized feedback has two disadvantages. It cannot operate properly if the channel step response has considerable oscillations before reaching the decision threshold. Also any distortion which shifts the time of detecting the transitions causes errors in the feedback signal. This causes a cumulative effect which emphasizes the distortion.

In Sec. 7-8, the duobinary technique was discussed as a means of increasing signaling speed in exchange for noise margin. Instead of compensating for the intersymbol intereference as does quantized feedback, the intersymbol interference becomes quantized with respect to the steady-state response so as to permit interpretation of the received wave as a multilevel signal.

REFERENCES

1. Zobel, O. J.: Distortion Correction in Electrical Circuits with Constant Resistance Recurrent Networks, *Bell System Tech. J.*, vol. 7, pp. 438–534, July, 1928.

2. Bennett, W. R.: Synthesis of Active Networks, *Proc. Polytech. Inst. Brooklyn Symp. Series*, vol. 5, Modern Network Synthesis, pp. 45–61, April, 1955.
3. Kallman, H. E.: Transversal Filters, *Proc. IRE*, vol. 28, pp. 302–310, July, 1940.
4. Wheeler, H. A.: The Interpretation of Amplitude and Phase Distortion in Terms of Paired Echoes, *Proc. IRE*, vol. 27, pp. 359–385, June, 1939.

CHAPTER 16

MEASURING THE PERFORMANCE OF DATA TRANSMISSION SYSTEMS

The final criterion of performance of a digital communication system is how well the final receiving device makes decisions as to what was transmitted. Errors of decision are determined by a comparison of the sent and received messages. The quality of transmission can be stated as the decision error probability. In this chapter we consider means of measuring the quality of data signals and the margin against error.

16-1 DATA SIGNAL DISTORTION

Most of the time a useful communication system operates below the threshold of error. Thus a measurement of errors often gives no information as to how much margin there is against a wrong decision. It is under these no-error conditions that data signal quality measurements are particularly valuable in determining how close to error the system may be. A number of terms describing the quality of binary telegraph signals have been generally accepted. The term distortion is used to mean a change in the received signal from that transmitted. After the received binary signal has been restored to a rectangular shape, distortion takes the form of change in the relative times of the signal transitions. Thus, if the marking and spacing intervals as received differ in duration from those transmitted, they are said to be distorted.

The time distortion of the signal elements can be resolved into two components commonly termed *systematic* and *fortuitous*. The systematic component is the average distortion which occurs when a particular signal wave is repeatedly transmitted through a system. The fortuitous component is the variation from the average. The sum of the systematic and fortuitous components makes up the total distortion.

The systematic distortion can be further broken down into components of *bias* and *characteristic* distortion. Bias distortion is that type which changes sign when the functions of the signaling states are interchanged. For example, a case of bias exists if a marking interval is lengthened in transmission over a system while a spacing interval is shortened. Bias which lengthens marking intervals is termed "marking bias" and is commonly considered as "positive bias." The opposite condition resulting in shortened marking intervals and lengthened spacing intervals is known as "spacing" or "negative bias." Characteristic distortion is that type which changes neither sign nor magnitude when the functions of the two signaling states are interchanged. For example, if an isolated short marking interval is shortened in transmission by the same amount that a similarly short spacing interval is shortened, a case of characteristic distortion exists. For this particular example the sign is considered negative, while a case in which short marks and spaces are both lengthened is considered positive characteristic distortion.

Bias distortion is brought about by a lack of symmetry in the system. For instance, the decision threshold may not be set at the midpoint between the steady-state mark and space conditions, or the shape of the transition from mark to space may differ from that of space to mark. Characteristic distortion is brought about by intersymbol interference resulting from bandwidth restriction or a nonlinear phase-vs.-frequency transmission characteristic. Fortuitous distortion is caused by extraneous factors such as noise, crosstalk, relay chatter, and carrier-phase effects, all of which may occur at random with respect to the signal sequence.

The amount of distortion can be stated in time units such as milliseconds, but more commonly it is expressed in per cent of a unit-length signaling element. It then becomes necessary to state the speed of transmission at which the per cent distortion applies. Figure 16-1 gives examples of binary signals having the various types of distortion described.

In determining the time distortion of binary signals, a comparison between the transmitted and received signal is implied. This brings up the question as to the orientation of the two signals to be compared. For instance, the original signal might be oriented to give equal early and late time distortions of the received transitions. This would minimize the peak distortions and is a reasonable approach when applied to Morse signals or to synchronous-type signals. When start-stop operation is employed, as with most teleprinters, it is usual to measure distortion as it affects a start-stop receiver. This calls for orienting the reference signal with respect to the beginning of the start element of each received character. The distortions of the start transition then add to the distortions of the following transitions in the character. The fortuitous component of distortion consequently has a peak value double that measured with reference to the mean transition position as for synchronous signals. If the start transition

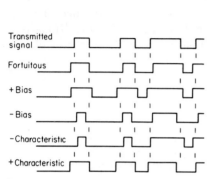

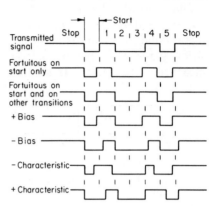

FIG. 16-1. Examples of synchronous signal distortion.

FIG. 16-2. Examples of start-stop signal distortion.

is mark-to-space (M–S), the bias distortion appears entirely at the space-to-mark (S–M) transitions. Therefore, a given amount of bias distortion appears as double value to a start-stop receiver as compared with a synchronous receiver. Figure 16-2 illustrates several cases of distortion of start-stop signals.

16-2 MEASUREMENT OF BIAS DISTORTION

Bias distortion is probably the most common type of data signal distortion. The bias distortion of a transmission link can be readily determined by transmitting a dotting or reversal signal and observing the received signal for equal durations of the mark and space intervals.

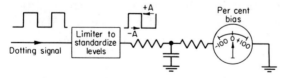

FIG. 16-3. Measurement of signal bias.

Since a dotting signal is not subject to characteristic distortion, a measure of its average distortion is a measure of bias. A simple means of obtaining a meter indication of bias distortion is shown in Fig. 16-3.

The meter deflection is proportional to the average value of the rectangular wave and is, therefore, linearly related to the percentage of the time the signal is in one of its binary states. The meter scale can be calibrated to indicate the bias in per cent of the unit signal duration.

Bias can also be measured from an observation of an eye pattern on an oscilloscope. The appearance of an eye pattern of biased rectangular reversals is shown in Fig. 16-4. In the absence of transition jitter, the opening between the M–S and S–M transitions is a measure of the bias. If the M–S transitions occur early, the bias is

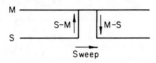

FIG. 16-4. Eye pattern of biased rectangular reversals.

FIG. 16-5. Oscilloscope display giving polarity separation of transitions.

spacing or negative. If the transitions have considerable jitter, the bias is indicated by the difference in the average position of the M–S and S–M transitions. If the ranges of M–S and S–M transitions overlap, the bias may not be apparent because of the inability to differentiate between the M–S and S–M transitions.

If the received signals are observed before they have been squared up by the slicer, the different slopes of the M–S and S–M transitions provide sufficient separation to observe bias by an eye-pattern scope display. A type of oscilloscope display which insures the necessary separation of M–S and S–M transitions is shown in Fig. 16-5. The rectangular data signal is differentiated to obtain short impulses which differ in polarity for M–S and S–M transitions. These are used for the vertical deflection and appear on the scope face as positive and negative pips on the horizontal base line. The average position of M–S and S–M transitions can thus be determined even under conditions of overlap.

Methods for measuring bias of miscellaneous data signals will be discussed in the next section in conjunction with more general distortion measurements.

16-3 MEASUREMENT OF PEAK DISTORTION AND BIAS OF RANDOM SYNCHRONOUS DATA SIGNALS

In general, the measurement of data signal distortion involves the measurement of the time displacement of the signal transitions from their normal undistorted positions. A suitable time base for comparison is thus basic to such measurements. For synchronous signals, where in the absence of distortion all transitions occur at multiples of the unit signal element, a continuously running time base phase-locked to the incoming signal is required. Figure 16-6 shows a sawtooth time base for use with a synchronous data signal. It passes

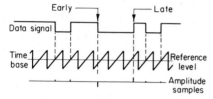

FIG. 16-6. Sawtooth time base for measuring synchronous distortion.

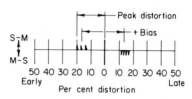

FIG. 16-7. Oscilloscope display using time base of Fig. 16-6.

through a reference level in the center of its amplitude range at the nominal transition time. The time-base wave thus has a value below reference value for early transitions and a value above reference value for late transitions. Sampling of the timing wave at the signal transitions results in pulses proportional to the time distortion. The samples can be integrated to form an error signal controlling the phase of the timing wave in a manner to keep the average distortion near zero. This basic timing wave can be used to obtain a number of distortion displays.

In many cases a measure of peak distortion without regard to sign is sufficient. This is accomplished by applying the samples to a rectifier followed by a peak-reading circuit. A measure of bias can be obtained

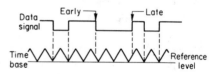

FIG. 16-8. Triangular time base for the display and measurement of synchronous distortion.

by separately averaging the M–S and S–M samples and using a differential-type circuit to measure the difference between the two averages.

Various types of oscilloscope displays can also be used with the basic timing wave of Fig. 16-6. For instance, the timing wave can be used for the horizontal sweep and the transitions used to modulate the intensity of the beam. A display of spots for each transition is thus obtained with their spread indicating the amount of total distortion. A more useful display which also permits the reading of bias can be had by deflecting the beam vertically with the differentiated transitions as described for measuring bias. Such a display is indicated in Fig. 16-7.

Modification of the timing wave as indicated in Fig. 16-8 permits reading of peak distortion directly on a single calibrated scale. The modified timing wave is the same as would be obtained by rectifying the wave of Fig. 16-6 about the reference level. A scope display using such a timing wave is shown in Fig.

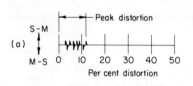

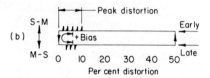

FIG. 16-9. Oscilloscope displays using time base of Fig. 16-8. (a) Display of peak synchronous distortion; (b) modified display to separate early and late transitions.

16-9a. This modification, however, makes it impossible to distinguish early from late transitions. Consequently, the sign of bias distortion is not indicated. With relatively pure bias distortion the M–S and S–M readings can be added to obtain the amount of bias. Bias in the presence of comparable amounts of fortuitous or characteristic distortion cannot be determined. Figure 16-9b shows a modified display that separates the early and late portions of the sweep. This is accomplished by applying a rectangular wave to the vertical deflection. It then becomes possible to estimate the average M–S and S–M times and to determine the amount and sign of bias present. Another method of separating the early and late transitions is described in connection with start-stop measurements.

16-4 MEASUREMENT OF PEAK DISTORTION AND BIAS OF START-STOP DATA SIGNALS

The measurement of distortion and bias of start-stop signals requires a start-stop time base. Figure 16-10 shows examples of suitable timing waves similar to those discussed for synchronous measurements. The wave starts at the beginning of the start pulse and stops after about

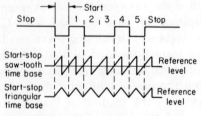

FIG. 16-10. Timing waves for the display and measurement of start-stop distortion.

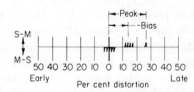

FIG. 16-11. Oscilloscope display of start-stop distortion using sawtooth sweep.

one-half unit of stop interval. A character timing arrangement is required for determining the stopping of the wave. With the sawtooth timing wave in Fig. 16-10, the scope display shown in Fig. 16-11 can be obtained. As described before, differentiated data transitions are applied to the vertical deflection. The S–M transitions indicate the amount of bias, and the peak distortion is indicated by the maximum

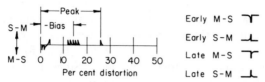

FIG. 16-12. Separation of early and late transitions by exponential pips.

transition deviation from the zero center. Using the triangular timing wave of Fig. 16-10, the display is folded over about zero to facilitate the reading of peak distortion. The sign of bias in such a display is determined by whether the timing wave is approaching or leaving the zero reference at the S–M transition times. The time constant of the transition differentiator can be chosen to cause enough of a tail on the pip to indicate the direction of the beam as shown in Fig. 16-12. This also permits recognition of early and late M–S transitions often referred to as spacing and marking end distortion. The separation in direction of the sweep can also be provided by applying a square wave to the vertical deflection to give a rectangular sweep as previously shown in Fig. 16-9b.

Another type of display which has been used for start-stop measurements is indicated in Fig. 16-13. The sawtooth timing wave shown in Fig. 16-10 is used together with a vertical sawtooth sweep at the character rate. The data transitions modulate the intensity of the beam. This permits the separation of the transitions by their positions in the

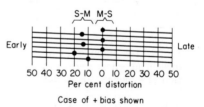

FIG. 16-13. Display separating transitions within a start-stop character.

character. Switching arrangements to view S–M and M–S transitions separately as well as together allow determination of bias and of end distortion. Such an instrument is mainly of value as a laboratory tool in determining variations in start-stop transmitters. A spiral sweep provides a similar display on a circular scale. Meter-type displays for start-stop bias and peak distortion can be obtained by suitable measurements of amplitude samples taken of the timing wave.

16-5 SHORTEST-PULSE DISTORTION MEASUREMENTS

A relatively simple type of peak-distortion measurement consists of determining the shortest pulse occurring with random signals. Where the distortion is made up mainly of bias, fortuitous, and negative characteristic distortions, the maximum shortening of a unit pulse is likely to agree closely with the peak start-stop distortion. Such measurements can be made with simple timing circuitry without the need for an accurate timing wave. Where accuracy is not of great importance, the shortest-pulse method has been found useful, particularly as a simple monitoring device. Since the measurement is not made with respect to a proper timing wave, the results do not always agree closely with the methods described before. The discrepancies are larger for synchronous signals than for start-stop signals.

16-6 MEASUREMENT OF CHARACTERISTIC DISTORTION

With the distortion measuring arrangements described, characteristic and fortuitous distortion of random signals appear alike. The fortuitous component can be filtered out by averaging the distortion

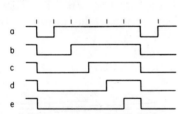

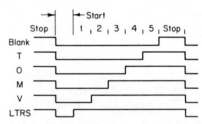

FIG. 16-14. Signal sequences for measuring characteristic distortion of synchronous signals.

FIG. 16-15. Repeated start-stop characters for measuring characteristic distortion.

obtained with repeated signal sequences. The maximum amount of characteristic, or intersymbol, distortion usually occurs when isolated short marks or spaces are transmitted. The effect of intersymbol interference typically does not extend more than three or four signal units, and hence a test sequence five or six elements long is ordinarily sufficient. A symmetrical series of sequences, as shown in Fig. 16-14, can be used. The variation in bias distortion obtained with these sequences is a measure of the characteristic distortion. For example, a case of negative characteristic distortion would cause sequence *a* to show marking bias and sequence *e* to show spacing bias. The variation from the true bias distortion as indicated by sequence c is characteristic distortion. The repeated teletypewriter characters BLANK, T, O, M, V, and LTRS as indicated in Fig. 16-15 are often used to obtain an indication of characteristic distortion. Such repeated characters can either be measured by regular start-stop measuring arrangements or by simple bias measuring arrangements as presented in Sec. 16-2. Where the channel is to handle signals already distorted by previous links, the testing sequence should include isolated single mark and space pulses shorter than the normal unit.

16-7 METHODS OF MEASURING ERROR RATE

Errors are determined by a comparison between the transmitted message and the received message. In experimental systems it is often convenient to loop back the channel so as to have the transmitter and receiver adjacent. For such cases the transmitted message can be locally delayed an amount equal to the transmission time and directly compared with the received signal. This permits the use of purely random sequences. An arrangement of this type is shown in Fig. 16-16.

A more useful arrangement is shown in Fig. 16-17 in which a predetermined sequence known to the receiver is transmitted. This

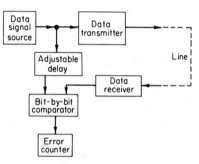

FIG. 16-16. Error counting arrangement for looped-back lines.

permits use on a point-to-point basis over real communication circuits. A convenient type of data signal source for this type of testing can be

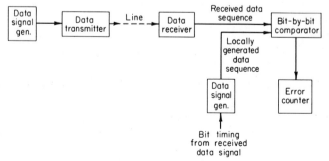

FIG. 16-17. Error counting arrangement for point-to-point lines.

built around a shift register and a modulo-2 adder. The modulo-2 addition of the output stage and one of the other stages is used as the input to the shift register. A register of n stages can thus be arranged to generate a sequence of $2^n - 1$ bits.[1] The sequence includes all combinations of n bits except n zeros. A similar generator at the receiver is driven by the recovered bit timing. By synchronizing the pattern to be in step with the received data, a bit-by-bit comparison can be made to determine the occurrence of errors. This synchronization of patterns at the receiver is readily accomplished by impressing the received pattern as the input to the shift register for a brief period. Once the content of the register is a piece of the proper sequence, it will proceed to generate the whole sequence in synchronism.

From an intersymbol interference standpoint a five- or six-stage shift register is usually sufficient. Longer sequences are useful, however, in the testing of bit synchronization, carrier recovery, automatic gain control, and other features that may have time constants lasting over many bits.

16-8 ERROR RATE IN PRESENCE OF RANDOM NOISE

The error rate in the presence of random noise provides a good measure of data transmission performance. As illustrated in previous chapters the theoretical error performance of a given type of system in the presence of white gaussian noise can usually be calculated. Random noise sources are readily available which are sufficiently close to being white and gaussian that a measure of noise power in a known band completely determines the noise density across that band. The shape of the curve relating error rate to signal-to-noise ratio is as shown in Fig. 7-11. The curve is steep with the error rate changing from 10^{-4} to 10^{-5} for only 1 db change in signal-to-noise ratio. The signal-to-noise ratio is sometimes expressed as the ratio of average signal energy per bit to the noise power per cycle of bandwidth. For double-sideband binary systems where the minimum band required is equal to the bit rate, this ratio is the same as that of the average signal power to the average total noise power in this minimum band.

The closeness of agreement between measured and theoretical error rates in the presence of random noise is a good indication of the quality of implementation. For instance, a fluctuating decision threshold shows up as a less steep curve. The effect of other transmission impairments such as delay distortion and frequency offset, which by themselves are not sufficient to cause errors, can be expressed in terms of loss in signal-to-noise performance by measuring the displacement they cause in the error rate curve.

Figure 16-18 gives a block diagram of the essential parts of a setup for measuring signal-to-noise performance. The filter limiting the noise spectrum to a specific frequency range should encompass the pass-band of any data receiver to be tested. The signal and noise powers can be separately measured by providing means of cutting one off at a time without disturbing the impedance terminations. Since the curves of error rate vs. signal-to-noise ratio are typically of similar

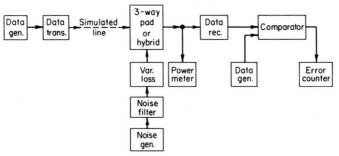

FIG. 16-18. Measuring arrangement for signal-to-noise performance.

shape, they can usually be extrapolated to lower error rates than those measured. This enables measurements to be made at higher error rates where less measuring time is required.

16-9   USE OF EYE-PATTERN OBSERVATIONS

The general concept of the eye pattern was described in Sec. 7-7. Its use in measuring bias and peak distortion of the transitions has also been discussed. When the eye pattern is observed at a point where noise adds linearly to the signal, the vertical eye opening is a measure of system tolerance to additive noise. For instance, if the eye is observed to be half closed because of intersymbol interference or other types of distortion, then the amount of added noise which can be tolerated before errors occur at a specified rate will be 6 db less than would be the case for a fully open eye. Observation of the eye pattern also gives a quick indication of the effectiveness of equalization measures to combat delay distortion and of the general quality of the transmission channel for digital signals.

16-10   MARGIN TESTS ON DIGITAL RECEIVERS

We are here concerned with that portion of a digital communication receiving system which makes the decision as to which symbol was

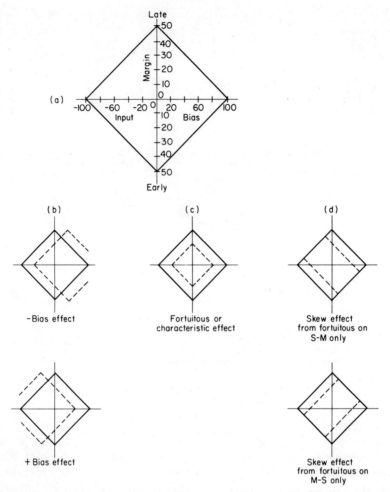

FIG. 16-19. Parallelograms of orientation margins for a synchronous selector.

transmitted. We will specifically consider the case of sampling a binary wave which has been squared up but not regenerated. The sampling may be on either a synchronous or a start-stop basis. With undistorted signals the orientation or phasing of perfectly timed sampling can be varied over a full bit interval or 100 per cent. Normally the sampling would be set at the center of the bit interval thus giving a maximum tolerance to distortion of the transitions of ± 50 per cent. The presence of signal distortion or of imperfect sampling reduces the orientation range over which no errors are made. The characteristics of such a binary decision arrangement can be conveniently measured by observing the margins of the orientation with

known amounts of signal bias distortion.   A plot of the orientation
margins vs. input signal bias forms a parallelogram.   Figure 16-19 at
a shows a parallelogram of a perfect synchronous selector.   The
orientation scale is referred to the nominal center of the bit intervals as
determined by the long-time average position of the transitions.
Asymmetry in the selecting circuitry or mechanism causes bias dis-

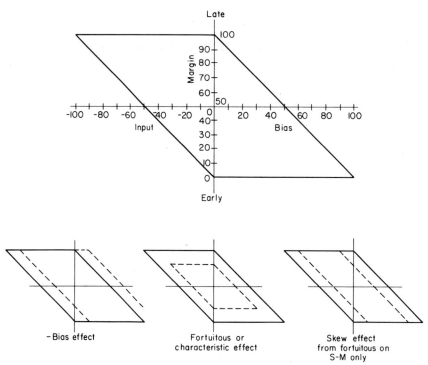

FIG. 16-20. Parallelograms of orientation margins for a start-stop selector.

tortion.   Presence of bias shifts the parallelogram as indicated at
b in Fig. 16-19.   Fortuitous effects equally reduce the margin at both
ends of the range as indicated at *c* in Fig. 16-19.   If there are any
long time-constant memory effects in the selecting arrangement, a
form of characteristic distortion occurs which also appears as fortuitous
distortion.   If the fortuitous or characteristic distortions affect the
M–S and S–M transitions by different amounts, the parallelogram takes
on a twisted or skewed shape as indicated at *d* in Fig. 16-19.

Selectors which operate on a start-stop basis[2] have parallelograms as
shown in Fig. 16-20.   The change in shape from the synchronous case
results from having only the S–M transitions move with respect to the
sampling times when biased signals are applied.   The orientation

scale in this case is referred to the beginning of the start pulse.   Electro-mechanical selectors as used in teletypewriters are more likely to suffer from various types of distortion than are purely electronic selectors. In either case a measurement of the parallelogram characteristic indicates the presence and type of any internal distortion.

REFERENCES

1. Peterson, W. W.: "Error-correcting Codes," sec. 7–4, pp. 118–123, The M.I.T. Press, Cambridge, Mass., and John Wiley & Sons, Inc., New York, 1961.
2. Rea, W. T.: Effect of Telegraph Distortion on the Margins of Operation of Start-Stop Receivers, *Bell System Tech. J.*, vol. 23, pp. 207–233, July, 1944.

CHAPTER 17

ERROR CONTROL

The problem of what to do about errors is one of basic importance in data transmission. The ideal objective is the delivery of error-free messages. A more practical requirement is expressed in terms of an error rate which must not be exceeded. If the actual channel makes more errors than allowed, it may still be possible to meet requirements by use of auxiliary techniques for detection and correction of errors.

17-1 ERROR DETECTION

Isolated errors can be detected in a relatively simple manner by adding redundant elements to the message. For example, it is possible to detect the existence of a single error in a block of data symbols if all single errors lead to sequences which have not been assigned meanings as parts of legitimate messages. The constant ratio, or "m-out-of-n," codes detect errors in this way. As an illustration consider a 3-out-of-7 code applied to binary data. Here there would be 2^7 possible seven-digit words, but only those containing exactly three 1's and four 0's are assigned as meaningful sequences. A single error in a word results in either two or four 1's. It can then be recognized that the word is wrong, but the location of the error in the word cannot be determined. A word with two errors could not be recognized with certainty because a 1 could be changed to 0 and a 0 to a 1, which would make the incorrect word acceptable. An odd number of errors would always be detected but an even number could escape recognition. The number of admissible seven-digit words would be reduced from 128 to 35. In general, an m-out-of-n code permits $n!/[m! \, (n - m)!]$ words out of 2^n possible ones.

A still simpler way of detecting single errors in a binary word is a parity check based on one added bit. The extra bit could be added at the transmitter according to the rule that the total number of 1's after the addition must be even. The augmented word is then said to have *even parity*. Thus if the message word contains an even number of 1's, the symbol 0 is inserted after the word at the transmitter, while if the message contains an odd number of 1's, the symbol 1 is inserted. A total of $n + 1$ bits is transmitted for each n-bit word in the original message. At the receiver a count is made of the number of 1's in each received $(n + 1)$-bit word and if the parity is odd, the word is known to be in error. A total of 2^n message words is obtained from 2^{n+1} possible words in a sequence of $n + 1$ bits. The ratio of number of message bits to total bits transmitted is thus $n/(n + 1)$. This ratio approaches unity as n is made large, but the advantage thereby attained must be balanced against the increased probability of undetected multiple errors.

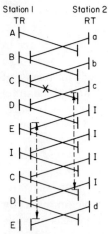

FIG. 17-1. Signaling sequences in van Duuren's ARQ system.

In some classes of service it may be sufficient to indicate words that are received in error without attempting a correction. For example, in telemetry the data may consist of successive readings of a time-varying quantity. If one of the readings is known to be received in error, it can merely be discarded. If a return channel is available, the error can be corrected by requesting retransmission of the erroneous word. In order for the transmitter to comply with the request, the message must remain in storage there until enough time has elapsed to allow a request from the receiver to reach the transmitter.

In the van Duuren ARQ system[1] extensively used on radio telegraph circuits, a two-way channel is operated full duplex with a 3-out-of-7 code. When an error is detected at either receiver, transmission in the opposite direction is interrupted, and a special signal indicating a request for retransmission is inserted. The duration of the interruption depends upon the delay of the transmission path between stations.

Figure 17-1 illustrates the operation of the system when the interval of interruption includes four words. Station 1 sends a sequence of words $A, B, C, \ldots$ to station 2 while station 2 sends simultaneously the sequence $a, b, c, \ldots$ to station 1. In the example shown an error is assumed to be detected at station 2 in the received word C. Station 2 thereupon interrupts the message it is transmitting to station 1 to insert four special signals indicated by I. When the first I signal is received at station 1, that station interrupts the message being transmitted to station 2 and sends one I signal followed by a repetition of words C, D, and E. The original message is then continued.

An analog-domain version of error detection, which can be used either as an alternative or supplement to the digital variety, is called *null zone detection*. In this scheme the results of marginal decisions are discarded at the receiver. For example, if binary decisions are made as to whether the received signal samples are positive or negative, all decisions based on samples in the range $-\epsilon$ to $+\epsilon$ could be rejected as being in doubt. To be worthwhile the null zone should be wide enough to pick up a significant number of errors. At the same time it must not be so wide as to cause excessive loss of good data. The method fails to detect errors in which the wrong value is indicated decisively.

17-2 ERROR CORRECTION

By adding still more redundancy it is possible to correct as well as to detect isolated errors. We recall that single-error detection is possible when all words differing in one position from a legitimate word are excluded from the message alphabet. In order to correct a single error, the minimum difference between acceptable words must be increased to three positions. The word which results from a single error then remains closer to the original word than to any other acceptable word. The number of positions in which two binary words of the same length differ is called the *Hamming distance*, after R. W. Hamming, who gave the first systematic treatment of error-correcting codes.[2] Single-error detection requires that the minimum Hamming distance between words is 2. If the minimum Hamming distance is 3, single errors can not only be detected but also corrected. A minimum distance of 4 permits detection of two errors and correction of one, while if the minimum distance is 5, two errors can be corrected.

A principal difficulty with error-correcting codes is the complexity of apparatus required to identify the correct word associated with each possible incorrect one. A simple method of performing single-error correction was given by Hamming in terms of parity checks. The method is most efficient when the number of bits in a word is $2^n - 1$ where n is an integer. The first, second, fourth, and in general the (2^m)th bits are check bits, and the remaining ones are used as information bits. The first bit is chosen to form even parity in the sequence of bits 1, 3, 5, 7, ... The second bit is chosen to form even parity with the sequence 2, 3, 6, 7, 10, 11, ... In general, the (2^m)th bit is the first term of a parity sequence including 2^m consecutive bits, omitting the next 2^m bits, including the next 2^m bits, etc. The result of parity checks on these sequences at the receiver is expressed as a binary number with 0's for even parity and 1's for odd parity, and with the order proceeding from right to left. The binary number thus represented gives the position of the single bit which is in error. Thus if all parities are found to be even, the binary number consists of all 0's, and no digit of the original word is in error. For example, if the number of digits is 7 and the result of the three parity checks is expressed by 011, an error is indicated in the third bit.

Table 17-1. Code for Single-error Correcting and Double-error Detecting

Decimal number	Position in sequence							
	1	2	3	4	5	6	7	8
0	0	0	0	0	0	0	0	0
1	1	1	0	1	0	0	1	0
2	0	1	0	1	0	1	0	1
3	1	0	0	0	0	1	1	1
4	1	0	0	1	1	0	0	1
5	0	1	0	0	1	0	1	1
6	1	1	0	0	1	1	0	0
7	0	0	0	1	1	1	1	0
8	1	1	1	0	0	0	0	1
9	0	0	1	1	0	0	1	1
10	1	0	1	1	0	1	0	0
11	0	1	1	0	0	1	1	0
12	0	1	1	1	1	0	0	0
13	1	0	1	0	1	0	1	0
14	0	0	1	0	1	1	0	1
15	1	1	1	1	1	1	1	1

In serial binary transmission the parity conditions of the Hamming code are conveniently inserted by gating the appropriate pulses into flip-flop circuits whose states at the end of the parity sequences indicate the binary values for the check bits. At the receiver a similar operation measures the parity of the received sequences and thereby indicates which bit if any should be corrected.

Table 17-1 shows a Hamming code which corrects single errors and detects the presence of two errors in a word containing four information bits and four check bits. Columns 3, 5, 6, and 7 give the message values and represent in binary notation 0, 1, 2, ..., 15. Columns 1, 2, and 4 are check pulse values for single-error correction. Column 8 gives check pulse values for double-error detection.

At the receiver four parity checks are made: pulses 1, 3, 5, and 7; pulses 2, 3, 6, and 7; pulses 4, 5, 6, and 7; pulses 1, 2, 3, 4, 5, 6, 7, and 8. If no error is made, all four checks give even parity. If a single error is made, the fourth check shows odd parity. The results of the first three checks in the order 3, 2, 1 then form a binary number indicating which position is in error. If the number is 000, the error is in position 8. The number 001 indicates an error in position 1, 010 in position 2, 011 in position 3. etc. Identification of bits in error enables correction to be accomplished by changing 1 to 0 or 0 to 1. If two errors are made check 4 gives even parity, and at least one of the other checks shows odd parity. Since this result is inconsistent with either no error or a single error, the word is known to be wrong, but there is insufficient information to perform a correction.

In the example just given, single-error correction and double-error detection are obtained at the cost of a reduction in information rate to one-half the number of binary symbols transmitted per second. If the double-error-detecting feature were omitted, the information rate would be increased to 4/7 of the number of symbols per second. As noted before, the efficiency of Hamming single-error-correcting codes is greatest when the number of bits in a word is of form $2^n - 1$. Since n bits of the word are used for checking purposes only, the ratio of message bits to total binary symbols is $(2^n - n - 1)/(2^n - 1)$. As in the case of single-error detection, the efficiency increases with n, but so does the probability of more than one error. Words of other lengths than the most efficient ones can be used, and their coding tables can be derived from that of the nearest higher value of n by omitting the highest numbered positions.

17-3 CODING AND DECODING BY SHIFT REGISTERS

Codes which enable more than one error to be corrected in a word are necessarily quite complicated. Relatively simple methods of encoding have been found, but the decoding requires what amounts to a special purpose computer. A particularly convenient method of encoding employs a shift register with multiple feedback. An example is shown in Fig. 17-2. The shift register itself consists of a number of cascaded bistable devices or binary stages. Under the control of a timing pulse supplied to all stages in common, the state of each stage can be transferred to the next following stage. An external source is applied as input to the first stage, and the output of the last stage is delivered to an external sink.

In Fig. 17-2 internal connections are shown by means of which some of the stages are driven by the sum of outputs from other stages. A particularly simple theory of operation can be constructed when the modulo-2 sum is used instead of the ordinary arithmetical sum. In modulo-2 addition the rules are the same as in ordinary addition except that $1 + 1 = 0$. In the present description we shall assume that all sums are modulo 2. When a binary message sequence is applied to a shift register with a specified set of interconnections, with all stages initially at state 0, say, the state values of the stages after n message bits is a unique function of the n-bit message sequence. The shift register can, therefore, be used to generate check bits.

The mode of operation for use of a shift register for error detection is as follows: With an m-stage shift register cleared to state 0 for all stages, send n sequential message bits to the line and to the input of

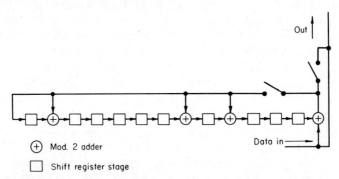

Out

⊕ Mod. 2 adder

▢ Shift register stage

Data in

FIG. 17-2. Shift register for encoding Bose-Chaudhuri (31, 21) code.

the first stage of the shift register. The latter is timed to shift in synchronism with message bits. After n message bits, interrupt the message source and shift out to the line the m values stored in the shift register. At the receiver an identical shift register receives the incoming message bits at the same time as they are delivered to the message sink. After n bits have been received, the input to the shift register is disconnected, and the next m bits from the output of the shift register are compared one by one with the next m bits received from the line. Any disagreement indicates that there are one or more errors in the received $(m + n)$-bit word including the n message bits and the m check bits.

The effectiveness of error detection depends critically upon the interconnections of the stages. If there are no feedback loops, the shift register functions only as a storage device and in the mode of operation described serves to repeat part of the message. This is a crude form of error detection which can be greatly improved upon by the highly developed theory of the codes obtainable by different interconnection patterns. The diagram of Fig. 17-2 actually shows a 10-stage shift register with connections appropriate for encoding a message by the Bose-Chaudhuri (31,21) code.[3] The sum of the incoming data and the output of the tenth stage acts as the input to the first stage and is added to the outputs of the first, sixth, and seventh stages. The encoding plan consists of transmitting 21 serial message bits to both the line and the register input. Transmission from the message source is then stopped, and the 10 stored check bits are shifted out to form a serial output from the last stage. The resulting 31-bit word on the line has a minimum Hamming distance of 5 and, therefore, permits either double-error correction or quadruple-error detection. The former requires a fairly complicated series of computations. The latter is very simply done by a duplicate shift register at the receiver. A set of 10 check bits is generated locally from the possibly erroneous incoming 21 message bits and then compared bit by bit with the 10 check bits arriving from the line.

The Bose-Chaudhuri codes are based on a complete mathematical theory furnishing a systematic procedure for constructing words of length $2^m - 1$ in which k errors can be corrected by use of no more than mk check digits. They may be regarded as a generalization of the Hamming code, which achieves the same result when $k = 1$. Instead of correcting k errors we can detect $2k$ errors. Actually the effectiveness as an error detector is much greater in practical situations than indicated by the number positively detected. Many of the error patterns containing more than $2k$ errors will also be detected. In fact if, as is often the case in real channels, the errors appear in bursts, it becomes extremely improbable that an erroneous word will not be detected. Correction of the many errors associated with the burst requires a much more powerful code than would be needed for highly reliable error detection.

A straight probabilistic analysis of a code performance can be deceptive in that a weakness against systematic defects may be over-looked. For example, even though a Bose-Chaudhuri code of moderate length detects practically all error sequences when used in the normal way, it is relatively ineffective against the simple fault of a "slipped synch," i.e., a displacement between the word framing at receiver and transmitter. To illustrate this for the (31,21) example, assume that the information bits in a word are $b_1, b_2, \ldots, b_{20}, b_{21}$ and that they generate the check bits $c_0, c_1, \ldots, c_9$ in the shift register stages 1, 2, 3, ..., 10 respectively. The message sent on the line then consists of the sequence $b_1, b_2, \ldots, b_{20}, b_{21}, c_9, c_8, \ldots, c_1, c_0$, since the states of the higher-numbered register stages are shifted out to the line first. Suppose now that the receiver timing is delayed by one bit from its proper position relative to the incoming signal. The information bits are then read as $b_2, b_3, \ldots, b_{20}, b_{21}, c_9$ and the check bits as $c_8, c_7, \ldots, c_1, c_0, \beta_1$ where β_1 is the first information bit of the next word. The local shift register is driven by the erroneous set $b_2, b_3, \ldots, b_{21}, c_9$ to generate the fallacious check bits $d_9, d_8, \ldots, d_1, d_0$ which are compared bit by bit with the also incorrect sequence $c_8, c_7, \ldots, c_0, \beta_1$. At first glance it might seem incredible that all 10 of these parity checks would indicate correct reception, but here is a case where more careful scrutiny is rewarded.

In order to calculate what actually happens in our example without a tedious enumeration of the sequential operations, we introduce some appropriate algebraic technique. Assume that all states of the shift register have the value 0 at the beginning of the word. Represent the states of the stages after the application of the nth message bit by the coefficients of the polynomial

$$P_n(x) = a_{0n} + a_{1n}x + \cdots + a_{9n}x^9 \qquad (17\text{-}1)$$

where a_{kn} is the state of stage $k + 1$ after the nth bit is applied. That is, the state of the first stage is a_{0n}, that of the second is a_{1n}, etc., and each of these coefficients can have either the value 0 or 1. Using modulo-2 addition, we can write the following equation applicable to the connections shown in Fig. 17-2

$$P_{n+1}(x) = xP_n(x) + b_n(1 + x + x^6 + x^7) = xP_n(x) + b_nx^{10} \quad (17\text{-}2)$$

where the convention

$$x^{10} \equiv 1 + x + x^6 + x^7 \qquad (17\text{-}3)$$

is to be applied where necessary to reduce all exponents to values less than 10. The state of the shift register after the 21 information bits have been applied is then

$$
\begin{aligned}
P_{21}(x) &= b_1x^{30} + b_2x^{29} + \cdots + b_{20}x^{11} + b_{21}x^{10} \\
&= c_0 + c_1x + c_2x^2 + \cdots + c_8x^8 + c_9x^9 \qquad (17\text{-}4)
\end{aligned}
$$

By use of Eq. (17-3) as needed, the values of the c's can be expressed in terms of the b's.

The fallacious check bits generated by the mistimed register at the receiver are defined by

$$
\begin{aligned}
Q_{21}(x) &= b_2x^{30} + b_3x^{29} + \cdots + b_{20}x^{12} + b_{21}x^{11} + c_9x^{10} \\
&= d_0 + d_1x + d_2x^2 + \cdots + d_9x^9 \\
&= x(b_1x^{30} + b_2x^{29} + b_3x^{28} + \cdots + b_{20}x^{11} + b_{21}x^{10}) \\
&\quad + c_9x^{10} + b_1x^{31} \\
&= xP_{21}(x) + c_9x^{10} + b_1x^{31} \\
&= b_1x^{31} + c_0x + c_1x^2 + \cdots + c_8x^9 \qquad (17\text{-}5)
\end{aligned}
$$

We now make use of a general property of the Bose-Chaudhuri code of word length $2^m - 1$. The "primitive element" represented by a polynomial X, which in our example is defined from (17-3) as

$$X = 1 + x + x^6 + x^7 \tag{17-6}$$

is a root of the equation

$$X^{2m-1} = 1 \tag{17-7}$$

In our case $2^m - 1 = 31$, and we deduce accordingly that $x^{31} = 1$. The skeptic can verify this by a straightforward although somewhat tedious calculation.

If the check bits from the line are now arranged in one-to-one comparison with the locally generated check bits, we note that every parity check succeeds except possibly the last, which compares b_1 and β_1. These two symbols are the first information bits of two adjacent words and typically have a probability of 0.5 that they are alike. Hence, a one-bit slip in word synchronism has only a 50-50 chance of being detected.

The defect is very easily remedied once the problem is recognized. One solution is to invert the check bits before transmission. A second inversion is performed at the receiver before the parity checks are made. In the example we have computed, the coefficient of x^{10} in the first expression for $Q_{21}(x)$ in Eq. (17-5) would then be replaced by $1 + c_9$. This in effect adds x^{10} or $1 + x + x^6 + x^7$ to the final result. The one-to-one comparison of line and local check bits is then as follows:

Line	c_8	c_7	c_6	c_5	c_4	c_3	c_2	c_1	c_0	$1 + \beta_1$
Local	c_8	c_7	$1 + c_6$	$1 + c_5$	c_4	c_3	c_2	$1 + c_1$	$1 + c_0$	$1 + b_1$

Hence if there is no error except for the synch slip, four of the parity checks must fail and a fifth fails half the time. Thus, not only are the errors caused by the slipped timing detected with exceedingly high probability, but a valuable diagnostic clue is also obtained.

In addition to the Bose-Chaudhuri codes, many others have been discovered which have interesting error-detecting and error-correcting properties. The theory of the various kinds of codes has, in fact, become a significant mathematical domain in its own right.[4] Classification and description are not very simple. The Reed-Muller codes[5,6] provide words of length 2^m in which $2^{m-r-1} - 1$ errors can be corrected in reasonably straightforward manner by majority testing of redundant relations. The minimum Hamming distance is 2^{m-r}, and the number of information bits per word $\sum_{n=0}^{r} m!/[n!(m-n)!]$. A Hamming single-error-correcting–double-error-detecting code is a Reed-Muller code with $r = m - 2$. A Reed-Solomon code[7] is a special case of a Bose-Chaudhuri code which is useful for correcting multiple bursts of errors

in a word. Fire codes[4] correct a single burst of errors in a word
without requiring many check digits.

Practical evaluation of the performance of specific codes requires a
knowledge of the statistical distribution of errors. Even when the
error statistics are known, analytical evaluation of the probabilities
of undetected and uncorrected errors is a formidable task. Computer
simulation can be helpful, but a direct test on a real channel gives the
most conclusive results.[8,9]

The codes so far discussed are all of block type, meaning that blocks
of fixed length are checked independently. Codes exist in which there
are no divisions of the message into blocks. We shall discuss two
examples of these, namely, the recurrent code of Hagelbarger[10] and
the sequential coding and decoding system of Wozencraft.[11]

17-4   RECURRENT CODING FOR BURST ERROR CORRECTION

Hagelbarger's code is aimed at correcting errors which occur in
bursts with relatively long error-free intervals of time between bursts.
The principle is to insert parity
check bits associated with message
bits spread out in time so that error
bursts are not likely to include more
than one bit of the group whose
parity is checked. A simple example with 50 per cent redundancy,
which corrects all errors in a burst
of length 6 or less provided that
there are 19 or more correct bits between bursts, is shown in Fig. 17-3.
The message is applied as input to the first stage of a seven-stage shift
register. The input to the line is switched alternately between the
output of the last stage of the shift register and the modulo-2 sum
of the states of the first and fourth stages. Each shift of the register
thus generates a message output bit and a parity check bit, which are
transmitted alternately to the line. Each message bit is involved in
a parity check with the fourth preceding message bit and the fourth
following message bit.

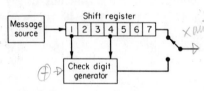

FIG. 17-3. Encoder for Hagelbarger
code.

At the receiver an alternating switch directs the message and check
bits into separate shift registers as shown in Fig. 17-4. Two parity
checks designated by R and S are made simultaneously, one on stages
1 and 4 and the other on stages 4 and 7 of the message register. When
only one of the two parity checks fails, no error in the message is
indicated. When both checks fail, the bit in stage 4 is judged to be in
error and is reversed while being shifted to stage 5. An error in a

check digit is indicated when the R parity check holds and the S parity check fails. When this happens the state of the tenth stage of the check shift register should be reversed if the message is to be retransmitted. More complicated encoding and decoding arrangements have been given by Hagelbarger to correct longer bursts of errors with less redundancy.

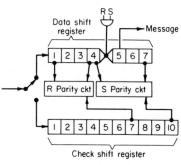

FIG. 17-4. Decoder for Hagelbarger code.

17-5 SEQUENTIAL CODING AND DECODING

Shannon proved[12] that a coding method exists by means of which the probability of error in communication over a noisy channel can be made smaller than any assignable value provided that the information rate is less than a uniquely defined number called the channel capacity C. In the case of a binary symmetric channel with probability p that an error is made in the reception of any digit, he showed that the channel capacity is given by

$$C = 1 + p \log p + (1 - p) \log (1 - p) \qquad (17\text{-}8)$$

If the logarithms are taken to the base 2, C is expressed in bits of information per received binary digit.

To approach errorless transmission at a rate comparable with but less than the channel capacity requires very long code words. No optimum choice of a coding method has ever been demonstrated. It can be shown, however, that when long codes are selected at random, the chance of choosing one that fails to perform almost as well as the best is slight. Shannon's result shows that as the code length is increased the average of the probabilities of error for all the codes approaches zero. Let P represent the average probability of error for a set of N codes of fixed length. Divide the codes into two groups, one containing the k codes with probability of error greater than αP and the other group containing the remaining $N\text{-}k$ codes. Let p_n and q_n represent the probabilities of error of the nth codes in the first and second groups repectively. Then

$$P = \frac{1}{N} \sum_{n=1}^{k} p_n + \frac{1}{N} \sum_{n=1}^{N-k} q_n \qquad (17\text{-}9)$$

By hypothesis

$$\sum_{n=1}^{k} p_n > k\alpha P \qquad (17\text{-}10)$$

Also $q_n \geq 0$. Therefore, $NP > k\alpha P$ and hence,

$$k < \frac{N}{\alpha} \qquad (17\text{-}11)$$

This means that the fraction of the codes having probability of error greater than αP must be less than $1/\alpha$. For example, if the average probability of error for all codes were 10^{-12}, then no more than one code in a million could have a probability of error greater than 10^{-6}.

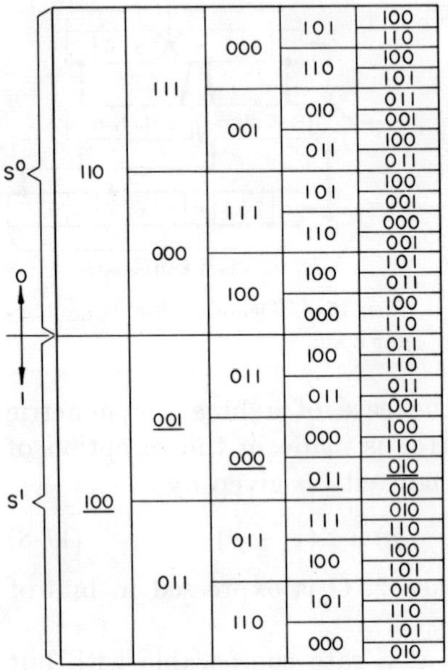

Unless there were a run of incredibly bad luck, a randomly chosen long code approaches the most reliable performance of which the channel is capable. The big difficulty in the use of a random code is the size of the code book. In the absence of any systematic coding procedure, the decoder must have available in storage a set of sequences increasing exponentially in number with word length. To decode the message, the received sequence must be compared with each possible sequence to determine the identification most likely to be correct. The exponential growth in amounts of storage and computation required for decoding has discouraged application of long random block codes.

Fig. 17-5. Random tree code. The underlined digits form the transmitted sequence when the information sequence is 10110.

The sequential coding and decoding method of Wozencraft[13] seeks to escape from the tyranny of exponentially increasing complexity by substituting a treelike structure for the block-type code book. Figure 17-5 shows a sample random tree code suggested by Wozencraft and Reiffen. The message information is contained in the choice of branches at each node. In the example shown a "1" is represented by a choice of the lower branch and a "0" by the upper branch. The actual digits transmitted are those given in the table for the branches chosen. The entries of the table are originally established by a random process and must be available at both the transmitter and receiver. The decoder tries to make its decisions successively on the basis of probabilities of two sequences at a time. The criterion of acceptance is that the Hamming distance between the received sequence and a hypothesized true sequence of the same length must be less than a prescribed number. If a decision cannot be made at a node, the previously unrejected sequences are retained, and the different possible ensuing sequences are compared for the next interval. The number of possible sequences increases exponentially as we proceed along the tree, but most of them will have been discarded as improbable when the later branches are reached. An advantage may thereby be obtained over methods which require consideration of all the possible sequences in a block.

Evaluation of the effectiveness is difficult except by actual trial.[14,15] Theoretical analysis indicates that the storage grows at a rate less than the square of the word length instead of exponentially. Practical advantages can be obtained on a two-way channel by providing for the receiver to request transmission at a lower speed when the computing time becomes excessive. Repetition is requested for portions of the message which cannot be decoded within the requirements of the acceptance criterion.

REFERENCES

1. van Duuren, H. C. A.: Error Probability and Transmission Speed on Circuits Using Detection and Automatic Repetition of Signals, *IRE Trans. Commun. Systems*, vol. CS-9, pp. 38–50, March, 1961.
2. Hamming, R. W.: Error Detecting and Error Correcting Codes, *Bell System Tech. J.*, vol. 26, pp. 147–160, April, 1950.
3. Peterson, W. W.: Encoding and Error-correction Procedures for the Bose-Chaudhuri Codes, *IRE Trans. Inform. Theory*, vol. IT-6, pp. 459–470, September, 1960.
4. *Ibid.*: Error-correcting Codes, The M.I.T. Press, Cambridge, Mass., and John Wiley & Sons, Inc., New York, chap. 9, pp. 162–182, 1961.
5. Reed, I. S.: A Class of Multiple-error-correcting Codes and the Decoding Scheme, *IRE Trans. Inform. Theory*, vol. IT-4, pp. 38–49, September, 1954.
6. Muller, D. E.: Application of Boolean Algebra to Switching Circuit Design and to Error Detection, *IRE Trans. Electron. Computers*, vol. EC-3, pp. 6–12, 1954.
7. Reed, I. S., and G. Solomon: Polynomial Codes over Certain Finite Fields, *J. Soc. Ind. Appl. Math.*, vol. 8, pp. 300–304, 1960.
8. Bennett, W. R., and F. E. Froehlich: Some Results on the Effectiveness of Error-control Procedures in Digital Data Transmission, *IRE Trans. Commun. Systems*, vol. CS-9, pp. 58–65, March, 1961.
9. Reiffen, B., W. G. Schmidt, and H. L. Yudkin: The Design of an Error-free Data Transmission System for Telephone Circuits, *AIEE Trans.*, part I (Communications and Electronics), vol. 80, pp. 224–231, July, 1961.

10. Hagelbarger, D. W.: Recurrent Codes: Easily Mechanized, Burst-correcting Binary Codes, *Bell System Tech. J.*, vol. 38, pp. 969–984, July, 1959.

11. Wozencraft, J. M., and B. Reiffen: "Sequential Coding," The M.I.T. Press, Cambridge, Mass., and John Wiley & Sons, Inc., New York, 1961.

12. Shannon, C. E.: A Mathematical Theory of Communication, *Bell System Tech. J.*, vol. 27, pp. 379–423, July, 1948; vol. 27, pp. 623–656, October, 1948.

13. Perry, K. E., and J. M. Wozencraft: SECO: A Self-regulating Error-correcting Coder-Decoder, *IRE Trans. Inform. Theory*, vol. IT-8, pp. 128–135, September, 1962.

14. Fano, R. M.: A Heuristic Discussion of Probabalistic Decoding, *IEEE Trans. Inform. Theory*, vol. IT-9, pp. 64–74, April, 1963.

15. Lebow, I. L., D. G. McHugh, A. C. Parker, P. Rosen, and J. M. Wozencraft: Application of Sequential Decoding to High-rate Data Communication on a Telephone Line, *IEEE Trans. Inform. Theory*, vol. IT-9, pp. 124–126, April, 1963.

CHAPTER 18

IDEALIZED OPTIMIZATION THEORY

The objective of optimization theory is to find systems which are best in accordance with specified criteria of goodness. It is too much to expect that the results obtained by a theoretical optimization procedure will actually enable the designer to choose the best system in a real life situation. Of all the conditions which govern the performance of a system, there are usually only a few which give a precise mathematical formulation. Optimization theories deal with idealized models which represent only a part of the total problem and do not even simulate that part exactly. Such important considerations as cost, complexity, maintenance, use of existing facilities, compatibility with other systems, and time schedules are difficult to include with any precision in a tractable mathematical model.

Nevertheless idealized optimizations have their uses. They establish bounds on performance under specified constraints. These bounds tell us how much better our actual system could perform if it were idealized. If the difference is small, a wasted effort toward a significant improvement can be avoided. Also if we find by analysis or experiment a result that appears better than the ideal, the work leading to this result should be carefully reexamined. It is possible that a way has been found to beat the constraint imposed in the idealized model, but more likely a mistake will come to light.

We shall examine some of the idealized optima from information theory and statistical decision theory.

18-1 THE IDEALIZED CHANNEL OF INFORMATION THEORY

In the previous chapter we referred to Shannon's theorem on maximum information rate over a binary symmetrical channel with specified probability of error in reception of any digit. Another theorem given by Shannon gives the capacity of a band-limited channel with fixed average signal power and additive white gaussian noise. The theorem is expressed by the equation

$$C = W \log_2 \left(1 + \frac{S}{N}\right) \qquad (18\text{-}1)$$

The capacity C is the maximum number of bits per second which can be received with arbitrarily small probability of error. The bandwidth W is defined only for a system which has unity gain and linear phase shift over a range of frequencies W cps wide and zero gain for all other frequencies. The average signal power is S and the average noise power in the band is N. The spectral density of the noise is constant and equal to N/W. For nongaussian noise or colored gaussian noise the value of C would be greater than the amount given by the theorem.

Blind application of the theorem to specific channels is likely to give a capacity far greater than the practically attainable information rate. For example, suppose the bandwidth of a telephone channel were stated to be 3,000 cps and the signal-to-noise ratio 30 db. The theorem would then give the capacity as $3{,}000 \log_2 (1 + 10^3)$ or 30,000 bits per second. Practical experience would say that 3,000 bits per second would be a more reasonable rate to use. One reason for the discrepancy is that the actual channel is not perfectly equalized for constant gain over a 3-kc band and zero gain outside the band. Also the phase shift of the channel is not equalized for perfect linearity with frequency. But even if these conditions were met with arbitrarily small error, a gap would remain between theory and practice. The reason is that it would not be practical to construct the elaborate coding and decoding arrangements necessary to come close to the ideal capacity.

Figure 11-2 in Chap. 11 shows the limiting rate of Shannon's theorem on the same chart with the ideal performance of various n-ary systems. The amount by which these systems fall below the ideal can be expressed in two ways. By drawing horizontal lines we obtain the difference between intercepts which give the increase in signal-to-noise ratio required in specific systems over that indicated by the Shannon formula for the same bit rate. Likewise by drawing vertical lines, we obtain differences in intercepts showing the reduction in bit rate from the ideal at a given signal-to-noise ratio. The best systems shown require about 6 db more signal power than called for by the Shannon formula to attain their bit rates. With a particular signal-to-noise ratio the best systems fall short of the maximum possible speed of transmission by about 2 bits per second per cycle of bandwidth. The ratio of bit rates approaches unity at high signal-to-noise ratios when the number of signal levels is made large enough to take advantage of the ability to recognize small differences.

18-2 RESULTS FROM STATISTICAL DECISION THEORY*

The theorems from information theory previously cited deal in general with channels which have finite bandwidth and no limit on the time occupied by the message. The optimal performance under these conditions can be approached asymptotically as the message length is increased. The problem of intersymbol interference is solved by using Nyquist's band-limited signal waves which can be sampled independently at instants at which all except one have null values.

Somewhat different optima can be found for the dual case in which the bandwidth is not limited, but the decision must be made on the basis of the wave received during a finite time interval. The assumption of the unlimited band takes intersymbol interference out of the problem, since the band can be made wide enough to keep successive signal responses within their own time slots. The optimum results are then attainable asymptotically as the bandwidth is increased. Any case of finite bandwidth is included as a possible strategy since a receiving filter can precede the detector. The finite band system must cope with channel memory and can, of course, do no better than the optimum no matter how well the resulting intersymbol interference is suppressed.

Consider the case of binary signaling through a channel with unlimited bandwidth and additive white gaussian noise. During each successive time interval of duration T, a decision is made at the receiver as to which of two equally likely functions $a(t)$ and $b(t)$ has been impressed by the transmitter during that interval. The average signal power W_s and the average noise power n_0 per unit bandwidth are given. What is the minimum probability of error and how can it be attained?

Let $v(t)$ represent the added gaussian noise wave. The decision is to be made as to whether the complete received wave $V(t)$ is to be identified with

$$V_a(t) = a(t) + v(t) \qquad 0 < t < T$$

or with

$$V_b(t) = b(t) + v(t) \qquad 0 < t < T \tag{18-2}$$

The waves $a(t)$ and $b(t)$ are known, but the information about $v(t)$ is of a statistical nature. We assume that for the decision we have available the complete wave $V(t)$ from $t = 0$ to $t = T$. To describe this information in convenient mathematical form, we expand $V(t)$

---

* Assistance in the preparation of this section was contributed by J. Salz.

in a series of orthonormal functions over the interval 0 to T, thus

$$V(t) = \sum_{n=0}^{\infty} c_n \phi_n(t) \qquad 0 < t < T$$

$$c_n = \int_0^T V(t)\phi_n(t)\, dt \tag{18-3}$$

The set $\{\phi_n(t)\}$ can be chosen with considerable freedom. For example, a Fourier series expansion could be used, in which case $\phi_n(t)$ would include the functions $T^{-\frac{1}{2}}$, $(2/T)^{\frac{1}{2}} \cos(2n\pi t/T)$, $(2/T)^{\frac{1}{2}} \sin(2n\pi/T)$, with $n = 1, 2, 3, \ldots$. The infinite set of numbers $\{c_n\}$ is then equivalent to a complete description of the received waveform during the interval.

The coefficients c_n resolve naturally into two components, that is,

$$c_n = a_n + v_n \quad \text{or} \quad b_n + v_n \tag{18-4}$$

where

$$a_n = \int_0^T a(t)\phi_n(t)\, dt$$

$$b_n = \int_0^T b(t)\phi_n(t)\, dt$$

and

$$v_n = \int_0^T v(t)\phi_n(t)\, dt \tag{18-5}$$

The decision problem is to choose which one of the two possible sets of values $\{a_n\}$ or $\{b_n\}$ is correct. Since each v_n is derived by a linear operation on the gaussian variable $v(t)$, the v_n's are gaussian variables. We calculate

$$\text{av}(v_m v_n) = \iint\limits_0^T \text{av}\,[v(t_1)v(t_2)]\phi_m(t_1)\phi_n(t_2)\, dt_1\, dt_2 \tag{18-6}$$

But since $v(t)$ is white gaussian, the autocorrelation function $R_v(\tau) = \text{av}\,[v(t)v(t+\tau)]$ vanishes except at $\tau = 0$. The general relation expressing autocorrelation as the Fourier transform of spectral density can in this case be written as $R_v(\tau) = n_0\delta(\tau)$. Then

$$\text{av}\,[v(t_1)v(t_2)] = n_0\delta(t_2 - t_1) \tag{18-7}$$

It follows that

$$\text{av}(v_m v_n) = n_0 \int_0^T \phi_m(t)\phi_n(t)\, dt = \begin{cases} n_0 & m = n \\ 0 & m \neq n \end{cases} \tag{18-8}$$

Vanishing of the crosscorrelation of gaussian variables implies independence. Therefore, it follows from Eq. (18-8) that the joint distribution of the set of variables $\{v_n\}$ is independent multidimensional gaussian. The joint probability density function of the first m values

$v_0, v_1, \ldots, v_{m-1}$ can be written

$$p(v_0, v_1, \ldots, v_{m-1}) = (2\pi n_0)^{-m/2} \exp\left(-\sum_{n=0}^{m-1} \frac{v_n^2}{2n_0}\right) \tag{18-9}$$

Depending on which signal was transmitted, we have either $v_n = c_n - a_n$ or $v_n = c_n - b_n$. The conditional joint probability density function of $c_0, c_1, \ldots, c_{m-1}$ given that $a(t)$ was transmitted is

$$p_1(c_0, c_1, \ldots, c_{m-1} \mid a) = (2\pi n_0)^{-m/2} \exp\left[-\sum_{n=0}^{m-1} \frac{(c_n - a_n)^2}{2n_0}\right] \tag{18-10}$$

The corresponding conditional probability density function, given that $b(t)$ was transmitted, is

$$p_2(c_0, c_1, \ldots, c_{m-1} \mid b) = (2\pi n_0)^{-m/2} \exp\left[-\sum_{n=0}^{m-1} \frac{(c_n - b_n)^2}{2n_0}\right] \tag{18-11}$$

To maximize the probability of a correct decision, we choose $a(t)$ if $p_1 > p_2$ and choose $b(t)$ if $p_1 < p_2$. Equivalently the decision can be made on the basis of whether or not p_1/p_2 exceeds unity or on whether or not $\log(p_1/p_2)$ is positive. The latter gives the simple decision function

$$L_m = \sum_{n=0}^{m-1} [(c_n - b_n)^2 - (c_n - a_n)^2] \tag{18-12}$$

If $L_m > 0$, $a(t)$ is chosen, and if $L_m < 0$, we choose $b(t)$. Geometrically this is seen to be equivalent to comparing the distances between the point $(c_0, c_1, \ldots, c_{m-1})$ and the points $(a_0, a_1, \ldots, a_{m-1})$ and $(b_0, b_1, \ldots, b_{m-1})$ in Euclidean m-dimensional space. To make use of all the available information, we take the limit as m goes to infinity.

Equation (18-12) can also be written

$$L_m = \sum_{n=0}^{m-1} (b_n^2 - a_n^2) + 2\sum_{n=0}^{m-1} c_n(a_n - b_n) \tag{18-13}$$

Now observing that

$$a(t) = \sum_{n=0}^{\infty} a_n \phi_n(t)$$

$$b(t) = \sum_{n=0}^{\infty} b_n \phi_n(t) \tag{18-14}$$

it follows that

$$\int_0^T a^2(t)\,dt = \int_0^T \sum_{m=0}^{\infty} \sum_{n=0}^{\infty} a_m a_n \phi_m(t)\phi_n(t)\,dt = \sum_{m=0}^{\infty} a_n^2 \tag{18-15}$$

$$\int_0^T b^2(t)\,dt = \sum_{n=0}^{\infty} b_n^2 \tag{18-16}$$

$$\int_0^T V(t)[a(t) - b(t)]\,dt = \int_0^T \sum_{m=0}^{\infty} \sum_{n=0}^{\infty} c_m(a_n - b_n)\phi_m(t)\phi_n(t)\,dt$$

$$= \sum_{n=0}^{\infty} c_n(a_n - b_n) \tag{18-17}$$

Therefore

$$L_\infty = \int_0^T [b^2(t) - a^2(t)]\, dt + 2\int_0^T V(t)[a(t) - b(t)]\, dt \qquad (18\text{-}18)$$

With the optimum decision function established we next proceed to evaluate the probability of error. There are two conditions under which errors occur:

(1) $L_\infty < 0$ when $a(t)$ is transmitted.

(2) $L_\infty > 0$ when $b(t)$ is transmitted.

Let P_1 be the probability of the first event and P_2 that of the second. Then since we have assumed $a(t)$ and $b(t)$ equally probable, the actual probability of error is the average $P = (P_1 + P_2)/2$. Replacing $V(t)$ appropriately by $a(t) + v(t)$ or $b(t) + v(t)$, we find then

$$P_1 = \text{Prob } (u > k \text{ if } a(t) \text{ is sent})$$
$$P_2 = \text{Prob } (-u > k \text{ if } b(t) \text{ is sent}) \qquad (18\text{-}19)$$

where

$$u = 2\int_0^T v(t)[b(t) - a(t)]\, dt \qquad (18\text{-}20)$$

and

$$k = \int_0^T [b(t) - a(t)]^2\, dt$$

Since $v(t)$ is gaussian and u is defined by a linear operation on $v(t)$, u is also a gaussian variable. A gaussian distribution function is completely determined by the mean and variance. Since v has zero mean, the mean of u is also zero. The variance of u is then equal to the mean square and is calculated as follows:

$$\text{av } u^2 = 4\iint_0^T [b(t_1) - a(t_1)][b(t_2) - a(t_2)] \text{ av } [v(t_1)v(t_2)]\, dt_1\, dt_2$$

$$= 4n_0 \iint_0^T [b(t_1) - a(t_1)][b(t_2) - a(t_2)]\, \delta(t_2 - t_1)\, dt_1\, dt_2$$

$$= 4kn_0 \qquad (18\text{-}21)$$

It follows that the probability density function of u is

$$p(u) = (8\pi kn_0)^{-1/2} \exp\left(-\frac{u^2}{8kn_0}\right) \qquad (18\text{-}22)$$

Referring back to Eq. (18-19) and noting the even symmetry of $p(u)$, we deduce

$$P = P_1 = P_2 = \int_k^\infty p(u)\, du = \frac{1}{2} \text{erfc } \sqrt{\frac{k}{8n_0}} \qquad (18\text{-}23)$$

The probability of error is seen to decrease monotonically as k is increased. For minimum probability of error, we make k as large as possible. We are limited by the amount of available average signal power:

$$W_s = \frac{1}{2T} \int_0^T b^2(t)\, dt + \frac{1}{2T} \int_0^T a^2(t)\, dt \qquad (18\text{-}24)$$

We note that

$$k = 2TW_s - 2\int_0^T a(t)b(t)\, dt \qquad (18\text{-}25)$$

Maximizing k is therefore equivalent to minimizing the integral of $a(t)b(t)$. The constraint is that the integral of $a^2(t) + b^2(t)$ is fixed. The variational problem is accordingly formulated as

$$\delta \int_0^T [a(t)b(t) + \lambda a^2(t) + \lambda b^2(t)]\, dt$$

$$= \int_0^T [a(t) + 2\lambda b(t)]\, \delta b(t)\, dt$$

$$+ \int_0^T [b(t) + 2\lambda a(t)]\, \delta a(t)\, dt = 0 \qquad (18\text{-}26)$$

The variational equation can only be satisfied by setting $a(t) + 2\lambda b(t)$ and $b(t) + 2\lambda a(t)$ equal to zero. Eliminating the parameter λ, we find $b(t) = \pm a(t)$ as the condition for stationarity. Since we wish to make k maximum, we choose the negative sign and obtain for the minimum probability of error

$$b(t) = -a(t)$$

$$W_s = \frac{1}{T} \int_0^T a^2(t)\, dt$$

$$k = 4TW_s \qquad (18\text{-}27)$$

$$P = \frac{1}{2} \operatorname{erfc} \sqrt{\frac{TW_s}{2n_0}}$$

We note that T is the reciprocal of the bit rate f_s. We have assumed a spectral density function in which the power is equally divided between positive and negative frequencies. The average total power in a bandwidth numerically equal to the bit rate when contributions from both positive and negative frequencies are included is $2n_0 f_s$. Setting M equal to the ratio of average signal power to average noise power in the bit-rate bandwidth, we then have

$$M = \frac{W_s}{2n_0 f_s} \tag{18-28}$$

$$P = \tfrac{1}{2} \, \mathrm{erfc} \, \sqrt{M} \tag{18-29}$$

Equation (18-29) has been cited a number of times in the previous chapters as the ideal performance for binary data transmission. Equation (18-18) indicates one method by which the ideal performance can be obtained. If we substitute the optimum condition $b(t) = -a(t)$, the decision function becomes

$$L_\infty = 4 \int_0^T V(t)a(t) \, dt \tag{18-30}$$

Hence the idealized result is obtained by integrating the product of the received wave $V(t)$ and the noise-free signal wave $a(t)$ over the time interval from 0 to T and making the decision on the basis of the sign of the integral. The receiver must have the function $a(t)$ available and must know when to start and stop the integration. A detector making decisions on the basis of the integrated product of the received wave and some reference function is called a correlation detector, since it evaluates a crosscorrelation of two waves. The optimum functions for $a(t)$ and $b(t)$ have the largest possible difference between their crosscorrelation with each other and their autocorrelations. A better performance is obtained in this way than if $a(t)$ and $b(t)$ were orthogonal to each other over the interval 0 to T.

Another method of realizing optimum detection can be deduced from the fundamental equation for the response of a linear network to a specified impressed voltage wave. If $V(t)$ is the voltage impressed, starting at $t = 0$, and $g(t)$ is the impulse response of the network, the current at $t = T$ is given by

$$I(T) = \int_0^T V(t)g(T - t) \, dt \tag{18-31}$$

The decision function of Eq. (18-30) can therefore be generated as the response of a network to which the received wave $V(t)$ is applied if the impulse response of the network satisfies the equation

$$g(T - t) = a(t) \tag{18-32}$$

This implies
$$g(t) = a(T - t) \tag{18-33}$$

That is, the impulse response of the network is equal to the signal function reversed in time. Such a network is called a *matched filter*.[1] In the frequency domain, writing $G(\omega)$ for the Fourier transform of

$g(t)$, and $A(\omega)$ for the Fourier transform of $a(t)$, we have for the trans-mittance function of the network

$$G(\omega) = e^{-j\omega T}A^*(\omega) \tag{18-34}$$

A third method of realizing optimum performance has already been described in the previous chapters. This method consists of binary signaling with positive and negative signal waves having their spectra so shaped that regularly spaced nulls occur in the time domain. Inter-symbol interference is thereby suppressed by sampling each signal wave at the nulls of the others. This can be accomplished with band-limited spectra, and we have found that the ideal formula for error probability, Eq. (18-29), holds for these cases. The signal elements are not limited in time, but this does not matter when samples are taken only at their axis crossings.

It is of interest to compare the optimum time-limited channel with the idealized channels of information theory. The latter theory tells us that our optimum binary channel is actually a binary symmetric channel with capacity

$$C = [1 + P \log P + (1 - P) \log (1 - P)]/T \tag{18-35}$$

Instead of sending $1/T$ bits per second with probability of error P, we can send C or less bits per second with probability of error arbitrarily small. To do this we require external coding in which final decisions about the message are made from a long block of individual decisions in each interval T. When P is small the difference between $1/T$ and C is also small.

The problem of optimum n-ary decisions is more difficult and has not been completely solved. In terms of the geometric picture, it is desirable to choose signal waves whose representative points in signal space are as far apart as possible. In binary transmission the problem was solved by choosing signals $a(t)$ and $b(t)$ such that

$$\int_0^T a(t)b(t)\, dt = -E \tag{18-36}$$

where
$$E = \int_0^T a^2(t)\, dt$$

$$= \int_0^T b^2(t)\, dt \tag{18-37}$$

Here E represents the total energy associated with each signal wave. For more than two signals, say, $a_1(t), a_2(t), \ldots, a_n(t)$, the best that can be done is to satisfy relations of the form

$$\int_0^T a_r(t)a_s(t)\,dt = -\frac{E}{n-1} \qquad r \neq s \tag{18-38}$$

$$\int_0^T a_r^2(t)\,dt = E \tag{18-39}$$

To show that Eq. (18-38) gives the most negative correlation possible, write

$$\int_0^T a_r(t)a_s(t)\,dt = -cE \qquad r \neq s \tag{18-40}$$

We observe that

$$\int_0^T \left[\sum_{r=1}^n a_r(t)\right]^2 dt \geq 0 \tag{18-41}$$

But also

$$\int_0^T \left[\sum_{r=1}^n a_r(t)\right]^2 dt = \sum_{r=1}^n \sum_{s=1}^n \int_0^T a_r(t)a_s(t)\,dt$$

$$= [n - n(n-1)c]E \tag{18-42}$$

By comparison of Eqs. (18-41) and (18-42) we see that

$$c \leq \frac{1}{n-1} \tag{18-43}$$

As the value of n is increased, we approach the condition in which the best result is obtained by orthogonal signals, that is, when the integrals of the product of two unlike functions vanish. Extensive studies of n-ary signaling are given in the literature.[2-5]

REFERENCES

1. Turin, G. L.: An Introduction to Matched Filters, *IRE Trans. Inform. Theory*, vol. IT-6, pp. 311–329, June, 1960.
2. V. A. Kotel'nikov: "The Theory of Optimum Noise Immunity," translated by R. A. Silverman, McGraw-Hill Book Company, New York, 1959.
3. D. Middleton: "Introduction to Statistical Communication Theory," McGraw-Hill Book Company, New York, 1960.
4. A. H. Nuttall: Error Probabilities for Equicorrelated M-ary Signals under Phase-coherent and Phase-incoherent Reception, *IRE Trans. Inform. Theory*, vol. IT-8, pp. 305–314, July, 1962.
5. H. Debart: Détection optimale d'un message codé au milieu d'un bruit blanc, *Cables & Transmission*, vol. 17, pp. 98–105, April, 1963.

CHAPTER 19

STATISTICS OF DIGITAL SIGNALS

Digital transmission can be regarded as a discrete random process. The transmitter makes a choice from an alphabet of possible waves. The waves which the transmitter can choose are known to the receiver, but the sequence, of course, cannot be known until the complete message has been delivered. We have already observed that it is helpful to deal with statistical quantities which are characteristic of the signal wave transmitted. The average signal power is one such quantity which we have used over and over again. More general functions which we have made use of, primarily in relation to the effects of noise, are the spectral density and the correlation. In the present chapter we shall examine the statistical description of the signal itself apart from the noise which may accompany it.

19-1 SPECTRAL DENSITY

The spectral density function $w_v(f)$ of a wave $v(t)$ is defined in terms of the response $i(t)$ of a bandpass filter of bandwidth Δf to the wave $v(t)$ as follows:

$$w_v(f) = \lim_{\Delta f \to 0} \frac{\text{av } i^2(t)}{\Delta f} \qquad (19\text{-}1)$$

The bandpass filter is assumed to be ideal with unit absolute value for its transmittance throughout a band of width Δf centered at f, and zero response outside this band.

As noted in Chap. 7, the integral of the spectral density function from 0 to f defines the spectral distribution function:

$$W_v(f) = \int_0^f w_v(f) \, df \qquad (19\text{-}2)$$

Here we have assumed that all the power is contained in the positive frequency range, which is consistent with physical measurements. For convenience in mathematical analysis, the power is sometimes

315

divided between positive and negative frequencies. The spectral density function would then be divided by two. If the wave $v(t)$ contains discrete sinusoidal components, the spectral distribution function increases discontinuously by the amount of power in a component as the frequency of the component is reached. Correspondingly the spectral density contains a δ function weighted by the amount of power in the component and centered at the frequency of the component.

Relation of Spectral Density and the Fourier Transform.
The spectral density can be related to the Fourier integral representation of a wave.[1,2] Consider a signal wave $s(t,T)$ which vanishes outside the range $-T < t < T$. Represent this wave by a Fourier integral as follows:

$$s(t,T) = \int_{-\infty}^{\infty} S(f,T)e^{j2\pi ft}\, df \tag{19-3}$$

$$S(f,T) = \int_{-\infty}^{\infty} s(t,T)e^{-j2\pi ft}\, dt \tag{19-4}$$

Truncation of the signal to the finite range $-T$ to T enables us to avoid the question of convergence of the integrals. By Parseval's theorem, the mean-square value of $s(t,T)$ over the time interval from $t = -T$ to $t = T$ is given by

$$\frac{1}{2T}\int_{-T}^{T} s^2(t,T)\, dt = \frac{1}{2T}\int_{-\infty}^{\infty} s^2(t,T)\, dt = \frac{1}{2T}\int_{-\infty}^{\infty} |S(f,T)|^2\, df$$

$$= \int_{0}^{\infty} \frac{|S(f,T)|^2}{T}\, df = \int_{0}^{\infty} w_s(f,T)\, df \tag{19-5}$$

where
$$w_s(f,T) = \frac{|S(f,T)|^2}{T} \tag{19-6}$$

We have thus exhibited the mean square of the truncated signal wave as the integral of a density function in frequency. It is tempting to define the spectral density of the complete signal as the limit of $w_s(f,T)$ as T goes to infinity. Actually this limit fails to exist in most cases of interest. The difficulty can be overcome in either of two ways. We can calculate the mean square of the response of a bandpass filter of fixed bandwidth to $s(t,T)$ over the truncated time interval. This quantity approaches a limit dependent on the bandwidth as T goes to infinity. The ratio of this limit to the bandwidth then defines the spectral density at midband when the bandwidth is made to approach zero. The other method makes use of the concept of an ensemble of signal waves. Before attempting to take the limit of $w_s(f,T)$ for large T, we average $w_s(f,T)$ over all members of an ensemble in accordance with their probabilities of occurrence. The resulting ensemble average then approaches a definite limit as T is allowed to go to infinity.

We illustrate by calculating the spectral density of a random binary telegraph signal[3] such as shown in Fig. 19-1. In intervals of duration $T_s = 1/f_s$ centered at multiples of $1/f_s$, a choice is made between two standard pulses defined by the functions of time $g_1(t)$ and $g_2(t)$ when the origin of time is taken at the center of the interval. The probability

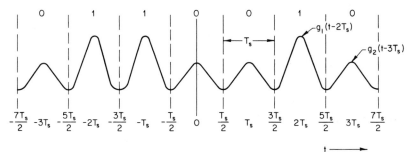

FIG. 19-1. Binary signaling wave.

that $g_1(t)$ is selected in any interval is p and the probability that $g_2(t)$ is selected is $1 - p$. The choice in each interval is independent of the choices in all other intervals. It is convenient to think of each pulse as confined to its own interval, although it will appear in the analysis that the results hold also for overlapping pulses.

If we let $2T = (2N + 1)T_s$, the truncated signal $s(t,T)$, can be represented by

$$s(t,T) = \sum_{n=-N}^{N} s_n(t) \tag{19-7}$$

where

$$s_n(t) = \begin{cases} g_1(t - nT_s) & \text{with prob } p \\ g_2(t - nT_s) & \text{with prob } 1 - p \end{cases} \tag{19-8}$$

The computation is expedited if we can separate out at the beginning the portion of $s(t,T)$ which leads to discrete spectral lines. In this case the separation is accomplished by subtracting steady-state waves consisting of repeated g_1- and g_2-functions weighted in accordance with their respective probabilities. Let

$$v(t,T) = \sum_{n=-N}^{N} [pg_1(t - nT_s) + (1 - p)g_2(t - nT_s)] \tag{19-9}$$

We then consider the wave $u(t,T) = s(t,T) - v(t,T)$. We verify that we can write

$$u(t,T) = \sum_{n=-N}^{N} u_n(t) \tag{19-10}$$

where $\qquad u_n(t) = a_n[g_1(t - nT_s) - g_2(t - nT_s)]$ $\qquad$ (19-11)

and $\qquad a_n = \begin{cases} 1 - p & \text{with prob } p \\ -p & \text{with prob } 1 - p \end{cases}$ $\qquad$ (19-12)

The Fourier transform of $u(t,T)$ is found to be

$$U(f,T) = \sum_{n=-N}^{N} a_n \int_{-\infty}^{\infty} [g_1(t - nT_s) - g_2(t - nT_s)]e^{-j2\pi f t} \, dt$$

$$= \sum_{n=-N}^{N} a_n e^{-j2\pi n T_s} [G_1(f) - G_2(f)]$$ $\qquad$ (19-13)

where $\qquad G_k(f) = \int_{-\infty}^{\infty} g_k(t)e^{-j2\pi f t} \, dt$ $\qquad$ (19-14)

Then

$$|U(f,T)|^2 = U(f,T)U^*(f,T)$$

$$= \sum_{m=-N}^{N} \sum_{n=-N}^{N} a_m a_n e^{j2\pi(n-m)T_s}[G_1(f) - G_2(f)][G_1{}^*(f) - G_2{}^*(f)]$$

(19-15)

To evaluate the expectation, we note that the only variables are the a's. When $m = n$ we find

$$a_n{}^2 = \begin{cases} (1 - p)^2 & \text{with prob } p \\ p^2 & \text{with prob } 1 - p \end{cases}$$ $\qquad$ (19-16)

Therefore

$$\langle a_n{}^2 \rangle = (1 - p)^2 p + p^2(1 - p) = p(1 - p)$$ $\qquad$ (19-17)

When $m \neq n$

$$a_m a_n = \begin{cases} (1 - p)^2 & \text{with prob } p^2 \\ p^2 & \text{with prob } (1 - p)^2 \\ -p(1 - p) & \text{with prob } 2p(1 - p) \end{cases}$$ $\qquad$ (19-18)

Therefore

$$\langle a_m a_n \rangle = (1 - p)^2 p^2 + p^2(1 - p)^2 - 2p^2(1 - p)^2 = 0 \quad \text{(19-19)}$$

Hence

$$\langle |U(f,T)|^2 \rangle = |G_1(f) - G_2(f)|^2 \sum_{n=-N}^{N} p(1 - p)$$

$$= (2N + 1)p(1 - p) |G_1(f) - G_2(f)|^2$$ $\qquad$ (19-20)

If we let $u(t)$ represent the function $u(t,T)$ when N goes to infinity in Eq. (19-10), the spectral density of $u(t)$ is given by

$$w_u(f) = \lim_{N \to \infty} \frac{\langle |U(f,T)|^2 \rangle}{(2N + 1)T_s/2}$$

$$= 2p(1 - p)f_s |G_1(f) - G_2(f)|^2$$ $\qquad$ (19-21)

Now let T go to infinity in Eqs. (19-7) and (19-9) and call the resulting functions $s(t)$ and $v(t)$. From the expression

$$v(t) = \sum_{n=-\infty}^{\infty} [pg_1(t - nT_s) + (1 - p)g_2(t - nT_s)] \qquad (19\text{-}22)$$

we verify that $v(t + T_s) = v(t)$, and hence that $v(t)$ is periodic in t with period T_s. Therefore we expand $v(t)$ in a Fourier series as follows:

$$v(t) = \sum_{m=-\infty}^{\infty} c_m e^{j2\pi mf_s t} \qquad (19\text{-}23)$$

$$c_m = \frac{1}{T_s} \int_{-T_s/2}^{T_s/2} e^{-j2\pi mf_s t} \sum_{n=-\infty}^{\infty} [pg_1(t - nT_s) + (1 - p)g_2(t - nT_s)] \, dt$$

$$= f_s \sum_{n=-\infty}^{\infty} \int_{-nT_s-T_s/2}^{-nT_s+T_s/2} [pg_1(t) + (1 - p)g_2(t)]e^{-j2\pi mf_s(t+nT_s)} \, dt$$

$$= f_s \int_{-\infty}^{\infty} [pg_1(t) + (1 - p)g_2(t)]e^{-j2\pi mf_s t} \, dt$$

$$= f_s[pG_1(mf_s) + (1 - p)G_2(mf_s)] \qquad (19\text{-}24)$$

The expression for $v(t)$ can be written

$$v(t) = c_0 + \sum_{m=1}^{\infty} (c_m e^{j2\pi mf_s t} + c_m^* e^{-j2\pi mf_s t})$$

$$= c_0 + \sum_{m=1}^{\infty} |c_m| [e^{j(2\pi mf_s t + ph\, c_m)} + e^{-j(2\pi mf_s t + ph\, c_m)}]$$

$$= c_0 + \sum_{m=1}^{\infty} 2 |c_m| \cos (2\pi mf_s t + ph\, c_m) \qquad (19\text{-}25)$$

Thus $v(t)$ consists of a constant term and a series of harmonics of the signaling frequency f_s. The amplitude of the mth harmonic is $2 |c_m|$ and the average power is $2 |c_m|^2$. The complete spectral density function consists of the continuous function $w_u(f)$ plus weighted δ functions representing the power concentrated at frequency zero and the harmonics of f_s. Collecting the terms we have

$$w_s(f) = w_u(f) + w_v(f)$$

$$= 2f_s p(1 - p) |G_1(f) - G_2(f)|^2 + f_s^2[pG_1(0) + (1 - p)G_2(0)]^2 \, \delta(f)$$

$$+ 2f_s^2 \sum_{m=1}^{\infty} |pG_1(mf_s) + (1 - p)G_2(mf_s)|^2 \, \delta(f - mf_s) \qquad (19\text{-}26)$$

From Eq. (19-26) we observe that the continuous part of the spectrum depends on the difference between the Fourier transforms of the two pulses. The amplitudes of the spectral lines depend upon the Fourier transforms of the pulses at the line frequencies. If the Fourier transforms of both g_1 and g_2 vanish at a particular harmonic of f_s, there can be no discrete component in the spectrum at the frequency of that harmonic. The harmonic amplitude will also vanish if the weighted contributions from the Fourier transforms of g_1 and g_2 at the harmonic frequency are equal in magnitude with opposite signs. These phenomena are of fundamental importance in the problem of recovering the signaling frequency from the received pulse sequence. A circuit tuned to any harmonic of nonzero amplitude delivers a sine wave at that frequency which can be used for synchronizing purposes. The d-c component has special interest in telegraphy since many

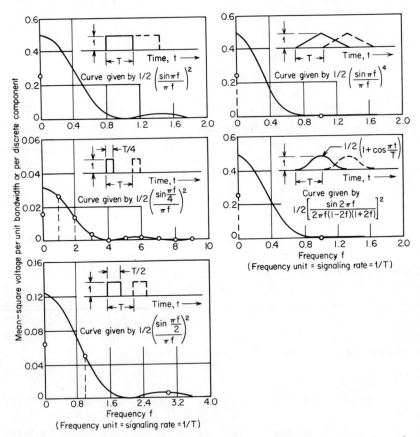

FIG. 19-2. Continuous and line spectral density components for independent binary on-off signaling with specific pulse shapes. Probability that any pulse is present $= p$; ordinate scale is for $p = 1/2$; multiply ordinates by $4p(1-p)$ for continuous spectrum; multiply ordinates by $4p^2$ for discrete terms. (W. R. Bennett, Bell System Tech. J., vol. 37, p. 1511, November, 1958.)

channels have zero response at zero frequency. If the d-c component of the signal can be adjusted to zero magnitude, the effect of d-c suppression by the channel may be reduced. The effect will not be entirely eliminated because suppression of direct current is necessarily accompanied by low response at frequencies near zero which may represent inportant parts of the continuous signal spectrum. Figure 19-2 shows spectral density functions for a variety of on-off pulse trains.

Use of a Random Signal Process as a Noise Source. The continuous part of the signal spectrum resembles the spectrum of a noise source, and indeed a random telegraph source can serve as a noise generator. An important practical difference between telegraph noise and gaussian noise is that the former can be generated deterministically if the message values are known or can be found. This follows because the waveform is completely determined by the sequence of message values and the standard unit pulse waveforms. Use of telegraph noise for masking other waves is therefore subject to the qualification that if the telegraph message can be read, the noise can be removed. Reading the message becomes more and more difficult as the ratio of bandwidth to signaling frequency is made smaller, and the overlapping of adjacent pulses in time becomes correspondingly greater. From the standpoint of digital transmission, reading the message is, of course, a paramount objective, and the bandwidth of the transmission medium must be made large enough and the noise and distortion small enough to enable a correct reading to be made.

The deterministic character of a signal process imparts a phase structure to the spectral components. In contrast to gaussian noise, it is possible to have regularly spaced axis crossings. It is also possible to generate discrete spectral components when none such exist in the actual wave. We have seen that no discrete spectral component can appear in the spectrum at a frequency for which the Fourier transforms of the standard pulses vanish. It is still possible, however, to generate a discrete component at such a frequency by performing a nonlinear operation on the signal wave. Nonlinear processes can convert the pulse shapes into new ones which have nonzero Fourier transforms at the frequency in question. From the spectral point of view, the discrete term is thereby created from the components in the continuous spectrum, which although individually infinitesimal have systematic phase relations enabling a discrete sum to be formed at one frequency.

Carrier-type Signals. When the signal is a modulated carrier wave, the spectral density can be easily expressed in terms of that of the baseband wave if the carrier wave is derived by simple product modulation. For example, if the spectral density function $w_s(f)$ is known for the signal wave $s(t)$, the spectral density of the carrier signal $\mu(t) = s(t) \cos(\omega_c t + \theta)$ is readily found. For, consider any single frequency component of $s(t)$, say, $A \cos \omega t$. This component contributes upper- and lower-sideband terms to $\mu(t)$ thus

$$A \cos \omega t \cos(\omega_c t + \theta) = \frac{A}{2} \cos[(\omega_c + \omega)t + \theta]$$

$$+ \frac{A}{2} \cos[(\omega_c - \omega)t + \theta] \quad (19\text{-}27)$$

The baseband component has mean-square value $A^2/2$ at frequency f. The resulting sideband components have mean-square values $A^2/8$ at frequencies $f_c + f$ and $f_c - f$. We translate these relations into the conclusion that an element of mean signal power $w_s(f)\,df$ at f in the baseband gives a pair of elementary modulated components of mean power $w_s(f)\,df/4$ at the frequencies $f_c + f$ and $f_c - f$. There are in general, therefore, two contributions to the spectral density of the carrier signal at frequency f. One is that from either the upper or lower sideband depending on whether f is above or below the carrier frequency. The value of this spectral density contribution is $w_s(f - f_c)/4$ if $f > f_c$ and $w_s(f_c - f)/4$ if $f < f_c$. The other contribution is from the folded-over lower sideband and has the value $w_s(f_c + f)/4$. If the carrier frequency is not harmonically related to the signaling frequency, the direct and folded sideband contributions have unrelated phases and simple power addition is valid. The resulting formula can be written as

$$4w_\mu(f) = w_s(|f_c - f|) + w_s(f_c + f) \quad (19\text{-}28)$$

When the signaling and carrier frequencies are harmonically related, Eq. (19-28) does not apply, and the exact solution is preferably obtained by considering $\mu(t)$ as the signal process itself rather than by decomposing into the product of baseband and carrier waves. In many cases of interest, however, the foldover sideband is negligible, and hence the phase relation is of no consequence.

Binary Phase Modulation. As an example of a case in which the signaling frequency and carrier frequency are harmonically related, consider the case of binary phase-shift keying when a differentially coherent detector is to be used. Here, as shown in Chap. 10, the carrier phase difference between the delayed and undelayed signals affects the output of the detector. A favorable situation is that in which $\omega_c T_s$ is a multiple of 2π. As an example consider the signal process:

$$s(t,T) = \sum_{n=-N}^{N} Ah(t - nT_s)a_n \cos{(2r\pi f_s t + \theta)}$$

$$\frac{nT_s - T_s}{2} < t < \frac{nT_s + T_s}{2} \qquad (19\text{-}29)$$

where
$$a_n = \begin{cases} 1 & \text{with prob } p \\ -1 & \text{with prob } 1 - p \end{cases}$$

r is a positive integer and $f_s T_s = 1$

The function $h(t)$ shapes the transition between two successive values of phase. If the bandwidth is large compared with the signaling frequency, $h(t)$ can be substantially constant throughout the signaling interval and zero elsewhere. When economy of bandwidth is important, the transitions are necessarily rounded off. We can now apply the previously developed theory, setting

$$g_1(t) = -g_2(t) = Ah(t) \cos{(2r\pi f_s t + \theta)} \qquad (19\text{-}30)$$

The spectral density function can then be obtained from Eq. (19-26), and is

$$w_s(f) = 8f_s p(1 - p) |G_1(f)|^2 + f_s^2(1 - 2p)^2 G_1{}^2(0)\delta(f)$$

$$+ 2f_s^2(1 - 2p)^2 \sum_{m=1}^{\infty} |G_1(mf_s)|^2 \, \delta(f - mf_s) \qquad (19\text{-}31)$$

The value of $G_1(f)$ is given by Eqs. (19-14) and (19-30), that is,

$$G_1(f) = \frac{A}{2} e^{j\theta} H(f - rf_s) + \frac{A}{2} e^{-j\theta} H(f + rf_s) \qquad (19\text{-}32)$$

where

$$H(f) = \int_{-\infty}^{\infty} h(t)e^{-j2\pi ft} \, dt \qquad (19\text{-}33)$$

The second term of (19-32) represents foldover of the lower sideband and is often negligible in the frequency range of interest. When it must be taken into account, the resultant spectral density function is seen to depend on the carrier phase θ. Note that when the two phases are equally likely, $p = \frac{1}{2}$, and the discrete terms vanish, leaving only the continuous spectrum.

The Fourier transform of the amplitude transition function $h(t)$ is seen to play a key role in the spectral density of the phase-modulated wave. If the transitions are abrupt at the beginnings and ends of the intervals, $h(t)$ is a rectangular pulse of duration T_s. The value of $H(f)$ is then

$$H(f) = \int_{-T_s/2}^{T_s/2} e^{-j2\pi ft} \, dt = \frac{\sin{(\pi f/f_s)}}{\pi f} \qquad (19\text{-}34)$$

The corresponding spectral density function consists of upper- and lower-sideband contributions of squared $(\sin x)/x$ shape. There is a discrete component at the carrier frequency except when $p = \frac{1}{2}$. There can be no other discrete components no matter what value p has since $H(f)$ is zero when f/f_s is an integer.

In practice a signal is subjected to some band limiting by the channel and its associated sending and receiving filters. The effect of band limiting on the spectral density of the received signal is easily computed from the properties of linear networks. A linear system with transmittance function $Y(f)$ transforms the spectral density function $w_s(f)$ of an input signal to $|Y(f)|^2 w_s(f)$. Except for the effect of sideband overlap, this can be considered as equivalent to using a different transition function, which in general is rounded off and has longer duration than $h(t)$. The rounding off can also be performed directly on the baseband signal before modulating the carrier phase. The spreading of transition functions over more than one signaling interval does not affect the validity of the analysis since we can always start with a time-limited function and can derive other cases from it by linear operations in the frequency domain.

Multilevel Phase Modulation. The case of n-ary phase modulation can be handled in a manner similar to that of binary. We illustrate by analyzing a random four-phase signal in which the four values are equally probable. We write for the signal over a finite interval

$$s(t,T) = \text{Re} \sum_{n=-N}^{N} Ah(t - nT_s)a_n e^{j(2k\pi f_s t + \theta)}$$

$$= \sum_{n=-N}^{N} \frac{A}{2} h(t - nT_s)[a_n e^{j(2k\pi f_s t + \theta)} + a_n{}^* e^{-j(2k\pi f_s t + \theta)}] \quad (19\text{-}35)$$

The coefficient a_n is a random variable which we shall assume takes one of the four values $e^{\pm j\pi/4}$, $e^{\pm j3\pi/4}$ independently with probability $\frac{1}{4}$. The number k represents the ratio of carrier frequency to signaling frequency. We have represented the signal for a type of phase modulation in which the phase changes by an odd multiple of $45°$ in each signaling interval. Proceeding in the same manner as in the earlier examples, we find

$$S(f,T) = \frac{A}{2} H(f - kf_s)e^{j\theta} \sum_{n=-N}^{N} a_n e^{-j2\pi nT_s(f - kf_s)}$$

$$+ \frac{A}{2} H(f + kf_s)e^{-j\theta} \sum_{n=-N}^{N} a_n{}^* e^{-j2\pi nT_s(f + kf_s)} \quad (19\text{-}36)$$

Then
$$|S(f,T)|^2 = \frac{A^2}{4} \sum_{m=-N}^{N} \sum_{n=-N}^{N} [a_m e^{j\theta} H(f - kf_s) e^{-j2\pi m T_s(f-kf_s)}$$
$$+ a_m^* e^{-j\theta} H(f + kf_s) e^{-j2\pi m T_s(f+kf_s)}]$$
$$\times [a_n^* e^{-j\theta} H^*(f - kf_s) e^{j2\pi n T_s(f-kf_s)}$$
$$+ a_n e^{j\theta} H^*(f + kf_s) e^{j2\pi n T_s(f+kf_s)}] \tag{19-37}$$

Averaging over the ensemble requires averaging the products $a_m a_n^*$, $a_m a_n$, $a_m^* a_n^*$, and $a_m^* a_n$. When $m = n$

$$\langle a_n^2 \rangle = \frac{1}{4} (e^{j\pi/2} + e^{j3\pi/2} + e^{-j\pi/2} + e^{-j3\pi/2}) = 0 \tag{19-38}$$

$$\langle a_n a_n^* \rangle = 1 \tag{19-39}$$

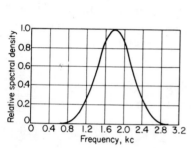

FIG. 19-3. Spectral density of four-phase data signal with random code input.

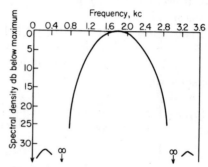

FIG. 19-4. Spectral density expressed in decibels for four-phase data signal with random code input.

When $m \neq n$, the ensemble average of each of the products is zero because with any choice of a_m, the average of the a_n's is

$$(e^{j\pi/4} + e^{j3\pi/4} + e^{-j\pi/4} + e^{-j3\pi/4})/4 = 0$$

Therefore

$$\langle |S(f,T)|^2 \rangle = \frac{A^2}{4} (2N + 1)[|H(f - kf_s)|^2 + |H(f + kf_s)|^2] \tag{19-40}$$

and hence
$$w_s(f) = \frac{A^2 f_s}{2} [|H(f - kf_s)|^2 + |H(f + kf_s)|^2] \tag{19-41}$$

Figures 19-3 and 19-4 show the resulting spectral density plotted for the case of raised-cosine transitions, that is,

$$h(t) = \frac{1 + \cos \pi f_s t}{2} \qquad -T_s < t < T_s \tag{19-42}$$

Setting $x = f/f_s$, we then obtain from Eq. (19-41):

$$w_s(f) = \frac{A^2}{16\pi^2 f_s}\left[\frac{1 - \cos 4\pi(x - k)}{(x - k)^2(1 + 2k - 2x)^2(1 - 2k + 2x)^2}\right.$$

$$\left. + \frac{1 - \cos 4\pi(x + k)}{(x + k)^2(1 - 2k - 2x)^2(1 + 2k + 2x)^2}\right] \quad (19\text{-}43)$$

The curves are drawn for $f_s = 1.2$ kc and $k = 1.5$. The amount of sideband overlap for this case is negligible, and the spectral density is for all practical purposes equal to the squared Fourier transform of a raised cosine with the center shifted to the carrier frequency. Figure 19-4 shows the ordinates on a decibel scale and indicates how far down the secondary lobes are relative to the main components of the signal. No discrete lines appear because of the symmetry of the four equiprobable phases.

Frequency-shift Keying with Discontinuous Phase. The case of frequency modulation is easily analyzed when it can be considered as switching between two independent oscillators. For example, consider the signal process

$$s(t) = \begin{cases} A \cos(\omega_1 t + \theta) & \text{with prob } p \\ A \cos(\omega_2 t + \phi) & \text{with prob } 1 - p \\ & nT_s - \dfrac{T_s}{2} < t < nT_s + \dfrac{T_s}{2} \quad (19\text{-}44) \end{cases}$$

This does not quite fit Eqs. (19-7) and (19-8) because the presence of carrier phase angles relative to the signaling intervals prevents reduction to standard forms $g_1(t)$ and $g_2(t)$ referred to the center of each interval. It also does not fit the switching of two independent carrier waves to which we could apply the results of Eq. (19-28) because this would assume that we sometimes have both waves and sometimes neither. The solution can be obtained by writing

$$s(t) = u(t) + v(t) \quad (19\text{-}45)$$

where $\quad v(t) = pA \cos(\omega_1 t + \theta) + (1 - p)A \cos(\omega_2 t + \phi) \quad (19\text{-}46)$

$$u(t) = \sum_{n=-\infty}^{\infty} a_n A[\cos(\omega_1 t + \theta) - \cos(\omega_2 t + \phi)]$$

$$nT_s - \frac{T_s}{2} < t < nT_s + \frac{T_s}{2} \quad (19\text{-}47)$$

$$a_n = \begin{cases} 1 - p & \text{with prob } p \\ -p & \text{with prob } 1 - p \end{cases} \quad (19\text{-}48)$$

Then

$$w_s(f) = w_u(f) + \frac{p^2 A^2}{2} \delta(f - f_1) + \frac{(1 - p)^2 A^2}{2} \delta(f - f_2) \quad (19\text{-}49)$$

The function $u(t)$ is defined in terms of modulating two carriers simultaneously with a choice between the two signals

$$g_1(t) = (1 - p)A \qquad \frac{-T_s}{2} < t < \frac{T_s}{2} \qquad (19\text{-}50)$$
$$g_2(t) = -pA$$

From Eq. (19-28) we therefore have

$$w_u(f) = \frac{p(1 - p)f_s A^2}{2\pi^2} \left[\frac{\sin^2 \pi(f - f_1)/f_s}{(f - f_1)^2} + \frac{\sin^2 \pi(f + f_1)/f_s}{(f + f_1)^2} \right.$$
$$\left. + \frac{\sin^2 \pi(f - f_2)/f_s}{(f - f_2)^2} + \frac{\sin^2 \pi(f + f_2)/f_s}{(f + f_2)^2} \right] \qquad (19\text{-}51)$$

Thus the solution comes out to be the same as random on-off independent switching of the two oscillators.

Continuous-phase FSK. If the frequency of a single oscillator is shifted with continuous phase, the problem becomes more difficult. The solution has been given in papers by Pushman,[4] Postl,[5] and Bennett and Rice.[6] We shall give a brief summary of the method and results, using the same notation as in the third paper. Consider the signal wave

$$u(t) = \begin{cases} A \cos(\omega_1 t + \theta_n) \\ \text{or} \\ A \cos(\omega_2 t + \phi_n) \end{cases} \begin{array}{l} nT \le t < (n + 1)T \\ n = 0, 1, 2, \ldots \end{array} \qquad (19\text{-}52)$$

where the choice is made independently and with equal probability for each interval of length T. The initial values at $t = 0$ of the phase are $\theta_0 = \phi_0 = \phi$, and the succeeding values θ_n, ϕ_n are to be chosen so as to make the phase of $u(t)$ continuous at the transition points.

Let $\qquad \alpha = \frac{1}{2}(\omega_2 + \omega_1) \qquad \beta = \frac{1}{2}(\omega_2 - \omega_1) \qquad (19\text{-}53)$

Then $\qquad \omega_1 = \alpha - \beta \qquad \omega_2 = \alpha + \beta \qquad (19\text{-}54)$

Set $\quad u(t) = A \cos B_n(t), \; nT \le t < (n + 1)T, \, n = 0, 1, 2, \ldots \quad (19\text{-}55)$

$$B_0(t) = (\alpha + x_1 \beta)t + \phi \qquad (19\text{-}56)$$

$$B_n(t) = \alpha t + x_{n+1}\beta(t - nT) + \phi + \beta T \sum_{r=1}^{n} x_r \qquad n > 0 \quad (19\text{-}57)$$

We assume $x_1, x_2, \ldots$ to be independent random variables each of which is equally likely to have the value $+1$ or -1. We verify that within the interval beginning at $t = nT$, the frequency is $\alpha + x_{n+1}\beta$,

which is equal to ω_2 if $x_{n+1} = 1$ and equal to ω_1 if $x_{n+1} = -1$. Therefore, the function $B_n(t)$ satisfies the condition of an equiprobable
choice between the two frequencies in each interval. We also note
that the phase at the beginning of the typical interval is

$$B_n(nT) = \alpha nT + \phi + \beta T \sum_{r=1}^{n} x_r \qquad (19\text{-}58)$$

while the phase at the end of the previous interval is

$$B_{n-1}(nT) = \alpha nT + \phi + x_n \beta[nT - (n-1)T]$$

$$+ \beta T \sum_{r=1}^{n-1} x_r = B_n(nT) \quad (19\text{-}59)$$

Thus the function $B_n(t)$ also satisfies the required condition of continuous phase.

The spectral density $w_u(f)$ of $u(t) = A \cos B_n(t)$ is the limit of
$2\langle |S_N(f,NT)|^2 \rangle / NT$ as $N \to \infty$. In this expression

$$S_N(f,NT) = \int_0^{NT} e^{-j\omega t} u(t)\, dt = \sum_{n=0}^{N-1} s_n \qquad (19\text{-}60)$$

$$s_n = Ae^{-j\omega nT} \int_0^T e^{-j\omega t} \cos B_n(t + nT)\, dt \qquad (19\text{-}61)$$

where s_n is a function of $f = \omega/2\pi$. The ensemble average of

$$|S_N(f,NT)|^2 = \sum_{n=0}^{N-1} \sum_{m=0}^{N-1} s_n s_m{}^*$$

$$= \sum_{n=0}^{N-1} s_n s_n{}^* + \sum_{k=1}^{N-1} \sum_{n=0}^{N-k-1} (s_n s_{n+k}{}^* + s_{n+k} s_n{}^*) \quad (19\text{-}62)$$

is the sum of terms of the form

$$\langle s_{n+k} s_n{}^* \rangle = A^2 e^{-j\omega kT} \int_0^T e^{-j\omega t}\, dt \int_0^T e^{j\omega \tau}$$

$$\langle \cos B_{n+k}(t + nT + kT) \cos B_n(\tau + nT) \rangle\, d\tau \quad (19\text{-}63)$$

We calculate

$$2 \langle \cos B_n(t + nT) \cos B_n(\tau + nT) \rangle$$

$$= \operatorname{Re} \langle [e^{jB_n(t+nT)-jB_n(\tau+nT)} + e^{jB_n(t+nT)+jB_n(\tau+nT)}] \rangle$$

$$= \operatorname{Re} \left\langle \left[e^{j\alpha(t-\tau)} e^{jx_{n+1}\beta(t-\tau)} \right. \right.$$

$$\left. \left. + e^{j\alpha(t+\tau+2nT)+j2\phi} e^{jx_{n+1}\beta(t+\tau)} \prod_{r=1}^{n} e^{j2x_r\beta T} \right] \right\rangle \quad (19\text{-}64)$$

Since the x's are independent, the average of a product of functions in which the variables appear separately is equal to the product of the averages of the individual functions. Since each x has only two possible values with a probability of one-half for each, we evaluate the expectations of individual terms by inserting the sum of the two possible functions with weighting factor one-half. Performing the necessary operations we find

$$2 \langle \cos B_n(t + nT) \cos B_n(\tau + nT) \rangle = \cos \alpha(t - \tau) \cos \beta(t - \tau)$$
$$+ \cos [\alpha(t + \tau + 2nT) + 2\phi] \cos \beta(t + \tau) \cos^n 2\beta T \quad (19\text{-}65)$$

Similarly when $k > 0$

$$2 \langle \cos B_{n+k}(t + nT + kT) \cos B_n(\tau + nT) \rangle$$
$$= \cos \alpha(t - \tau + kT) \cos \beta t \cos \beta(\tau - T) \cos^{k-1} \beta T$$
$$+ \cos [\alpha(t + \tau + 2nT + kT) + 2\phi]$$
$$\times \cos \beta t \cos \beta(\tau + T) \cos^{k-1} \beta T \cos^n 2\beta T \quad (19\text{-}66)$$

If $2\beta T$ is not a multiple of π the terms in (19-65) and (19-66) containing $\cos^n 2\beta T$ contribute nothing to the left-hand sides of

$$\lim_{N \to \infty} N^{-1} \sum_{n=0}^{N-1} \langle s_n s_n^* \rangle$$
$$= 2^{-1} A^2 \int_0^T e^{-j\omega t} \, dt \int_0^T e^{j\omega\tau} \, d\tau \cos \alpha(t - \tau) \cos \beta(t - \tau) \quad (19\text{-}67)$$

$$\lim_{N \to \infty} N^{-1} \sum_{n=0}^{N-k-1} \langle s_{n+k} s_n^* \rangle$$
$$= 2^{-1} A^2 e^{-j\omega kT} \cos^{k-1} \beta T \int_0^T e^{-j\omega t} \, dt \int_0^T e^{j\omega\tau}$$
$$\cos \alpha(t - \tau + kT) \cos \beta t \cos \beta(\tau - T) \, d\tau \quad (19\text{-}68)$$

Performing the integrations and summing with respect to k as indicated in (19-62), we obtain

$$w_u(f) =$$
$$\frac{2A^2 \sin^2 [(\omega - \omega_1)/2]T \sin^2 [(\omega - \omega_2)/2] \, T}{T[1 - 2 \cos (\omega - \alpha)T \cos \beta T + \cos^2 \beta T]} \left[\frac{1}{\omega - \omega_1} - \frac{1}{\omega - \omega_2} \right]^2$$
$$+ \frac{2A^2 \sin^2 [(\omega + \omega_1)/2]T \sin^2 [(\omega + \omega_2)/2]T}{T[1 - 2 \cos (\omega + \alpha)T \cos \beta T + \cos^2 \beta T]} \left[\frac{1}{\omega + \omega_1} - \frac{1}{\omega + \omega_2} \right]^2$$
$$(19\text{-}69)$$

In contrast to the case of discontinuous phase at switching instants, there are no discrete components when the phase is continuous if no harmonic relations between the frequency shift and the signaling rate exist. The general formula Eq. (19-69) must be modified for certain integer relationships among the frequencies involved, and in some cases discrete components appear at the marking and spacing frequencies, f_2 and f_1. Details of the special cases are given in the reference cited.[6] Figures 19-5 to 19-9, taken from the reference, show the illustrative spectral density functions for various ratios of the shift frequency to the signaling frequency.

Figure 19-5 shows a typical curve for the spectral density function when the phase is discontinuous at the instants of transition. The

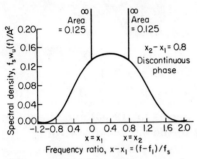

FIG. 19-5. Spectral density of random binary FSK wave with discontinuous phase at transitions. Frequency shift = 0.8 times signaling frequency.

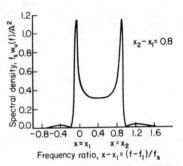

FIG. 19-6. Spectral density of random binary FSK wave with continuous phase at transitions. Frequency shift = 0.8 times signaling frequency.

portion of the spectrum folded back is assumed to be negligible. In the notation used $x_1 = f_1/f_s$ and $x_2 = f_2/f_s$. The parameter $x_2 - x_1$ is then equal to the ratio of frequency shift to signaling frequency. The steady-state terms are represented by spikes of infinite height and infinitesimal width at $x = x_1$ and $x = x_2$. Each of these spikes has an area of $\frac{1}{8}$. The area under the continuous curve is $\frac{1}{4}$. The total area is $\frac{1}{2}$, which is the mean-square value of the signal wave per unit of squared amplitude. The frequency shift in Fig. 19-5 is equal to 0.8 times the bit rate. Figure 19-6 is drawn for the same conditions as Fig. 19-5 except that the phase is continuous at all times. The infinitely sharp spikes change into horns of finite height and width. As the frequency shift is made to approach the bit rate, the horns increase in height and decrease in width and move toward the marking and spacing frequencies. Figure 19-7 shows a close approach in which $x_2 - x_1 = 0.95$. Figure 19-8 shows the limiting case when $x_2 - x_1 = 1$. This is the case previously described in Chaps. 5 and 9 for which Sunde has shown that intersymbol interference can be

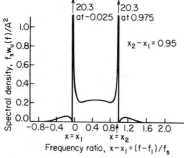

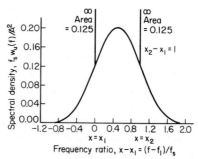

FIG. 19-7. Spectral density of random binary FSK wave with continuous phase at transitions. Frequency shift = 0.95 times signaling frequency.

FIG. 19-8. Spectral density of random binary FSK wave with continuous phase at transitions. Frequency shift = signaling frequency.

avoided. The presence of the steady-state components at the marking and spacing frequencies represents wasted signal power as far as information is concerned and leads to performance 3 db poorer than binary phase modulation when average signal power is constrained.

When the frequency shift is made greater than the bit rate, the horns again reappear as shown in Fig. 19-9 with the peaks now inside the interval bounded by the marking and spacing frequencies. It will be noted also on this figure, which is drawn for $x_2 - x_1 = 1.2$, that nulls now appear in the spectral density within the marking-to-spacing interval. Further increase in $x_2 - x_1$ takes us into the region of large-index frequency modulation in which the signal power is spread out over a wide range compared with the bit rate.

If we proceed toward lower ratios of shift frequency to bit rate, we have the case of low-index FM. It has been shown by Postl[5] that the horns disappear when $x_2 - x_1 = 2/\pi = 0.636$.

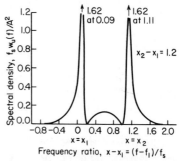

FIG. 19-9. Spectral density of random binary FSK wave with continuous phase at transitions. Frequency shift = 1.2 times signaling frequency.

It does not follow that this is a particularly good operating value. Although the resulting spectral density function is more definitely localized near the center of the band, the reduction in signal frequency deviation gives less margin over noise.

The spectral density function of signal processes is seen to be generally useful for indicating at what frequencies the average power of the signal is concentrated.   It does not tell us exactly what will happen to the signal waveform if the bandwidth is restricted or if the amplitude and phase relations within the band are not preserved.   We can only say the waveform will be changed, but we can not say how much and in what way.   Since the power density is averaged over all possible signal sequences, the more infrequent messages do not have much weight.   It could happen that a channel of sufficient bandwidth to transmit the most important frequencies represented in the spectral density curve would perform badly on some unusual sequence.   This could happen, for example, if the principal components resulting from the sequence were at or beyond the edges of the band.

The spectral distribution function furnishes useful information when constraint on the channel is expressed in terms of average power. The peak power cannot in general be determined from the spectral distribution since the averaging process removes effects of phase structure from the description.

Cross-spectral Density.   We have so far dealt with what can be called the self-spectral density of a signal.   The concept of cross-spectral density between two signals is also useful.   The cross-spectral density is a measure of the coherence between two signals and is conveniently expressed in terms of complex values to show the phase relations.   Corresponding to the definition of Eq. (19-1), we define the real part of the cross-spectral density of $x(t)$ and $y(t)$ by

$$\operatorname{Re} w_{xy}(f) = \lim_{\Delta f \to 0} \frac{\operatorname{av} [x(t)y(t)]}{\Delta f} \qquad (19\text{-}70)$$

The imaginary part is formed by replacement of $y(t)$ by its Hilbert transform $\hat{y}(t)$.   The latter is defined as the function of time which results when the phases of all components of $y(t)$ are retarded by $90°$ without disturbing the amplitudes.   In terms of Fourier transforms of $x(t)$ and $y(t)$ over the finite range from $-T$ to T, we have in analogy with Eqs. (19-3) to (19-6):

$$w_{xy}(f) = \lim_{\Delta f \to 0} \left[\lim_{T \to \infty} \int_{f-\Delta f/2}^{f+\Delta f/2} \frac{S_x{}^*(f,T)S_y(f,T)}{2T\Delta f} \, df \right] \qquad (19\text{-}71)$$

Note from this definition that the cross-spectral density $w_{yx}(f)$ is the complex conjugate of $w_{xy}(f)$.   We also see that if $x(t)$ is transmitted through a linear network with transmittance $Y_1(f)$, and $y(t)$ is transmitted through a network with transmittance $Y_2(f)$, the cross-power spectral density of the two output waves is obtained by multiplication of $w_{xy}(f)$ by $Y_1{}^*(f)Y_2(f)$.

The real part of the cross-spectral density gives the average in-phase power of the two signals as a function of frequency. The imaginary part gives a similar measure of the components which are in quadrature with each other. Totally unrelated components of the two signals make no contribution to the cross-spectral density. It can be verified from the definitions that the cross-spectral density can be determined experimentally from four self-spectral density measurements made on the sums and differences of the original waves and of one wave and its Hilbert transform. The required relation is expressed by

$$4w_{xy} = w_{x+y} - w_{x-y} + j(w_{x+\hat{y}} - w_{x-\hat{y}}) \qquad (19\text{-}72)$$

Cross-spectral density functions are helpful in analyzing the persistence of phase structure in the relations between two signals after undergoing various stages of processing. They are also useful in the study of random noise waves which contain contributions from a common origin.

19-2 CORRELATION

In dealing with single random variables, we have found it possible to express a considerable amount of useful information in terms of averages of the first and second powers of the variable. In the case of signal waves, we identify the average itself with the d-c component and the average square with the mean total power in a load of unit resistance. The difference between the mean square and the square of the mean gives the average a-c power. The latter quantity can also be obtained by first subtracting the average or d-c component from the wave and then calculating the mean square of the remainder. Statisticians call the resulting average the *variance* of the process and write the definition as

$$\text{var } x = \text{av } (x - \text{av } x)^2 = \text{av } (x^2) - (\text{av } x)^2 \qquad (19\text{-}73)$$

The square root of the variance is called the *standard deviation* and will be designated here by σ_x for a random variable x. The standard deviation is equal to the rms value of the a-c component.

When there are two random variables to be considered jointly, it is convenient to introduce another important second-order average called the covariance of the two quantities. We define

$$\text{cov } (x,y) = \text{av } [(x - \text{av } x)(y - \text{av } y)] \qquad (19\text{-}74)$$

Evidently $\qquad \text{cov } (x,x) = \text{var } x \qquad (19\text{-}75)$

The correlation coefficient of two random variables is found by dividing their covariance by the product of their standard deviations, thus

$$\rho_{xy} = \frac{\text{cov }(x,y)}{\sigma_x \sigma_y} \tag{19-76}$$

It can be shown that the values of the correlation coefficient lie in the range -1 to $+1$. If the value is zero, the variables are said to be uncorrelated. Uncorrelated variables are not necessarily independent. An exception is the case of gaussian variables, which must be independent if their correlation coefficient is zero.

When we consider the joint properties of two variables evaluated at different times, it is convenient to define correlation functions in which the time appears as a parameter. In general the crosscorrelation function of two random variables $[x(t)]$, $[y(t)]$ is defined by

$$R_{xy}(t_1,t_2) = \langle x(t_1)y(t_2)\rangle \tag{19-77}$$

In the case of stationary random processes, the crosscorrelation function depends only on the time difference $\tau = t_2 - t_1$. For this case we have

$$R_{xy}(\tau) = \langle x(t)y(t + \tau)\rangle \tag{19-78}$$

If x and y are the same process, we obtain the autocorrelation function

$$R_{xx}(\tau) = R_x(\tau) = \langle x(t)x(t + \tau)\rangle \tag{19-79}$$

It would be more consistent with the preceding correlation coefficient if we had normalized these functions by dividing by the product of the standard deviations. However, the unnormalized definitions have such widespread usage that it seems futile to insist on a change. We note that as a consequence of the definitions

$$R_{xy}(\tau) = R_{yx}(-\tau) \tag{19-80}$$

$$R_x(\tau) = R_x(-\tau) \tag{19-81}$$

Wiener-Khintchine Relations. Since the correlation and spectral density functions are both second-order statistics of random processes, it is not surprising that there are relations between them. They are in fact Fourier transforms of each other in accordance with the Wiener-Khintchine formulas. We state these here first for the case in which the spectral density is "two-sided," that is, defined for both positive and negative frequencies, and second for the "one-sided" case in which all the power is assumed to be contained in the positive frequency range. Note that the one-sided w_f is twice the two-sided w_f.

Two-sided spectra, $-\infty < f < \infty$

$$w_x(f) = \int_{-\infty}^{\infty} R_x(\tau)e^{-j2\pi f\tau} \, d\tau \tag{19-82}$$

$$w_{xy}(f) = \int_{-\infty}^{\infty} R_{xy}(\tau)e^{-j2\pi f\tau} \, d\tau \tag{19-83}$$

$$R_x(\tau) = \int_{-\infty}^{\infty} w_x(f)e^{j2\pi f\tau} \, df \tag{19-84}$$

$$R_{xy}(\tau) = \int_{-\infty}^{\infty} w_{xy}(f)e^{j2\pi f\tau} \, df \tag{19-85}$$

One-sided spectra, $0 < f < \infty$

$$w_x(f) = 4\int_{0}^{\infty} R_x(\tau) \cos 2\pi f\tau \, d\tau \tag{19-86}$$

$$R_x(\tau) = \int_{0}^{\infty} w_x(f) \cos 2\pi f\tau \, df \tag{19-87}$$

We note that as a consequence of these formulas, W_x, the average total signal power, is given by

$$W_x = \int_{-\infty}^{\infty} w_x(f) \, df = R_x(0) \tag{19-88}$$

Also W_{xy}, the average total correlated volt-amperes, is given by

$$W_{xy} = \int_{-\infty}^{\infty} w_{xy}(f) \, df = R_{xy}(0) \tag{19-89}$$

This is a complex number with real part giving in-phase volt-amperes and imaginary part giving quadrature volt-amperes.

We recall that the presence of a sine-wave component in a random process creates a δ function in the spectral density at the frequency of the component. The corresponding behavior of the autocorrelation is exhibited by calculating $R_x(\tau)$ when $x(t)$ is a sine wave. Let

$$x(t) = A \cos (2\pi f_0 t + \theta) \tag{19-90}$$

Then $\quad x(t)x(t + \tau) = \dfrac{A^2}{2} \cos 2\pi f_0\tau + \dfrac{A^2}{2} \cos [2\pi f_0(2t + \tau) + 2\theta]$

$$\tag{19-91}$$

The ensemble average of $x(t)x(t + \tau)$ can be computed by regarding θ as a random parameter uniformly distributed throughout the range from 0 to 2π. Or we can integrate the product over a long time interval, divide by the length of the interval, and take the limit as the length of the interval goes to infinity. In either case the oscillating term in t averages to zero giving the result

$$R_x(\tau) = \frac{A^2}{2} \cos 2\pi f_0 \tau \tag{19-92}$$

The mean total power is, of course, $A^2/2$, which is seen to be the value of $R_x(0)$. Therefore the presence of a sinusoidal autocorrelation component $B \cos 2\pi f_0\tau$ indicates mean power B in a line-spectral term at a frequency $f = f_0$. In other words, in the example cited

$$w_x(f) = \frac{A^2}{2} \delta(f - f_0) \tag{19-93}$$

If we wish to define the spectral density at both positive and negative frequencies the corresponding formula would be

$$w_x(f) = \frac{A^2}{4} \delta(f - f_0) + \frac{A^2}{4} \delta(f + f_0) \qquad -\infty < f < \infty \tag{19-94}$$

A d-c term equal to A in the signal process gives

$$R_x(\tau) = A^2 \tag{19-95}$$

$$w_x(f) = A^2\delta(f) \tag{19-96}$$

Calculations are usually expedited if d-c and sinusoidal components are subtracted from a random process at the beginning of the analysis.

We further note that

$$\begin{aligned}
R_{x+y}(\tau) &= \langle [x(t) + y(t)][x(t + \tau) + y(t + \tau)] \rangle \\
&= \langle [x(t)x(t + \tau) + y(t)y(t + \tau) \\
&\quad + x(t)y(t + \tau) + x(t + \tau)y(t)] \rangle \\
&= R_x(\tau) + R_y(\tau) + R_{xy}(\tau) + R_{xy}(-\tau) \\
&= R_x(\tau) + R_y(\tau) \quad \text{if} \quad R_{xy}(\tau) = 0 \tag{19-97}
\end{aligned}$$

Thus the autocorrelation function is an additive property of uncorrelated random processes.

Examples of Autocorrelation Functions. By means of the Wiener-Khintchine formulas, we can calculate correlation functions from the spectral densities when the latter are known. We can also compute the autocorrelation directly and then obtain the spectral density as a Fourier transform. The relative difficulties in the two procedures vary considerably, and it is often an advantage to choose one function over the other as the initial goal of the analysis. We illustrate by calculating the autocorrelation function for the random binary telegraph signal process of Fig. 19-1, for which we previously computed the spectral density. Using the same resolution as before, we write

$$s(t) = u(t) + v(t) \tag{19-98}$$

where

$$u(t) = \sum_{n=-\infty}^{\infty} a_n g_{12}(t - nT_s) \tag{19-99}$$

$$v(t) = \sum_{n=-\infty}^{\infty} [pg_1(t - nT_s) + (1 - p)g_2(t - nT_s)] \tag{19-100}$$

$$a_n = \begin{cases} 1 - p & \text{with prob } p \\ -p & \text{with prob } 1 - p \end{cases} \tag{19-101}$$

$$g_{12}(t) = g_1(t) - g_2(t) \tag{19-102}$$

At any fixed value of t we have

$$\langle u(t)u(t + \tau) \rangle = \sum_{m=-\infty}^{\infty} \sum_{n=-\infty}^{\infty} \langle a_m a_n \rangle g_{12}(t - mT_s)g_{12}(t + \tau - nT_s)$$

$$= p(1 - p) \sum_{n=-\infty}^{\infty} g_{12}(t - nT_s)g_{12}(t + \tau - nT_s) \tag{19-103}$$

It appears that the expectation of the product $u(t)u(t + \tau)$ is a function of t as well as of τ. Strictly speaking, therefore, we do not have a stationary process, and the autocorrelation function cannot be expressed as a function of the lag time τ alone. We observe, however, that if we increase t by T_s, the value of the expectation is unchanged. The autocorrelation is, therefore, a periodic function of t with period T_s. Since in obtaining $u(t)$ we have subtracted from $s(t)$ the portion $v(t)$ which gives line-spectral components, the process $u(t)$ has a continuous spectral density. The corresponding autocorrelation function dependent on τ only is obtained by averaging $\langle u(t)u(t + \tau) \rangle$ over one period in t, thus

$$R_u(\tau) = \frac{p(1 - p)}{T_s} \sum_{n=-\infty}^{\infty} \int_{-T_s/2}^{T_s/2} g_{12}(t - nT_s)g_{12}(t + \tau - nT_s) \, dt$$

$$= p(1 - p)f_s \sum_{n=-\infty}^{\infty} \int_{-nT_s-T_s/2}^{-nT_s+T_s/2} g_{12}(t)g_{12}(t + \tau) \, dt$$

$$= p(1 - p)f_s \int_{-\infty}^{\infty} g_{12}(t)g_{12}(t + \tau) \, dt \tag{19-104}$$

Averaging the autocorrelation function over a signaling interval is equivalent to assuming a random phase angle between the various members of the ensemble of possible signal waves.

By means of Parseval's formula,

$$\int_{-\infty}^{\infty} y_1(t)y_2(t)\,dt = \int_{-\infty}^{\infty} Y_1(f)Y_2^*(f)\,df \qquad (19\text{-}105)$$

where the Y's are Fourier transforms of the y's, we can write Eq. (19-104) in the alternate form

$$R_u(\tau) = p(1 - p)f_s\int_{-\infty}^{\infty} |G_{12}(f)|^2\,e^{j2\pi\tau f}\,df \qquad (19\text{-}106)$$

We note that $R_u(\tau)$ is thus exhibited as the Fourier transform of $p(1 - p)f_s\,|G_{12}(f)|^2$. We thus deduce directly the two-sided spectral density of $u(t)$, which when multiplied by 2 gives the one-sided spectral density function $w_u(f)$ of Eq. (19-21).

As a second example, consider alternate bipolar or pseudoternary signal transmission[7] in which the binary symbol 0 is always represented by no signal on the line, and the binary symbol 1 is represented alternately by positive and negative standard pulses. This coding method has the advantage of reducing the effects of zero wander since a pulse of one polarity is certain to be followed eventually by a pulse of the opposite polarity. The effects of d-c suppression and reduction of transmitted amplitude at frequencies near zero are then tolerable if a single isolated pulse can be satisfactorily received.

An appropriate representation of the transmitted wave is

$$s(t) = \sum_{n=-\infty}^{\infty} a_n g(t - nT_s) \qquad (19\text{-}107)$$

$$a_n = \begin{cases} 0 & \text{with prob } 1 - p \\ \pm 1 & \text{with prob } p \end{cases} \qquad (19\text{-}108)$$

The choice of sign of a_n is opposite to that of the most recent sign in the sequence. The ensemble expectation of the product $s(t)s(t + \tau)$ at fixed t and τ is given by

$$\langle s(t)s(t + \tau)\rangle = \sum_{m=-\infty}^{\infty} \sum_{n=-\infty}^{\infty} \langle a_m a_n\rangle g(t - mT_s)g(t + \tau - nT_s) \qquad (19\text{-}109)$$

When $m = n$ we have

$$a_n{}^2 = \begin{cases} 0 & \text{with prob } 1 - p \\ 1 & \text{with prob } p \end{cases} \qquad (19\text{-}110)$$

Hence $$\langle a_n{}^2\rangle = p \qquad (19\text{-}111)$$

When $m \neq n$

$$a_m a_n = \begin{cases} 0 & \text{with prob } 1 - p^2 \\ 1 & \text{with prob } p_{|n-m|} \\ -1 & \text{with prob } q_{|n-m|} \end{cases} \qquad (19\text{-}112)$$

where p_k and q_k are to be calculated for $k > 0$. We note that

$$p_k + q_k = p^2 \tag{19-113}$$

We also note that

$$p_1 = \text{prob}\,(a_m a_{m+1} = 1) = 0$$
$$q_1 = p^2 - p_1 = p^2 \tag{19-114}$$

We define x_k by the relation

$$p_k = x_k\,\text{prob}\,(a_m = 1,\, a_{m+k} = 1) = p^2 x_k \tag{19-115}$$

We observe that x_k is the probability that there is an odd number of 1's in the sequence $a_{m+1},\, a_{m+2},\, \ldots,\, a_{m+k-1}$. Then $1 - x_k$ is the probability of an even number of 1's in the same sequence. We can express x_{k+1} in terms of x_k by noting that the number of 1's retains its parity when a 0 is added to the sequence and changes parity when a 1 is added. Hence

$$x_{k+1} = (1 - p)x_k + p(1 - x_k)$$

or

$$x_{k+1} = p + (1 - 2p)x_k \tag{19-116}$$

The solution of this first-order difference equation* with the boundary condition $x_1 = 0$ is found to be

$$x_k = \frac{1}{2}\,[1 - (1 - 2p)^{k-1}] \tag{19-117}$$

Therefore

$$p_k = \frac{p^2}{2}\,[1 - (1 - 2p)^{k-1}] \tag{19-118}$$

and with $m \neq n$

$$\langle a_m a_n \rangle = p_{|n-m|} - q_{|n-m|} = 2p_{|n-m|} - p^2$$
$$= -p^2(1 - 2p)^{|n-m|-1} \tag{19-119}$$

It follows that

$$\langle s(t)s(t + \tau) \rangle = p \sum_{n=-\infty}^{\infty} g(t - nT_s)g(t + \tau - nT_s)$$

$$- p^2 \sum_{\substack{m=-\infty \\ m \neq n}}^{\infty} \sum_{n=-\infty}^{\infty} (1 - 2p)^{|n-m|-1}\, g(t - nT_s)g(t + \tau - nT_s) \tag{19-120}$$

We verify by substitution that the value of the right-hand member of (19-120) is unchanged when t is increased by T_s. Hence the ensemble average of the lag product is periodic in t with period T_s. We can average over t by taking the average over one period and dividing by

---

* This is the same one encountered in Chap. 7, Eq. (7-76), for the growth of error probability in a chain of regenerative repeaters.

T_s. We also rearrange the double summation by substituting $n - m = l$. The result is

$$
\begin{aligned}
R_s(\tau) &= pf_s \sum_{n=-\infty}^{\infty} \int_{-T_s/2}^{T_s/2} g(t - nT_s)g(t + \tau - nT_s)\, dt \\
&\quad - p^2 f_s \sum_{n=-\infty}^{\infty} \sum_{l=\pm 1}^{\pm\infty} (1 - 2p)^{|l|-1} \\
&\quad \times \int_{-T_s/2}^{T_s/2} g[t - (n - l)T_s]g(t + \tau - nT_s)\, dt \\
&= pf_s \sum_{n=-\infty}^{\infty} \int_{-nT_s - T_s/2}^{-nT_s + T_s/2} g(t)g(t + \tau)\, dt \\
&\quad - p^2 f_s \sum_{l=\pm 1}^{\pm\infty} (1 - 2p)^{|l|-1} \sum_{n=-\infty}^{\infty} \int_{-nT_s - T_s/2}^{-nT_s + T_s/2} g(t + lT_s)g(t + \tau)\, dt \\
&= pf_s \int_{-\infty}^{\infty} g(t)g(t + \tau)\, dt - p^2 f_s \sum_{l=\pm 1}^{\pm\infty} (1 - 2p)^{|l|-1} \\
&\quad \times \int_{-\infty}^{\infty} g(t + lT_s)g(t + \tau)\, dt
\end{aligned} \tag{19-121}
$$

We now apply Parseval's formula (19-105) to obtain

$$
\begin{aligned}
R_s(\tau) &= pf_s \int_{-\infty}^{\infty} G(f)G^*(f)e^{j2\pi f\tau}\, df \\
&\quad - p^2 f_s \sum_{l=\pm 1}^{\pm\infty} (1 - 2p)^{|l|-1} \int_{-\infty}^{\infty} G(f)e^{-j2\pi flT_s}G^*(f)e^{j2\pi f\tau}\, df \\
&= pf_s \int_{-\infty}^{\infty} |G(f)|^2 e^{j2\pi f\tau}\, df - p^2 f_s \int_{-\infty}^{\infty} |G(f)|^2 e^{j2\pi f\tau} \\
&\quad \times \sum_{l=1}^{\infty} (1 - 2p)^{l-1} (e^{j2\pi flT_s} + e^{-j2\pi flT_s})\, df \\
&= 2p(1 - p)f_s \int_{-\infty}^{\infty} \frac{(1 - \cos 2\pi fT_s)\,|G(f)|^2}{1 + 2(2p - 1)\cos 2\pi fT_s + (2p - 1)^2} e^{j2\pi f\tau}\, df
\end{aligned} \tag{19-122}
$$

Since $R_s(\tau)$ is exhibited in the form of a Fourier integral, the spectral density function can be written down immediately as the coefficient of $e^{j2\pi f\tau}$. With a slight rearrangement we obtain

$$
w_s(f) = \frac{8p(1 - p)f_s\,|G(f)|^2 \sin^2 \dfrac{\pi f}{f_s}}{1 + (2p - 1)^2 + 2(2p - 1)\cos \dfrac{2\pi f}{f_s}} \tag{19-123}
$$

We note that $w_s(0) = 0$ and hence that suppression of direct current by the channel should cause no impairment of the pulse train. We note also that if 1's and 0's are equally likely in the binary message, corresponding to $p = \frac{1}{2}$,

$$w_s(f) = 2f_s \, |G(f)|^2 \sin^2 \frac{\pi f}{f_s} \qquad (19\text{-}124)$$

In this case the spectral density reduces to that of the square of the Fourier transform of the standard pulse multiplied by the square of a sine function with nulls at multiples of the signaling rate.

It is of interest to compare this result with that of the dicode method, which reduces zero wander by sending the difference between an on-off pulse train and itself delayed by one bit. The standard pulses then become

$$g_1(t) = g(t) - g(t - T_s)$$
$$g_2(t) = 0 \qquad (19\text{-}125)$$

Then
$$G_1(f) = (1 - e^{-j2\pi f T_s})G(f)$$
$$G_1(mf_s) = 0, \quad \text{and} \quad G_2(f) = 0 \qquad (19\text{-}126)$$

From (19-126)

$$w_s(f) = 8f_s p(1 - p) \, |G(f)|^2 \sin^2 \frac{\pi f}{f_s} \qquad (19\text{-}127)$$

It is seen that the spectral densities of dicode and alternate bipolar become equal when $p = \frac{1}{2}$.

REFERENCES

1. Bennett, W. R.: Methods of Solving Noise Problems, *Proc. IRE*, vol. 44, pp. 609–638, May, 1956.
2. *Ibid.*: "Electrical Noise," chap. 10, McGraw-Hill Book Company, 1960.
3. *Ibid.*: Statistics of Regenerative Digital Transmission, *Bell System Tech. J.*, vol. 37, pp. 1501–1542, November, 1958.
4. Pushman, H. J.: Spectral Density Distributions of Signals for Binary Data Transmission, *Radio and Electron. Engr.*, vol. 25, pp. 155–165, February, 1963.
5. Postl, W.: Die spektrale Leistungsdichte bei Frequenzmodulation eines Trägers mit einem stochastischen Telegraphiesignal, *Frequenz*, vol. 17, pp. 107–110, March, 1963.
6. Bennett, W. R., and S. O. Rice: Spectral Density and Autocorrelation Functions Associated with Binary Frequency-shift Keying, *Bell System Tech. J.*, vol. 42, pp. 2355–2385, September, 1963.
7. Aaron, M. R.: PCM Transmission in the Exchange Plant, *Bell System Tech. J.*, vol. 41, pp. 99–141, January, 1962.

NAME INDEX

Aaron, M. R., 341
Abrams, I. J., 197, 199
Alexander, A. A., 95
Alexanderson, E. F. W., 17
Ampère, A, M., 5
Anderson, R. R., 194
Arago, D. F., 6
Armstrong, E. H., 246

Bain, A., 10, 14
Baker, P. A., 251
Balakrishnan, A. V., 197, 199
Bark, L. S., 155, 163
Barker, R. H., 265, 267
Baudot, J. M. E., 13
Becker, F. K., 259
Becquerel, A. C., 6
Bennett, W. R., 132, 163, 200, 276, 303, 327, 341
Berger, J. M., 200
Bessel, F. W., 154
Betancourt, 3
Black, H. S., 132
Bose, R. C., 296
Bowyer, L. R., 199
Brand, S., 131
Branly, E., 16
Braun, F., 17
Brett, J., 14
Buchanan, J., 14
Bunsen, R. W. E., 6
Buterbaugh, J. N., 251

Cahn, C. R., 219, 224
Carslaw, H. S., 48
Carter, C. W., Jr., 131
Caruthers, R. S., 95
Cavallo, T., 3
Chappe, C., 1, 3, 5

Clokey, A. A., 123, 132
Cooke, W. F., 7, 8, 11
Costas, J. P., 254, 259
Crafts, C. A., 251
Cramér, H., 200
Crater, T. V., 251
Cravis, H., 251
Crick, F. H. C., 25

Daniell, J. F., 6
Davey, J. R., 239, 259
Davy, E., 11
Debart, H., 314
DeForest, L., 17
de Heer, V., 5
de Jager, F., 259
Dyar, H. G., 5

Edison, T. A., 13, 242, 244, 247
Emde, F., 100, 131

Fahie, J. J., 18
Fano, R. M., 304
Faraday, M., 6
Field, C., 14
Fleming, J. A., 17
Fourier, J. B. J., 15
Freebody, J. W., 18
Froehlich, F. E., 303

Gauss, J. K. F., 6, 10
Gilbert, E. N., 25
Goldschmidt, R., 17
Golomb, S. W., 25
Goodall, W. M., 131
Gordon, B., 25
Graham, R. S., 259

343

Gray, F., 117, 219
Griffith, J. S., 25
Grove, W. R., 6
Gryb, R. M., 95
Gulstad, K., 123, 131

Habib, S., 127, 189
Hagelbarger, D. W., 300, 301, 304
Hamming, R. W., 293, 303
Hancock, J. C., 239
Hartley, R. V. L., 15, 18
Heaviside, O., 15, 18
Henry, J., 6, 10, 16
Hertz, H. R., 16
Highleyman, W. H., 199
Hilbert, D., 214
Hofman, E. J., 251
Hollerith, H., 25
Hollis, J. L., 251
Hopner, E., 259
Horne, 10
Horton, A. W., Jr., 94
House, R. E., 11
Huffman, D. A., 21, 25
Hughes, D. E., 12

Jackson, C. T., 10
Jahnke, P. R. E., 100, 131

Kallman, H. E., 276
Kelvin (Sir William Thomson), Lord,
    14, 15
Kendall, B. W., 90
Khintchine, A., 334, 336
Knopp, K., 200
Koenig, W., 251
Koll, V. G., 194
Kotel'nikov, V. A., 314
Krarup, C. E., 16
Kuznetzov, P. E., 155, 163

Lagrange, A. M., 187
Lawton, J. G., 213, 224
Lebow, I. L., 304
Leggett, B., 18
Lender, A., 125, 132, 239
LeSage, G. L., 3
Lodge, O. J., 16

Lommel, E. C. J., von, 155
Lomond, M., 3
Losch, F., 131
Lucky, R. W., 239

MacColl, L. A., 127, 132
McHugh, D. G., 304
Mandelbrot, B., 200
Marcatili, E. A., 150
Marconi, G., 16
Marcum, J. I., 163
Marshall, C., 3
Maxwell, J. C., 16
Meissner, A., 17
Mertz, P., 95
Meyers, S. T., 251
Middleton, D., 314
Mitchell, D., 95
Moore, E. F., 25
Morrison, C., 3
Morse, S. F. B., 7, 8, 240
Mosier, R. R., 251
Muller, D. E., 303
Munk, 16
Murray, Lord George, 2

Nast, D. W., 95
Nuttall, A. H., 314
Nyquist, H., 55–70, 79, 82, 307

Oersted, H. C., 5
Ohm, G. S., 6
Oliver, B. M., 131
Orgel, L. E., 25

Pareto, V., 191
Parker, A. C., 304
Parseval, M. A., 104, 222
Peirce, B. O., 100, 131
Perry, K. E., 304
Peterson, W. W., 290, 303
Pierce, J. R., 131
Polybius, 1
Popov, A. S., 16
Postl, W., 327, 341
Pouillet, C. S. M., 6
Poulsen, V., 17
Prescott, G. B., 18
Pushman, H. J., 327, 341

Queen Victoria, 14

Ray-Chaudhuri, D. K., 296
Rayleigh, J. W. Strutt, Lord, 155
Rea, W. T., 290
Reed, I. S., 303
Reiffen, B., 303, 304
Reizen, 3
Rice, S. O., 155, 163, 174, 182, 199, 327, 341
Rieke, J. W., 259
Ronalds, F., 5, 12
Rosen, P., 304

Sabine, R., 18
Saltzberg, B. R., 259
Salz, J., 197, 198, 200, 307
Schilling, P. L., 5, 7, 10
Schmidt, W. G., 303
Schweigger, J. S. C., 5, 8
Shannon, C. E., 15, 18, 131, 228, 301, 304–306
Soffel, R. O., 251
Solomon, G., 303
Sömmering, S. T., von, 4
Spack, E. G., 251
Stein, S., 197–200
Steinheil, C. A., 7, 8, 10
Still, A., 18
Sunde, E. D., 70–77, 82, 103, 118, 120, 131, 161–163, 166–168, 183–189, 239

Susskind, C., 16, 18
Swerling, P., 163

Thomson, Sir William (see Kelvin), 14, 15
Titchmarsh, E. C., 131
Toeffler, J. E., 251
Turin, G. L., 314

Vail, A., 7, 10
van Duuren, H. C. A., 292, 303
van Gerwen, P. J., 259
Vaughan, H. E., 94
Volta, A., 4
von Arco, G., 17

Watson, G. N., 131, 163
Watson, W., 3
Weber, W. E., 6, 10
Welch, L. R., 25
Wheatstone, C., 7, 8, 11
Wheeler, H. A., 276
Whittaker, E. T., 131
Wien, W., 17
Wiener, N., 334, 336
Wozencraft, J. M., 300, 302, 304

Yudkin, H. L., 303

Zobel, O. J., 275

SUBJECT INDEX

ACF data system, 248
Adjacent-sideband overlap, 146, 147
Alternators as radio-frequency transmitters, 17
AM (*see* amplitude modulation)
American standard code for informa-
tion interchange, 24
Amplifiers, parametric, 17
Amplitude-frequency distortion, 83
of telephone circuits, 84
Amplitude jumps, 92
Amplitude modulation, data systems,
247, 248
effect of phase characteristic on, 87
general discussion of, 133–161
on-off, 29
signal space diagram for, 232
sinusoidal, 34, 151
square-wave, 35
suppression of intersymbol inter-
ference in, 66
Amplitude-modulation index, 35
Analog information, 19
Analog vs. regenerative links, 129
Analog repeaters, 128, 129
Analog signals, 26, 30
Angle modulation, 36
distortion by nonlinear phase charac-
teristic, 87
Angular velocity, 36
AN/TSQ data system, 247
A1 data system, 247
Arc transmitter, 17
Artificial impulse noise, 194
Asymmetrical sidebands, 138
Asymptotic error rate for differential
four-phase system, 219
Asymptotic expansion, 181
Asynchronous data, 28
Asynchronous transmission, 20, 27
Atlantic Telegraph Company, 14

Attenuation, of cables, 83
of carrier channels, 84
effect of nonuniform, 84
equalization of, 269
of typical telephone circuit, 84
Audion, 17
Autocorrelation function, 334
of random binary telegraph signal,
336–338
of white gaussian noise, 308
Automatic gain control, 246
Average power, of AM signal at carrier
pulse peak, 157
of multilevel baseband signals, 115
in phase-modulation systems, 220–
224
of random on-off carrier pulses, 159
of random variables, 333
Axis-crossing detector, 171

Bain telegraph system, 10
Bandwidth, 15
Barker sequence for framing indication,
265
Baseband signal, 29–32, 53, 114
Baseband system, basic functions of, 96
Baud, 20
Baudot code, 13
Bell System, A1 data system, 247
301B data system, 251
T1 carrier system, 251
201-type data system, 249
202-type data system, 248, 249
Bessel function, 37, 154
Bias distortion, 98, 278, 279
measurement of, 279–283
Binary-coded decimal code, 23
Binary error probability, in AM, 177
in baseband signaling, 110–114
in envelope detection, 156
in FM, 177, 182

Binary pulse train, with generalized waveforms, 317
  with raised-cosine spectra, 111
Binary signaling above the Nyquist rate, 121
Bipolar signal, 27, 28, 338
Bit, 20
  error rate, 117
  timing, 260, 263
Bit-rate bandwidth, 112, 114
Bivariant cylindrical function, 155
Bose-Chaudhuri code, 296–299
Bridge duplex, 12, 242
Burst error correction, 300
Business machine codes, 22, 23

Cables, attenuation of, 82
  delay distortion of, 89, 90
Cadence signal, 13
Calculus of variations, 105, 311
Carrier, phase ambiguity, 254
  pulse, 67
    spectrum, 159
  recovery, 253–259
    Costas's method of, 253, 254
    for quadrature AM, 258
  signal, 34
  systems, attenuation vs. frequency, 83
  telegraph systems, 246
  wave, 29
Carrier-frequency offset, 89
Carrier-shift keying, 29
CCITT recommendation for maximum frequency offset, 91
Chappe semaphore telegraph, 1, 2
Character, 19
Character timing, 21, 260
  in parallel systems, 267
  for start-stop systems, 263
  for synchronous systems, 264
Characteristic distortion, 278
  measurement of, 284, 285
Chirp, 193
Choice of data systems, factors affecting, 237–239
Circular coverage function, 156
Clock, 26
Closed-circuit telegraph system, 240
Codes, American standard, 24
  Baudot, 13

Codes, binary-coded decimal, 23
  business machine, 22, 23
  comma-free, 21
  constant ratio, 291
  cyclic binary, 117
  dots and dashes, 10
  8-level, 22
  5-level, 22
  five-unit, 13
  4-out-of-8, 25
  Gauss and Weber, 8
  Gray, 117, 201, 202, 219
  Hagelbarger, 300, 301
  Hamming, 293–295
  Hollerith, 25
  International Morse, 31
  m-out-of-n, 291
  minimum-redundancy, 21
  Morse, 10, 21
  natural binary, 220
  recurrent, 300
  Reed-Muller, 299
  Reed-Solomon, 299
  reflected binary, 117
  Schilling, 7
  self-synchronizing, 21
  sequential, 302
  7-level, 23
  Sperry-Rand, 25
  Steinheil, 9
  step-by-step, 117
  tree, 302
Coherent detection, 136, 253
Coherer, 16
Collins data systems, 248
Collins Radio Company, 248
Comma-free codes, 21
Compandors, 91
Comparisons of data systems, 227–232
Complementary error function, 218
Composite set, 245
Conditional probability, 178
  density function, 177, 178
Continuous loading method, 16
Continuous phase, 42, 43
Continuous spectrum, 49, 319
Convolution, 66, 167
Cooke and Wheatstone telegraph system, 8, 9, 11
Correlation, 333, 334
  detector, 312
Cos^r-filters, 107–109

Cosine filter, 187
Cosine pulse, 51
Costas's method of carrier recovery, 253, 254
Covariance, 333
  matrix, 198
Cross-spectral density, 332, 333
Crosscorrelation, 334
Crosstalk, 94
Crystal detector, 17
Cube-law phase-frequency distortion, 118, 119
Cycle-counting detector, 171
Cyclic binary code (see Gray code)

Dash, 31
Data distortion, 195, 277
Data set (see data systems)
Data systems, amplitude-modulation, 247, 248
  comparison of performance, 227–232
  factors affecting choice of, 237–239
  frequency-modulation, 248
  high-speed, 250, 251
  phase-modulation, 248–250
  T1 carrier, 251
Data terminals (see data systems)
Data waveforms, 26–29
D-c component, elimination of, 28
  of periodic on-off pulses, 33
  of random on-off signals, 113
  of random variable, 333
D-c telegraphy, 244, 245
Decision threshold, 26, 96
Decoherer, 16
Delay, 85
Delay distortion, 85, 88, 120, 161
  in baseband systems, 118
  of cables, 89, 90
  of carrier channels, 89
  effect on data system performance, 230
  effect on waveform distortion, 89
  equalization of, 268
  linear, 162, 230
  square-law, 118, 162, 230
  of telephone circuits, 90
δ functions in spectral density, 335
Demodulator, 137
Derivative of the signal envelope, 183

Detector, axis-crossing, 171
  crystal, 17
  cycle-counting, 171
  electrolytic, 17
  envelope, 140
  frequency, actual, 171
    ideal, 170
      response of, to FM signal plus gaussian noise, 175
    noncoherence of, 184
  threshold decision, 104
  wireless telegraph, 17
  zero-crossing, 171
Dicode signal, 28, 341
Difference equation, 130, 339
Differential detection, 28
  of eight-phase signal, 206, 207
  of four-phase signal, 205, 206
Differential duplex, 12, 242, 243
Differential encoding, 28, 125
Differential four-phase system, average power in signal on line, 223
  calculation of error rate, 214–220
  error probability curve for, 218
Differential phase detection, 204–208
  noise margin of, 211
Digital computer, 180
Digital information, 19
Digital phase modulation, Fourier series expansion of, 47
Diplex, 12
Discontinuous function, Fourier series expansion of, 47
Discontinuous phase, 42, 46
Distortion, amplitude-frequency, 83
  bias, 98, 278, 279
    measurement of, 279–283
  characteristic, 278
    measurement of, 284, 285
  data, 195, 277
  delay (see delay distortion)
  fortuitous, 277
  harmonic, 90
  nonlinear, 90
  peak, 280
  shortest-pulse, 284
  systematic, 277
Distortion measurements, of start-stop data, 282, 283
  of synchronous data, 280–282
Distortionless transmission, 53, 85
Dot, 31

Dot signal, 33
Dots and dashes, 10
Dotting speed, 123
Double-needle telegraph system, 8
Double-sideband suppressed carrier, 151–153
  signal space diagram for, 232
Doubling the dotting speed, 123, 125
Drop outs, 92
Duality of frequency and time, 54
Duobinary frequency modulation, signal space diagram for, 235–237
Duobinary signaling, 125–127, 275
Duplex telegraph systems, 12, 16, 242–244
Duty factor, 30

Early and late transitions, 281
Early telegraph systems, 240, 241
Echo suppressors, 93
Echoes, 92, 272
8-level code, 22
Eight-phase signal, detection by fixed reference, 204
  differential detection of, 206, 207
  generation of, 202
  noise margin of, 211
Electrochemical telegraphy, 4, 10
Electrolytic detector, 17
Electromagnetic telegraphy, 5
Electrophysiological telegraphy, 5
Electrostatic telegraphy, 3
Electrothermal telegraphy, 10
Ensemble of data sequences, 221
Envelope, distortion by nonlinear phase characteristic, 87
  effect of large carrier component, 139
  of sine wave plus gaussian noise, 155
  of symmetrical narrow-band gaussian noise, 155
Envelope delay, 85–90
  measurement of, 88
Envelope detection, 137–141, 144, 145
  compared with synchronous detection, 160
  of on-off carrier pulses, 153–160
Envelope distribution function, 155
Equalization, of attenuation, 84, 269
  of delay, 268
  of phase, 90, 121
  by predistortion, 273
  by quantized feedback, 274, 275

Error correction, 293–295
Error detection, 23, 25, 291–293
Error function, 179
Error probability (see probability of error)
Error-rate measurements, 285–287
Euclidean distance, 309
Even parity, 292
Even symmetry of amplitude, 137
Exponential pulse, 52
Eye pattern, 119, 162, 210, 280, 287

Fading, 94
Filters in phase-modulation system, 208–210
5-level code, 22
Five-needle telegraph system, 8
Five-unit code, 13
Fixed-reference phase, derivation from resistance summing networks, 208
  detection by, 203, 204
Flanking channel, 147–151
FM telegraph systems (see frequency modulation)
Foldover, 134, 175
  of lower sideband, 68, 74
Fortuitous distortion, 277
4-out-of-8 code, 25
4 × 4 system, 196
Four-level signal, 29, 115
Four-phase signal, asymptotic error rate for, 219
  detection by fixed reference, 203
  differential detection of, 205, 206
  generation of, 202
  noise margin of, 211
  postdetection filtering of, 209, 210
  probability of error in, 218, 211
  symbol timing for, 262
Four-wire circuit, 93
Fourier analysis, 42
Fourier integral, 49, 67, 69
Fourier series, 32, 49
  expansion of discontinuous function, 47
Frequency detection, effect of additive gaussian noise on, 174
Frequency detector, actual, 171
  ideal, 170
    response of, to FM signal plus gaussian noise, 175
  noncoherence of, 184

Frequency discriminator, 173, 174
Frequency-division multiplex AM channels, 145–151
Frequency modulation, 29, 30, 70
  analysis of, by AM synthesis, 166
  data systems, 164, 248
  duobinary, signal space diagram for, 235–237
  nonsinusoidal, 38
  signal space diagram for, 234, 235
  of single oscillator, 81
  sinusoidal, 36
  square-wave, 38–40
  telegraph systems, 246
Frequency modulators, 165
Frequency offset, 89, 91, 231
Frequency-shift, 70
Frequency-shift keying, 17, 29, 165, 168
Frequency shift pulse spectrum, 79
Frequency-shift signal, analysis by AM synthesis, 77
  calculation of spectral components, 42
Frequency spectrum, 32
  of AM, 36
  of FM, 42
FSK wave, 195
Full-cosine roll-off, 57, 58
Full duplex, 12
Full-length rectangular pulses, modification to preserve axis crossings in band-limited response, 58
Full-wave linear rectifier, 140
Fundamental, 33

Galvanometer, Kelvin, 14
  Schweigger, 5
Gauss and Weber, telegraph code, 8
  telegraph system, 6, 7
Gaussian distribution, 100
Gaussian filter, 150
Gaussian frequency spectrum, 58
Gaussian noise, 100–102
  effect on performance of data systems, 225–229
  insensitivity to delay distortion, 193
  narrow-band, resolution into in-phase and quadrature components, 144
  white, 106, 113, 114
Gaussian pulse, 52

Gaussian variables, addition of, 177
  linear transformation of, 214
  multiplication by a constant, 177
Gray code, 117, 201, 202, 219
Grinder, 12
Group-band data systems, 250
Group timing, 260
Gutta-percha, 14
Hagelbarger code, 300, 301
Half duplex, 12
Hamming distance, 293
Hamming single-error-correcting code, 293–295
Harmonic distortion, 90
Harmonics, 33
Heaviside distortionless line, 15, 16
Heterodyning, 175
High-index FM, 168
High-speed data systems, 250, 251
Hilbert transform, 214
Hits, 92
Hollerith code, 25
Homodyne detection, 136
House printing telegraph system, 11
Hughes printing telegraph system, 12
Hughes quaternary phase-modulation data system, 250
Hybrid circuit, 93
Hybrid-modulated wave, 166

IBM, 23
Ideal frequency detector, 170
Ideal low-pass filter, 53, 54
Ideal performance for binary data transmission, 312
Ie function, 182, 199
Impulse, spectrum of, 33
Impulse noise, 94, 102, 107
  approach to gaussian noise in narrow-band circuit, 103
  artificial, 194
  effect on FM signal, 190
  relative effects on FM and AM, 192
Impulse response, 53–60
Impulses, signaling with, 65
In-phase component, 139, 141, 144, 162, 170
Index of modulation (see modulation index)
Information waveforms, 26
Instantaneous frequency, 36
  deviation, 183

Interchannel interference, 145–151
Interference in telephone channels, 94
International Morse code, 31
Intersymbol interference, 99, 100, 121
 in AM, 66, 67
 in FM, 72, 79–82, 183
 suppression, by equally spaced axis
  crossings, 61
  by equally spaced transitions, 63
  by preservation of pulse areas, 65

Jitter, 128
 in binary FSK system, 195
Joint distribution of in-phase and
 quadrature components and their
 derivatives, 176
Jumps, amplitude and phase, 92

Kelvin's mirror galvanometer, 14
Kendall effect, 90
Keying loss, 134
KR law, 15
Krarup loading, 16

Lagrange multipliers, 187
LC oscillator as frequency modulator,
 167
Lenkurt quaternary FM data system,
 248
Level variations, 230, 231
Limiter, 169
 double-acting, 96
Lincoln Laboratories phase-modulation
 data system, 249
Line spectra, 319
Linear delay distortion, 162, 230
Linear transformation of gaussian
 variables, 214
Listener echo, 93
Loaded cables, 16, 83
Lommel's functions, 155
Low-frequency cutoff, 59, 127
 in telephone channels, 84
Low-frequency restoration, 255
Low-index FM, 168
Lower sideband, 35
Lumped-coil loading method, 16

m-out-of-n codes, 291
Magnetic tape, 23

Margin tests, 287–290
Mark, 26
Marking bias, 98, 278
Marking frequency, 70
Matched filter, 312
Matrix of error probabilities, 215
 for differential four-phase trans-
  mission, 219
Maximally flat filter, 150
Maxwell's theory, 16
Mean-square value of FM wave, 182
Measures of performance, 225
Metallic circuit, 12, 245
Method of steepest descents, 181
MF, 196
Minimization of product of two inte-
 grals, 105
Minimum-bandwidth binary FM sys-
 tem, 166
Minimum-redundancy code, 21
Modified ideal low-pass filter with zero
 crossings preserved, 55
Modulated carrier signals, 29
Modulation index, of amplitude modu-
 lation, 35
 of frequency modulation, 36
 of phase modulation, 36
Modulator, 134
Modulo-2 addition, 286
Morse, telegraph code, 10, 21
 telegraph system, 10, 11, 26, 240
Multifrequency system, 196
Multilevel signals, AM, 160
 average power of, 115
 baseband, 114, 160
 FM, 196
 symbol timing for, 262
Multipath, 94
Multiphase signal, generated by fre-
 quency step-down, 203
 generated by phase-shifting net-
  works, 203
Multiplex, 12, 13
Multivibrator as frequency modulator,
 167
Murray's six-shutter telegraph, 2, 3

n-ary, baseband signals, 114
 data, 131
 FM, 196
 slicer, 160

Natural binary code, 220
Negative bias, 278
Negative-resistance repeaters, 92
Neutral relay, 26
Neutral signal, 26
Neutral telegraph circuit, 241
New York-Azores permalloy-loaded submarine cable, 16
Noise, 94, 99
  gaussian, 100–102
    insensitivity to delay distortion, 193
    narrow-band, resolution into in-phase and quadrature components, 144
    white, 106, 113, 114
  impulse, 94, 102, 107
    approach to gaussian noise in narrow-band circuit, 103
    artificial, 194
    effect on FM signal, 190
  nongaussian, 158
  white, 101
Noise margin in phase-modulation system, 210
Noise-to-signal ratios in FM, 186
Noncoherence of frequency detector, 184
Nongaussian noise, 158
Nonlinear distortion, 90
Nonlinear phase, 86
Nonpolarized relays, 12
Nonreturn-to-zero signal, 27, 59
Null zone detection, 293
Nyquist bandwidth, 112, 114, 159
Nyquist interval, 55, 57, 99, 109, 119, 123, 162
Nyquist rate, 122, 126
  definition of, 121
Nyquist's condition for no distortion at the half-amplitude point, 57
Nyquist's criteria for suppression of intersymbol interference, applied to AM, 69
  applied to FM, 70, 79
  first, 61
  second, 63, 126
  third, 65

Octonary signal, 206
Odd parity, 292

Odd symmetry of phase, 137
Offset, frequency, 89, 91
On-off amplitude modulation, 29
  signal space diagram for, 232
  synchronous detection of, 252
On-off, baseband signal, 26, 34, 111, 113, 114
  carrier signal, 29, 35, 36
  keying, 17
  switching, 134
Open-circuit telegraph system, 240
Optical telegraphy, 2
Optimum decision function, 310
Optimum filters, in AM systems, 141–145, 225, 226
  in baseband systems, 99–110
  in binary FM, 186–188
  effect of deviating from, 107–109
  for frequency-division multiplex systems, 145–151
Optimum n-ary decisions, 313
Optimum receiving filter, 106
Orthonormal functions, 308

PAM, 30
Parabolic delay distortion, 118, 162, 230
Parallel-to-serial conversion, 201
Parallel transmission, 20, 21, 29, 30
Parallelogram, orientation margin vs. input signal, 288–290
Parametric amplifier, 17
Pareto's distribution, 191
Parity check, 25, 292
Parseval's theorem, 104, 222, 338
PDM, 30, 40
  —AM, 41
  —FM, 42
  —PM, 42
Peak clipper, use in FM, 193
Peak distortion, measurement of, 280
Peak instantaneous signal power in AM wave, 157
Performance, measures of, 225
Permalloy-loaded cable, 16
Phantom circuit, 245
Phase characteristic, effect on waveshape of modulation, 86
Phase continuity in FM, 79
Phase detection by fixed reference, 203
Phase deviation, 36

Phase differentiator, 171
Phase discontinuities in FM, 77
Phase-frequency distortion, 84
  in AM systems, 161
  in baseband systems, 118
  cube-law, 118, 119
Phase intercept, 86, 89
Phase jumps, 92, 231
Phase-locked loop, 254, 256
Phase-modulated component of FM
    wave, 188
Phase modulation, 30
  average signal power in, 220–224
  data systems, 248–250
  filters for, 208–210
  noise margin in, 210
  nonsinusoidal, 40
  probability of error vs. signal-to-
      noise ratio in, 212–220
  signal space diagram for, 232, 233
  signals, generation of, 202
  sinusoidal, 36
  square-wave, 40
  triangular-wave, 40
Phase optimization, 103
Phasing function in start-stop synchro-
    nization, 265, 266
Pith-ball telegraphy, 3
Polar binary signals, 111, 113, 114
Polar return-to-zero signal, 27
Polar signal, 26, 29, 33
Polar telegraph system, 241
Polarized relays, 12
Polybius's telegraph system, 1
Positive bias, 278
Postdetection filter, 210
Postdetection filtering in FM, 190
PPM, 30, 31, 40
  —AM, 41
  —FM, 42
  —PM, 42
Predetection filter, 209
Predistortion, 273
Preequalization, 103
Press Wireless Corporation, 246
Printing telegraph systems, House, 11
    Hughes, 12
Probability of error, in binary AM,
    151–160
  in binary angle modulation, 177–182
    approximation for, 181
  for binary baseband signals, 110–114

Probability of error, in binary envelope
    detection, 153–160
  in binary FM, 177, 182
  for differential four-phase system,
      211, 218
  in envelope detection of multilevel
      AM signals, 161
  in ideal digital systems, 114, 312
  matrix for, 215, 219
  in multilevel baseband transmission,
      116, 117
  vs. number of links, 129
  vs. signal-to-noise ratio in phase-
      modulation system, 212–220
  for Sunde's FM system, 189
Probability density function, 100, 215,
    310
Probability distribution function, 100
Product detection, 70
Propagation constant, 15
Pseudo-random sequence, 183, 286
Pseudoternary signal, 338
Pulse amplitude modulation (PAM), 30
Pulse duration modulation (PDM), 30,
    40
Pulse frequency modulation (PFM), 42
Pulse modulation, 30, 40
Pulse position modulation (PPM), 3,
    30, 40
Pulse shapes, generalized, 65
Pulse spectrum, 148
Punched cards, 25
Punched paper tape, 22

Q function, 156, 182, 198, 199
Quadratic delay distortion, 118, 162,
    230
Quadratic form, 177, 213
Quadrature AM, synchronous detection
    of, 258
Quadrature carrier multiplex, 141
Quadrature component, 140, 162, 170
Quadruplex, 13, 242–244
Quantized feedback, 255, 274, 275
Quaternary baseband signal, 114
Quaternary phase modulation (see four-
    phase signals)
Quaternary signal, 29, 115
Quaternary signaling at the Nyquist
    rate, 124
Quenched-spark transmitter, 17

Raised-cosine pulse, 51, 52, 166
Raised-cosine spectrum, 98, 99, 106, 109, 111, 114, 121, 125, 149, 159, 209, 223
Random binary signals, 152
Random data sequence, 104
Random signal as noise source, 321
Rank ordering of binary systems, 193
Rayleigh distribution, 155, 158, 174
Ready function in start-stop sychronization, 265, 266
Receiving filter, 99
Rectangular pulse, 50, 58
Rectangular switching in FM, 73
Recurrent code, 300
Reed-Muller code, 299
Reed-Solomon code, 299
Reference carrier, for binary double-sideband AM, 252
    for binary vestigial-sideband AM, 254
    for quadrature AM, 258
Reflected binary code, 117
Regeneration, 97, 128
Regenerative links, 129–131
Regenerative payoff, 131
Relay, 11, 241
    nonpolarized, 12
    polarized, 12
Reliability of synchronization, 264
Repeater, analog, 128, 129
    negative-resistance, 92
    for open-close signals, 241
    regenerative, 129–131
Reshaping, 128
Rest frequency, 170, 173
Retransmission, 292
Return loss, 93
Return-to-zero signal, 27, 34, 262
Reversal rate, 123
Reversals, 33
Rice distribution, 155, 158, 174
Rixon-Sebit data system, 247
rms value, 102
Robertshaw-Fulton, multi-lok data system, 250
Roll-off of baseband signal, 55–57
    in FM, 168
Ronald's synchronous clockwork telegraph, 5, 12

SAGE data system, 247
Schilling's telegraph code, 7
    telegraph system, 5, 6
Self-clocking signal, 27
Self-synchronizing codes, 21
Semaphore systems, 1, 2
Sequential coding and decoding, 301–303
Serial-to-parallel conversion, 201
Serial transmission, 20, 28, 29
7-level code, 23
Shannon's formula, for capacity of band-limited channel, 228, 306
    for capacity of binary symmetric channel, 301
Shaping of FM signal, 168
Shaping network, 74–76
Shift register, use in coding and decoding, 295, 296
    use in equalization, 273
    use for generation of pseudo-random sequence, 286
Shortest-pulse distortion measurements, 284
Side-frequency components, 34
Sideband, 35, 137, 142
    foldover, 68, 167
    overlap, 137
    adjacent, 146
    spectra in frequency modulation, 167
Signal, 26
Signal-to-interference ratio, 148, 149
Signal-to-noise impairment, 108, 109, 121
Signal-to-noise ratio, 15
Signal power constraint, 104
Signal space diagrams, 232–237
Simplex, 12
    circuit, 244
Simplex-phantom circuit, 245
$(\sin x)/x$, function, 33, 50, 54, 58
    pulses, 109
    spectrum, 78
Single-needle telegraph system, 5, 8
Single-sideband suppressed carrier, 152
Sinusoidal, amplitude modulation, 34
    frequency modulation, 36
    phase modulation, 36
Siphon recorder, 14
Slicer, 96
    n-ary, 160

Slicer, thresholds for minimum error rate in binary envelope detection, 158

Slipped synch, 297

Smear-desmear, 193–195

Sömmering telegraph system, 4

Sounder, 26

Space, 26

Spacing bias, 98, 278

Spacing frequency, 70

Spark-gap transmitter, 17

Spectral density, of binary FM signals, continuous phase, 327–331
    discontinuous phase, 326, 327
    of binary phase-modulated signals, 322–324
    of carrier signals, 321, 322
    δ functions in, 335
    of multilevel phase-modulated signals, 324–326
    of noise at input to phase detector, 221
    one-sided and two-sided, 335
    of output related to that of input, 101
    of random binary telegraph signal, 317–321
    relation to Fourier transform, 316

Spectral density function, 101, 142, 311, 315

Spectral distribution function, 101, 315

Spectrum of impulse, 33

Sperry-Rand code, 25

Square-law delay distortion, 118, 162, 230

Square-wave, amplitude modulation, 35
    frequency modulation, 38–40
    phase modulation, 40

Stacked systems, 42

Standard deviation, 333

Start function in start-stop sychronization, 265

Start-stop synchronization, 97, 265
    phasing function in, 265, 266
    ready function in, 265, 266
    start function in, 265

Start-stop system, 21, 263
    measurement of distortion in, 282, 283

Statistical decision theory, 307

Steady-state components of FM wave, 188

Steinheil, telegraph code, 9
    telegraph system, 7, 8

Step-by-step code, 117

Submarine cables, 14, 16, 123
    New York-Azores permalloy-loaded, 16

Sunde's minimum-bandwidth solution for binary FM, 70, 183

Supergroup-band data system, 251

Suppressed-carrier AM, synchronous detection of, 252

Sweep-frequency modulation, 193

Switch-type modulator, 135

Switched telephone network, attenuation vs. frequency, 84
    delay vs. frequency, 90

Symbol, 19
    error rate, 117, 219
    timing, 21, 260–263

Symmetry with respect to carrier frequency, 69

Synchronization, reliability of, 264

Synchronous data, 26
    measurement of distortion in, 280–282

Synchronous detection, 68, 136, 144, 148, 151, 153, 209
    of on-off carrier pulses, 153, 252
    of quadrature AM, 258
    of suppressed-carrier AM, 252
    of vestigial-sideband AM, 254

Synchronous telegraphy, 5

Synchronous transmission, 20, 21, 28

Systematic distortion, 277

Tails of the noise distribution, 213

Talker echo, 93

Tape, magnetic, 23
    punched paper, 22

Tape-recorded noise, 195

Tapped delay line, 269

Telegraph repeater, 241

Telegraph systems, Bain, 10
    carrier, 246
    closed-circuit, 240
    Cooke and Wheatstone, 8, 11
    double-needle, 8
    duplex, 12, 16, 242–244
    early, 240, 241
    five-needle, 8
    FM, 246
    Gauss and Weber, 6, 7
    Morse, 10, 11, 26

Murray, 2, 3
open-circuit, 240
polar, 241
Polybius, 1
Ronalds synchronous clockwork, 5,
  12
semaphore, 1, 2
single-needle, 5, 8
Schilling, 5, 6
Sömmering, 4
Steinheil, 7, 8
Telegraphy, d-c, 244, 245
electrochemical, 4, 10
electromagnetic, 5
electrophysiological, 5
electrostatic, 3
electrothermal, 10
optical, 2
pith-ball, 3
submarine cable, 14, 16, 123
synchronous, 5
wireless, 16
Telemetry, 42
Telephone circuits, amplitude-frequency distortion of, 84
delay distortion of, 90
Telephotography, 91
Teletypewriter, 23
Ternary data, 122
Ternary signaling, 127
Time delay, 85
Time division, 13
Time domain, 167, 271
Timing of digital information, 20, 21
digital phase control of, 261
from modulation of the data signal,
  262
in regenerative repeaters, 97
from signal transitions, 260
T1 carrier systems, 251
Transatlantic cable, 14, 16, 123
Transformation from rectangular to
  polar coordinates, 154, 179, 180
Transition from passband to stop band
  of filter, 122
Transition coding, 28
Transitions, 98
Transmittance function, optimum for
  receiving filter, 103
Transmitters, wireless, 17
Transmitting filter, 99
optimum for uncurbed pulses, 109

Transversal filters, 269–273
Tree code, 302
Triangular pulse, 50, 51
Two- to four-wire conversion, 92

Unbalanced modulator, 135
Unconditional probability density
  function, 178
Uncurbed rectangular pulses, 113
Upper and lower bounds for error rate
  in FM, 186
Upper sideband, 35

Vacuum-tube rectifier, 17
van Duuren ARQ system, 292
Variable channels, 94
Variance, 333
Vector diagram, for amplitude modula-
  tion, 35
for angle modulation, 37
for frequency modulation, 80–82
Vestigial-sideband system, 66, 142
signal space diagram for, 233, 234
synchronous detection in, 254
Vestigial symmetry, 61, 70, 73
Vibrating relay, 123
Voice-band data transmission at higher
  speeds, 246, 247
Voice-frequency carrier telegraph, 246

Wandering zero, 61
Western Union Telegraph Company,
  246
Wheatstone and Cooke telegraph sys-
  tem, 8, 9, 11
White gaussian noise, 106, 113, 114
White noise, 101
Wide-swing FM, 168
Wiener-Khintchine relations, 334, 335
Wireless Telegraph and Signal Com-
  pany, 17
Wireless telegraphy, 16, 17
Word, 19
Word timing, 21

x-db Nyquist rate, 121
x per cent Nyquist rate, 121

Zero-crossing detector. 171
Zero crossings, 138
Zero wander, 61